THE
RUSSIAN AUTOCRACY
IN CRISIS
1878-1882

Peter A. Zaionchkovsky

THE RUSSIAN AUTOCRACY
IN CRISIS, 1878-1882

Edited, Translated, and with a
New Introduction by
GARY M. HAMBURG

Academic International Press

1979

THE RUSSIAN SERIES / Volume 33

Peter A. Zaionchkovsky, *The Russian Autocracy in Crisis, 1878-1882*. Translation of *Krizis samoderzhaviia na rubezhe 1870-1880-kh godov* (Moscow, 1964).

ISBN: 0-87569-031-9

Composition by Beverly Echternacht, Jean MacNeil and Jeanette Rawlinson.
Title page by King & Queen Press

Printed in the United States of America

A list of Academic International Press publications is found at the end of this volume.

ACADEMIC INTERNATIONAL PRESS
Box 555 Gulf Breeze FL 32561 USA

CONTENTS

Peter Andreevich Zaionchkovsky is perhaps the most distinguished historian of nineteenth-century Russian politics in his generation. In his thirty-plus years of scholarly work Zaionchkovsky has accounted for more than eighty publications. His definitive editions of sources, such as the diaries of D.A. Miliutin, A.A. Polovtsov, and P.A. Valuev, and the collection of documents on peasant rebellions in the 1870s, testify to his erudition and ability to select revealing materials. His monographs on the abolition of serfdom, on the implementation of the 1861 peasant reforms, on the 1874 military reforms, on the condition of the Russian army at the turn of the century, and on government politics during the reactionary reign of Alexander III illuminate nearly every aspect of state policy in the period from the mid-1850s to the reign of Nicholas II. The four-volume directory to Russian memoirs now being published under his editorship, his guide to sources on nineteenth-century Russian history, and other invaluable reference works have been of great assistance to scholars both in the Soviet Union and the West.

Zaionchkovsky's scholarly activity has had considerable impact on Russian historiography. As professor at Moscow University since 1951 he has imparted to a generation of specialists his insights on political and military affairs, and his knowledge of archival source materials. His methodology, concentration on bureaucratic politics, and influence in the academic community have enabled him to establish the first "school" of historiography to exist in the Soviet Union since the death of Stalin.

Like all reputable scholars Zaionchkovsky insists that all available unpublished and published sources be used in the preparation of a monograph, and that these sources be examined critically. However, it is possible that no scholar since Lord Acton has attributed so much importance to archival materials or spent such a large part of his career assiduously analyzing unpublished documents. Zaionchkovsky and his students frequently cite page after page from archival sources. This practice makes their monographs on Russian politics heavy reading, but it has the singular advantage of placing the most important facts before the reader and permitting the reader to draw conclusions directly from primary sources. By emphasizing the use of archival documents and refraining from over-interpretation in historical narratives, Zaionchkovsky has contributed to a more scientific and professional historiography in the Soviet Union.

There is a tendency in the West and in the Soviet Union to regard political history with some disdain, as a discipline inferior to social and economic history. In the words of the noted French historian Jacques Le Goff: "Once the backbone of history, political history has sunk to being no more than an atrophied appendix: the parson's nose of history." Soviet scholars particularly have been inclined to reject political history in favor of histories of the working class, the peasantry, the revolutionary movement, and Russian literary culture. Zaionchkovsky and his school have attempted to rescue political history from oblivion, partly by the expedient of combining administrative and bureaucratic history with aspects of social and economic history. The term used to describe Zaionchkovsky's subject matter is "internal politics," an elastic category that encompasses the composition and mentality of various social groups, the politics of class relationships, intellectual and revolutionary history, as well as "the record of what one clerk said to another clerk."

Zaionchkovsky has done more, however, than expand the domain of political history. He has emphasized a fact that had been obscured by the demolition of the old regime in 1917: namely that Russian history cannot be understood apart from the workings of the state. The pretensions of the tsar and his ministers always had been enormous, and with time the state apparatus began to achieve the power to match its pretensions. This power was never absolute, and in moments of crisis like 1881, 1905, and 1917 the government proved weak or impotent. Nevertheless, the gradual aggrandizement of the state at the expense of society makes of vital concern Zaionchkovsky's studies of bureaucratic maneuvers, the personalities of government officials, and the evolution of legislative proposals.

Of all his books *The Russian Autocracy in Crisis* is the most impressive, perhaps because the subject is perfectly tailored to Zaionchkovsky's method. This book analyzes four pivotal years in Russian historical development—1878 to 1882—and relates the terrorist campaign of the Populist groups Land and Liberty and The People's Will to the evolution of government policy. The limited time span covered in the book and the peculiar pattern of repressive legislation and reforms adopted by the government lend themselves to analysis through official archival documents, officials' memoirs, correspondence, and journalistic sources. In *The Russian Autocracy in Crisis* Zaionchkovsky takes his readers inside the government and exposes the conflicting ideologies, prejudices, and blindness of Russia's ruling elite. One watches with fascination as the tsar's ministers fight to eradicate the revolutionaries, now by force, now by guile and demagogy, and occasionally by sound legislation. One sees clearly the history of bureaucratic ineptitude, mistakes, and missed opportunities as the crisis of the autocracy becomes more profound.

Zaionchkovsky divides the political crisis into four distinct stages. He begins with the first episodes of the Populist terror campaign in early 1878, and shows how swiftly the government was compelled to abandon its normal administrative procedures in favor of repressive emergency measures designed to suppress the revolutionary movement. When repression alone failed to halt the Populists, the government started to debate concession and reform. The debate was interrupted by the bomb explosion of 5 February 1880 inside the Winter Palace itself. The bomb blast, which killed eleven people and wounded fifty-six and narrowly missed Alexander II, set off the second stage of political crisis. To this second stage belong the rise of Loris-Melikov and the so-called "dictatorship of the heart," the drafting of economic and political reform packages, and the discussion of Loris-Melikov's plan for representative government on a limited basis. The third stage of the crisis commenced with the assassination of Alexander II on 1 March 1881. Zaionchkovsky is at his best in presenting the intense drama of this period as the successor to the throne, shaken by the death of his father, permitted the rival liberal and conservative factions to struggle for control of the government. The fourth period was one of cautious transition to reaction; after 29 April 1881 the government was dominated by the ultra-conservative Pobedonostsev and his protege N.P. Ignatiev. In periodizing the crisis of the autocracy according to major terrorist acts and government decisions, Zaionchkovsky illustrates the significance of political voluntarism in historical development.

One virtue of *The Russian Autocracy in Crisis* is the comprehensive treatment of disparate aspects of government policy. It is natural to expect a narrative on the government's reaction to the revolutionary movement to contain long sections on the police and the gendarmerie, on the temporary Governors-General, on censorship, and on the construction of a powerful and unprecedented police organization under the Minister of Internal Affairs. Yet Zaionchkovsky also reviews educational policy, the zemstvos, reform of the rural economy, and the moral stature and role of the Russian clergy, and demonstrates how these areas of government interest were influenced by the political crisis.

A second virtue of this book is in its accurate description of the personalities of Russian statesmen. Zaionchkovsky gives a convincing account of Alexander II's weakness as a leader. The unfortunate tsar, dominated by his strong-willed morganatic wife, Princess Yurievskaia, and without any strong political convictions of his own, was the object of intrigues by a succession of ministers and courtiers rather than the source of a consistent government policy. Alexander II was "capable of holding simultaneously two diametrically-opposed opinions." In the end the tsar was nervous and irritable, a "half-ruined sovereign . . . with a dim presentiment of disaster." Alexander III, who came to the throne under the pall of tragedy, was a person of little education and meager talent but, in contrast to his father, Alexander III possessed a strong will and reactionary convictions. According to Zaionchkovsky, Alexander III fought for reactionary ideals "with all the intolerance inherent in his limited mind."

Zaionchkovsky makes short shrift of most of the reactionaries in the government. He dismisses Count Tolstoy with Loris-Melikov's diatribe against "that evil genius of the Russian land." Zaionchkovsky labels Ignatiev a demagogue and a consummate liar, a political illiterate, and an anti-Semite. Ignatiev's ministerial career began with Pobedonostsev's advice to speak the truth, and ended in humiliation as Ignatiev tried to deny sponsorship of a more-than-ceremonial Zemsky Sobor (Assembly of the Land). The Minister of Internal Affairs was doomed by Alexander III's repeated interruptions of these disingenuous denials: "That is untrue," the tsar twice observed.

Zaionchkovsky is most devastating in his treatment of the Ober-Procurator of the Holy Synod, K.P. Pobedonostsev. Most of Chapter Four is an anatomy of Pobedonostsev's maneuvers from the shameful speech to the tsar and the ministers on 8 March 1881 to the secret and duplicitous preparation of the Manifesto of 29 April. On the evening of 28 April the ministers met for the last time in Loris-Melikov's office to discuss a unified government approach to Russia's problems. At the end of the meeting in the very early hours of the morning, the Minister of Justice let slip Pobedonostsev's dark secret about the reactionary manifesto to be published later on the 29th. The Ober-Procurator was surrounded immediately by the irate Miliutin, Abaza, and Loris-Melikov, who demanded explanations for Pobedonostsev's faithless conduct. The powerful Ober-Procurator was "pale, embarrassed, and silent like an accused man before his judges." Pobedonostsev had pulled off a great political stroke, but now he stood humiliated in the presence of honorable men, who later refused even to shake his hand.

If Pobedonostsev is the villain of the piece and the object of Zaionchkovsky's irony, the heroes are Valuev and the liberal bureaucrats Miliutin, Abaza, and Loris-Melikov. As the aging chairman of the State Council, Valuev possessed an unrivalled knowledge of bureaucratic politics and a healthy suspicion of nearly everyone in the government. At first, Valuev resented Loris-Melikov because of the latter's arrogance and tendency to meddle in all aspects of decision-making. Valuev referred to the dictator as "Michel Ier." Yet in the crucial showdown between liberals and reactionaries after 1 March 1881 Valuev threw all his weight behind Loris-Melikov. Miliutin and Abaza were Loris-Melikov's closest political allies and his confidants; this trio of liberals formed the "triumvirate" that controlled the government before Alexander II's death. Zaionchkovsky is obviously impressed by Loris-Melikov's political acumen, although he recognizes clearly enough Melikov's shortcomings as a statesman. Zaionchkovsky is circumspect in his analysis of Loris-Melikov's plan to bring public representatives into government deliberations, and observes that the project cannot be construed as a constitution. But he does note repeatedly that the Loris-Melikov plan was an important step toward a constitution, and toward the liberalization of Russian political life. The government's failure to follow the liberal course was tragic in Zaionchkovsky's view because the reactionaries retarded the natural progress of Russia from a backward feudal society to a modern bourgeois democracy. Russia might have achieved transformation from autocratic absolutism to constitutional monarchy by decree instead of revolution.

A third virtue of *The Russian Autocracy in Crisis* is Zaionchkovsky's contribution to our understanding of the Populist's role in Russian history. By analyzing in detail the government's reaction to the terrorist campaign, Zaionchkovsky proves that the Populists were the immediate cause of a terrible disarray in the ruling elite. He disagrees sharply with earlier Soviet writers, who claim that the political crisis was produced by peasant disturbances and workers' strikes, and his criticisms of these Soviet historians are decisive. While the Populists were the immediate cause of the crisis of the autocracy, they blundered tragically in their single-minded effort to assassinate the tsar. Zaionchkovsky implies that they would have been wiser to have given up terror in 1880 in order to organize dissident workers in Moscow and St. Petersburg, and to agitate for revolution in the countryside. The Populists' failure of political judgment meant that they would exhaust themselves trying to murder the tsar. Ultimately their success in conspiracy meant their political defeat. The death knell for Alexander II was also the death knell for the Populists and, by implication, for constitutional reform.

In his analysis of the political crisis Zaionchkovsky never forgets the long-term historical and social context in which the events of 1878-1882 occurred. For Zaionchkovsky the fatal error of the autocracy was the decision not to sweep away all the elements of serfdom in 1861. In an attempt to placate the landed gentry the government liberated the serfs without providing sufficient land to support a robust peasant economy. The autocracy preferred temporary political advantage and the maintenance of privilege to long-term social stability and economic efficiency. During the dictatorship of Loris-Melikov the liberal bureaucrats instituted several reforms that ameliorated some of the worst features of the emancipation. The state of "temporary obligation" was eliminated, redemption of land was made obligatory, and the hated salt tax was abolished. Yet Loris-Melikov was neither strong enough nor wise enough to devise a more permanent solution to the peasant question. The liberals outside the government, such as the Moscow group headed by S.A. Muromstov and V.O. Skalon, were full of righteous indignation about violations of free speech and free press, but they were less worried about the condition of the peasantry. Zaionchkovsky condemns the short-sighted liberal social policy, and notes that none of the constitutional projects sponsored by the liberals would have meant much to the lower classes, at least initially.

Zaionchkovsky is also careful to explain that the waves of government reaction that occurred between 1878 and 1882 were preceded by more than a decade of increasingly reactionary rule. The high liberal hopes of the early 1860s had been shattered by the government's response to the 1866 assassination attempt by Dmitry Karakozov. Totleben, Baranov, D.A. Tolstoy, Pobedonostsev and Ignatiev had not simply materialized after the first terrorist acts in 1878; there had been a strong reactionary party in the government for years.

The Russian Autocracy in Crisis is a masterful piece of extended historical analysis and its virtues will be readily apparent to the reader. One can, however, take issue with certain points of emphasis and interpretation in the book. First, it is possible that Zaionchkovsky has not paid sufficient attention to the impact of zemstvo and gentry liberalism on the government. In the historiographical introduction he justly criticizes liberal historians like Kornilov, Bogucharsky, and Golitsyn for their exaggerated accounts of the impact of liberal opinion on the government. Yet regardless of the general weakness of liberal figures and institutions, one suspects that they were much more influential before March 1881 than Zaionchkovsky will allow. Zaionchkovsky mentions in passing the role of I.I. Petrunkevich in organizing the Moscow zemstvo congress of 1879, but he fails to recount Petrunkevich's attempt to unite the revolutionaries and liberals before the Moscow congress. Moreover, Zaionchkovsky ignores the constitutional campaign in zemstvo and gentry assemblies that lasted up to the very eve of the 1881 assassination. No less a personage that A.A. Bobrinsky, one of Russia's richest landowners and leader of the Petersburg provincial gentry, petitioned the regime for a constitution in early 1881. During the long lull in the terrorist campaign of The People's Will the most visible and effective pressure on the government came from zemstvo and gentry leaders.

Second, Zaionchkovsky divides the government into liberal and reactionary factions, and asserts that liberals spoke for the nascent bourgeoisie and a more progressive political system while the reactionaries defended the aristocracy and the inviolability of the autocratic principle. Thus, it was natural for the liberals to back the development of rural capitalism on the one hand, and to defend a limited freedom of the press, and the independence of the judiciary on the other. Conservatives, of course, opposed both ideas. The problem with Zaionchkovsky's approach is that the links between politics in the bureaucracy and the social configuration in post-reform Russia are assumed but never proven to exist. However, Zaionchkovsky's reticence on this point is understandable because the subject verges on one of the most sensitive issues in Marxian theory: the nature of the state and its relation to social classes.

The Russian Autocracy in Crisis already has had a marked impact on the thinking of historians concerned with the nature and fate of the old regime. A recent case in point may be mentioned. Drawing on Zaionchkovsky's work, one American historian has argued that between 1878 and 1881 the legal and institutional foundations for a bureaucratic-police regime took shape in Russia.[1] According to this historian, one may seek the "roots of modern totalitarianism" in the crisis of the Russian autocracy. The most important statute enacted during this period was the law of 14 August 1881, which declared emergency rule in various provinces. This law supposedly has served as the basis for Russian government ever since, save during brief interludes. It also is asserted that the police system devised in Russia in the early 1880s was historically unprecedented in two respects. It made Russia the only European nation before the First World War with two police forces: one to protect the citizenry, and the other—the secret political police—to guard the state. The laws also eliminated police accountability to the judiciary. This police-bureaucratic system allegedly developed in Russia because government officials were heirs to a "patrimonial mentality" with deep roots in the Russian past, and because the Populist terror campaign

1. See Richard Pipes' provocative essay *Russia Under the Old Regime* (New York, 1974), especially the chapter called "Toward the Police State."

played into the hands of the reactionaries in the government, rein-
forcing their pleas for police control.

Zaionchkovsky, it should be observed, would not agree with such a
formulation of the problem. He explains the genesis and development of
the crisis of 1878-1882 by reference to a series of concrete historical
circumstances in a well-defined social milieu, and the interplay of various statesmen at the highest level of government. There are no references to any "patrimonial mentality" as an important factor in the
government's response to the terrorists. Zaionchkovsky probably would
agree that the assassination of Alexander II ultimately strengthened the
reactionaries' hand. Yet he also notes that the Populists' mistake was
not their original turn to terror, but rather their failure to engage in
full-time political work in 1880. Zaionchkovsky is much more generous
in his treatment of the Populists than are some American scholars, who
believe that by 1881 the Populists were trying to kill the tsar for frivolous reasons, that they engaged in "terror for the sake of terror."[2]

As to the statute of 14 August 1881, Zaionchkovsky writes with
irony that the law was no mere temporary regulation, but a permanent
basis for repression in effect until the overthrow of tsarism. He appre-
ciates and stresses the significance of this legislation, but he does not
overstate its importance. In writing *The Russian Autocracy in Crisis*
Zaionchkovsky obviously did not seek "the roots of modern totalitarianism," nor did he hope to describe the end of the autocracy in Russia
and the beginning of a modern police-bureaucratic state. Indeed, the
central fact of Zaionchkovsky's book is that the autocracy survived the
grave political crisis of 1878-1882.

It is the measure of a good book that it excites curiosity and arouses
controversy. Zaionchkovsky's *The Russian Autocracy in Crisis* has led
already to new insights and hypotheses by scholars working in the field
of Russian history. It is a book that deserves to be read by everyone interested in the evolution of modern Russia and in modern history in general. The publication of *The Russian Autocracy in Crisis* in English is a
great tribute to P.A. Zaionchkovsky. In him one finds, as Voltaire discovered in Bolingbroke, "all the erudition of his country. . . .This man
. . .has found the means to learn and remember everything."

Gary M. Hamburg

Stanford, California

2. *Ibid.*

A NOTE ON THE TRANSLATION

This translation presents the original text in its entirety, but some of the scholarly apparatus (the original bibliography) and two memoranda published by Zaionchkovsky in the appendix have not been included.

Several common Russian terms (zemstvo and Zemsky Sobor, for example) have been retained in the English because there are no exact and economical English equivalents. The plural of zemstvo has been rendered as "zemstvos," although the Russian plural is *zemstva*. When the Russian text refers to newspapers or other periodicals, the titles are transliterated in the English but not translated. (Thus, *Golos* and *Novoe Vremia*, not *Voice* and *New Times*.)

It has not always been possible to translate Zaionchkovsky's longest and most complex sentences without breaking them up into shorter English sentences. When forced to alter the syntactical arrangements of the Russian, I have been careful not to tamper with the meaning of the original.

In dealing with proper names and transliteration of Russian terms, the Library of Congress system has been used with a few minor modifications. The diphthongs "ia" and "iu" are transliterated "ya" and "yu" at the beginning of names. Soft signs and hard signs have not been indicated in transliterations.

I should like to thank Professor Terence Emmons who suggested the translation and read the text, saving me from many errors. Robin Elaine Rider worked hard to improve my English. Linda Johnson and David Newell helped in the proof-reading. Joan H. Neuberger, Michael Shaw, R.E. Rider, and Terence Emmons criticized the introduction, and Professor Gordon Wright graciously shared with me his insights on the police in Western Europe.

Peter von Wahlde of Academic International Press was generous in his support of this project, and very kind to allow me extra time to complete it.

Finally, I wish to thank Peter Andreevich Zaionchkovsky who took time out from his own research to talk with me about this book and to exchange pleasantries. Professor Zaionchkovsky is a delightful and courteous human being, as well as a great scholar.

FOREWORD

The crisis of the autocracy in the late 1870s was ultimately the consequence of the peasant reforms of 1861. The peasant reforms had failed to abolish completely the feudal order and had set the stage for later political reforms that one can only describe in retrospect as half measures.

This work is the logical continuation of my books *The Abolition of Serfdom* and *The Implementation of the Peasant Reforms*; it is intended to illuminate the internal politics of the government during the crisis period. This book is based on the study of numerous sources, most of them unpublished, relating primarily to the activities of the various institutions of government in the Russian empire. The book covers the period from Spring 1878 to Summer 1882. I decided to start the narrative in early 1878 because at precisely that time the autocracy, faced by a growing revolutionary situation, already seemed unable to govern on the basis of existing legislation. The institutional framework of the state appeared unable to cope with the revolutionary movement. Hence, the government began to consider rule by emergency laws, and it created a special institution of power—the Special Conferences "for the formulation of measures contributing to the better protection of domestic tranquility in the Empire." These steps are proof of a serious governmental crisis.

The book concludes with the dismissal of the Minister of Internal Affairs, N.P. Ignatiev, and the accession to power of D.A. Tolstoy. The appointment of Tolstoy, a rabid reactionary, as Minister of Internal Affairs, indicated that the autocracy had basically overcome the crisis.

Since the subject of this monograph is the political crisis of the autocracy, I will deal with other facets of socio-political life only to the extent necessary for comprehension and illumination of questions of internal politics.

P.A. Zaionchkovsky

INTRODUCTION

Background, Sources, Historiography

In the late 1870s a revolutionary situation matured in Russia. V.I. Lenin indicated that there are three major signs of such revolutionary situations: "1) The ruling classes can no longer govern by traditional means .... The desire of the 'have-nots' for change is usually an insufficient precondition for revolution; the 'haves' must also be unable to live as before. 2) The needs and poverty of the oppressed classes intensify. 3) There is a significant increase in the activism of the masses as a result of these factors ...." [1]

These three symptoms were evident to some extent in the late 1870s. A complicated situation had been created by the whole course of the socio-economic and political development of Russia, particularly by the nature of the peasant reform. The popular and revolutionary movement of this period objectively constituted a struggle against those vestiges of feudalism left by the reform. The economic circumstances of most Russians had deteriorated significantly. The peasantry was affected especially by the confiscatory nature of the peasant reform.

According to the Special Conference set up by the Ministry of Finance to formulate proposals for the reduction of redemption payments, the causes of the deteriorating situation in the countryside were the terms of the reform. "The land alloted to the peasants in many areas did not provide the wherewithal for redemption payments. ... The inadequacy of assets, especially of meadows and pastures, the consequent need to rent more parcels of land at high prices, the poor quality and sometimes complete infertility of peasant allotments, the scarcity of cattle, which made profitable agriculture impossible, the inability of peasants to solve their problems given inadequate monetary resources, that is, insufficient pasture and meadow lands, and the existence of the 'mutual responsibility' rule that impelled even prosperous farmers to hold a comparatively low number of cattle in order to avoid their sale for payment of arrears—this whole series of conditions adversely affected peasant life. In addition, many peasant allotments were difficult to cultivate, or located far away from the villages, and peasants were deprived of the right to cut wood in the forests." In its summary the Conference argued that the "result of these unfavorable conditions had been described by various government agencies: 'The arable land, without improvement, is depleted from year to year; this explains in part the poor harvests of the last half decade.'" [2]

During the 1870s arrears in redemption payments increased every-where in Russia. In 1871 arrears exceeded 50 percent of the annual base payment in eight provinces (in five of them, arrears exceeded 100 percent). By 1881 there were fourteen such provinces (in ten provinces, arrears exceeded 100 percent and in one—Smolensk—the rate was 222.2 percent).[3]

The war with Turkey in 1877-1878 caused additional problems. First, 565,427 reservists were called into active military service,[4] the overwhelming proportion from the rural population. Second, the war further complicated an already extremely serious financial situation, and this also affected the populace. The war required 1,020,578,489 rubles in extraordinary expenses.[5] These expenditures were covered by a new issue of banknotes in the sum of 500 million rubles, and also by domestic and foreign loans.[6] The call-up of reserves primarily from the vigorous young men of the countryside, additional financial burdens, and a rise in prices led to a drop in the people's standard of living, particularly in rural areas. An intensification of class contradictions was the natural result. Data on the peasant movement from 1875 to 1884 is relevant here.[7]

Peasant disturbances occurred unevenly in individual provinces.[8] The statistical data on peasant disturbances in general, and the data used here in particular, are imperfect because the concept "peasant disturbance" itself encompasses peasant demonstrations in a single village or estate, as well as a movement involving tens of thousands of peasants and lasting for several years. Therefore, one must examine the relevant statistics with great care.

Disturbances among former serfs, connected with the prolonged implementation of the reform of 1861 (transition to redemption, land surveys, resettlement, etc.) have their own special features. All these demonstrations, though they were localized in character and did not spread beyond the confines of a rural district (volost), involved activity which led not infrequently to confrontation with representatives of local authority and to suppression by armed force. Disturbances among state peasants were an important feature of the larger peasant movement. These demonstrations arose in connection with the introduction of proprietary records (vladennye zapisi). The state peasants' movement affected broad geographical areas, but as a rule did not constitute such a threat to authority as the movement among former serfs.

Among the more massive disturbances was the movement of state peasants in Kiev province from 1875 to 1878. The disturbance centered in Chigirinsky county (uezd). According to the figures of the Kiev provincial procurator, some 40,000 peasants from nineteen districts participated in the movement.[9] The peasants demanded transfer from household land tenure to individual tenure. Most violent was the disturbance of 1875, when the authorities were obliged to send military detachments to a number of villages. In 1875 a disturbance involving about 5000 state peasants occurred in Voronezh province; it was also put down by troops.[10]

In 1878 state peasants took part in large demonstrations in Asovskaia and Tazovskaia districts (Kungurskii county) in Perm province[11] and in four districts of Orenburg province.[12] These disturbances were related to the compilation of proprietary records. The second of them was suppressed with the aid of troops. In 1878-1879 a numerically significant movement of Tatar peasants developed in Kazan province and lasted two years. It involved a series of counties (Kazan, Tetiushsky, Chistopolsky, Spassky, Laishevsky, Mamadyshsky) and spread to neighboring provinces (Viatka, Samara).[13] The movement was prompted by rumors about the forced conversion of Tatars, but was not distinguished by unusual activity and was terminated basically by military means.[14]

Serious and persistent disturbances among the state peasants of Novo-Grigorsky county, Stavropol province, occurred in 1879. These disturbances, caused by the issuance of proprietary records, spread to Vinodelenskaia, Petrovskaia, and Kultinskaia districts before they were crushed by military force.[15]

In 1880 the disturbances continued among state peasants in Perm province, and in thirty-one hamlets in Orlovsky county, Viatka province. These demonstrations also were connected with the issuance of proprietary records and the conduct of land surveys. In the early 1880s there were no more large-scale disturbances among state peasants, although the actual number of incidents increased.

In examining the dynamics of the peasant movement in the late 1870s and early 1880s (Table 1), it is essential to note that the total number of disturbances for the decade is a rather imposing figure—more than 300. Troops were used to halt eighty of these disturbances. However, if one compares the peasant movement of this period with that of the 1860s (after 1863), one notices a clear decline. Such a decline is not unnatural because during the 1860s the implementation of the Statute of 19 February was far from complete, and there were thus constant confrontations of peasants and landlords.

Even though the implementation of the peasant reform was essentially complete by the mid-1870s, peasant disturbances did not cease.

In 1878 and 1879 the movement intensified; at the beginning of 1880 it diminished. There was thus a certain growth of the movement immediately after the conclusion of the war. It must also be noted that the peasant movement in the second half of the 1870s was distinguished by mass participation. In the early 1880s, after a certain decline, the movement grew again both in the quantity of demonstrations and in their scale.[16] The number of disturbances suppressed by military force also increased significantly.

The situation in the countryside in the late 1870s and early 1880s cannot be described merely by reference to peasant disturbances. One must also bear in mind the generally tense atmosphere in rural areas in 1878-1879, when rumors spread concerning a "black [land] partition." These rumors were a cause of greater anxiety to authorities than were individual local peasant disturbances. In the author's opinion, rumors about land partition were the naive expression of the peasants' loyal hopes for the tsar's charity, which they thought would be forthcoming at the end of the war. Retired soldiers initiated most of these rumors. In the summer of 1879 the governor of Kiev informed the Minister of Internal Affairs of rumors that "soldiers who returned home would be given land as a reward for service performed during the war."[17] Several months later the governor of Simbirsk indicated that rumors about land partition were spread "by low-ranking officers, discharged from active service to the reserves and retirement, and particularly those who had served in Turkey."[18]

The governor of the Polish province of Kelecz reported to the Minister of Internal Affairs that in one *gmina* (village) a group of retired soldiers had appeared "with the request that he explain to them when and in what form they would receive rewards for service in the last war . . . ."[19]   The Turkish campaign was not the first to occasion hopes of tsarist benevolence. They had surfaced after the war in 1812 and after the Crimean War. Faith in the "good tsar" had been preserved among the peasants.[20]

The dissemination of such rumors strengthened the peasants' struggle against landlords and led to a peculiar form of disturbance. On 25 July 1881, the governor of Mogilev wrote the Minister of Justice that "recently in almost all counties of Mogilev province there have been land seizures by local peasants involving noble estates."[21]

Along with rumors about land partition, voluntary peasant migration to Siberia reached a significant scale. The Minister of Internal Affairs sent a special circular on the subject to the governors in 1879.[22]

While taking note of a certain growth in the peasant movement in the late 1870s, one must concede that it was certainly less impressive than the rise of the peasant movement in the years when serfdom was abolished. Yet in the 1870s the situation in the countryside had become much more complex, and therefore the peasant movement provoked greater concern in government circles. Unlike 1861 there was a party which expressed the peasants' interests and tried to involve the peasants, albeit unsuccessfully, in the fight for social revolution. This was the government's deepest fear, and so it is no wonder that the peasant question occupied a large, even central place in domestic politics.

During the industrial boom of 1878-1879 strikes grew more frequent. A series of big strikes hit the St. Petersburg area in 1878; at the New Cotton Factory two thousand workers walked out. In Serpukhov, Moscow province, some 2500 workers struck, while 1500 workers struck the Tretiakov Factory in Moscow county, and 3000 were involved in a strike in Teikovo-Shuisky county, Vladimir province. In late 1878 the Northern Union of Russian Workers appeared in Petersburg. It enrolled several hundred workers and dedicated itself to the struggle for political liberty.

In 1879 there were eight large strikes, each involving more than 1000 workers. In 1880 over 13,000 workers participated in five major strikes. In 1881 and 1882 there were no large strikes. The walkouts all were motivated by purely economic issues.

The modest growth of the strike movement was marked by a rise in worker activism. However, the labor movement at this time was still too small to have real significance. The dynamics of disturbances and strikes in the decade between 1875 and 1884 are shown in the following data:[23]

Year	Disturbances	Year	Disturbances
1875	24	1880	26
1876	27	1881	25
1877	16	1882	22
1878	44	1883	29
1879	54	1884	25

The late 1870s and early 1880s also witnessed a decline in living standards and a certain growth of both the peasant and the worker movements.

The Russo-Turkish war was a boon for the opposition movement and the revolutionaries alike for it laid bare the complete ineptitude of the government. The senseless sacrifices near Plevna, massive abuses and graft, and the behavior of the tsar and his brothers in the military theater, could not but hasten the erosion of imperial authority.

Concerning the shortcomings of the governmental system which were revealed so starkly during the war, K.D. Kavelin wrote in his anonymous brochure "Political Phantoms": "The government's bankruptcy, which until then only a few recognized, was now painfully evident even to its recent defenders."[24]

Unquestionably the war transformed many well-intentioned men into potential critics of government policy. "The reason for our failures," wrote M.A. Gazenkampf, an officer of the General Staff, "lies not in individual errors, but in something much more profound. Otherwise, the same thing could not occur in two parts of the world. In Asia—Zivin, in Europe—Plevna. If we had had domestic order, then partial defeats would have served as a lesson to us, and not as a cause of complete stagnation and general confusion."[25]

In 1878 the half-successful war led to the threat of an anti-Russian coalition in Europe. The decisions of the Congress of Berlin significantly changed the provisions of the Peace of San Stefano. During the Berlin Congress I.S. Aksakov, who considered its very deliberations to be a national humiliation for Russia, told the Moscow Slavic Committee: "Loyalty commands us all to hope and believe; loyalty also commands us not to keep silent in these days of lawlessness and untruth, which are erecting a wall between the tsar and the nation, between his thought and the nation's thought."[26]

Finally, the liberation of Bulgaria and the installation of a constitutional regime there engendered hopes for a constitution in Russia. Together these factors radicalized the democratic elements of society and strengthened the liberal opposition.

It is a peculiarity of the socio-political circumstances of the late 1870s that the crisis of the autocracy was not directly provoked by the popular struggle, but rather by the actions of a party which expressed the interests of the people. "Despite a utopian theory which rejected political struggle," wrote V.I. Lenin, "the movement led a handful of heroes into desperate battle with the government over political liberty. Because of this struggle, and only because of it, circumstances changed again, and the government was again forced to make concessions. . . ."[27]

Friedrich Engels evaluated the situation in the same way.[28] The group Zemlia i Volia (Land and Liberty) directed the revolutionary struggle of the Populists at this time. The failure of the organization's propaganda among the peasantry precipitated a crisis. Terrorist activity, which at first took the form of reprisals against traitors and widely hated officials, soon was transformed into the basic weapon of revolutionary struggle. "Political murder is the realization of revolution," wrote N. Morozov in the periodical *Listok Zemli i Voli*.[29] In addition, some of the revolutionary Populists began to understand the need to fight for political liberty.

The crisis within Zemlia i Volia ended with a schism and a new party called Narodnaia Volia (The People's Will) was created. It recognized the necessity of winning political liberty. Members of the People's Will (narodovoltsy) considered the peasantry to be the "chief popular force," but they also attached great importance to support from the workers and soldiers. "The urban working population, which has particular importance for the revolution because of its strategic position and comparatively progressive views, must attract the serious attention of the party," said one of the programmatic documents of the People's Will. "The success of the first attack hinges entirely on the behavior of workers and troops."[30] A.I. Zheliabov composed a "Program for Working Class Members of The People's Will." Party members founded a newspaper called *Rabochaia Gazeta* (The Workers' Gazette) and agitated among workers in the capital. Zheliabov formed a special combat section within the People's Will consisting of officers.

However, the People's Will concentrated on terrorist activity. "A skilfully-executed series of terrorist offensives that would liquidate ten to fifteen persons, the pillars of the present government, will drive the government to panic, deprive it of unity of action, and will arouse simultaneously the people—that is, will create the proper atmosphere for attack."[31] The Executive Committee of the People's Will concentrated all its efforts on preparations to kill Alexander II. Thus the practical activity of the People's Will amounted to political conspiracy.

One cannot help but note that this terrorism evoked fear and confusion among the ruling classes. As A.A. Planson, a gentry landowner and government official, wrote later: "Only in the midst of an armed uprising does there occur such a panic as that which gripped everyone in Russia in the late 1870s and early 1880s. All over Russia people fell into silence: in clubs, hotels, on the streets, at bazaars . . . . People awaited something unknown but terrible. No one was certain what tomorrow would bring."[32] Naturally this account is somewhat exaggerated since the author tried to attribute a panicky disposition to virtually all classes of society. But there is no doubt that high government officials and the top stratum of the ruling class experienced these feelings.

The growth of the liberal opposition movement also contributed to the crisis of the autocracy. In 1878 the zemstvo movement stepped forward through various addresses to the tsar. While most of these addresses contained protestations of loyalty, several zemstvos spoke critically of government policy, and demanded that the sphere of zemstvo activity be broadened, and that political freedom be granted. The zemstvo of Chernigov province, headed by I. Petrunkevich and A. Lindfors, was the most radical in its views. On Petrunkevich's initiative a zemstvo congress met in Moscow in early 1879. Eminent liberal figures (the Bakunin brothers, Goltsev, Rodichev, Chuprov, and others) spoke about the need for a constitution in Russia.

However, now as earlier the liberal movement was not able to exert serious pressure on the government. The reason for this was the weakness of the Russian bourgeoisie, and its direct dependence on the autocracy. The liberal movement was led primarily not by the bourgeoisie, but by the gentry intelligentsia, who had no broad-based support among the gentry as a whole.

SOURCES

The sources for this study may be subdivided into four groups: (1) official documents; (2) diaries and memoirs; (3) letters; and (4) journalistic publications. Most of the sources belong to the first group which may be further divided into subgroups. The first subgroup includes materials of a legislative character in the broad sense of the word—that is, materials relating to the preparation of various laws examined in the State Council, the Committee of Ministers, or the Council of Ministers. The records of these three institutions are kept in the Central State Historical Archive in Leningrad.

In Imperial Russia there was no precise delimitation of functions for individual governmental institutions. Therefore, while the State Council as the highest legal consultative agency was responsible for the drafting of much legislation, a number of important laws were prepared not by the State Council, but by the Committee of Ministers. During the reign of Alexander III the Committee of Ministers was extremely active as a legislative group. For example, the Statute of 14 August 1881, which strengthened police powers, the Temporary Decree on Jews in 1882, and other laws were formulated in the Committee of Ministers. Since the Committee of Ministers was a smaller and more conservative body than the State Council, it usually wound up discussing the more reactionary proposals of the regime.

Several laws having to do with state security were the products of the Council of Ministers. Examples include the laws of 3 April 1878, adopted after the trial of Vera Zasulich, and the law of 8 August 1878, which was promulgated only after the assassination of the Chief of Gendarmes General Mezentsov. On 8 March 1881 the Council of Ministers also dealt with Loris-Melikov's proposal to convoke representatives of the educated public for preliminary discussion of a number of legislative projects.

The completeness of archival materials in this subgroup depends on the institution which considered each law. For example, the materials of the State Council are the most complete. They contain the original reports of the responsible minister, responses to this report by other departments, a second ministerial report commenting on these responses and, finally, records of deliberations in joint sessions and general meetings. In several instances complete protocols of meetings have been preserved. Using such material, the evolution of legislation may be studied in detail.

State Council materials include the documentary compilations "On Changes of Jurisdiction and Procedure in Crimes under Articles 263-271, 285, and 393 of the 1866 Penal Code, and in Other Very Grave Crimes against Officials;"[33] "On Changes in the Law of 7 June 1872 concerning Criminal Procedure in State Crimes;"[34] "On the Supervision of Students;"[35] "On the Reduction of Redemption Payments;"[36] "On the Gradual Replacement of the Poll Tax by Other Taxes"[37] and others.

The records of the Committee of Ministers are more germane to this study, but less complete than the State Council materials. There are found only the original reports of a responsible minister or department chief and the journal of the session in which a given question was discussed. Moreover, these journals are less detailed than those of the State Council. Protocols of meetings have not been preserved. In addition to the laws mentioned earlier (the *Statute of 14 August 1881*,[38] and the *Temporary Decree on Jews* in 1882[39]), the reports of the Committee of Ministers examined decisions of the Special Conference of Spring 1879,[40] the reports of the Governors-General, particularly of the Temporary Governor-General of Odessa, Totleben,[41] the reports of the Ministers of Internal Affairs, particularly those about rumors of land partition in 1879,[42] on interprovincial zemstvo congresses,[43] on the activity of the Kakhanov Commission,[44] and on peasant resettlement in free lands.[45]

As a rule these documents were part of the "special journals" of the Committee of Ministers. The Committee's decisions, which had binding legal force after the tsar ratified them, were not subject to publication. Therefore they are absent from the Complete Collection of Laws.

It is terribly difficult to follow the discussions of the Council of Ministers in archival materials. The Council archive for the nineteenth century[46] contains only 96 volumes, a modest number to be sure. The Council of Ministers was most active during the 1860s, so it is not surprising that the records for those years contain both ministerial reports and an indication of action taken. Such information is lacking for later decades. As a rule the volumes on the late 1870s and early 1880s include notations that the Council met on certain dates and also lists of persons present at the meetings. In volume 94, entitled "On the Disposition of Imperial Directives for Meetings of the Council of Ministers on 3 April and 8 August 1878," are found (a) telegrams from Alexander II calling the meeting of 8 August; (b) a report from Kakhanov, who supervised the Council of Ministers, on the execution of the tsar's orders; (c) invitations for the session; (d) notes from those who found it impossible to attend; (e) a list of those present at the meeting. In volume 95 there were similar documents: (a) a letter from Loris-Melikov to Valuev on the calling of a meeting on 8 March 1881; (b) announcements of the meeting; and (c) a list of participants.

Finally, it must be noted that certain laws were adopted simply on the recommendation of the responsible minister without further discussion. For instance, the salt duty was abolished after a report by the Minister of Finance.

This first subgroup of documents also contains the materials of the Special Conferences set up in 1878-1879 to devise measures to combat the revolutionary movement. These conferences, whose composition was always nearly the same, were established by special decree of the tsar and functioned under the chairmanship of P.A. Valuev, Minister of State Domains.

The first Special Conference, or as it originally was called, the Advisory Agency (Soveshchatelnoe prisutstvie), was asked in late March 1878 to discuss methods of combatting the revolutionary movement. Besides Valuev its members included the Ministers of Internal Affairs, Justice, Education, the Head of the Second Section of His Majesty's Chancellery, and the Chief of Gendarmes. A second Special Conference was constituted in late June in connection with the activity of an "underground socialist circle operating in Kiev, Kharkov, and Odessa—namely the 'Executive Committee of the Russian Socialist-Revolutionary Party'." This conference had the same membership as its predecessor, except that the War Minister replaced the Minister of Education and the Head of the Second Section. After an unsuccessful attempt to kill Chief of Gendarmes Drenteln, a third Special Conference met on 15 March 1879. P.A. Shuvalov, a former Chief of Gendarmes, was added to its membership. After Soloviev's attempt on Alexander II's life in April 1879 a fourth conference convened. It was supposed to "investigate and elucidate the reasons for the rapid dissemination of destructive doctrines among the young," and to work out measures to fight such subversion. The fourth conference involved three additional members—the Ministers of Finance and Education, and the Head of the Second Section. In June 1879 this conference debated the educational reforms proposed by the Kharkov Governor-General Loris-Melikov.[47]

The materials of the four Special Conferences are invaluable sources for this study. Unfortunately for the historian, the materials lie in various archives. Documents on the spring 1878 conference (March-May) are located in the archive of the Third Section of His Majesty's Chancellery.[48] Here are found journals, verbatim protocols of meetings, unsigned copies made by clerks, and the original general journal of the conference with Valuev's hand-written note on the first page summarizing Alexander II's intentions in creating the conference. The conference's decisions were discussed neither in the Council of Ministers, nor in the Committee of Ministers; they were simply ratified by the tsar.

The original journal of the second Special Conference is also in the Third Section's archive.[49] Copies of the journal for the conference of 22 March 1879 may be found in the Third Section archive and in the personal papers of Miliutin.[50] The Council of Ministers' archive contains the journal of the Special Conference of April-May 1879, and a rough copy of the journal is in Valuev's personal papers.[51] A printed copy of the discussion of Loris-Melikov's proposals is the Third Section archive, and a rough copy is in the Valuev papers.[52]

The journals of the Supreme Administrative Commission also belong to the first subgroup. The Supreme Administrative Commission was neither legally nor factually a collegial institution; it was a consultative body whose executive was in essence a dictator. The commission met only in the first few months after its establishment, and altogether there were only five sessions—on 4, 11, and 24 March, 15 April, and 1 May 1880. Printed versions of its journals were not preserved. However, in Loris-Melikov's papers there are rough copies of all journals (handwritten with corrections made by an unknown individual). Uncorrected printed copies may be found in various repositories, but in none of these is there a complete set. [53]

Finally, to this subgroup of legislative materials one must assign the relevant decrees for the years 1878-1882. These have been published in the Complete Collection of Laws.[54]

Ministerial reports and top-level memoranda from other high officials constitute a second subgroup of sources. It must be said at the beginning that not a single annual report from the Ministry of Internal Affairs or the Third Section of His Majesty's Chancellery relevant to this investigation has survived. The last extant annual report for the Ministry of Internal Affairs is dated 1863, and for the Third Section, 1869. However, all the annual reports of the War Ministry—including even the ones written after the turn of the century—have been preserved.[55] The same holds for the annual accounts of the War Ministry, the State Council, and the State Controller.[56] Annual governors' reports relevant to this period are also still extant. It would be logical to assume that the annual reports of the Ministry of Internal Affairs and those of the Third Section existed at one time, but apparently they have perished.[57]

Whatever the fate of the annual reports, ministerial reports on individual political issues still exist. These documents, particularly the reports of the Minister of Internal Affairs, the head of the Supreme Administrative Commission, and the Chief of Gendarmes, constitute an extremely important source. Such reports analyze the situation prevailing in the country, and recommend political solutions to various problems. One can often judge by the tsar's written comments (marginalia) how he reacted to events.

There can be no certainty that all the relevant documents in this subgroup have been read, since the archives of the Ministry of Internal Affairs and that of the Supreme Administrative Commission are far from intact. In the repository of the Chancellery of the Ministry of Internal Affairs for a period of 107 years (1811-1917) only 5074 volumes of documents have been preserved. Literally, not more than thirty volumes pertain to our period. The archive of the Supreme Administrative Commission has fared little better; at best, only one-fourth of its documentary material has survived.[58] Most ministerial reports and official memoranda were found in personal papers. Only two relevant reports from the Minister of Internal Affairs can be found in the General Business section of the Ministry archive; a third turned up in the Chancellery archive.[59] There is, of course, no assurance that documents missing from the larger archives have found their way into personal repositories.

The personal archives of Alexander II and Alexander III are helpful in this regard; they contain a number of important ministerial reports, although the number of such reports is still modest.[60] Apparently, it was standard procedure to read such documents and then return them to the author.[61] The historical journal *Krasny Arkhiv* published a series of reports from the Minister of Internal Affairs and the Chief of Gendarmes. For example, S.N. Valk published Loris-Melikov's reports from 2-4 March 1881 on preparations for the trial of Alexander II's assassins,[62] V. Dalago and S. Vaksman edited reports of the Chief of Gendarmes for August-December 1878 concerning measures to combat the revolutionary movement,[63] and finally, P.E. Shchegolev published reports on the same matter for April-November 1879. This last group of reports discusses the terrorist campaign of Land and Liberty.[64]

Circulars and other directives issued by the Ministry of Internal Affairs and police agencies comprise a third subgroup of official sources. This kind of source is of value for the study of actual government measures affecting domestic politics. Circulars sent by the Ministry of Internal Affairs to provincial governors and bearing on administration of government policy are of great interest. However, it must be reiterated that not one of the repositories of the Ministry of Internal Affairs or the Third Section has survived fully intact. Moreover, the most important circulars—the secret or confidential ones—did not appear in the collections of circulars published by the Ministry of Internal Affairs. Still, this source is of extreme value for the study of daily governmental activity. Therefore I looked for these circulars in the Central Historical Archive of the Ukraine, and in regional archives such as those of the Governors-General of Moscow, Petersburg, Kiev, and Kharkov. My search was successful because these archives contain a large number of circulars for the period 1878-1882.[65]

The situation is much worse with regard to the official correspondence of the Minister of Internal Affairs, which includes detailed instructions to local authorities. Such correspondence has vanished almost entirely. Only in rare instances can one compensate for this gap with materials scattered in various archives. For example, the directive of Loris-Melikov on the situation of political prisoners in Siberian labor camps, contained in an official letter to the Governor-General of Eastern Siberia, was discovered in excerpted form in the archive of the Third Section. All circulars to local gendarme offices have been preserved in the Central State Historical Archive in Leningrad.

The final subgroup of official sources includes miscellaneous reports, projects, estimates, and resolutions of local governmental agencies. These materials are kept in the archives of the Ministry of Internal Affairs (Chancellery of the Minister, General Business section, Department of the Police), of the Supreme Administrative Commission, of the Ministry of Education, of the Third Section, particularly in its secret archive. They are found also in the personal papers of P.A. Valuev, M.T. Loris-Melikov, N.P. Ignatiev, D.A. Miliutin, V.K. Plehve and others. In the archives of the Chancellery of the Minister of Internal Affairs, the General Business section, and the Third Section, for instance, there are documents concerning the staff of the Third Section and its budgets,[66] and the organization of the secret police in Russia and abroad.[67] In the archive of the Supreme Administrative Commission there is information on its staff,[68] on the composition of the Petersburg police,[69] and information about crimes against the state.[70] As I noted earlier, the repository of the Supreme Administrative Commission is far from complete. Several commission documents were filed in the archive of the

Chancellery of the Minister of Internal Affairs.[71] The Ministry of Education archive has materials concerning the regulation of students.[72]

Many documents may be found in personal collections. P.A. Valuev's enormous archive contains materials on the Special Conferences and his notes on establishment of the Supreme Administrative Commission,[73] on the institution of the temporary Governors-General,[74] on preparation of the censorship reform,[75] and so on.

Among Loris-Melikov's papers are seventy-five tomes concerning his activity as head of the Supreme Administrative Commission and as Minister of Internal Affairs. Among them are his memorandum on police reform, dated 1 August 1880,[76] a report from Kakhanov about relations between the gendarmes and the courts,[77] a report from Senator Markov concerning state crimes,[78] Senator Kovalevsky's memorandum on administrative exile,[79] among others.

The repository of N.P. Ignatiev is very extensive.[80] In it are 322 folders relating to his activity as Minister of Internal Affairs, including a bewildering variety of reports, frequently annotated by Alexander III, official correspondence, and memoranda on the preparation of reforms. Particularly noteworthy are two memoranda neatly summarizing governmental policy,[81] a report on the state of the police force,[82] a report entitled "The Principal Bases of Internal Order,"[83] the draft of a decree offering amnesty to revolutionaries,[84] secret communiques from the Petersburg Chief of Police about the Holy Retinue,[85] anti-Semitic disorders,[86] and the like. Most of the aforementioned documents are clean copies done by clerks; unfortunately, they are unsigned and hence it is difficult to trace their provenance. Such documents have been cited only when their reliability has been established through other sources.

The personal papers of D.A. Miliutin and V.K. Plehve also include interesting materials. For example, the Plehve collection includes a pencil copy of a suggestive memorandum on the situation in universities. Plehve himself wrote on the first page: "Memorandum presented to the Emperor in May 1881—led to the formation of the Delianov Commission."[87]

It would be remiss not to mention two reports by P.A. Valuev and Grand Duke Konstantin Nikolaevich which outlined their proposals for government reforms.[88] The Valuev report on the reform of the State Council was written in 1863, and resurrected for discussion in January 1880. The original has not survived, but the report was published in the journal *Vestnik Prava* (Number 9, 1895).

In 1866 Grand Duke Konstantin Nikolaevich and Prince Urusov had proposed the formation of a Special Assembly of Deputies, to be elected by the gentry and the zemstvos. The proposal was revived in early 1880. Not surprisingly, there are two variants of the Grand Duke's report, one dated 1866 and the other 1880. After the original project was debated and rejected in 1880, the Grand Duke wrote the second variant with the help of E.A. Peretts; this variant reflected objections raised during the deliberations of the government. The 1866 version was quoted verbatim by Peretts in the typed copy of his memoirs (Central State Archive of the October Revolution, Alexander III papers); the 1880 version was published by Bermansky in *Vestnik Prava* (Number 9, 1905).

A special place in this subgroup is occupied by local archival materials such as the repositories of the Governors-General of Kiev,[89] Kharkov,[90] Moscow,[91] and Petersburg.[92] These archives contain government circulars plus mandatory orders by the governors and their various communications.[93]

Finally, there are the reports of the Austro-Hungarian ambassador in Petersburg to the Austrian Minister of Foreign Affairs, Hamerlei. I am indebted to the historian C. de Gruenwald for these reports, which were checked by the staff of the Main Archival Administration of the USSR Council of Ministers.[94] The reports describe the atmosphere prevailing at court and in high society in this period.

Diaries and memoirs comprise the second group of sources. They make possible a fuller and more concrete understanding of the political situation in the country and of the disposition of forces within the government. Diaries and memoirs acquaint us with a whole series of details concerning domestic politics and with the hidden side of governmental activity which is not reflected in official documents. Diarists and memoirists naturally view events through the prism of their own experience. Their perceptions depend both on their position in society and their political biases. Moreover, diaries and memoirs usually have an apologetic character. When an official, despite his loyalty to the government, sometimes reacts critically to the actions of the tsar and his retainers, his personal role is usually exaggerated and narrated apologetically. The historian must be aware of this at all times. Nevertheless, diaries and memoirs are of enormous assistance to the scholar. Without them one would be literally unable to fathom many problems central to the years 1878-1882.

We are blessed with a large quantity of diaries and memoirs. Among them are the diaries of P.A. Valuev, D.A. Miliutin, E.A. Peretts, A.A. Polovtsov, A.A. Kireev, Alexander III, Grand Duke Konstantin Nikolaevich, and the memo books of Alexander II. Outstanding memoirs include the notes of A.V. Golovnin, "Materials for Future Historians of Russia," which elucidates the government's policies in the late 1870s and early 1880s, and the memoirs of N.P. Ignatiev.

With few exceptions, all of these sources reflect the viewpoint of a high government official, or a member of the imperial family. Although these people shared an attitude common to their class, they nevertheless differed, albeit insignificantly, in their views on various political questions. Personal qualities also influence perspective on events and the character of writing. Disparities among authors offer a fine opportunity to check the reliability of statements made by an individual diarist or memoirist.

P.A. Valuev was Minister of State Domains and later chairman of the Committee of Ministers; he also served as chairman of the Special Conferences established to combat the revolutionary movement. This determines the great value of his diary. In it there is found information about the Special Conferences, on the establishment of the Governors-General, on the creation of the Supreme Administrative Commission, and on sessions of the Committee of Ministers. Valuev devotes much attention to the characters and mutual relations of statesmen. He discusses the so-called "constitutional projects" of 1880-1881, including the proposals of Grand Duke Konstantin Nikolaevich, Loris-Melikov and his own project. Valuev's notes offer not only unvarnished facts, but sweeping judgments about political events. He is critical of his fellow ministers, and of Alexander II himself. However, Valuev is apologetic about his own role. Valuev's political attitudes are rather complex. He did not belong to the reactionary clique of Pobedonostsev and Katkov, nor to the liberal bureaucrats like Miliutin and Abaza. Valuev occasionally supported the liberal bureaucrats; otherwise, he occupied a distinct position. [95]

The diary of D.A. Miliutin is also of great importance. Naturally Miliutin's perspective differed from that of Valuev. By conviction Miliutin sided with the liberal bureaucrats. He was the most intimate adviser to Loris-Melikov, and an important actor at the center of the political arena. After the 29 April 1881 Manifesto, Miliutin retired along with Abaza and Loris-Melikov. Therefore, his description of events in late 1881 and 1882 is much less interesting. Miliutin's notes are more complete than those of Valuev; he describes events in detail and then offers his own evaluation. The Miliutin diary is valuable for its analysis of the Special Conferences, and other government steps in domestic politics. Entries on the period of struggle within the government in March and April 1881 are especially interesting. The diary covers nearly thirty years—from 1873 to 1900. [96]

The diary of State Secretary E.A. Peretts is of equal significance, although his position within the government was rather different from that of Valuev and Miliutin. For a time he moved in different circles than these two men, and he rarely conferred with Alexander II. Yet Peretts compensated for this by his otherwise broad conclusions, his intimacy with Grand Duke Konstantin Nikolaevich, and most importantly, by his conscientiousness as a diarist. His notes are extensive and precise.[97] A good example of Peretts' skill is his description of the celebrated session of the Council of Ministers on 8 March 1881—a description more detailed and exact than that of any other witness. The Peretts diary was published in 1927 by A.A. Sergeev, with a foreword by A.E. Presniakov. It covers the period from 28 September 1880 to 31 December 1883. However, the published version does not include the whole text. One may consult a typed copy, called "Extracts from the Memoirs of State Secretary Peretts for the Period 1880 to 1881" in the papers of Alexander III. This copy was prepared in the pre-revolutionary period and written in the old orthography.[98] The "extracts" deal solely with the "constitutional projects" of 1880-1881. The first thirty-five pages recount the deliberations that occurred in late January 1880 relating to these projects. The rest is devoted to the Loris-Melikov project, and includes an account of the session of 8 March 1881. The comments covering January 1880 make it clear that the published version of Peretts' diary is incomplete, and suggest that Peretts may have made entries even before January 1880.

The diaries of Senator A.A. Polovtsov are rather less interesting for our present purposes. A man of moderately conservative views, a friend of Count P.A. Shuvalov, and an intimate of Grand Duke Vladimir Alexandrovich, Polovtsov served his government and kept his diaries for half a century.[99] The diaries lack grand generalizations and penetrating insights, but they are nevertheless distinguished by the abundance of factual information conscientiously included by their author. Despite his conservatism, Polovtsov was not uncritical, and his comments about the emperor himself are frequently none too flattering. The entry for 18 November 1880, for example, upbraids "dim-witted Alexander Nikolaevich."[100]

The diaries kept by Polovtsov during his tenure as State Secretary (1883-1892)[101] are fascinating, but in 1878 he was merely a senator in the First Department. In the autumn of 1880 he participated in the inspection of Kiev and Chernigov provinces. He recorded Loris-Melikov's speech to the senators departing for inspection tours. He also wrote down conversations with Alexander III and Loris-Melikov in March 1881.

The diary of General A.A. Kireev, Adjutant to Grand Duke Konstantin Nikolaevich, describes the atmosphere in government circles. The Kireev diary is not a first-class source.[102] Kireev bases most of his entires on second-hand information. He himself, of course, was not present at sessions of the State Council or Committee of Ministers, nor did he have access to either Alexander II or Alexander III. Nor did Kireev speak with the ministers as an equal. However, he conveys the mood prevailing in the court very clearly. Kireev was a reactionary Slavophile by conviction.

The diary of the 22-year-old Grand Duke Konstantin Konstantinovich is interesting only insofar as it discusses attitudes prevalent among the upper level of the ruling class during the crisis of the autocracy. The notes for February 1880 after the bomb explosion in the Winter Palace are worth reading carefully.[103]

The diaries of Alexander Alexandrovich, the heir to the throne, and the memo books of Alexander II are also of some interest. The future Alexander III kept a diary from his youth until January 1881.[104] His notes are rarely of value for the historian. Most entries are devoted to the tsarevich's daily personal life: diversions, the weather, personal guests. Sometimes he unblushingly records intimate experiences about which most persons would have preferred not to write. Minimal attention is devoted to political matters. Almost every day the tsarevich writes the following phrase: "Was at Papa's for ministers' report." He almost never jots down the subject of the meeting.[105] Nevertheless, occasionally one may find entries of some significance: a short account of the conclusions reached at the deliberations on the constitutional projects in January 1880, terse notes on his relations with Loris-Melikov, records of his visits with ministers. All of these entries are made in a very lapidary fashion.[106]

For more than a half century, from 1829 to 1881, Alexander II made daily notations in a memo book.[107] On each of the 12 x 8 centimeter pages he made entries in microscopic handwriting, often abbreviating words and phrases. Besides descriptions of his diversions, Alexander left his comments on ministerial reports and the most important events of the day. The tsar tells us about the establishment of the Supreme Administrative Commission, the hanging of Mlodetsky, the arrest of Zheliabov, and so on. By studying these notebooks can determine how often Loris-Melikov visited Alexander II. It is a great effort to read the tsar's memos. In view of the abbreviations and tiny handwriting every precaution must be observed. Under such circumstances, what is read not infrequently is not what is actually written, but rather that which one wishes to find.[108]

Memoirs also may be of great assistance to the historian. The recollections of N.P. Ignatiev, Minister of Internal Affairs, contain much information pertinent to the crisis of the autocracy, but given the author's irresistable passion for falsehood and the impossibility of checking many of his statements, these memoirs must be treated with extreme care. In this connection it is necessary merely to mention Ignatiev's "Thoughts on the Zemsky Sobor."[109] Comparison with other sources proves that Ignatiev's account is inaccurate. Ignatiev tries to pass off all projects for the Zemsky Sobor as his own, and fails to mention the role of D.P. Golokhvastov, who was in fact their author.

The notes of A.V. Golovnin, entitled "Materials for Future Historians of Russia,"[110] are not without interest. They contain an analysis of domestic politics, and deal with the problem of enlisting representatives of society to examine legislative proposals. However, in my opinion these memoirs are not of exceptional value. In the late 1870s Golovnin was merely a member of the State Council and did not serve the government in an executive role. Golovnin borrowed his material from conversations with Grand Duke Konstantin Nikolaevich and D.A. Miliutin. Moreover, his accounts are less detailed than those of Miliutin, Valuev, and Peretts.

In his memoirs M.I. Semevsky analyzes government policy toward the press. He also describes the activity of the Temporary Council of the Petersburg municipal governor (the "Parliament of Sheep" in contemporary parlance), created after the events of 1 March 1881.[111]

It is necessary to comment on the memoirs of M.T. Loris-Melikov, particularly on the account of the Council of Ministers meeting of 1881 which he gave to Bilbasov, the editor of the newspaper *Golos*. Bilbasov has testified that he was summoned by Loris-Melikov on 12 March 1881 to hear a description of the Council of Ministers meeting four days earlier. Loris-Melikov's account was clearly tendentious, and was apparently calculated to win public opinion over to his project. Even if one ignores the careless citation of participants' speeches and the lack of detail, Loris-Melikov did not recount faithfully the results of the meeting. Loris-Melikov asserted that Alexander III had accepted his proposals with the words: "Well, gentlemen, a majority has spoken in favor of the proposal to convoke a preparatory commission from the elected representatives of all classes for the welfare of the state. I agree with the majority .... The Minister of Internal Affairs will prepare a decree in accordance with our decision."[112] This account did not correspond to reality.

Finally, there must be mentioned the memoirs of Laferté, "Alexander II. Details inedits sur la vie intime et sa mort," published in Paris in 1882. Contemporaries attributed these memoirs to the morganatic wife of Alexander II, Princess E.V. Yurievskaia (Dolgorukaia). In my opinion, these recollections which appeared so soon after the tsar's death are of no interest since they are a mere apology for Alexander. The Laferté memoirs allege that before departing to review his troops on 1 March 1881, the tsar signed an order to convoke a preparatory commission to discuss political reforms. According to the memoirs, the order was to have been published on 2 March.[113] Actually, on the day of his death, Alexander merely called a meeting of the Council of Ministers for 4 March where the issue was finally to be decided.

Let us now consider the third major group of sources—letters. Like memoirs, letters are of crucial importance to the student of internal politics and their hidden aspects. If memoirs provide a more systematic illumination of politics than letters, which usually are confined to a narrow range of issues, letters recount events more directly and by their very nature are seldom apologetic in character. Therefore, letters are generally more reliable than memoirs as historical sources.

Most of the letters cited in this book have been published previously. Let us mention the more important among them. One may begin with the correspondence between Loris-Melikov and the future Alexander III in 1880.[114] These letters help to clarify not only the personal relations between these two figures, but also reveal Alexander III's attitude toward the activity of the Supreme Administrative Commission and the former Minister of Internal Affairs.

Of still greater importance is the correspondence of K.P. Pobedonostsev, preserved in his personal papers, in the Ignatiev papers, and the archives of Alexander III. This correspondence may be subdivided into several parts. First, there are the 225 letters which Pobedonostsev wrote to Alexander between 1878 and 1882.[115] The letters after 1 March 1881 are especially intriguing, since for several years Pobedonostsev exerted an enormous influence on the young tsar. These letters make it possible to discern the role of Pobedonostsev in preparing the Council of Ministers meeting on 8 March 1881, to peer behind the scenes at the drafting of the Manifesto of 29 April 1881, and also to discover the persons who were Pobedonostsev's creatures and were appointed on his recommendation to various government posts. Second, there is the correspondence between Pobedonostsev and other persons.[116] The letters from Alexander III to Pobedonostsev are especially interesting.

Third, there are the letters from Pobedonostsev to Ignatiev, preserved in Ignatiev's papers and heretofore unavailable to historians. The overwhelming portion of these letters (79 out of 90) were written during Ignatiev's service as Minister of Internal Affairs.[117] They make it possible to study Pobedonostsev's influence on Ignatiev, and thus on the internal politics of this period. Without consultation with Pobedonostsev, Ignatiev almost literally took not a single step (with the exception of attempts to call a Zemsky Sobor, where he acted quite independently). The final part of Pobedonostsev's correspondence consists of his letters to E.F. Tiutcheva, whom he regularly (once a week) informed about political events and his relationship to them. These letters are again of special interest for the year 1881. Pobedonostsev describes in detail the session of 8 March, his mutual relations with the ministers, and particularly with Loris-Melikov; he recounts the meeting of 21 April in Gatchina, and talks about the Manifesto of 29 April which he prepared.[118]

For study of Ignatiev's attempt to convoke a Zemsky Sobor and the infighting which characterized the struggle over this issue, the extensive correspondence of D.P. Golokhvastov with I.S. Aksakov is of unquestionable importance.[119]

These are the most significant letters, but the letters of other statesmen and public figures are of some value: M.E. Saltykov-Shchedrin,[120] Katkov,[121] Golovnin's and Loris-Melikov's letters to Miliutin,[122] Loris-Melikov's letters to Belogolovy,[123] and to Shalkovsky in which he gives a rather detailed picture of his activity in 1880 and 1881,[124] and others.

The last group of sources is journalistic material. It may be subdivided into two categories: (1) various projects and memoranda of an unofficial character concerning the contemporary policy of the government and recommending reforms; and (2) articles published in the press.

The memoranda and projects of P.P. Shuvalov, D.A. Miliutin, B.N. Chicherin, A.V. Golovnin, and others are part of the first subgroup. Two memoranda of Pavel Petrovich Shuvalov, or "Bobby Shuvalov" as he was known in society, have survived. The first memorandum raises the question of the introduction of a bicameral representative system; according to textual references, it must be dated to the period of late 1879 to early 1881, when the ruling classes began to understand the need for definite political concessions. Thanks to the testimony of Polovtsov, it may be dated even more precisely: on 21 February 1881 Polovtsov mentions a memorandum "sent from Bobby Shuvalov to the tsar and concerning the calling of a parliament."[125] The second memorandum, dated May 1881, contains a more moderate proposal, although the question of its realization is posed more concretely.[126] Neither of the Shuvalov memoranda became a topic for official discussion.

Let us turn to the memoranda written by D.A. Miliutin. In his personal papers there is a report entitled "Thoughts on Necessary Reforms in Administration, Education, and the Church," which proposes the reform of all elements of the governmental apparatus. This is merely a draft with numerous elisions. On the first page, he wrote "Livadia 1879." In light of Miliutin's residence in the Crimea, and of certain notes in his diary, this memorandum may be dated to fall, 1879. Miliutin's proposal apparently never was discussed; certainly none of his contemporaries ever mentioned it. The memorandum simply represents Miliutin's thoughts fixed on paper.[127]

A second memorandum entitled "Thoughts for a New Conference" also listed proposed reforms.[128] The opening lines refer to the assassination of Alexander II; therefore, it must be dated to March-April 1881 (after 29 April Miliutin was retired). However, one can establish the date even more precisely. On 21 April there was a meeting in Gatchina, where the warring governmental factions achieved a certain compromise. At this conference Alexander III asked his ministers to get together periodically for discussion of important issues. The tsar set out a number of issues for discussion, and recommended the convocation of a new conference under his chairmanship to decide these issues. Thus a *new conference* was proposed. Miliutin's memorandum was prompted by just this new conference. Hence it must be dated not earlier than 22 April and not later than 28 April 1881. Both of the Miliutin memoranda are helpful in reconstructing the political program of one of the most influential ministers of Alexander II.

B.N. Chicherin's report called "The Tasks of the New Regime," written on 10 March 1881, is an important source on the political views of the moderate liberals following the assassination of Alexander II.[129]

After the bomb blast in the Winter Palace on 5 February 1880, memoranda of a rather different type were addressed to Alexander II and Loris-Melikov. The explosion triggered a consolidation of the ruling elite and also an understanding of the need for definite political concessions. In the wake of this event there passed a whole stream of memoranda containing various recipes for the "salvation of Russia." People from diverse backgrounds contributed their ideas: A.V. Golovnin, a member of the State Council; the reactionary journalist P.A. Fadeev; the adventurist General Bogdanovich; and various obscure "saviors of the tsar and the Fatherland," who conjured up every conceivable device for the battle against "subversion."

In this category there must be included a long, unsigned memorandum dated April 1880—a document obviously written by A.V. Golovnin. The first lines prove his authorship: "The author, who has devoted himself to historical study and to the present conditions of schools, . . . took part in almost all the academic reforms of this reign."[130] Golovnin treats the reasons for the growth of the revolutionary movement and outlines reforms in the political and economic spheres (most notably new reforms in education).

On 7 April 1880 R.A. Fadeev, who was then an advisor to the head of the Supreme Administrative Commission, submitted a detailed memorandum on the reasons for the development of a revolutionary movement in Russia and on needed reforms. Although Fadeev was a reactionary, he did demand reforms of an objectively bourgeois character.[131]

General E.V. Bogdanovich who, despite his unenviable reputation, had served as expert advisor to Loris-Melikov, also wrote a memorandum. It dealt with those groups of the population which in Bogdanovich's opinion constituted the chief danger to the state—namely, the lumpenproletariat. Although Bogdanovich recognized the need for reforms, he refrained from specific proposals in his memorandum.[132]

A group representing Moscow liberalism, including S.A. Muromtsov, A.I. Chuprov, V.Yu. Skalon and others, authored a particularly important memorandum. They conveyed this document to Loris-Melikov in March 1880. The first and longest part of the memorandum attempted to establish the causes for the growth of the Russian revolutionary movement; the second part suggested methods to eliminate these causes.[133]

The second subgroup of journalistic materials is comprised of articles published in the periodical press. To characterize reactionary public opinion, which expressed the interests of gentry landowners, one may use M.N. Katkov's *Moskovskie Vedomosti*. This paper opposed any political concessions, and treated vigorous repression as the only answer to "subversion."

For various shades of liberal opinion there is A.A. Kraevsky and M.M. Stasiulevich's *Vestnik Evropy*, the left-wing *Otechestvennye Zapiski*, and the Geneva-based publication *Obshchee Delo*. Liberal papers founded in late 1880 or early 1881 also deserve attention; among the most interesting are *Strana, Poriadok,* and *Zemstvo*. With the exceptions of *Obshchee Delo* and *Otechestvennye Zapiski*, the liberal press set its hopes on government-sponsored reforms, and on a sympathetic hearing from Loris-Melikov.

Revolutionary-democratic opinion may be followed by reading illegal papers like *Zemlia i Volia, Narodnaia Volia, Listok Zemli i Voli* and

Listok Narodnoi Voli. The revolutionary press showed itself irreconcilable to government policy as a whole and to public officials, including Loris-Melikov. The pages of *Narodnaia Volia* continually attacked the duplicitous policy and hypocrisy of Loris-Melikov. Even so, the People's Will ignored the change of government tactics after 5 February 1880— the relaxation of the system of police terror—which was the result of their heroic struggle.

Karl Marx and Friedrich Engels displayed a lively interest in the Russian situation during this period. Marx studied in detail the economic condition of post-reform Russia.[134] Marx and Engels conducted an animated correspondence with Russian revolutionaries and public figures (P.L. Lavrov, G.A. Lopatin, V.I. Zasulich, M.M. Kovalevsky, and others).[135] In a number of Engels' works there are direct statements about the period from 1878 to 1882. In an article called "The Exclusionary Law against Socialists in Germany.—The Situation in Russia," Engels wrote: "For several years I have drawn the attention of European socialists to the situation in Russia where events of decisive significance are maturing. The struggle between the government and secret societies has become so sharp that it cannot last for long. The movement strikes again and again. Government agents respond with unbelievable cruelty. There is only one way to defend oneself against such animals—with powder and bullet. In Russia political assassination is the only weapon left to intelligent, brave and self-respecting individuals, who wish to defend themselves against the agents of a despotism unprecedented in history."[136]

Fourteen years later in the afterword to the book *On the Social Question in Russia*, Engels made another observation on the crisis of the autocracy; he underlined the decisive role of the People's Will in the struggle against the government. "These people, who were but a few hundred, by their selflessness and valor drove the tsarist regime to the point that it was forced to consider the possibility of capitulation and surrender. We cannot criticize these people for their belief that the Russian people are the chosen people of social revolution."[137]

V.I. Lenin's work "The Oppressors of the Zemstvo and the Hannibals of Liberalism" is of crucial importance for understanding the most important questions posed in this investigation. Lenin analyzed the reforms of the 1860s and 1870s, in particular the zemstvo reform, and the subsequent government policies during this period. He defined the underlying causes of the crisis of the autocracy, underlined the significance of the heroic campaign of the People's Will, and analyzed the policies of Loris-Melikov and his "constitution." Lenin discussed the reasons why the government survived the crisis following the assassination of Alexander II. "By 1 March the revolutionaries had exhausted themselves. There was neither a broad movement nor solid organization of the working class. Liberal society was so politically undeveloped that, even after the death of Alexander II, it confined itself to petitions alone."[138] Lenin's article on "The Break Up of the Second International," is also relevant to our study because it summarizes the preconditions of a revolutionary situation.

HISTORIOGRAPHY

It is no surprise that the first published works to deal with the crisis of the autocracy were journalistic. The authors were either European liberals or members of the Russian liberal movement. The first person to attempt an explanation of Russia's political crisis was the French journalist Leroy-Beaulieu. As early as April 1881 *Revue des deux mondes* carried an article called "L'Empereur Alexandre II et la mission du nouveau tsar." This article, written by Leroy Beaulieu on the basis of testimony from informed sources,[139] is largely devoted to an analysis of the personality of the recently-slain emperor and to commentary on the Russian political situation after 1 March 1881. Written from a liberal standpoint, the article gives a more or less accurate description of the personal qualities of Alexander II and of the inconsistencies in his reform program. Concerning Beaulieu's article, D.A. Miliutin wrote in his diary: "The article deserves attention. The author obviously had excellent sources to depict thus the personality of the late emperor and to explain many aspects of his reign by these personal traits. It seems to me that Beaulieu's explanations are quite correct and should be accepted by future historians of Alexander II."[140] Beaulieu's second article, "La Russie sous le tsar Alexandre III," dealt primarily with political circumstances in the first year of the new tsar's reign.[141]

During the 1880s Leroy-Beaulier authored a huge three-volume work, *L'Empire des tsars et les russes*. The fourth chapter in book six, volume II, deals with the final period in Alexander II's reign and the accession of Alexander III to the throne,[142] but this multi-volume history adds nothing new to what appeared in the articles in *Revue des deux mondes*.

The famous French journalist de Vogüé wrote an article called "Le général Loris-Melikov. Derniers mois du regne de l'empereur Alexandre II,"[143] a piece noteworthy if only because its author was an eyewitness to events—a perspective afforded by his position in the French embassy in Petersburg. It must be recognized that de Vogüé's testimony is not absolutely trustworthy since information received in the embassy was frequently less than reliable.

In 1893 the Free Russian Press in London published an anonymous pamphlet, "The Constitution of Loris-Melikov." [144] Written from a liberal standpoint, the pamphlet contains biographical information on Loris-Melikov, his participation in the Russo-Turkish war, his tenure as head of the Supreme Administrative Commission and as Minister of Internal Affairs. It includes also detailed notes on the planned senatorial inspection tours, a full draft by Loris-Melikov of a government communiqué of 6 March 1881, and a complete account of the reforms proposed by Loris-Melikov to Alexander on 28 January 1881. The pamphlet cites reports by B.N. Chicherin, A.L. Gradovsky, Marquis Wielopolski, and the Parisian Police Prefect Andrier dated after 1 March 1881. A letter from the German emperor to Alexander III on the introduction of a constitution in Russia is also of great interest.

The pamphlet makes a series of valuable historical sources available to scholars for the first time. However, it is an apology for Loris-Melikov, even to the dubious assertion that he requested a pardon for Presniakov, a member of the People's Will, and clemency for the would-be assassin Mlodetsky. Summarizing the narrative, the author writes: "Thus ended a modest attempt to reconcile the cultured classes with the bureaucracy and absolutism; thus was eliminated the sole path to peaceful development of the Russian nation, to the completion of those reforms begun on 19 February 1861." [145]

Who wrote this pamphlet? According to the historian B.E. Nolde, the author was M.M. Kovalevsky, who spoke to Nolde personally about it. The documents were provided by Dr. N.A. Belogolovy, who was close to Loris-Melikov. [146]

In 1894 the Free Russian Press published F.V. Volkhovsky's article "What are the Lessons of the Loris-Melikov Constitution?" Volkhovsky's main idea was that the revolutionaries who assassinated Alexander II could not be held responsible for the failure to implement Loris-Melikov's plan; instead, Loris-Melikov was himself responsible. ". . . It is quite incorrect to blame the People's Will and its tactics for the failure to carry through with the plan. The People's Will became a political force in the first place only because of its tactics; if Loris-Melikov, who advocated different tactics, did not understand the role and significance of this new political force, that is not Narodnaia Volia's fault." [147] The article also made a number of mistaken assertions.

Volkhovsky's work depends heavily on sources introduced by Belogolovy and Kovalevsky. As for new sources, Volkhovsky quotes only an "invaluable passage" in a letter from Alexander III to his brother Vladimir, which suggests that the tsar was ready to approve the Loris-Melikov proposals; however, no one was willing to help the tsar proceed in this direction, and thus he had been obliged to turn to Pobedonostsev, who had drafted the 29 April Manifesto.[148] The provenance of this letter from the tsar is more than dubious.[149] Saying nothing of the fact that the correspondence of the tsar with his brother could hardly have been known to an emigre group, it is necessary only to observe that Alexander III's statement is in complete contradiction to the facts.

Early in the twentieth century historians began to examine the crisis of the autocracy. In a two-volume biography entitled *Emperor Alexander II. His Life and Reign* the historian S.S. Tatishchev devoted three chapters to the political crisis of the late 1870s.[150] Written from the official-monarchical standpoint, Tatishchev's work scarcely could pretend to be an objective description of events, although it does deserve attention as a factual history which introduces many important sources. Tatishchev used extensively the materials of the Special Conferences of 1879 and quotes long passages from them.[151] He also gives detailed summaries based on the journals of the Supreme Administrative Commission, and on Loris-Melikov's reports to the tsar. The report of 11 April 1880, which proposed broad domestic political measures, is quoted almost in its entirety. The report for 11 August on senatorial inspections is also cited *in extenso*. In this way Tatishchev quoted a series of official documents that are of crucial import for the study of internal politics.

Let us consider the works of liberal historians. In 1909 A.A. Kornilov's historical essays on *The Social Movement in the Reign of Alexander II* were published in Moscow. One chapter treats the crisis of the autocracy. Unlike Tatishchev, Kornilov made available no new facts; instead he suggested a new interpretation. Analyzing the activity of Loris-Melikov and in particular the aboliton of the Third Section, Kornilov writes: "When he abolished the Third Section, Loris-Melikov had no intention of abolishing the secret police, the gendarmerie, or associated agencies; instead, with a view to concentration and intensification of repressive power, he transferred these functions to the Minister of Internal Affairs. He pursued revolutionaries mercilessly. . . . Temporary Governors-General, military tribunals and the whole apparatus of the white terror remained intact." Some details in this description are not quite accurate, but on the whole it portrays justly the dictatorship of Loris-Melikov. On the assassination of Alexander II, Kornilov remarks: "In any case, it would be extremely short-sighted to attribute responsibility for the unhappy outcome of the social movement in Alexander II's reign to the revolutionaries. An objective and thoughtful examination of the historical facts suggests that the actual culprit was the government."[152]

This interpretation was offered earlier by F.V. Volkhovsky. On the whole, however, A.A. Kornilov was far from correct in his description of events. He exaggerated the significance of the zemstvo liberal movement, ignored the mass movement, and so on.

In his course of lectures on nineteenth-century Russia published in 1914, Kornilov offered a rather more conservative view than that expressed in his earlier book. His lectures do not argue that the government was in some way responsible for the assassination of Alexander II, and they idealize Loris-Melikov. Kornilov rejects N.K. Mikhailovsky's argument that Loris-Melikov followed a hypocritical policy. According to Kornilov, "Loris-Melikov can hardly be accused of hypocrisy and guile. On the contrary, his policy was distinguished essentially by its forthrightness. . . . "[153]

In 1912 V.Ya. Bogucharsky, a historian of the revolutionary movement, dedicated a chapter in his book *From the History of the Political Struggle in the 1870s-1880s* to the crisis of the autocracy. This chapter deals with the discussion of the reform proposals made by Valuev and Grand Duke Konstantin Nikolaevich in January 1880, and with the Loris-Melikov proposals in early 1881. Bogucharsky also considered the session of the Council of Ministers of 8 March 1881 and cites extensively from the diaries of Valuev and Peretts.

Bogucharsky is far from idealizing Loris-Melikov, although one encounters in this narrative not a few liberal propositions. In his analysis of the early 1880s, Bogucharsky writes: "At this time the government by its very nature and by virtue of its opportunity to conduct the country along the path of prosperity and progress was in an unusually strong position. It would have been impossible to imagine more favorable conditions for reform, which would have buttressed the stability of the government and continued the movement forward on the path of reform *from above*."[154]

Another example of liberal historiography is N.V. Golitsyn's voluminous introductory article to the materials he collected on Loris-Melikov's "constitution."[155] The article is quite interesting as a piece of factual reportage; it provides a history of the "constitution" and covers the period of factional struggle within the government after 1 March 1881. Golitsyn draws not only on the documents he collected, but also on a broad range of memoirs, and his article represents an important step forward in research on the political crisis.

It seems fair to assert that pre-revolutionary historiography did rather little to illuminate the crisis of the autocracy. However, there were published a number of documents crucial to future research including the journals of the Supreme Administrative Commission and the most important memoranda of Loris-Melikov.

During the 1920s and 1930s Soviet historians left the problem virtually untouched. The sole exception was S.N. Valk, who wrote short but valuable introductory articles to documentary publications.[156] In 1938 Academic Yu.V. Gotie published a brilliant article called "The Struggle of Government Factions and the 29 April Manifesto."[157] Gotie used a wide range of memoirs and letters. With his characteristic mastery, Gotie depicts the condition of government leadership after 1 March, the Council of Ministers meeting on 8 March, the struggle of governmental factions, and also the preparation of the 29 April Manifesto. He introduces a number of new and interesting historical facts. However, Gotie set his sights rather narrowly: he did not attempt to describe the general situation prevailing in the country, much less portray the struggle of government factions against this background. The absence of historical background somewhat diminishes the value of this serious and detailed article.

After the Second World War two dissertations on the autocratic crisis were defended: the first was "The Political Project of Loris-Melikov" by I.V. Epaneshnikov, and the second, by M.I. Kheifets, was "The Revolutionary Situation in Russia in the Late 1870s: The Crisis of Government Politics." Epaneshnikov's dissertation treats the political program of Loris-Melikov, but without touching on the internal politics of the government as a whole. Moreover, Epaneshnikov essentially ignored important aspects of Loris-Melikov's policy. The author did not even analyze Loris-Melikov's reports on 11 April 1880 and 28 January 1881 as part of his general domestic political program. The "political project" of Loris-Melikov is therefore considered in isolation from the general course of government politics—a very grave shortcoming.

A second shortcoming, which explains to some degree the first, is the author's failure to examine a sufficient number of sources. Epaneshnikov wrote his dissertation without drawing on government institutional archives. He did not use the personal papers of Loris-Melikov or Valuev, which were absolutely essential to his research.[158] In fact, this dissertation is written primarily from memoirs. The author leans heavily on such poor sources as the Yurievskaia memoirs, published by Laferté. These factors seriously diminish the value of Epaneshnikov's research. It is scarcely possible to think that Epaneshnikov settled the questions he set out to answer.

M.I. Kheifets looks at the crisis of the autocracy more seriously in his voluminous dissertation.[159] "The theme of my research is the political

crisis of the ruling class during a growing revolutionary situation, a
crisis which found its clearest and most complete expression in the so-
called regime of Loris-Melikov."[160]   Kheifets deals with the period from
February 1880 to 1 March 1881. He uses a wide range of sources, introducing much new evidence in his discussion. Much space is devoted to a
historiographical survey, written with a polemical bent. The economic
situation of the country and the mass movement are treated in detail.
Public opinion is thoroughly described. Little space is allotted to analysis of internal governmental politics, about which only general information is provided.

As the preface says, the dissertation centers on the period of Loris-
Melikov's dictatorship (Chapters 3-5). However, even here the research
on internal politics is more of a summary than of a concrete historical
character. For example, Kheifets does not treat Loris-Melikov's basic
program and activity relating to the zemstvos, the university reform,
the politics of censorship, the campaign of the Special Conferences
against the press, or the structure and staff of the Supreme Administrative Commission, or the Department of State Police founded by Loris-
Melikov. Even the reports of 11 April 1880 and 28 January 1881 receive
insufficient attention. The last chapter (pages 693-772) is a compendium
of well-known facts concerning events after 1 March 1881; no new
material is cited.

Kheifets' dissertation also has its interpretive shortcomings. The author tries to prove that the crisis of the autocracy was caused directly
by the mass movement, primarily by the peasant movement. He depre-
cates the significance of the People's Will, which played a central role in
creating the crisis. Figures on the number of peasant disturbances are
extremely exaggerated. On page 215 the author cites the following data
on the number of provinces in which peasant demonstrations were
observed:

1877 – 11	1879 – 29	1881 – 12
1878 – 14	1880 – 34	

These figures mean nothing in and of themselves. More precise information is needed on the number and character of disturbances. Furthermore, the figures are exaggerated, and lack documentary foundation.[161]
Kheifets informs the reader that data for 1879 was derived from a manuscript *Materials on the History of the Peasant Movement* prepared by
the Institute of History from papers of the Third Section and the Ministry of Internal Affairs, and for 1880 from materials of the Third Section
and the Supreme Administrative Commission. However, Kheifets gives
no specific references whatsoever to papers in these archives.[162]   The

Institute of History publication reprinted documents on peasant demon-strations, and each document appeared with full archival references. Perusal of the Institute of History publication, which I edited, shows that Kheifets' statistics are erroneous. While he says that the number of peasant disturbances rose in 1880, the fact is that it decreased sharply. Table 1 in this book and the work of other historians undermine Khei-fets' conclusions.[163]

It must be said that Kheifets generally takes a great deal of liberty with his sources. Logically speaking, historians can only discuss the dynamics of a historical movement in a particular year if they have examined the preceding and following years. One needs a broad per-spective to speak of the growth or decline of the movement. Kheifets violates this logical rule. He cites no figures on the peasant movement in the years after 1881 even though the number of disturbances increased in 1883 and 1884.

Kheifets does not cite any data on the worker movement after 1879, presumably because he wishes to conceal the sharp decline in the num-ber of strikes that occurred just when the crisis of the autocracy was becoming most intense. In addition, Kheifets arbitrarily wrenches quo-tations out of their proper context.[164] The result is a patently mis-taken view.

Kheifets is also wrong in his assessment of Loris-Melikov's dictator-ship. The assertion that police terror increased under Loris-Melikov is absolutely incorrect. Kheifets argues this mistaken position not only in his dissertation but in his article on "The Second Revolutionary Situa-tion in Russia."[165] "While applying police repression in its most extreme form, Loris-Melikov simultaneously flirted with the liberals (by the re-tirement of the Minister of Education and Supreme Procurator of the Synod D. Tolstoy, a certain relaxation of press censorship, liberation of the zemstvo from its cruel tutelage, etc.)."[166]

Actually political terror was reduced significantly, although the policy of cruel repression of revolutionaries continued. Not only official docu-ments but the testimony of such authoritative observers as M.E. Saltykov-Shchedrin and V.N. Figner prove this point.[167] The "admirable mo-tives" of Loris-Melikov do not explain his flirtation with the liberals. This flirtation was part of a new phase in the crisis of the autocracy, when the government was forced to make real concessions by the activi-ty of the People's Will.

In spite of its shortcomings, Kheifets work helps to understand the sentiments prevailing in the ruling classes, and to form a clearer picture of the "crisis of the leadership." Still, the most important sources for the study of internal politics—the papers of the State Council, the Committee of Ministers, and Special Conferences—are ignored in Kheifets' study.

Finally, mention should be made of S.N. Valk's article "Internal Politics in the 1880s and Early 1890s" in *Essays on Russian History in the Second Half of the Nineteenth Century*, which also touches on the crisis of the autocracy, specifically on the first months of Alexander III's reign and on the appointment of D.A. Tolstoy as Minister of Internal Affairs.[168] This article, written on the basis of a broad range of historical sources, including archival sources, is interesting both from a factual and methodological perspective.

Table One
The Peasant Movement from 1875 to 1884

Year	Number of Disturbances	A	B	C	D	E	Disturbances Ended by Military Force
1875	17	3	4	4	4	2	4
1876	23	5	2	8	3	5	5
1877	9	1	1	6	--	1	3
1878	31	--	8	9	6	8	5
1879	46	3	6	8	12	17	8
1880	13	1	--	8	3	1	4
1881	21	--	2	11	6	2	4
1882	29	8	2	7	5	7	9
1883	62	10	6	16	23	7	19
1884	81	14	--	8	47	12	19
Total	332	45	31	85	109	62	80

Causes:

A -- Land disputes, demands to increase allotments, etc.
B -- Demonstrations against local administration
C -- Disputes over land surveys, resettlement, eviction
D -- Seizure of land, harvests, unauthorized use of pastures, forests
E -- Refusal to pay taxes, refusal to accept land allotted, etc.

CHAPTER I

POLITICAL REACTION IN THE LATE 1870s

During the first months of 1878 the revolutionary activity of the Russian Populists was gaining momentum. On 24 January Vera Zasulich shot and wounded the Governor of St. Petersburg, General Trepov. On 1 February the spy Nikonov was murdered in Rostov-on-the-Don. In Kiev on 25 February there was an unsuccessful attempt on the life of Procurator Kotliarevsky. On 30 January in Odessa a police search of a conspirator's apartment, where a printing press had been hidden, was met by armed resistance from the revolutionaries (Kovalsky, Vitashevsky, and others) inside. Proclamations were issued by the secret "Executive Committee of the Russian Social Revolutionary Party" which had arisen in southern Russia.

In early 1878 the situation in the countryside also became considerably more complex. The war worsened the plight of the populace (because of mobilization of the male population, consequent disruption of the economy, etc.). This coincided with bad harvests in a series of provinces, which caused a sharp rise in grain prices. The war prompted various rumors about the partition of land. All this created tension in the country, and against this background the Populists' revolutionary struggle was especially frightening to the ruling classes. In January and February St. Petersburg witnessed a number of strikes and disturbances. The largest of them was a strike at the New Cotton Mill and Textile Factory involving 2000 workers, which began in late February and continued until 20 March. The number of peasant demonstrations also increased slightly.

On 31 March there was a powerful demonstration in front of the St. Petersburg courthouse to celebrate Vera Zasulich's acquittal.[1] All this, particularly the Zasulich demonstration, caused the government serious concern. On the evening of 31 March, after Zasulich's acquittal, the Advisory Group, later called the Special Conference, convened for the first time.

According to the minutes of the Conference, it was created "in response to the continually increasing momentum of the Social-Revolutionary movement, whose members have tried recently to implement the extreme parts of their program." P.A. Valuev, the Minister of State Domains, was appointed chairman, and other Conference members included the Minister of Internal Affairs, A.E. Timashev, of Justice, Count K.I. Pahlen, of Education, Count D.A. Tolstoy, plus S.N. Urusov, Head of the Second Department of His Majesty's Chancellery, and N.V. Mezentsov, Chief of Gendarmes. Opening the session, Valuev stated that the Conference must examine carefully "the meaning of the revolutionary propaganda for the state as a whole. . . . "[2]

Various issues were raised at the first session. The Minister of Justice spoke of the need to refer all crimes "against the lives and health of officials" and all cases of armed resistance to military field tribunals.[3] Count Pahlen pointed to the "inconveniences" in legal proceedings concerning state offenses, and drew attention to the significant number of students involved in revolutionary propaganda. He recommended organizing a special punitive corrective educational institution for these youths. Valuev, expanding upon Pahlen's idea, advised such a punitive institution for young workers as well. The Chief of Gendarmes dwelled on the question of administrative exile, noting that the existing system, which scattered exiles to different provinces, was ineffective. He recommended the founding of colonies in remote areas to accommodate such persons. Mezentsov asserted that "workers should be included among the colonists," obviously meaning the participants in revolutionary agitation and the strike movement.

In his summary at the end of the session, Valuev formulated the following recommendations: "(a) it would be desirable for political criminals who were still under age to be sent to special corrective institutions analogous to boarding schools in remote locations, (b) it would be desirable to construct similar institutions for young workers as well, and (c) it would be advisable to set up colonies in remote areas for the remaining workers and other unreliables, and to provide means for their subsistence."[4] The meeting was adjourned on this note.

The next session, on 10 April, considered possible measures to halt the revolutionary movement in educational institutions and a proposal to increase police forces. Valuev called the Conference's attention to the widespread currency of revolutionary ideas among students, and proposed to reduce the enrollment in higher educational institutions, particularly in the capitals. He claimed that this decrease would "naturally end the disorders in educational institutions." The Minister of Education expressed complete solidarity in this, announcing that the commission for review of the university statute had reached similar conclusions.

Count Pahlen, the Minister of Justice, spoke at length about the noticeable increase in the desire of the lower classes for education "in light of the significant privileges granted to the educated by the statute on military obligation."[5]

The members of the Conference then discussed the questions referred to them by Alexander II, namely, (1) whether to create a special guard unit in the capitals, (2) whether to establish police tribunals in St. Petersburg, and (3) whether to consolidate all police units into one government department (that is, form a Police Ministry). These issues also were analyzed in subsequent sessions on 18, 22, and 28 April and 9 May and 20 May. In the first two sessions the Conference dealt with measures concerning educational institutions. I.D. Delianov, the director of the Public Library, also participated in these meetings. At the 28 April meeting, Makov, a friend of the Minister of Internal Affairs, spoke about police reform, advising the creation of village constabularies. At the May sessions participants again considered educational issues (projects for corrective educational institutions and the situation at the women's medical courses at the Nikolaev Military Hospital), the condition of the rural population, the press, and so forth. Alexander II received the minutes of the Special Conference (as the Advisory Group was now called) on 12 June.

"Having set out on 31 March to discharge its responsibilities," said the minutes, "the Conference tried first to clarify the causes of such deplorable events as Vera Zasulich's recent acquittal by sworn jurors, as well as street disorders and political demonstrations. The Conference did not consider Zasulich's acquittal to be an exceptional or isolated event; rather, this example demonstrated the jurors' inadequate understanding of their role as judges and the people's poorly developed allegiance to the state."[6]

Discussing the reasons for the success of revolutionary propaganda, the Conference noted that there had been a marked decline "in administrative power and, more to the point, in police power." This decline was said to be the result of social reforms, such as the zemstvo reform, which had narrowed the sphere of police administrative activity. "The police," continued the minutes, "were subordinated to a certain extent to the power of the courts and the procurator and shunted aside, with no more power than private individuals."

The Conference unanimously considered bolstering police strength in both the cities and rural districts to be an absolute necessity. In addition, the Chief of Gendarmes proposed to increase the number of gendarmes "especially in those factories most susceptible to revolutionary propaganda."[7] The Conference also indicated the need to reorganize the police

and to give them more power to suppress various types of "street disorders." It recommended drafting precise regulations for bearing arms,
for granting to the police the right to use firearms, and forbidding
private citizens to carry weapons. The minutes noted that "(the reorganization of the police) would be advantageous in that it might make
it unnecessary to call out military support, since military intervention
always excites people and exaggerates the political significance of the
suppressed disorder."[8]

The Conference believed that the "swift dispersal of every sort of ill-
intentioned crowd" ought to be accompanied by no less decisive punishment of the participants. For this purpose the Conference advocated the
creation of police tribunals in the capitals and large cities, especially
university towns, to deal with "street demonstrations and outrages."
This recommendation is conclusive proof of the growth of the mass
movement in the cities.

In addition to these questions of justice and administrative-police
power, the Conference minutes also discussed "means of guaranteeing
government influence among the rural populace." The Conference noted
that it had not been requested to draft any measures for basic reform of
the existing governmental system at the village or district level. The
minutes nonetheless mention "in passing" the more important inadequacies of this system, which constrained "the beneficial influence of
central governmental power." "At the present time," said the minutes,
"the dominance of loyal and sensible elements of the rural population is
not certain. Respectable homeowners are often afraid to participate in
meetings where a tiny vocal minority might sway public opinion. The
mutual responsibility rule (*krugovaia poruka*) is most onerous for those
peasants who are the most industrious, thrifty, and far-sighted, and it
weighs least on the negligent peasants." One suggestion for bolstering
government influence in the countryside was the creation of territorial
districts. The Conference hoped that this step would "increase contact
between the authorities concerned with the peasants and the more educated elements of the rural districts."[9]

The Special Conference thus saw two ways to strengthen government
influence in the countryside: reliance on the prosperous peasants and
increasing the influence of the landed gentry (whom the Conference
must have meant in speaking of "the more educated elements of the
rural districts"). This discussion of government influence in rural areas
bespoke fear about the spread of anti-government ideas among the
peasantry. The perception of the rural situation in these terms, which

dominated the Conference, evidently belonged to Valuev. It was he who had expressed these same ideas as early as the 1860s.

In a long section of the minutes devoted to the condition of higher educational institutions, the Special Conference stated that "the principal contingent of disseminators and adherents of socialist-revolutionary propaganda is concentrated in institutions of higher education." Guided by this observation, the Conference decided it was necessary to "reduce the influx of students who were insufficiently prepared to enter these institutions and who lacked the means to obtain a higher education without undue hardship."[10] The object of this verbose proposition was to deny to members of the less-wealthy stratum of society— that is, the most democratic part—admission to institutions of higher learning. The Conference then called for a reduction in the number of students at the Academy of Medicine and Surgery, since so many Academy students had participated actively in the revolutionary movement.

In one session of the Special Conference the members had talked about abolishing the courses for female doctors at the Nikolaev Military Hospital. But after the speech of N.I. Kozlov, the Chief Medical-Military Inspector, who had been invited to address the Conference, and Valuev's visit to the hospital, the opinion of the members changed. "The difficult question of higher medical education for women was not legally resolved," according to the minutes. "Meanwhile a *de facto* solution has been reached in the women physicians' courses at the Nikolaev Military Hospital. The classes have been running for several years. The number of auditors is very substantial. The value of the instruction is indisputable . . . . The Conference recommends that the Ministers of War, Internal Affairs, and Education jointly draft a bill for the consideration of the Committee of Ministers concerning women's medical courses and the general question of medical education, and of the rights of women to practice medicine."[11]

The minutes then deal with the corrective educational institute proposed by A.L. Apukhtin, director of the Surveyors' Institute.[12] He suggested establishing corrective schools, far from the capitals and large cities, for "pupils and students who had been subjected to judicial prosecution or who had been expelled from other institutions because of participation in anti-governmental or socialist activity."[13] The Conference planned to take further action on this proposal if in detailed discussions it could be proven feasible. Furthermore, the Conference explored the possibility of establishing a special military-disciplinary unit "where young people of this kind might be sent for a more or less extended period of time, and where they would be subject to strict military discipline. In observing military order, the young people could make up for past offenses by improved behavior, and might then be able to enter regular schools or military service."[14] The idea of founding such special military units aroused general support among Conference members.

In the final section of the minutes, administrative-police measures again received attention. The Minister of Internal Affairs and the Chief of Gendarmes spoke of the "growing inconvenience" of scattering political exiles throughout the country, and argued that it would be more efficient to "confine all the exiles to a few distant locations" where it would be easier to observe them and prevent the further dissemination of propaganda. However, the Conference concluded that this issue was complicated by differences in social background, age, and sex among exiles. It thus decided to begin by organizing the colonization of political exiles from the lower classes, "whose number is increasing and who would be capable of supporting themselves at such settlements." The northern section of Western Siberia was suggested to the Minister of Internal Affairs and the Chief of Gendarmes as a suitable place for agriculture.[15]

Another section of the minutes dealt with the violation of censorship regulations by the press: "In so-called scientific articles the dominant tendency is to weaken religious belief; on issues of political and economic relationships, thoughts and theories are aimed at shaking the present foundations of the government order and at stimulating inimical feelings among the different classes of the population . . . ." However, no concrete decisions were reached on these matters. Finally, the Conference decided to reexamine the laws of 19 May 1871 and 7 June 1872 concerning the elimination "of procedural shortcomings in political trials."[16]

The Conference reached these conclusions after more than two months of consultation. The minutes were approved by Alexander II, who asked the Conference to report on the fifteenth of every month concerning the implementation of these decisions. The founding of the Special Conference demonstrates the powerful impact of revolutionary propaganda and activity. The government was disturbed also by the increase in mass demonstrations. The decisions of the Special Conference reflected these concerns. According to the government, the chief danger was the activity of the revolutionary Populists, but the regime also was alarmed by worker demonstrations and worried by the situation in the countryside. The measures adopted by the Conference, except the proposal for all-class districts, were intended to intensify repression. The imperial government had become incapable of governing on the basis of existing laws, and was forced to adopt extraordinary measures violating normal statutes. This marked the onset of the crisis of the autocracy.

The Special Conference had worked out a number of proposals for changing government practices. One of the first to be instituted was the establishment of village constabularies. The Minister of Internal Affairs had asked that village constables be stationed in rural locations in 46 provinces, and 2000 men in mounted patrol units in large cities. These special police units were intended to assist district police officials "to discharge police duties and to maintain surveillance over the actions of the regular village police."[17] The mounted police units could be used "in unusual circumstances," when the presence of a large number of disciplined forces might be necessary for the suppression of disturbances.[18] Squads of thirty men were requested for each large city. In his presentation to the Conference the minister had outlined even regulations for the selection of the lowest police officials—the *sotskie* and *desiatskie*. The *desiatskie* [ten-men] would be elected at village meetings for terms no longer than one month; the *sotskie* [hundred-men] would be elected at district meetings. For each of the latter positions the assembly would elect two men, one to serve as district police officer, the other as his deputy. Their tenure would be three years. "*Sotskie* who seemed irresponsible or disloyal might be fired by a district police official and replaced through new elections."[19] The hundred-men thus were subordinated completely to police control.

The Minister of Internal Affairs' plan was discussed in the Committee of Ministers in late May and early June and approved in its entirety. The tsar confirmed the decision of the ministers on 9 June,[20] and on 1 August 1878 village policemen were installed. The number of constables in individual provinces varied: in 20 provinces there were fewer than 100 men; in 15 provinces between 100 and 125; in 9 provinces there were between 125 and 175; in two provinces, Volynia and Podolia, there were about 200.[21] The average county [uezd] had approximately eleven constables.[22]

In instructions published by the Ministry of Internal Affairs on 19 July 1878 the constables were ordered "to preserve social peace and watch for rumors or signs of any actions directed against the government, legal authorities, and social order, or which might undermine the moral integrity of society and the rights of property."[23] Naturally enough, the creation of these posts was prompted by the "unhappy situation" in the countryside,[24] just as the mounted police units in the cities were a response to the increased number of strikes.

The spread of revolutionary attitudes caused the government to attempt to broaden the definition of "state crime" to encompass every action against officials. As stated earlier, the acquittal of Vera Zasulich by the St. Petersburg Municipal Court served as the immediate pretext for this maneuver. Alexander II convoked the Council of Ministers on 3 April to consider this strategy.[25] "The purpose of the meeting," Miliutin wrote in his diary, "was to discuss the urgent need to eliminate cases like that of the Zasulich girl—that is, to make sure that crimes against officials who guard society against the encroachments of political propagandists will not go unpunished. The Minister of Justice read a report prepared with the cooperation of other ministers,[26] Count Pahlen finding no way to remedy the problem other than to refer such cases to military tribunals . . . ."

Miliutin continued that he himself had spoken out sharply against the proposal and that many other ministers had supported him. Pahlen's project consequently was rejected by the tsar. "It seemed," wrote Miliutin, "that a different view had prevailed, that such matters should be removed from the customary courts with jurors and tried instead in special hearings . . . ."[27] However, new arguments erupted over this suggestion as well, and Alexander II finally asked Pahlen, Valuev, and Miliutin to report later on the matter. According to Miliutin, the group met the next day and decided that it would be inadvisable to refer crimes against officials to military courts. They proposed instead that these cases be tried in judicial chambers—that is, without a jury present.

In my opinion, this decision proves that the government was still able to reject measures that directly violated existing laws. Later, however, when the crisis of the autocracy had grown more serious, the leadership would be incapable of governing on the basis of ordinary legislation.

On 6 April the Minister of Justice submitted to the State Council a proposal "On Changes of Jurisdiction and Procedure in Crimes under Articles 263-271, 285, and 393 of the 1866 Penal Code, and in Other Very Grave Crimes against Officials."[28] At the beginning of his presentation Pahlen cited an investigation of political crimes which showed that revolutionaries used a variety of methods in their fight against the government. "But most important are those cases in which the criminal resolve of the malefactors appeared in its most dangerous and audacious form—in the form of open armed resistance to the government's orders. Among such cases," continued Pahlen, "one can point to the events of 6 December 1876 at the Kazan Square in St. Petersburg, where after an outrageous appeal to the people and a display of revolutionary banners, a crowd of propagandists beat up police officers who had ordered them to disperse."[29]

The minister then referred to the events of 31 January 1878 in Odessa, where a police staff officer and several gendarmes were wounded during a search of an apartment occupied by Vitten and Merzhanovaia. He also cited the demonstration outside the St. Petersburg courthouse on 31 March following Vera Zasulich's acquittal. "It is obvious," wrote Pahlen, "that this ominous development requires immediate measures guaranteeing strict punishment in cases of violence and resistance to the government. One could achieve this objective by a temporary change in jurisdiction over these crimes: by referring such cases for trial in judicial chambers without jury but in the presence of public representatives."[30]

On 13 April an interdepartmental commission examined the Pahlen plan. It approved his suggestions, but offered several changes. First, the category of crimes to be transferred to judicial chambers was broadened somewhat to include all cases of resistance to government orders, of "insubordination to duly constituted authority," insults or disrespectful behavior toward "officials carrying out their proper duties," jailbreaks, and "freeing or concealing prisoners charged with serious offenses." Second, the commission recommended that these provisions be made permanent and not just temporary parts of the law.

The State Council discussed this issue at a general meeting on 24 April which revealed disagreement over the proposal to have public representatives present during hearings in judicial chambers. A minority (thirteen members) thought this provision unnecessary, and they argued that the security of government officials should be protected solely by government institutions and the courts. The minority opposed the presence of public representatives at trials for offenses against the state because this presence would be construed as a concession to activist critics of government policy.[31] The majority of members (thirty-two) thought it "wrong to distrust such persons as the gentry marshals, municipal governors, or district elders, especially since the selection of these representatives was approved by the provincial governors.[32] On 9 May Alexander II upheld the majority position.[33]

In conjunction with his first plan Pahlen had submitted to the State Council a second proposal "On Changes in Certain Articles of the Law of 7 June 1872 Defining the Trial Procedure in State Offenses." This statute had referred all offenses against the state to the Special Bureau of the Senate. Pahlen argued that "placing all such matters before the Special Bureau of the Senate as the supreme judicial body of the empire"[34] caused a number of problems. First, it slowed trial of the cases themselves; second, it burdened the treasury with unnecessary expenses for the transportation of the defendants to St. Petersburg. With these problems in mind, Pahlen recommended several changes in the law. He maintained that state crimes should be tried (1) in judicial chambers "when the punishment for the crime as defined in the Penal Code did not involve deprivation or limitation of an individual's civil rights," (2) in judicial chambers with public representatives present, or in the Special Bureau of the Senate if the emperor so specified, if the punishment did involve deprivation or limitation of an individual's civil rights," and (3) in a Supreme Criminal Court "in cases of organized conspiracy against government officials or against the legal, established form of government and the order of succession to the throne."[35]

The interdepartmental commission and a general meeting of the State Council approved Pahlen's second proposal, and on 9 May the tsar affirmed the State Council's decision.[36] These government policies approved in the spring of 1878, indicated that the class struggle in Russia had become more intense.

Disturbed by the further growth of the revolutionary movement, Alexander II quickly recalled the Special Conference and asked it to map out a series of proposals to combat revolutionary activity. This is evident from a letter that Chief of Gendarmes Mezentsov sent to Minister of Internal Affairs Makov. It mentioned appointment of a Special Conference with Valuev as chairman and consisting of the Ministers of Internal Affairs, War, and Justice, plus the Chief of Gendarmes. The Conference was to deal "with the activity of an underground socialist circle located in the cities of Kiev, Kharkov, and Odessa and calling itself 'The Executive Committee of the Russian Socialist-Revolutionary Party.'"[37] Miliutin commented in his diary on the Conference's 28 June meeting: "Yesterday I attended a meeting convoked by special imperial order to discuss steps that ought to be taken against secret revolutionary socialist circles, clustered primarily in university towns. . . . Valuev, Mezentsov, Nabokov (the new Minister of Justice) and Makov (an associate of the Minister of Internal Affairs) participated in the meeting. The result of our discussion was recognition of the absolute necessity to strengthen police and gendarme forces, and also to adopt a number of other, less important measures."[38]

The participants discussed and elaborated a series of proposals to intensify the campaign against the revolutionary movement. A memorandum recording their decisions was sent to Alexander II in Livadia.[39] At the meeting, as the memorandum noted, Chief of Gendarmes Mezentsov listed "those conditions which permit harmful propaganda to be as effective as it has been recently."[40] According to Mezentsov, these conditions included "the inadequacy of funds available to the Third Section, particularly for underground work. No observation of society is possible without secret agents, and the present resources of the Third Section are too limited to carry out such observation properly. The provincial offices of the Third Section—the provincial gendarme branches—find it difficult to carry out their duties and conduct surveillance in their regions because they lack sufficient funds to cover expenses incurred in this kind of work."[41] Mezentsov announced that he would increase the personnel at gendarme branches by using the 100,000-ruble credit allowed to him. As far as the organization of a secret service was concerned, he would submit his recommendations at a later time. The Special Conference also discussed the condition of the imperial police and their role in the fight against the revolutionary movement.

After all these questions had been analyzed, the Conference formulated a proposal consisting of eight points. The first recommended that the Chief of Gendarmes be granted an additional 300,000 rubles (above the original 100,000-ruble allocation)[42] to hire more gendarmes and police investigators. The second point concerned the "immediate need" to strengthen police forces in a number of cities; the third point dealt with detention of political prisoners. The Special Conference recommended that political prisoners be detained separately from other prisoners and that "at major detention centers special quarters with increased surveillance be set up for political prisoners." The fourth point referred to the need for better surveillance of political exiles, and recommended that regulations be drafted to improve this surveillance. The fifth point asked that public printing presses be subject to government inspection, with persons delegated by the Ministry of Internal Affairs or the Chief of Gendarmes permitted "to examine presses during their searches and seizures. . . ." The sixth point recommended that gendarmes be granted the right to enter factories at any time without permission, since "increased propagandist activity has been noticed among factory workers, and has been successful." The seventh point indicated the need to change article four of the law of 1 July 1874, concerning the conditions and procedures for arresting persons accused of anti-government activity. The Special Conference recommended that the Minister of Justice discuss this law with the commission established for review of two other statutes (those of 19 May 1871 and 7 July 1872). Finally, the last point suggested that the Minister of Internal Affairs act "to avert further unsubstantiated and systematic criticism of police agencies and government officials in our journals and newspapers."[43] Every point of the Special Conference's decision called for some form of repression. It is important to note that point six spoke of the success of Populist propaganda among workers.

The Council of Ministers reviewed the Special Conference's recommendations only after 4 August when Chief of Gendarmes Mezentsov, the main speaker at the Conference, was assassinated by S.M. Stepniak-Kravchinsky.[44] The assassination of Mezentsov, like every revolutionary act, further consolidated the ruling classes. The liberal newspaper *Golos* wrote, for example: "One must be fair, even to scoundrels. They have chosen the revolver and the dagger as their tools, weapons used only in war. Let them face military justice! .... They must be accorded only one honor: these criminals must be given a trial before they are hanged."[45]

Immediately after the burial of Mezentsov on 8 August the Council of Ministers convened in the Winter Palace in the presence of the tsar. "The purpose of the meeting," wrote Miliutin, "was again to plan the reaction to the insolent act of a secret revolutionary circle. The protocol of the meeting on 28 June was read, and then Valuev delivered a report he personally had composed. A memorandum over the two signatures of Makov and Seliverstov (director of the Ministry of Internal Affairs and acting head of the gendarmes) followed, and the Minister of Justice Nabokov then spoke. All the points made in these four memoranda were approved by the tsar, despite prolonged and heated debate over certain issues. Valuev's attack on the new Minister of Finance, Greig, was noteworthy for its uncharacteristic acerbity. The Minister of Justice defended the procurator, but with rather little success. Finally, a whole series of measures was proposed, but the questions of how and by whom they were to be implemented were not resolved."[46]

In addition to the eight-point program, the Special Conference adopted additional measures,[47] including the important regulations of 1 September 1878, which contained necessary special measures for maintaining social tranquility and security.[48] These regulations gave gendarme officers, and in their absence police chiefs and district superintendents, the right to arrest persons "suspected of state crimes" as well as "persons responsible for participation in street disorders or political meetings." Such individuals might not merely be arrested, but even exiled without the sanction of the procurator: "Persons arrested on these counts may be subject to administrative exile by agreement of the Minister of Internal Affairs and the Chief of Gendarmes, if there is sufficient evidence of their political disloyalty." According to appended remarks, this rule was "accepted without consulation with members of the procurator's staff, to whom a copy of the decree on exiles was forwarded."[49] The law of 19 May 1871 gave responsibility for trying offenses against the state to officials of the gendarmerie, who, however, were placed under the supervision of the procurator's office. Compared to this 1871 statute, the Temporary Regulations of 1 September 1878 were a significant step forward in administrative arbitrariness. Given Valuev's sharp polemic with Nabokov at the Council of Ministers meeting, it is probable that Valuev himself provided the initiative for this new law.

On 25 September a new top-secret circular explaining the Temporary Regulations of 1 September 1878 was sent to gendarme authorities.[50] The new circular first noted that "efficient application of these regulations in practice undoubtedly will facilitate achievement of the desired results." However, every error in interpretation "of the rights and responsibilities of the gendarmes . . . inevitably will arouse public opinion against the government, increase the number of malcontents, and deeply inconvenience those persons unjustly subjected to surveillance and deprived of their freedom, however briefly." Because of this, the Chief of Gendarmes instructed that "the disposition of cases through administrative channels," that is, by the rules of 1 September 1878, would occur only under the following conditions: "(1) when compromising information is obtained by absolutely secret means but cannot be confirmed factually, (2) when compromising information, though not secret, cannot be verified."

In practice there sometimes might "arise doubt over the disposition of cases through legal inquest or administrative procedure." In such instances the circular advised the "initiation of administrative procedures; should new evidence establishing more clearly the guilt of the individual become available, an administrative review could be converted into a legal inquest under the law of 19 May 1871. Other procedures will not be allowed under any circumstances."[51]

The very text of this explanatory circular testifies to the government's realization that the Temporary Regulations of 1 September 1878, if broadly applied, might intensify administrative arbitrariness to such an extent that the rules would prove counterproductive. However, the circular in no way limited arbitrariness. Indeed, it proposed applying the regulations precisely in those cases where a criminal charge could not be proven by legal means.

The second important provision adopted by the Council of Ministers was the transfer of "state crimes" to the jurisdiction of district military tribunals; this again violated existing laws. According to the Military Justice Statute of 15 May 1867, district military courts were established to try persons in military service. The courts consisted of officers who might be permanently empanelled or temporarily assigned to the court for six-month terms from the respective military district.[52]

A law "On Temporary Submission of Cases Involving State Crimes and Certain Crimes Against Government Officials to the Purview of Military Courts Operating Under Wartime Procedures" was promulgated on 9 August. This law provided that "persons accused of armed resistance to government officials or of attacks against military officers or policemen or any responsible officials carrying out legally prescribed duties, when the crimes committed are assassination, attempted assassination, assault, battery, or arson, will be transferred to military courts for trial under wartime procedures and sentencing according to article 279 of the Military Penal Code of 1875."[53]

On the same day a second law was promulgated defining the procedures for trying offenses against the state in military district courts.[54] This law stipulated that the district military commanders were responsible for bringing such cases to trial in military courts, and had the right to ratify sentences. Previously this right had been reserved in wartime to the commander-in-chief. Only staff officers (the senior and most conservative members of the officer corps) might be appointed by the district infantry commanders to be temporary members of the military courts. The referral of cases to military district courts, the composition of the court, and the ratification of sentences all depended upon one man, the district infantry commander. The potential for arbitrariness was obvious. This law thus gave to the government the institution about which the Minister of Justice had dreamed: a court which would dispose of cases "at the instance of government authorities."[55]

In the wake of these decisions by the Council of Ministers on 8 August, the Committee of Ministers examined the proposal of the Minister of Internal Affairs "On Increasing Police Forces in Several Provincial and District Capitals."[56] The minister's proposal was accepted in its entirety in mid-November, and the committee decided on two courses of action. The first was to increase police forces in ten cities—Odessa, Kharkov, Kiev, Kazan, Saratov, Samara, Nizhny Novgorod, Rostov-on-the-Don, and Nikolaev. These cities were chosen because they "recently had been the most important centers of agitation, and afforded agitators several advantages." The committee also approved Timashev's request for increased police funding—9795 rubles for immediate use and an annual appropriation of 267,400 rubles.[57]

The second course of action involved the organization of covert operations by the national police in 46 provinces, again to combat the revolutionary movement. The Committee of Ministers accepted this request despite the parallel existence of two other kinds of secret police in the gendarmerie and in police departments. The committee appropriated 138,000 rubles annually for covert activity as requested by the Minister of Internal Affairs.

One of the most severe measures enacted on 8 August was the "imperial decree" concerning persons under police surveillance. It required that "every political criminal exiled by administrative or judicial procedure who escapes or attempts to escape police surveillance be banished to the Yakut region."[58]

Together with these police-administrative measures the government took the extraordinary step of calling for the cooperation of the public. The journal *Pravitelstvenny Vestnik* published a "government report" which called the Mezentsov assassination "a heinous deed" and said that "the government's patience now has been completely exhausted." The article underlined the government's decision "to pursue with determination those individuals guilty of or connected with subversion of the existing governmental system." Moreover, it maintained that the Russian people would condemn revolutionary activity. This assertion was based on the numerous letters which the government supposedly received from private citizens and representatives of class and social institutions. The article said that "no matter how strong and persistent were the actions of the government," the government would "need support in society itself and therefore considered it essential to ask for the unanimous cooperation of all classes of the Russian people to help the government eradicate the evil created by falsehoods and terrible crimes." The end of the article included a special appeal to students to "reflect carefully upon the grave and lamentable consequences" that might befall them if they listened to "false teachings."[59]

By its very nature this appeal revealed the weakness of the government and of its attempt to find support in the conservative element of society and simultaneously to consolidate its social base. Here were unmistakable symptoms of the crisis of the autocracy.

A number of zemstvos responded to the appeal by promising "to eradicate evil." According to B.B. Veselovsky, fourteen provincial and twelve district zemstvos sent such messages to the tsar.[60]

On 20 November 1878 in Moscow Alexander II also appealed to representatives of the Estates to cooperate with the government in "stopping confused youths from travelling that unfortunate road which disloyal persons had urged them to follow."[61] Noteworthy in this regard is a secret instruction from the Ministry of Internal Affairs on 9 June 1878 that all telegrams, including various addresses and reports of gentry organizations, zemstvos and urban agencies, and individuals sent to members of Russia's ruling house or to foreign monarchs, "must first be submitted to local officials, who, together with the Ministry of Internal Affairs, will allow only authorized . . . telegrams to be transmitted."[62] The autocracy thus feared not only the revolutionary movement, but also demonstrations of political opposition.

After studying the measures taken by the government in domestic politics in 1878 one may make a series of observations. It is obvious that any government, be it feudal or bourgeois, exercises its power in two ways: by naked force, and by concessions, reforms, and appeasement of the populace. In reality both of these approaches function simultaneously and are closely related, although one usually dominates the other. Beginning in 1866 the method of violence and repression predominated in Russia. The second approach rarely was used. The year 1878—characterized by the rapid growth of the crisis of the autocracy— did not witness the introduction of any essentially new government policies. In attempting to suppress the revolutionary movement the government used only repression, applying it to a significantly greater extent than in previous years. The growing crisis was evident, primarily in the shift from ordinary statutes to extraordinary legislation (the Temporary Regulations of 1 September 1878, the extended functions of military courts, etc.). The attempt to broaden the government's base of social support by appealing to the "loyal" segments of society also provides some evidence of the crisis.

Despite the repression of the previous year, the revolutionary movement did not diminish in 1879, but instead grew stronger. The countryside witnessed a certain increase in peasant disturbances as compared to the preceding year. The tense situation in rural areas was characterized not only by peasant disturbances, but also by widespread rumors of a confiscation of gentry land. Nor did Populist terrorism diminish. On 9 February Governor-General Kropotkin was assassinated in Kharkov, and on 26 February Police Agent Reinstein was murdered in Moscow. In St. Petersburg on 13 March an unsuccessful attempt was made on the life of Chief of Gendarmes Drenteln.

Immediately after the attempted assassination of Drenteln, according to Miliutin's diary, the tsar ordered Valuev as chairman of the Special Conference to explore further measures to prevent future terrorism.

"This matter," wrote Miliutin, "had been discussed so frequently already that it seemed superfluous to waste time on a convocation. But the pretext for renewing discussion on this occasion was the arrival in St. Petersburg of Count Shuvalov, who took it upon himself to offer certain proposals."[63]

Indeed, former Chief of Gendarmes Shuvalov actively participated in the meeting of 15 March. "Members of the Conference," noted the minutes, "came to the unanimous conclusion that the time for equivocation had passed, and that governmental authorities no longer should be limited by instructions issued in the usual course of administrative and judicial proceedings. The quite exceptional, and even unprecedented circumstances required exceptional instructions." The minutes continued: "The suppression of revolutionary terrorism demanded the most decisive and extensive measures, whatever the discomforts to private citizens."[64]

The Conference endorsed proposals of a purely repressive nature. The first point of its resolution, adopted at Shuvalov's recommendation, called for a credentials check of the residents of St. Petersburg (including the homes of treasury and court officials) in order to expose individuals without internal passports. The punishment for violation of the passport law was also defined. Homeowners and landlords of hotels or apartments with furnished rooms [who housed people without passports] could be fined from 50 to 500 rubles; hall porters and yardkeepers might be dismissed from their posts and deprived of the right to hold such jobs in the future. These penalties could be imposed in St. Petersburg province, Moscow, Kiev, Kharkov, Odessa, and Yalta. The second point of the resolution granted Moscow and Kiev Governors-General the right to exile by fiat any persons "whose presence in these cities is inimical to social tranquility and security."[65]

The third point concerned the right of St. Petersburg police to carry revolvers, and confirmed the right of policemen to use their weapons in self-defense. "Anticipating future assassination attempts,"[66] the final point recommended that two mounted police convoys escort the Chief of Gendarmes, the Minister of Internal Affairs, and the Petersburg governor. The conference also approved the proposal of the Minister of Education to discuss the question of organizing a mounted police unit in Petersburg and the proposal of the Minister of Justice to transfer responsibility for sanitation from the police to the municipal government.

In conclusion, the Special Conference remarked that its decisions "involved measures of a preliminary or palliative nature aimed at the

immediate reduction of that problem threatening the basis of the state
and the social order; but for the final eradication of that problem it
would be necessary to go to its roots, to locate the soil in which it
germinated, to discover the conditions which permitted its pernicious
growth and spread, and to discuss a series of steps that could, if carefully and systematically followed, ensure final success in the battle."[67]

The session of 15 March had been limited to police measures, and
no general plan for defeating the revolutionary movement was devised,
but within two weeks, on 2 April, a new attempt was made on the life
of Alexander II. This event caused a powerful wave of reaction. In the
words of Senator Polovtsov, who had spent the day of 2 April in the
palace, the tsar told a deputation of nobles directly that "the gravity
of the situation forced him to employ extraordinary methods, that he
saw the need to depart from strictly legal methods, and that he hoped
the nobility would help rather than criticize him, as it had done so often
in the past."[68]

When Miliutin heard of the attack on the tsar, he also went to the
palace, where he saw a number of ministers, including Valuev and
Drenteln. According to Miliutin, "the tsar summoned Valuev, Drenteln,
Makov, and me to discuss possible responses to the abnormal situation
we faced. The tsar ordered us to meet that day and work out a proposal for establishing temporary military Governors-General in the two
capitals and other large cities and for enforcement of martial law."[69]
This offers the impression that the initiative for creating temporary
Governors-General came from the tsar himself, but this impression is
mistaken.

Valuev stated explicitly in his diary that the idea of temporary military Governors-General was his own. On 15 April he noted: "The idea
of Governors-General is mine, and was suggested even before 2 April."[70]
There is very solid evidence to support this assertion in Valuev's archive—
a memorandum in Valuev's own handwriting, dedicated to the struggle
with "sedition" and dated 2 April. In this memorandum Valuev spoke
of the need for temporary military Governors-General in St. Petersburg,
Kharkov, and in either Odessa or Nikolaev, and for granting analogous
powers to the Governors-General of Moscow, Warsaw, and Kiev.

Valuev defined these "powers" as follows: "Subordinate to the Governors-General all local authority in the law enforcement field. Subordinate to them all members of the procurator's office, and give the
Governors-General the right to form investigative and military judicial
commissions and to confirm their orders and sentences. Transfer from
the Chief of Gendarmes and Minister of Internal Affairs to the Governors-General the right to detain and banish participants in revolutionary

agitation. Subordinate to the Governors-General local infantry and military detachments. Grant them the right to close temporarily those public institutions openly cooperating with revolutionary agitators, and to halt those publications which attempt to strengthen or support antigovernment agitation. Grant them the right to draw up and implement all temporary police orders that they think essential for the maintenance of public security."[71]

According to Valuev, the introduction of temporary military Governors-General essentially would mean imposition of martial law. This had to be done suddenly, as the memorandum indicated. "On the very night before the extraordinary measures are announced," he noted, "the most important arrests should be made to smash the existing web of subversion."[72] Apparently Valuev wrote this before the Conference met at two o'clock on 2 April to discuss the institution of temporary Governors-General. According to Miliutin, the chief military prosecutor, Filosofov, attended the meeting along with the regular members of the Conference. "After three hours of argument and discussion, we concluded that the next day Filosofov and the Minister of Justice Nabokov would draft a decree on the temporary Governors-General for submission to the Senate."[73]

The decree to the Senate, published on 5 April, said that the Conference had accepted Valuev's basic proposal, but that certain points had been stricken. The first sentences of the decree described the situation in Russia not only with reference to dissemination of revolutionary ideas, but also with reference to the terrorist campaign and the attempt on the tsar's life. According to the decree, these factors had forced the government "to apply temporary emergency measures in order to punish the guilty appropriately as well as to preserve public order by granting special powers to government officials."[74]

The first and second points of the 5 April decree concerned the appointment of temporary Governors-General in St. Petersburg, Kharkov, and Odessa, and a temporary conferral of analogous powers on the Governors-General of Moscow, Kiev, and Warsaw. These Governors-General had authority both in their respective provinces and in adjoining provinces which would be specified later.[75] "In all these areas," said the third point, "the Governors-General will have authority over all those local administrative units which would fall under the provincial or regional military command during wartime (by authority of article 46 of the Regulations on Field Command during Wartime).[76] [The Governors-General] also would control the curricula of educational institutions insofar as they affect the preservation of public order and domestic tranquility."[77]

The fourth and fifth points broadened the rights of the Governors-General to hand over to military courts persons charged with offenses against the state. According to the law of 9 August 1878, persons accused of armed resistance to authority or attacks on govermental officials could be turned over to military courts. By the decree of 5 April, transfer to military courts also was provided "for other sorts of state crimes or attacks against the administrative system, and for other offenses defined by criminal laws, when they [the Governors-General] deem it necessary for the protection of public order and tranquility."

The sixth point granted the Governors-General special administrative rights: (a) the right to exile all persons "whose continued presence in a local area might be deemed harmful," (b) the right to arrest any person "regardless of professional or class background" when it was considered necessary, (c) the right to halt or prohibit periodical publications, (d) "the right to take those steps that are deemed necessary in view of local conditions to preserve order."[78] The sixth point of the 5 April decree thus granted the Governors-General extraordinarily extensive plenary powers, and turned them into a sort of proconsul. The introduction of the institution of temporary Governors-General was a very large step forward in the direction of administrative arbitrariness. This government action testified to the further intensification of the crisis of the autocracy, which was incapable of ruling by established laws.

Comparing the Valuev proposal with the decree, few differences are found. The decree did not speak directly about subordinating officials from the procurator's office to the Governors-General, although the granting of extensive powers to the Governors-General certainly deprived the judicial agencies of much of their independence. More importantly, the Conference rejected Valuev's proposal for the kind of St. Bartholomew's night that he desired on the eve of the imposition of his program.

Two days after the decree introducing the temporary Governors-General was published, another decree appointed Governors-General in St. Petersburg, Kharkov, and Odessa. Generals who had distinguished themselves during the last war were named to these posts, probably to invest some authority in the office. General Gurko became St. Petersburg Governor-General, Count Loris-Melikov was to serve in Kharkov, and General Totleben filled the Odessa position.[79] Alexander II nominated these men in consultation with War Minister Miliutin and Chief of Gendarmes Drenteln.

The reactionary press and some liberal newspapers greeted these new posts with enthusiasm. In its editorial of 7 April *Moskovskie Vedomosti*

[Moscow News] wrote: "Every honest person gladly will accept temporary abrogation of a certain measure of comforts and privileges if this
sacrifice is demanded in the interests of public order." However, the
paper expressed some concern that the appointment of persons en-
dowed with extraordinary plenary powers might lead to disarticulated
government. "No matter how similarly the Governors-General act in
different parts of the empire," wrote Katkov, "they and their actions
nevertheless will be somewhat uncoordinated. To annihilate swiftly the
evil of revolutionary activity, perhaps the government should appoint
a man with full authority over this operation, a man who would hold
all the strings in his hands."[80] The liberal *Golos* [Voice] also reacted
positively to the introduction of Governors-General. "This extraordinary
step, which is the direct legislative consequence of the social malaise
afflicting the body politic, should bring only peace to the disturbed and
agitated minds in all educated and uneducated parts of society."[81] A
month later *Golos* returned to this issue: "We wish complete success
to the efforts of the temporary Governors-General. We all feel that it
will be possible to breathe and think peacefully only when the whole
pirates' den has been uncovered and utterly destroyed."[82]

Other reactionary steps were taken also. The day after the attack
on Alexander II the Minister of Internal Affairs organized a "reception"
in the Ministry for journalists. On 4 April he invited to his office the
editors of all newspapers in the capital and delivered a crude didactic
speech in an unduly familiar, boorish manner.[83] "I called you together,
gentlemen," began Makov, "to point out that the behavior of the press
at the present time is highly unsatisfactory."[84] During his remarks Makov gestured several times toward the supervisor of the Main Press Administration, Grigoriev, and proposed that Grigoriev take action against
certain journals. "From now on," he continued, "I will not tolerate
[such unsatisfactory behavior] and any newspaper daring to violate my
orders will be shut down immediately, without any explanation, at my
insistence." According to M.I. Semevsky, the editor of *Russkaia Starina*,
[Russian Antiquities] Makov's speech was vulgar in the extreme. "Just
as in olden times a half-drunk town mayor might twaddle about a whore,
so State Secretary Makov spoke of the Russian press."[85]

The attempted assassination of Alexander II caused great dismay in
ruling society. "In the city," wrote Miliutin in his diary entry for 7
April, "people speak of nothing but criminal plots, new attacks on officials, dragnet arrests. It is as if the air itself were permeated by sinister
expectations of some dread event. The wildest rumors and factions are
rife. The police command has been shaken by secret warnings. Simultaneously here and in Moscow there have been hints that malefactors,

seeing that individual attacks had failed, now planned to carry out 'mass attacks.' As a preventative, soldiers in the St. Petersburg garrison have been placed on emergency alert. Some of the soldiers have been stationed in different areas of the city: regiments have been kept in barracks."[86] Miliutin's testimony is surely reliable. Certainly the War Minister would know of secret maneuvers of troops stationed in the capital's garrison.

In early summer even Valuev shared these moods of pessimism and hopelessness. On 3 June he recorded his impression of a visit to Tsarskoe Selo: "I saw Their Imperial Majesties. Everything surrounding them is as before, but they have changed. Both left me in a dolorous mood. The Tsar looks tired and himself speaks of nervous irritation, which he tried to hide. A half-ruined sovereign. In an epoch when he obviously must possess strength, it cannot be counted upon. At the court—the same Grot and Golitsyn, the same Fraulein Pilar, the same head waiter .... Surrounding the palace at every step there are police guards. Mounted Cossacks ride beside the traditional carriage prepared for the Tsar; one feels that the earth is quaking, the buildings threaten to fall, but the inhabitants do not notice the danger. The proprietor has a dim presentiment of disaster, but conceals his anxiety."[87]

The Governors-General distinguished themselves in office by extreme arbitrariness and arrogance. Even the heir to the throne, Grand Duke Alexander Alexandrovich, far from a determined opponent of administrative arbitrariness, was forced to observe that some of the Governors-General did "heaven-knows-what."[88] During the period of the Governors'-General activity—from April 1879 to June 1880—575 persons were exiled on the basis of the 5 April decree, 130 to Siberia.[89] In only eight months in 1879 (April through December) sixteen persons were sentenced to death by military-district courts and hanged.[90] Naturally, all these sentences were confirmed by the Governors-General.

It was impossible to examine all the data on exiles under the 5 April decree; this discussion therefore will be limited to the activity of the Governors-General in Kiev, Odessa, and Kharkov. Very detailed data is available about the Kievan governor. He exiled a total of 148 persons before August 1880; of these, 115 were exiled in 1879, 11 in January and February 1880, 15 in March, April and May, 7 in June and July. All these exiles were divided into two groups: those with political motives and those with motives "of not purely political character." 106 persons belonged to the first category, and 42 to the second. Examining the accusations levelled at members of the second group, one finds that half of them were actually political in nature. Instigators of peasant land seizures, leaders of worker strikes and others were included in the second group. It would thus not be unreasonable to assign another 22 persons to the category of political exiles, for a total of 128.[91] Of these, 17 were sent to Eastern Siberia and 68 to other distant provinces (Arkhangelsk, Vologda, Viatka and Olonets), 22 were sent to various regions outside their native provinces and placed under police surveillance, 18 remained in their home region under surveillance, and three were deported.[92]

Great scandals were perpetrated in the Odessa Governor-Generalship, but not so much by Totleben himself as by his lieutenant, Paniutin, to whom he delegated full authority. However, it would not be accurate to hold Paniutin solely responsible for the unrestrained arbitrariness evident in Odessa. Totleben himself clearly was disposed toward the most impudent petty tyranny. As *Narodnaia Volia* indicated on 1 October 1879, "Arrests and administrative exiles still continue. Anyone falling into the net is exiled without further inquiry. One may say in general that the chief characteristic of Totleben's administration is crude violence and reckless arbitrariness."[93] Eight persons sentenced by the court of the military district were hanged in Odessa and Nikolaev during eight months in 1879.[94]

According to his official report of 25 August 1879, Totleben exiled 104 persons during the four months preceding; of these, 79 were sent to Eastern Siberia, 11 to Arkhangelsk province, and 14 were deported. During this period 31 persons were turned over to the court of the military district; five of these were sentenced to death by hanging, eighteen to hard labor, and eight were sent to Siberia.[95] In justifying all this, Totleben argued that "although these steps might seem ruthless, they were directed exclusively against ill-intentioned persons, to serve the interests of security and to save many from criminal passions and legal penalties. Hence they were not really measures taken out of harshness, but rather because of actual and pressing need." Apparently Totleben considered all this repression to be aimed "at saving youth from criminal passions." Totleben's report mentioned actions which clearly exceeded even the extensive powers granted to Governors-General. For example, he maintained that Governors-General had to approve appointments of justices of the peace. He included spreading rumors about land partition on the list of state offenses. Hunters could buy gunpowder only after their political loyalty had been verified.[96] Alexander II approved all these innovations of Totleben, saying: "I consider all these measures sensible and expedient."[97]

Totleben concluded his report by claiming: "In a word, during this short period of time Odessa has changed beyond recognition, according to the open admission of its own residents."[98] To comprehend the extent of Totleben's arbitrary actions, consider the regulations for Yalta and Sevastopol he promulgated on 27 April 1879—four days after he became Governor-General.[99] The first regulation stipulated that "non-military ships may pull into the city of Yalta only in daytime hours; only passengers with tickets to Yalta may disembark, and all others must remain aboard the ship." Passengers were deprived of the right to walk ashore. The regulation continued: "There must be a detailed and careful search of all disembarking passengers and their luggage on the pier itself." Those persons lacking passports or "appearing suspicious" should be escorted forthwith to the municipal police and after interrogation "should be sent under guard to the Odessa city governor."[100] The same fate would befall passengers carrying contraband items (firearms, illegal literature, etc.) ashore. Finally, any person entering Odessa must be subject to personal search and might be arrested simply on suspicion and taken "without charge" to Odessa. The second point provided that "persons who travelled to Odessa by land would be subject to careful search immediately after securing accommodations in a hotel or private apartment."[101]

Subsequent regulations obliged landlords of hotels, furnished apartments, inns, and private homeowners to inform the police about their lodgers and visitors to ensure that no meetings, gatherings, or assemblies occur, and to inform the police quickly of such events." First violations of these regulations would result in a fine of 100 to 200 rubles for landlords and homeowners.[102] No guests could be received without police knowledge. These facts provide sufficiently convincing evidence of the petty tyranny and arbitrary activity of Totleben and his assistant Paniutin.

Totleben's activity and that of Chertkov in Kiev distressed many citizens and, according to Semevsky, "struck terror not in the hearts of the miscreant socialists, but in the hearts of the law-abiding public, which was prepared to support reasonable measures."[103] There was some truth to this assertion. The repression fell on average citizens as well as on revolutionaries, and created dissatisfaction among social strata loyal to the government.

Let us now consider the activity of Kharkov temporary Governor-General Loris-Melikov. Repression was no stranger to Kharkov. On 1 October 1879 *Narodnaia Volia* wrote: "If Kharkov has yet to see the death penalty imposed,[104] other forms of government repression are nonetheless just as much in evidence here as elsewhere."[105] Of course, administrative exiles occurred in Kharkov, although on a much smaller scale than in other provinces.[106] Repressive measures against local students[107] also occurred, despite Loris-Melikov's role as initiator of educational reforms throughout the Russian empire. When Loris-Melikov arrived in Kharkov, one of his first decisions was to increase the number of gendarmes.[108] But, unlike other Governors-General, Loris-Melikov did not rely solely on threats and repression. In conjunction with a merciless struggle against the revolutionary movement he thought it necessary to attract liberal public opinion to the side of the government.

In an official report on his activity in Kharkov, he described the tasks of the Governor-General: "To give the Governors-General punitive powers alone, however important this might be, will not be sufficient for discharge of all their responsibilities, which include not only the pursuit of evildoers, but the prevention of their crimes. . . . The supreme representative of the government in a region must be constantly vigilant and be able to exercise his influence anywhere it might be needed. This goal," he wrote, "can be attained only when the Governors-General are in contact with representatives of local interests, learn of local needs, act effectively on legal petitions submitted to them, and generally render support (to local interests) as circumstances require." Loris-Melikov remarked that "a Governor-General should be the highest representative of state authority in a region and hence he must not only be competent to dispose of all questions arising from local conditions, but also must be invested with enough authority so that without undue interference in local institutional operations he can unify local actions and create from local institutions a completely reliable and staunch bulwark against the enemies of the regime."[109] He also thought it advisable to decrease gradually the application of strict punitive measures, "whose strength and effectiveness are great only so long as society can manage to tolerate them; prolonged use of these measures will diminish their salutary impact."[110]

The revolutionary press described the political policy pursued by the Kharkov Governor-General with these words: ". . .The clever, equivocal policy of Loris-Melikov and several of his semi-liberal pronouncements calmed an agitated society and won over public opinion. . . . The Count is like one of Saltykov-Shchedrin's heroes: he wishes both to remain innocent and to acquire wealth. The politics of ambiguity and ingratiation, the struggle not to depart too far from the spirit of the age, preserving his high office while trying not to appear as a representative of extremist revolutionary elements—these are the intimate thoughts of a person who fancies himself the prime mover of the contemporary system."[111]

The activity of the St. Petersburg temporary Governor-General, Gurko, and of Moscow's Prince Dolgorukov did not depart from the basic pattern. They too pursued a reactionary political course, although arbitrariness was rather less crude in the capitals than elsewhere.[112]

Before departing for the Crimea in April 1879, Alexander II asked the Special Conference under Valuev's chairmanship to "investigate and elucidate the reasons for the rapid spread of destructive teachings among youth and to recommend realistic measures to limit their corrupting influence."[113]   Judging by Valuev's diary, the first session of the Special Conference occurred on 27 April. "Today I have a session of the *Comité de salut public*." he wrote.

"Having first invited the others to speak about our general situation and its causes and having heard a series of platitudes (Count Tolstoy's ideas were especially narrow and lamentable), I summarized my own ideas. I did not mince words about those subjects that have so disheartened me for more than fifteen years: from lies at the expense of society and the people, self-congratulation for 19 February and the substitution of the Muscovite dynasty for the Russian empire, to the judicial reforms, the systematic humiliation of all the natural allies of the state, the mirage of the peasant masses and the temples of science, and finally the progressive constitution granted to Bulgaria."[114]

Valuev proposed to begin discussion of the special topic a week later, on 4 May. The discussions continued weekly throughout May. On 24 May Valuev presented to the tsar a very thorough report on the policy recommended by the Special Conference. He began by explaining that the Conference's work had been somewhat impeded because of other demands on its members' time. In evaluating the domestic situation Valuev noted: "The Conference found that no matter how difficult the problems that prompted the tsar to appoint it, it could not and must not consider the problems insoluble, nor could it delude itself about the reality, significance, and urgency of the problems and dangers ahead. The ostensible apathy of almost all of educated society toward the government's current struggle against a handful of malefactors deserves special attention."[115]   Valuev then observed that the majority of educated society was frightened, yet preferred neutrality to working in behalf of the regime. This group, actually, was critical of government policy. This meant that most educated people, that is, the ruling classes, tended to oppose the government.

According to Valuev, among the people "there were two contradictory inclinations. They are ready at the first call to aid the government in combatting its enemies, but this assistance would be undirected, violent, capricious, and therefore too dangerous to rely upon. At the same time," continued Valuev, "they would fall prey easily to every insidious rumor, gossip, or promise of new privileges or material advantage. Under the influence of such rumors and promises, the masses would be liable to disobey the government agency closest to them and to act as vigilantes."[116] Valuev noted further that revolutionaries were active in a number of provinces.

The common people showed two attitudes: faith in a good, beneficent, anti-gentry tsar, who supposedly required help in fighting his enemies; and, on the other hand, dissatisfaction with conditions, which might lead to disobedience of the government. Valuev correctly perceived the danger to the government of either attitude. And despite their ostensible contradiction, both attitudes could lead to the same result: opposition to the existing system of government. Objectively, the consequences of such opposition would be the same whether the people fought out of a desire to aid a "beneficent" tsar or in order to overthrow him.

Valuev also described the mood in the countryside. "Generally, among all levels of the population there is a somewhat ill-defined but pervasive dissatisfaction. Everyone complains about something and desires and expects change. The multiplicity of grievances and the vague expectations are even more noteworthy since the Minister of Internal Affairs expects that zemstvo and gentry assemblies will draft new and troublesome petitions toward the end of the year."[117]

Then Valuev summarized the ten measures that the Conference recommended. The first sought to augment the authority and rights of the police, and to grant them greater independence "in discharging their crucial assignments and to raise their prestige and authority in the public eye." The Conference proposed (1) to abolish the right of justices of the peace to censure policemen "without asking the policeman to explain his conduct and without consulting his superior officer," and (2) to examine the possibility of giving police the right to take complaints against justices of the peace directly to a county session of justices, a sort of local appeals court, bypassing the procurator's office. The procurators possessed too much control over the police. The Conference also wanted to alter the legislation on justices of the peace by giving police depositions and protocols "the force of admissible evidence."[118] Finally, since it was thought that the existing police force could not meet its new assignments, the Conference asked for an increase in the police budget "to strengthen and raise the moral stature of police personnel."

The fifth point of the Conference recommendations concerned personnel of the zemstvos and municipal governments. Since "agents of revolutionary propaganda are not infrequently encountered in these institutions," the Special Conference recommended "broadening provisions of the 1866 regulations requiring prior approval by the governor for certain appointments to zemstvo and municipal agencies." It recommended that all employees of these agencies be approved by the governor prior to their appointment.

Point six condemned the press as "a consistently and systematically baneful influence." The Minister of Internal Affairs therefore was directed to "draft new rules for fining periodical publications." In addition, the Conference thought it expedient to discuss the Chief of Gendarmes' suggestion for "publication of a new government-funded daily paper under the Chief of Gendarmes' constant supervision and guidance."

The next section of the report was devoted to the situation in the countryside—more precisely, to rumors about land redistribution and the reduction of existing obligations. The Conference proposed "to take steps to stop agitation against the Statute of 19 February and to refute false hopes of additional land allotments."[119] Such rumors, as pointed out earlier, resulted from the naive monarchical hopes of the peasants, who expected the tsar's favor at the end of the war. The Minister of Internal Affairs had informed the governors that "not infrequently retired or even active soldiers pass these rumors among the rural population."[120] These rumors spread as early as the second half of 1877. On 22 November 1877 the governors received a circular asking them to silence various rumors.[121] In August 1878 the Minister of Internal Affairs indicated in a confidential note to the governors that they should, "watch with special care for the dissemination of similar rumors."[122] Rumors about land redistribution were especially rife in 1879.

The Special Conference also discussed the possibility of uniting all conservative elements in the struggle against the revolutionary movement; this question was addressed in points eight and nine of the Conference report. Valuev wrote: "Now we must reassure the traditionally conservative elements of the populace and unite them in opposition to revolutionary propaganda; one such conservative force is the hereditary nobility, because the nobles will be aroused and motivated by threats to their own interests. . . . Another conservative element might be found among the religious dissenters, who thus far have remained impervious to revolutionary propaganda."[123] The conservative forces thus consisted of the hereditary nobility and the Old Believers. The latter were members of merchant and other petty bourgeois groups, mostly in urban areas.

Accordingly, the Conference adopted the following plan. First, since the influence of the hereditary nobility was paralyzed "by the absence of any territorial unity among various segments of the population," the Conference returned to a proposal made by the Minister of Internal Affairs in the 1860s for the organization of territorial districts. This was nothing other than an attempt to place representatives of the hereditary nobility at the head of territorial districts, that is, to create land captains, as was actually done in 1889. This point also spoke of the need "for the government to reassure private landholders."

Second, the Conference recommended ending persecution of sects "not recognized as especially harmful." This proposal resembled a plan of the Minister of Internal Affairs in 1864 that the tsar previously had approved. The Special Conference thought it expedient that "these measures be adopted administratively, without legislative ratification."[124] Significantly, they also proposed immediate opening of the Rogozhsky prayer house in Moscow. The Rogozhsky cemetery was a center for Old Believers of the Belokrinskaia group.

It is interesting to observe that while stressing the conservative role of the Old Believers, the Special Conference said nothing about the importance of the official Church in the fight against the revolutionary movement. This was no accident. The twenty years since the emancipation had brought certain changes in the Church's position. Whereas in the period of the abolition of serfdom the Holy Synod and the local dioceses had appealed to the people for cooperation, now such appeals were not voiced. This change testified to a decline in the authority of the Church, which had been an open ally of the government.

The tenth point related to the preceding two since it also addressed the issue of broadening the social base of the government in its battle with the revolutionaries. "Since revolutionary agitation has not found congenial company in the Catholic and Polish population," the Special Conference recommended "abolishing the special orders and regulations that had been in force in the western provinces."[125] The Conference considered the inhabitants of the western provinces (in Latvia, Belorussia, and the Right Bank Ukraine) loyal, since the Populist movement had not obtained much support there.

In its final meeting the Special Conference dealt with problems of education—more precisely, with "measures that ought to be adopted to improve the existing structure of educational institutions." According to the minutes, this issue prompted "a lengthy exchange of ideas."[126] Greig, the Minister of Finance, thought it essential to limit the admission of needy youths to higher educational institutions. "Low tuition, tuition grants, numerous stipends, and other financial assistance offered to students," he remarked, "artificially increase the number of persons aspiring to higher education. Despite the privileges and aid given them," he continued, "they are subject to conditions of cruel privation in the universities, and therefore fall more easily under the pernicious influence of agitators, who earlier discovered that among poor students they might more readily find sympathizers and blind adherents." In conclusion, Greig noted that this parlous situation had been compounded by the periodical press, which had extolled a system "that overcrowds institutions with a harmful and dangerous contingent of students."[127]

Count Tolstoy claimed that the problems in universities could be attributed in large measure to the inadequacies of the 1863 University Statute, as the Conference already had acknowledged. It was this statute, by Tolstoy's reckoning, that had eliminated the control of school district trustees over university affairs and had granted "an inconvenient autonomy" to the professoriate. The Minister of Education said that these factors would be considered seriously when a new university statute was drafted. To prevent a flood of students into the universities of St. Petersburg and Moscow, the Minister of Education thought it wise to control all stipends himself "and to divide them among various universities, giving the trustees, rather than the colleges or councils, the right to allocate them among various departments." Moreover, Tolstoy saw the need to establish "more exacting standards of discipline," and to enforce the existing dress code.[128] Tolstoy remarked that the supervision of elementary schools was inadequate and that it would be logical for the marshals of the nobility and the clergy to oversee such institutions according to the provisions of the 1874 statute on elementary schools.

The Chief of Gendarmes and the Minister of Finance expressed their opinions concerning the political unreliability of elementary school teachers who had been trained in university seminars, and argued that "the task of primary instruction is not so complicated as to make improved pedagogical techniques absolutely essential (for elementary schools—P.Z.). The task of elementary schools is to teach children how to read, write, and pray to God, and it therefore can be entrusted primarily to the clergy, if certain material improvements in non-church schools are made."[129] Drenteln and Greig thus hoped to kill two birds with one stone: to imbue primary schools with a clerical character while simultaneously improving the material position of the clergy. This arch-reactionary plan was rejected by a number of Conference members, including Count Tolstoy himself.[130] Prince Urusov and Tolstoy maintained that the clergy could not teach for lack of time and other reasons. Urusov, Tolstoy and Makov noted that "it would be imprudent to abolish or limit zemstvo activity in the field of education."[131]

Valuev, the Conference chairman, allied himself with Drenteln and Greig. He argued that a number of factors (scarce financial resources, the extent of territory, etc.) made it impossible to structure village elementary schools "along any kind of perfected European pattern;" consequently he believed it particularly desirable to entrust these schools to the guardianship of the parish clergy, who also would find teachers and supervise them."[132] Valuev fully endorsed the Drenteln-Greig proposal. However, as indicated above, the Conference reached no final decision on public education.

In analyzing the issues debated by the Conference and the decisions made there, it is apparent that they touched on literally every field of internal politics and recommended a panoply of reactionary measures. One set of issues concerned broadened police powers. In this category one might include the proposal granting to governors the power to confirm individual appointments to the zemstvos, and also the measures taken against the press. A second category of decisions was in answer to problems in the countryside, and involved quashing rumors about land redistribution and strengthening gentry influence in the rural sector. The third category included attempts to broaden the social base of the autocracy by appealing to such conservative elements as the Old Believers, who had been opposed to the government in the not-so-distant past, and the Polish nobility, some of whom had participated in armed resistance against the regime. That the government could classify the Polish nobility as a conservative force is itself a historical curiosity, and illustrates the loss of revolutionary spirit within the Polish *szlachta* [petty nobility]. The final category consisted of measures to limit the spread of revolutionary propaganda among the young.

The minutes of the Special Conference were sent by Alexander II to the Committee of Ministers, which discussed these issues in three meetings on 26 June, 3 July, and 10 July. The Committee fully agreed with the Special Conference's general evaluation of conditions in Russia. During discussion of the Conference's recommendations about the role of the police (eventually ratified by the Committee), several additional suggestions were offered. For example, "in light of the increased importance of the police," Chief of Gendarmes Drenteln proposed "abolition of the procurator's right . . . to censure police officials for oversights and irregularities in investigations and to turn such cases over to the courts." The Committee of Ministers did not reject this reactionary proposal. According to the Committee minutes, "The Committee perceives in this a real subversion of the present system of subordinating investigations by police officials to the procurators, who are dependent on the Minister of Justice and similarly subject to justices of the peace. Nevertheless, in view of the particular importance of the issue raised by General Drenteln, the Committee proposes to grant to the Minister of Justice in cooperation with the Minister of Internal Affairs and the Chief of Gendarmes the right to step in and if necessary change the method for defining police responsibility for oversights and irregularities in investigations."[133] Clearly, the Committee found itself very much in accord with Drenteln's plan, which created fertile ground for police arbitrariness and entailed in essence the liberation of police officers from the control of the procurator's office.

In discussions about the mutual relations of the police and the justices of the peace, Minister of Finance Greig introduced a proposal "to abolish elections for the office of justice of the peace, since the elective principle had proven to be a failure . . . ."[134] In fact, Drenteln suggested replacing the institution of justices of the peace by a crown court. Greig also wanted to grant the police the right of summary disposition "of petty offenses against statutes protecting public services and officialdom."[135] This proposal meant a return to the pre-reform system where certain judicial functions were the responsibility of the police. In answer to Greig, Minister of Justice Nabokov noted that his ministry currently was reviewing the organizational problems of the justices of the peace. The Committee of Ministers thus not only affirmed the proposals of the Special Conference for a more powerful police force, but even added to them.

The Conference's decision to grant governors the power to confirm appointments to zemstvo and municipal bodies was also endorsed by the Committee of Ministers,[136] and extended to cover employees of private railroads.[137] The Committee also agreed to the anti-press laws proposed by the Conference.

The question of stopping rumors about land redistribution had been examined earlier, in connection with the text of a "Declaration" on land redistribution which Alexander II brought to the Committee's attention. The meetings of 5 and 13 June dealt with this problem. Makov wrote in his report: "For some time rumors and gossip about an imminent general redistribution of land have been circulating among the rural populace. These rumors are being spread through the villages either by subversives, who have only disreputable and criminal motives, or by peasants who have heard false rumors and gossip concerning various government orders and intentions . . . . "[138] According to Makov, from August 1878 to January 1879, reports of such rumors came from Riazan, Smolensk, Chernigov, Grodno, and Pskov provinces; from January to June 1879 reports were received from Kazan, Petrokov, Kaluga, Novgorod, Kherson, Kiev, Kursk, Smolensk, Tula, and Penza provinces.

The dynamics of the spread of these rumors during 1878-1879 is of interest. In August 1878 reports about rumors came from one province; in September also from one; in October from one; in November from two; in December from one. In January 1879 one province reported rumors; in February and March there were no such reports; in April two provinces reported rumors about land redistribution, and eleven provinces reported in May (with Kaluga and Kiev both reporting twice).[139]

Makov indicated that the peasants had taken concrete action in several localities because of rumors about land redistribution: "Land was seized from the nobility and merchants and divided among the peasants according to the number of souls [registered peasants] and in all these localities they said that the land was seized from owners of more than one hundred desiatins [2.7 acres, 1.0925 hectares]. Rumors about liberation from the poll tax and all other fiscal obligations accompanied those concerning land redistribution."[140] The Committee of Ministers agreed with the Minister of Internal Affairs' warning to approach the publication of the "Declaration" with extreme caution so that it might not serve as an indirect pretext for spreading such rumors. The Committee recommended that the "Declaration" not be read everywhere, but only when and where the need might arise. The "Declaration" said that "neither now nor in the future will there be nor could there be any additional parcels of land allotted to peasant fields."[141] It also asserted that it would be extremely unjust and contradictory to the principles of private ownership to transfer land legally acquired by one person to someone else.[142]

Rumors about land redistribution circulated widely not only among the peasantry, but also among soldiers. In a confidential message to the Moscow Governor-General, the Minister of Internal Affairs wrote that "rumors about land redistribution apparently have permeated the army; one local infantry commander[143] reported that capable junior officers were refusing a second tour of duty solely because they hoped to receive plots of land in some sort of general redistribution. From information available to the Ministry of Internal Affairs, retired soldiers and those on active duty are spreading these rumors to the villages."[144] Therefore Makov suggested publishing the "Declaration" concerning rumors about land redistribution in a directive to the infantry in the Moscow military district.[145]

As rumors about land redistribution created a tense situation in the countryside, peasants from many parts of Russia migrated of their own accord to Western Siberia. For this reason, in September 1879 Makov sent a confidential circular to the governors asking them not to permit such internal migrations.[146]

The Committee of Ministers fully endorsed the Conference's decision concerning creation of territorial units headed by the landed gentry. The proposal originally made by Valuev in the 1860s for creating land captains thus was approved by the Committee of Ministers in 1879. The Committee also agreed to changes in legislation affecting religious dissenters. On the final point of the Conference's decision on the abolition of emergency laws in Poland, the Committee took no action. After discussing the Special Conference's concrete proposals, the Committee of Ministers examined a series of supplementary observations made by members of the Conference. The Committee agreed with Minister of Finance Greig's opinion that admitting poor students to higher educational institutions was "extremely harmful." The Committee of Ministers proposed that the Ministers responsible for higher educational institutions should "take the lead in exposing the dangers arising from artificially inspired desires for higher education . . . ."[147] The second point of the decision on higher educational institutions concerned distribution of student stipends. The Minister of Education was asked to devise a plan to place control over stipend funds in the hands of a single department chief in his Ministry.

The Committee of Ministers generally expressed agreement even on the elementary school question. "Full spiritual and moral development of the people, which is the cornerstone of the whole state system," said the minutes, "cannot be achieved unless the clergy plays a dominant role in public educational institutions. This clerical participation is necessary to keep the demands for public instruction from being satisfied by a false course inimical to public morality and the social order."[148] This decision sought to determine the future development of popular education and to give it a clerical character. Finally, the Chief of Gendarmes warned other members of the Committee of Ministers about the high incidence of unreliable persons working in the civil service and indicated the need "to maintain the strictest, most vigilant watch over the loyalty of government employees."[149]

Alexander II approved the Committee of Ministers' minutes on 12 July and directed that the First Section report to him monthly on progress in implementing the Committee's recommendations.[150] The decisions of the Special Conference endorsed by the Committee of Ministers testified to a significant intensification of reaction. They were characteristic of the unity of domestic policy both late in the reign of Alexander II as well as in the 1880s under Alexander III, a unity interrupted only by the further development of the crisis of the autocracy. It is not difficult to discern the roots of the counter-reforms in all fields of state administration. One can see the basis of the future legislation on land captains, a clear attempt to abolish the justices of the peace, the universal strengthening of police-administrative power, the demand for clerical elementary schools, and many other manifestations of reaction.

The Governors-General interpreted broadly their right to remove various sorts of cases from judicial purview. For example, the Minister of Justice wrote in a secret memorandum to the Governors-General: ". . .the general removal from judicial purview of all cases, without exception, of a certain category [i.e., political cases—P.Z.] is not justified by the power granted to Governors-General, for such behavior is tantamount to a change in legally established jurisdiction over criminal cases."[151] Consequently, at the urging of the Minister of Justice, an ukase was sent to the Senate to clarify the powers of the Governors-General. In cases where the Governor-General might recognize the need "to remove certain categories of crime covered by the criminal code from judicial jurisdiction, they would be obliged to inform the Minister of Justice of their proposed action and their recommendation for disposition of the case." The Minister of Justice in accord with the Minister of Internal Affairs and the Chief of Gendarmes would then be obliged to refer the issue to "imperial inspection" through the Committee of Ministers.[152]

"At His Majesty's command" the Committee of Ministers examined the report by the Odessa Governor-General, Totleben, in September 1879. Totleben had exceeded considerably his authority in a number of ways, but the emperor had approved his actions. The Committee was supposed to examine the problems raised by Totleben and to recommend action upon them. Scrutiny of the report exposed the lack of consistency in the actions of the Governors-General. In Odessa the dissemination of rumors concerning land redistribution was classified as a crime against the state, while in Kharkov the same offense was punished by administrative sanctions.

The first point of the Committee of Ministers' decision was to give the Governors-General the right "as a temporary measure" to confirm candidates for jobs in zemstvo institutions, with the exception of justice of the peace positions. The right to confirm justices of the peace remained as before the prerogative of the Senate. The governors were given the right to report "to the Senate their observations about the moral qualities and reliability of persons selected by zemstvos and municipal dumas to be justices of the peace."[153] In this way the governors enjoyed the opportunity to exert decisive influence over appointments of justices of the peace. The wilfull initiative of the Odessa Governor-General thereby acquired the force of law. In addition, the Committee of Ministers thought it desirable to indicate to Totleben and the other Governors-General the need for strict adherence to "the imperial command of 13 July" concerning removal of cases from judicial jurisdiction. The Committee recommended the adoption of appropriate measures to ensure scrupulous conformance of the Governors-General in judicial cases. Finally, it was proposed to the Governors-General that their published decrees concerning administrative sanctions be approved by the appropriate departments and examined by the Committee of Ministers.[154]

On one hand the Committee of Ministers had broadened the power of government administration and to some extent had subordinated the justices of the peace to it, while on the other the Committee had attempted to limit, or at least direct by law, the actions of the Governors-General. The latter approach provoked dissatisfaction. In an official report in December 1879, for example, General Gurko wrote indignantly: "Henceforth, orders of the Governors-General to remove cases from the courts will not be enforceable until they are discussed by three departments [Ministries of Justice, Internal Affairs, and the Chief of Gendarmes—P.Z.] and examined by the Committee of Ministers; not only that, but even published decrees on this matter cannot be recognized as valid until they are confirmed in the prescribed fashion." In his opinion, "Governors-General limited in their rights would be deprived of His Majesty's trust, and the authority of their power and decrees would be shaken . . . ."[155]

The attempt to compel the Governors-General to act in accordance with the law did not bring tangible results. In late 1879 the Chief of Gendarmes and the Minister of Internal Affairs were forced to submit a report to this effect to the Committee of Ministers. In the beginning of this report they acknowledged the importance of the responsibilities of the Governors-General under the ukase of 5 April. "From this it undoubtedly follows that the broader the plenary powers vested in government officials to discharge the special emergency assignment to eradicate anti-government, anti-social elements, the more unalterable must be the statutory course of action pursued by local governments, in spheres unconnected with state security." On this premise they thought it necessary to warn the Governors-General that "the course of economic, judicial, and class affairs—that is, matters affecting municipal, zemstvo, and class institutions—must be determined by the legally constituted local authorities and establishments,"[156] provided there was no criticism of the government in these local bodies. The report then dealt with the authority of the Governors-General to publish mandatory orders and set a maximum monetary fine for violation of such orders.

On 18 December the Committee of Ministers discussed this report. According to E.M. Feoktistov's letter to Katkov, Grand Duke Konstantin Nikolaevich attended the session and stubbornly insisted that "the powers of the Governors-General could not be left ill-defined, that it was necessary to spell them out more precisely and to make them consistent with existing legislation." In opposition, Valuev defended the powers of the Governors-General in their existing form.[157] The report was endorsed by the Committee of Ministers and confirmed by the tsar on 20 December. The Minister of Internal Affairs was asked to inform the governors of its conclusions by confidential means.[158] The Committee of Ministers' discussion concerning the rights of the Governors-General was itself convincing proof of extensive arbitrary nature of the governors' activities.

The institution of Governors-General, introduced to strengthen the government's power at the local level in the struggle against the revolutionary movement, did not meet the expectations of the ruling elite. Arbitrariness and repression increased the prevailing dissatisfaction. The disagreements between the high bureaucrats and the Governors-General was another symptom of the crisis of the autocracy.

In special sessions on 17 and 19 July the Special Conference examined more concrete proposals concerning education. The discussion centered around the proposals of Kharkov Governor-General Loris-Melikov. From the official report of the Conference chairman, Valuev, it was clear that Loris-Melikov had outlined an entire plan for fighting the revolutionary movement. According to Valuev, Loris-Melikov had acquainted himself with the special journal of the Committee of Ministers and then concluded that "many questions and requests he had intended to raise or present had been resolved already by the orders in the journal."

Therefore, Loris-Melikov fully endorsed the Committee of Ministers' decisions. Moreover, he pointed to "the real shortcomings in the internal structure of educational institutions, the inadequacy of supervision, the lack of responsibility, the absence of any discipline, and the failure of instructors to fulfill their tasks properly."[159] Loris-Melikov then made several rather unoriginal proposals. His educational program anticipated that of Delianov, which was implemented during the 1880s. The first three points in Loris-Melikov's ten-point plan dealt with higher educational institutions. He proposed to (1) eliminate the elective procedure for selecting rectors, inspectors, and sub-inspectors at the university level, (2) introduce a mandatory form of dress—if not a uniform, then at least clothes with some kind of external distinguishing marks, (3) discuss the advisability of withholding student stipends."[160]

These proposals went even farther than the earlier discussions in the Conference and Committee of Ministers. Whereas the earlier meetings had referred to the "inconvenient autonomy of the professoriate" granted by the Statute of 1863, now Loris-Melikov spoke of eliminating the elective procedure for filling the chief administrative posts in the universities. The same must be said of the proposal to allow the administration the right to withhold stipends. Finally, neither the Special Conference nor the Committee of Ministers had wished to prescribe forms of dress. The fourth, sixth, and seventh points in Loris-Melikov's proposal dealt with high schools. The fourth point spoke of the need to strengthen "the teaching element in gymnasia and progymnasia," and proposed an increase in the number of teachers' assistants. Point six anticipated the policy later spelled out in the famous Delianov circular of 1887: "We must discuss the question of whether gymnasium preparatory classes attract an inconveniently large contingent of students to the gymnasia, and eventually lead to an overcrowding of the gymnasia and even the universities."[161] The Kharkov Governor-General guardedly raised questions of eliminating preparatory classes in order to deny poor students admission to gymnasia.

The seventh point recommended improvement of the religious seminaries and either a reduction in their number or in the number of their students. Two points, the fifth and ninth, related to primary schools. Point five spoke of the need for "more intense supervision of public schools and their teachers. . . for among these teachers there are numerous unreliable persons, and presently in some provinces there are only two inspectors for five hundred schools."[162] The ninth point concerned public school teachers who would lose their jobs as a result of the transformation of the public schools into schools run by the clergy. Loris-

Melikov pointed out that "we must consider the dangers which would result from the dispersion throughout Russia of those unemployed and unsupervised public school teachers who had been dismissed due to the public school reform."[163] Despite his recognition of the dangers of such a reform, Loris-Melikov actually endorsed the Drenteln-Greig proposal to transform primary schools into clerical institutions. The last point recommended that administrative districts of various departments coincide with educational districts.

All these proposals were extremely reactionary and received a basically sympathetic hearing from members of the Special Conference. Thus, even before the drafting of a new university statute, the Conference resolved to grant the Minister of Education the right to turn over university inspection directly to trustees of educational districts, and to deprive elected rectors or university councils of the right of inspection. "Royal permission" was to be sought for this change in university inspection policy, and if it was thought necessary by the Governors-General, trustees would appoint new inspectors. The Conference also approved Loris-Melikov's proposals concerning universities (appointment of rectors, prescribed clothing, stipend distribution). All these suggestions were to be examined as the new university statute was drafted. The Conference endorsed the proposal for intensified supervision of public schools and surveillance of dismissed teachers.

On the question of abolishing preparatory classes, Count Tolstoy spoke decisively against Loris-Melikov. Tolstoy said that "he considered preparatory classes to be indispensable pedagogical appurtenances of gymnasia, for they do not increase the number of students, but rather facilitate the preliminary discipline of those pupils who might enter either the preparatory classes or the beginning classes in the gymnasia."[164]

In addition to the issues raised by Loris-Melikov, the Conference dealt with the question of women's education. The Minister of Education spoke about college-level courses for women and "restrictive measures and orders keeping these courses under tighter supervision." The Conference approved these measures and "reached the conclusion that increasing the number of women's courses was undesirable and in any case should not be undertaken without the consent of the Minister of Internal Affairs, the Chief of Gendarmes and the Governors-General." The same judgment was expressed on high school education for women. Delianov apparently opened the discussion of this issue. "In the Conference," wrote Valuev, "the general opinion was that future increases in women's gymnasia were undesirable; indeed, in accord with State

Secretary Delianov's proposal, the government should look favorably upon the establishment of elementary women's institutes in the cities, and in these institutes or separate from them, the government should establish professional schools and courses to prepare women for professions not requiring a higher or secondary education."[165] Alexander II confirmed the Conference's decision on 23 July.

The Special Conference thus defined very precisely the prospects for women's education in Russia. Analyzing the proposals of Loris-Melikov, it is impossible not to see their arch-reactionary character. They cancelled out literally every accomplishment made in public education since the abolition of serfdom. Loris-Melikov's program anticipated the Tolstoy-Delianov policy of the reactionary 1880s.

One of the more important measures to be worked out on the basis of Loris-Melikov's proposals changed the nature of student regulation and surveillance. In early November 1879 the "Regulation for Students of Imperial Russian Universities" was drafted.[166]

The rules carried a distinctly repressive flavor and contained a checklist of student obligations and prohibited activites. The first paragraph said that students were obliged to obey "all general laws of the state and university regulations as well as their direct superiors and other authorities responsible for preserving law and order in the state." The second paragraph was the most characteristic of the rules. "Students do not constitute a special corporation," it said, "and therefore they are most strictly prohibited from engaging in any kind of collective activity, any presentation of complaints, addresses, or petitions, any sending of deputations, any posting of announcements in the name of students in general, and so on."[167] The next three paragraphs prohibited meetings, the discussion of any issues in groups, public speeches by students, and the opening of any dining hall, library, reading room, common monetary fund or any other organization within or without the university, if said organization was not controlled by the university administration.

A special note indicated that "outside university buildings students were subject to police authority like other citizens but, in addition, as students they fell under the special jurisdiction of university inspectors and, in general, of the university administration, and unconditional obedience was demanded just as in university buildings."[168] The final points dealt with student obligations. Twice a year, at the beginning of the semester, a student was obliged to appear before the university prorector or inspector to obtain a residence permit and student body card and to submit his home address or to request permission to take a leave of absence. Students were supposed to speak personally to the inspector if they desired waiver of their tuition fees. Private tutoring was to be permitted by university officials "only when the tutors are morally reliable individuals not under police suspicion."[169] A number of paragraphs covered norms for student behavior. They were required to arrive at lectures on time and "under no circumstances" were they permitted to express either approval or disapproval of their instructors.

The regulations even specified the penalties for violations: (a) reprimand, either oral or written; (b) arrest for not more than seven days; (c) warning of possible expulsion; (d) suspension from the university for one year with the right of immediate admission to an institution of higher education in another city; (e) unconditional suspension for one to two years; (f) complete expulsion. A student might also be denied his stipend.

"Temporary instructions for supervising university students" were drawn up simultaneously with the "Regulations."[170] Supervision of "student morals and discipline" was entrusted to the university inspector and his assistants. The inspectors were completely subordinate to the trustee of the respective educational district; they were selected by the trustees together with the Governor-General and were appointed by the Minister of Education. "Students receiving stipends from the state or private philanthropy or with any kind of privilege relative to tuition are entrusted to the special attention of the inspector and his assistants. The government will tolerate no longer the use of these advantages and privileges by students careless in this regard or by students who, because of their manner of thinking and living or their character and inclination, cannot serve as good examples for their comrades."[171] Inspectors were obliged to keep records of student conduct to ensure "strict observation" of students.

The "Regulations" and "Temporary Instructions" were directed toward a single objective—the eradication of free thought in institutions of higher education. The inspector of students was made completely independent of the university administration, and functioned solely as a police administrator. In fact, the "Temporary Instructions" created a lesser version of the pre-emancipation inspector of students. On 5 November the "Regulations" and "Temporary Instructions" were approved by Alexander II,[172] who added this comment: "I hope that the new rules will be conscientiously enforced and will achieve the desired results."[173]

The results of these actions, however, were meager. Students were not so easily pacified, and both the "Regulations" and the "Temporary

Instructions" eventually were abolished. Even as the regulations were being drafted the Minister of Education was preparing a new university statute. The framers of the new statute attempted primarily to minimize university autonomy, to expand significantly the functions of the trustees, and finally to curtail the rights of the rector and the academic council. Whereas the statute of 1863 had granted the trustees and the rector full authority to act in emergency situations, the new draft project gave this power to the trustees alone. "In emergency situations the trustee is empowered to act in any manner, even if this should exceed his statutory authority; he will be obliged to bring such actions immediately to the attention of the Minister of Education." The trustee might attend meetings of the university council "and in particularly grave situations might assume its chairmanship."[174] Student inspection was established in accordance with the "Temporary Instructions." Surveillance of student behavior was entrusted to the inspector, who acted "under the direct supervision of the trustee." Formerly the university council had the right to dispense stipends, but this right was now given to the inspector. The university court was eliminated. The principle of election of rectors and deans was preserved, but in altered form: rectors earlier had been elected for four-year terms; under the provisions of the new draft they might serve two years but could not be re-elected.

The draft statute, depriving the university administration of authority over students, created in the person of the inspector a police administrator with extensive rights to interfere in university life. The professoriate no longer would have the right to discipline students. The result of the new inspection system was the creation in the university a kind of "state within a state." The entire academic and scientific life of the university now became very dependent on the educational district trustee. These were the basic changes in the university statute encompassed by the project of 1880. In early February 1880 the project was handed over to the State Council, but it was never considered because of political changes following the explosion in the Winter Palace. The 1880 statute was a prototype for the statute of 1884, which in fact did destroy university autonomy.

In the years 1878-1879 the government thus adopted a series of measures intended to intensify reaction in all spheres of state life. Alongside the measures aimed against the revolutionary movement (increasing administrative-police repression, persecuting the press and higher education), the government tried to "pacify" the countryside (creating village policemen, combating rumors about land redistribution). It also tried to assure peace in the cities by organizing a mounted-police guard. The complex of proposals, planned by the Special Conference and confirmed by the Committee of Ministers, took a large step toward establishing a regime of naked reaction. One action symptomatic of this reactionary trend was the establishment in February 1879 of a Main Prison Administration in the Ministry of Internal Affairs, centralizing jurisdiction over all penal institutions.[175] In late 1879 the arbitrariness of the administration and police reached its apogee. The replacement of existing legislation by emergency laws and the creation of the Governors-General testified to the political crisis of the autocracy.

The crisis of autocratic power, characterized by the impossibility of governing in the normal manner, was in its first stage—essentially one of transition from regular laws to emergency laws. However, even in this stage there were attempts to make minor concessions in order to involve representatives of the provincial elite in solving a number of questions.

Concessions were logical, given the efforts to keep intact the principle of the autocracy itself. Objectively this meant that the tsar attempted to broaden the social base of his power. This was not the first time such a step had been taken. Projects for "state constitutionalism" were put forward more than once during the nineteenth century as a means of averting revolutionary danger. M.M. Speransky drafted the first such project in 1809—a plan of state reform entitled "Introduction to a Code of State Laws." Speransky did not conceal his intention of preventing revolutionary shocks to the state. "Constitutions in almost all states have been introduced at various times, in bits and pieces and for the most part amidst violent political upheavals," said Speransky. "The Russian constitution will owe its inception not to the inflaming of passions and extremity of circumstance, but to the virtuous inspiration of the Supreme Authority . . . ."[176] In 1818 there were renewed signs of revolution in Europe and a huge peasant disturbance broke out in the Don region of Russia. Consequently Alexander I asked his friend Novosiltsev, a former member of the Secret Committee, to draft a Russian constitution, later entitled "State Statutory Charter of the Russian Empire."[177]

In the early 1860s, or more precisely in 1863, Valuev worked out a project to include elected members in the State Council.[178] The Valuev project was an object of discussion even in the period that concerns us.[179] Valuev began his report by discussing the situation prevailing in Russia because of the Polish rebellion. He indicated that it might be possible to make certain concessions in Poland that could not be made in a native Russian region. In describing Russia's domestic position,

Valuev spoke of several shortcomings, particularly in the areas of finances and communications, and argued that incomplete reforms explained the poor coordination among government departments. He underscored the growing dissatisfaction of the upper classes with the government while noticing a continuing devotion to the tsar. "One thought obsessed everyone. It manifested itself in different ways and acquired different names . . . but in essence it was everywhere the same. It was that in all European states various classes had acquired a certain share of participation in legislative affairs or general state administration, and if it was thus in Europe, it also must be so here."[180]

Valuev observed that this idea was very skilfully exploited in revolutionary propaganda. He noted that it had been included in a number of addresses of the nobility and would be expressed in resolutions by gentry congresses and zemstvo assemblies. Valuev therefore maintained that it would be impossible to deny all these petitions, and wondered "if it would not be better to anticipate them."[181] He linked the inclusion of elected representatives in the State Council with the creation of the zemstvos since he thought that the zemstvos should elect these representatives. The "zemstvo or class" representatives in the State Council would serve as consultants who might discuss legislative administrative operations, and so forth. These representatives would be elected from all regions of the Russian empire (save Finland and Tsarist Poland), with from one to four elected from each province. The capitals and other large cities might elect additional candidates. The other members of the State Council would be appointed from officials in the state apparatus, including the Church.

This report was written by Valuev on 13 April 1863,[182] and discussed by a meeting of the tsar and what was essentially the Council of Ministers on 15 April. According to Valuev, the majority of those present (Reutern, Prince Gagarin, Prince Gorchakov, Count Panin, Bludov, Baron Korf), led by Prince Gorchakov, spoke against his proposal. "The tsar, in view of the majority opinion, decided that nothing should now be done."[183] Valuev, however, apparently retained some hope that his proposal would be adopted, and he wrote out a more detailed plan for organization of the State Council. The "Project for a New Organization of the State Council"[184] was a very verbose document, with seven chapters and 201 paragraphs. There was an appendix entitled "The Distribution of Elected Officials in Individual Provinces."

This document considered in detail the foundation of a Congress of State Representatives elected by provincial zemstvo assemblies. The Congress would consist of elected members (151 in one variant, 177 in another) and appointed members not to exceed forty percent of the elected number. Ministers and other government officials might attend the Congress but would not have a decisive vote. The zemstvos could elect representatives for three years (The first group would be elected for only one year.). The larger cities also might elect representatives. The government would appoint the chairman of the Congress, but the Congress itself would select two vice-chairmen. It would convene every year, each time "at imperial command."

According to article 47, a number of very important matters might be examined by the State Council without the participation of the elected representatives. These matters included declaration of war and conclusion of peace, "issues that demand clear guiding principles in laws, statutes, and institutions," high budgetary allocations, and so forth. Other issues also outside the elected representatives' competence included: "(1) matters assigned directly to Ministers; (2) matters under consideration in the Committee of Ministers"; (3) matters under consideration in other committees in the Senate; and (4) military or naval affairs. Since there was no exact definition of matters reserved for examination by the State Council, Committee of Ministers, or other high instances of authority, any question might in fact be excluded from the purview of the Congress of Elected Representatives. At a plenary session of the State Council sixteen representatives of the Congress, including the two vice-chairmen, had to be present.

The provisions of Valuev's project certainly did not encroach on the prerogatives of autocratic power. The State Council would have remained, as before, a legal consultative body possessing no power of legislative initiative. The Congress of Elected Representatives would not have changed that situation in the least. Moreover, the formation of the Congress, by involving the nobility in preliminary discussion of various issues, would have satisfied the desires expressed in numerous addresses and resolutions of gentry assemblies. All this fully accorded with the personal views of Valuev, who thought that the nobility should enjoy certain clearly defined political rights but that the principle of autocracy should be preserved without alteration.

The second variant of Valuev's project suffered an even sadder fate. In late 1863 Alexander II simply returned it to its author. Changes in the domestic political situation seem to have been responsible for the rejection of Valuev's project. The suppression of the Polish uprising was nearly complete by late 1863, and the waves of revolutionary agitation within Central Russia itself had diminished. Valuev's project thus was forgotten.

In 1866 Grand Duke Konstantin Nikolaevich and State Secretary Prince Urusov composed a memorandum recommending that representatives of the nobility and zemstvos be involved in discussions of issues that the government deemed appropriate.[185] "After the events this year in Riazan and St. Petersburg provinces," wrote the Grand Duke at the beginning of his memorandum, "the tsar himself, dealing with the difficult situation of the nobility, deigned to analyze the question of what to do to remedy it."[186] These ideas led the Grand Duke to attempt to formulate a number of general principles upon which concrete proposals might be based. These principles were: (1) "At present and in the foreseeable future, constitutional government for Russia would be disastrous, because it soon would turn into oligarchy or anarchy." It therefore becomes essential to support the autocracy without reservation. (2) It is incorrect to destroy existing class privileges, but since these privileges are no longer absolutely exclusive, it is expedient to extend them to lower classes. (3) The toleration "of a certain degree of liberalism in the outward appearance of various measures is not dangerous so long as their essence remains unchanged." (4) Russian legislation should reflect the lessons of foreign models. (This apparently referred to various methods of involving the ruling classes in the solution of certain issues.)

With these general premises the Grand Duke portrayed the mind of a nobility dissatisfied with its position. Despite the periodic expression of constitutional aspirations, "the nobility does not seriously desire a constitution because it recognizes the dangers inherent in constitutional government; the nobility's constitutional allusions are nothing but an expression of its discontent."[187] According to the Grand Duke, the nobility's expectations might be satisfied "without the slightest infringement of the sacred rights of the autocracy" were the regime to be guided by the gentry rights included in existing legislation: the right to petition about gentry needs (*le droit de petition*) and the right to elect deputies "when the government requests explanation of these petitions."[188]

Accordingly, Grand Duke Konstantin Nikolaevich "constructed a project" consisting of fifteen points. Noble assemblies and zemstvo assemblies would elect two to three deputies. "The government would reserve the right to convoke a meeting of deputies when and however it might find one useful."[189] In these instances the deputies would assemble as part of the State Council. The assemblies of deputies would have no power of legislative initiative and might study only those questions placed before them by the government. Their function would be purely consultative. Two assemblies of deputies—an assembly of nobles and a zemstvo assembly—were envisioned. The former might consider petitions and requests of local assemblies of nobles; the latter, petitions of zemstvos (points nine and ten). Members of the State Council would preside over these assemblies. The last three points dealt with the discussion in the State Council of the assemblies' conclusions. Assembly deputies could be invited to the State Council "for presentation of their personal views, but they could not be present for the deciding votes." The journals of the assemblies of deputies would be presented to the tsar along with the journal of the State Council.[190]

Such were the provisions of a program that was far from clear. However, one thing is evident: the project not only failed to impinge upon the prerogatives of the autocracy but also proposed no new legislation. Assemblies of deputies from the nobility already existed but were inactive. Zemstvo assemblies already held the right to send petitions or addresses to the tsar on certain issues. The Grand Duke's project hence involved merely a slight extension or modification of existing legal procedures. Valuev's project was rather more liberal than the Grand Duke's proposal, since under Valuev's plan the State Council would have consisted mostly of elected members, not only in the Congress of Elected Representatives but in plenary meetings as well. According to Konstantin Nikolaevich (as quoted by Peretts), his project never was considered widely: "The tsar read the memorandum but never spoke to me about it, and I therefore concluded that he did not approve of my thoughts."[191]

Similar projects appeared as the crisis of the autocracy deepened.[192] The governing circles began to understand the necessity for reform and for the involvement of educated individuals in the preparation of reforms. This idea gained currency in early 1879. For example, Valuev noted in his diary on 27 April: "Yesterday Abaza dropped by.[193] There was a long conversation. He is pushing for a representative element, and mentioned my proposal of 1863. Of course, he is thinking of his own role in all this, but even so he utters the conviction that to continue just as before, without certain changes, is no longer feasible."[194]

Abaza was not the only one in the mood for change. On 12 June Miliutin wrote in his diary: "On returning from the Crimea,[195] I found a strange mood in St. Petersburg; in the highest spheres of government they talk of the need for radical reform, and the word 'constitution' is even heard. No one believes that the existing order of things can last."[196] Miliutin himself perceived the need for reform at all levels of government. While in the Crimea in late April he had read Professor

Gradovsky's article, "Socialism in Western Europe and Russia,"[197] and had jotted down in his diary some thoughts about the condition of the state apparatus and its organization: "Naturally, it is impossible not to recognize that our entire state structure requires basic reform, from top to bottom. The structure of village self-administration, the zemstvo, local administration at the district and provincial levels, as well as central and national institutions—all have outlived their usefulness, all should be recast in new forms, in accord with the Great Reforms of the 1860s. It is very regrettable that this colossal work is beyond the capacity of the present generation of statesmen, who are incapable of opinions more sophisticated than those of a policeman." Miliutin noted that the government recently had adopted merely police measures "instead of measures directed against the root of the evil."[198] Miliutin's admissions testify to the deepening crisis of government authority. His memorandum, "Thoughts on Necessary Changes in Government, Education, and the Clergy,"[199] composed in the fall of 1879, expressed the same sentiments as his earlier reflections. There is no direct evidence that this memorandum was ever a subject of government discussion or even that Alexander II knew of it.[200] Nevertheless, Miliutin's project of state reforms is of indisputable historical interest since it represents the thoughts of one of Alexander II's most intelligent ministers.

Miliutin wrote first[201] about the abnormal, chaotic division of functions among the various bureaucratic instances—a division that complicated the administration of the state.[202] He then outlined a number of changes for central and local institutions of government. Serious changes would have to be made in the State Council. "The State Council could become a purely legislative assembly were the Department of Civil Affairs detached from it and if elected representatives from the zemstvos were included in it. It seems to me that half the members might be appointed and half elected from provincial zemstvos without any danger of overthrowing or weakening the government." Two departments—Laws and State Economy—should be maintained for preliminary discussion of issues for submission to plenary sessions of the State Council; special commissions might also be created to examine certain issues. Decisions in the plenary sessions would be made by majority vote, and the tsar would retain the right of veto. Miliutin's project changed the supreme consultative body to a kind of Western European legislative body without infringing on the prerogatives of the autocratic power.

Miliutin wanted to transform the Committee of Ministers into a Council of Ministers, whose chairman would in fact be a prime minister.

The Senate would also be changed in important ways. Miliutin believed the Senate to have a dual significance: on one hand it was the supreme judicial body and Court of Appeals, but on the other it was the supreme guardian of the law. Miliutin thought it expedient either to remove the judicial functions from the Senate and to set up a special Supreme Court, or to preserve the Senate as the supreme judicial instance and to eliminate its other functions. Were a Supreme Court created, the Senate would become the general guardian of legality, resolving disputes between various institutional authorities, "announcing the law and preserving it."[203] In this instance, the Senate might be given the functions of legislative supervision, since a State Controller could not have authority commensurate with that of members of the Committee of Ministers.

According to Miliutin, it was advisable to abolish the Senate as an institution, and create in its place a Supreme Court and Supreme State Controller. The State Controller would then be the guardian of the law. Miliutin firmly recommended abolition of all four departments of His Majesty's Chancellery. The First Section would merge with the Chancellery of the Council of Ministers, the Second (Codifications) with the State Council, the Third with the Ministry of Police. The Fourth Section would be split between the Ministry of Education and a specially-created department devoted to welfare services, including medicine.

The second part of Miliutin's memorandum dealt with reforms of local government. Describing the organization of provincial and district administration, Miliutin wrote: "The structure of our provincial and district governments is a kind of mosaic, or more appropriately, a kaleidoscope, made up of the accidental aggregation of a large number of colored rocks. This structure is the consequence of gradual, long-term alterations and changes, made by different agencies without mutual agreement." The situation was complicated by the isolated existence of the zemstvo, which was a sort of counterweight to other administrative units. Miliutin advocated a number of very sweeping reforms. He thought that provincial administration should be headed by an independent official appointed by the tsar from candidates presented by the Council of Ministers. "I would even propose to draw a sharper line between the old and new systems, to change the very titles 'governor' and 'province' to the Russian appellations 'region'—*oblast'*—and 'regional chief' [oblastnoi nachal'nik]."[204] The regional chief would govern through a "regional chamber" consisting of various ministries and agencies. Zemstvo institutions would "share government of the province" with the regional chamber. According to Miliutin, district government should be a replica of the regional system. Miliutin also thought it essential to unite the municipal and district police: "One needs to have one police force, not various sorts of police." The assistant regional chief would control the police under Miliutin's plan.

The third part of the memorandum set out two tasks in education: "First, to extend, and make universal, elementary public education; second, to specialize and give a more practical character to secondary and higher education."[205] The first task could be achieved by the massive preparation of teachers "loyal" in the political sense, and then by the establishment of mass public schools supported by society itself and not by separate classes or the national treasury. Miliutin supposed that this was the only way to create the required number of public schools since it was a project beyond the financial capacity of the state alone. The second task was to increase specialization in secondary and higher education, and to teach students practical skills, as distinguished from the general humanistic education provided in gymnasia and universities. Miliutin thought that this approach would not only provide better training for specialists but also would impede the spread of revolutionary ideas among youth. Miliutin considered in detail a number of issues in education. He criticized the existing classical system of education in which instruction in ancient languages had become "an absurd fetish," and he dealt with high school curricula and the preparation of textbooks, and so forth. All this was done with the intention of controlling enthusiasm "for every variety of frivolous political theory and dream."[206]

The last part of Miliutin's memorandum was devoted to the clergy and contained an analysis of measures for raising its educational and material level. Miliutin also reached a general conclusion about financial reforms. "Obviously the whole question is one of diminution of direct taxes and general reform in the financial and economic system. This is the cornerstone of all necessary future reforms."[207]

Analysis of D.A. Miliutin's project for state reforms reveals that his proposals went significantly beyond those of Grand Duke Konstantin Nikolaevich or even Valuev. The entire project bore an objectively bourgeois stamp, especially the provisions concerning reorganization of government agencies. Miliutin asked that archaic, essentially feudal, institutions be abolished and replaced by contemporary bourgeois ones. Miliutin's government reforms envisioned a relatively precise system for organization of the higher institutions of governance. The legislative, executive, and judicial powers would have been rather strictly defined.

The State Council would have approximated the legislative institutions of Western European states. The autocracy would have remained inviolate, since the State Council could not have initiated legislation and the tsar would have retained his veto power.

The projected provincial and district reforms envisaged considerable change, which also implied a certain evolution toward bourgeois principles of government. Provincial administration would have become independent of the Minister of Internal Affairs, and in the process would have lost its repressive character. The political police would have lost their independence and would have been subordinated to the provincial administration. The project recommended an extension of zemstvo powers. Although the educational proposals were somewhat defensive, they were nonetheless essentially bourgeois in character. Their implementation would have facilitated the development of public schools under zemstvo control. The increase in specialized secondary and college-level institutions would have corresponded to the interests of socio-economic development in Russia.

Toward the end of 1879 the need for reforms was discussed with increasing frequency in government circles. On 26 November D.A. Miliutin recounted the following conversation with A.A. Abaza: "He asserted the compelling need for new fundamental reforms in the state. I objected that there was no immediate hope for any fundamental changes that would avert the disastrous problems now threatening Russia. For this a complete change in personnel and attitude would be required in high government spheres."[208] In early December Miliutin discussed the same theme with Grand Duke Konstantin Nikolaevich and said that he held no hope even for partial reforms, and that general changes were needed to alter the existing situation. "I told the Grand Duke that, given the present climate of dissatisfaction, one could not limit oneself to a single measure, particularly a measure so purely cosmetic as the proposed appointment of a certain number of temporary zemstvo delegates to the State Council. What would these zemstvo representatives do in the State Council when the imperial government cares only for intensified repression, when administrators at all levels govern with utter arbitrariness, when all of Russia, it may be said, has been declared in a state of siege?"[209] Miliutin said much the same thing to Valuev[210] and Golovnin.

In this connection Golovnin's memoirs are of great interest. He recorded there his conversation with Valuev on the need for government reforms. "In the fall of 1879 Valuev told Golovnin that in the present circumstances it was necessary to call to action the conservative forces of the empire and somehow to satisfy the demand of educated society to participate in affairs, and that therefore he [Valuev] cautiously would revive his proposal of 1863 calling for provincial representatives in the State Council. He hoped for the help of certain ministers, naming in particular the Minister of Internal Affairs and the Minister of War Count Miliutin."[211]

This evidence suggests that sometime in the latter half of 1879 government officials began persistent discussions about the need for definite concessions. With the exception of Valuev who had his own political views, the advocates of concession were representatives of the liberal bureaucracy: Miliutin, Abaza, Golovnin (a member of the State Council), and Senator Artsimovich.[212] Even Grand Duke Konstantin Nikolaevich warmly supported the liberal bureaucracy. Rumors about concessions reached even the tsar himself, who did not initially define his attitude toward them. At the beginning of January 1880 Alexander II first showed interest in the "constitutional" proposals of Valuev and Grand Duke Konstantin Nikolaevich. According to Valuev's diary, Alexander spoke with him on 9 January about the 1863 project, and also read to him Konstantin Nikolaevich's memorandum. "It is clear already that the narrowness of the [Grand Duke's] proposal constitutes its advantage in the tsar's eyes. His Majesty announced that he will meet us later for discussion with the Minister of Internal Affairs, the Chief of Gendarmes, and others." Valuev noted that the successor to the throne, who was present at the discussion, "obviously desires no organic change in the *status quo* and considers all forms of constitutionalism to be ruinous."[213]

According to State Secretary E.A. Peretts in the unpublished part of his diary, the tsar went to see Grand Duke Konstantin Nikolaevich on 13 January, and they discussed the Grand Duke's project. Peretts related Konstantin Nikolaevich's account as follows: "His Majesty informs me now that he would like to show Russia a sign of his trust on the twenty-fifth jubilee of his accession, to make a new and important step toward the completion of state reforms. He would like to grant society a greater voice in discussion of important affairs."[214] According to Peretts, Alexander II proposed that Konstantin Nikolaevich head a Special Conference consisting of the successor to the throne, Valuev, Prince Urusov, Chief of Gendarmes Drenteln, and Minister of Internal Affairs Makov. The Conference would consider the refom projects of both Konstantin Nikolaevich and Valuev. Golovnin offered a similar account in his memoirs.[215] There is insufficient evidence to explain the immediate causes of Alexander II's decision to show favor to his subjects on his twenty-fifth jubilee; however, it may be suggested that his decision was symptomatic of the crisis of the autocracy and of his realization that definite concessions were now necessary.

According to Valuev's diary, the reform issue was discussed at four meetings. The first session met in the Winter Palace on 21 January. It was chaired by the tsar himself and met in utmost secrecy. Grand Duke Konstantin Nikolaevich, the heir to the throne, Prince Urusov, Drenteln, Makov, and Valuev were present. "In order best to maintain secrecy," wrote Valuev, "everyone was admitted into the library by the first corridor doors. His Majesty offered the general question for discussion. The Grand Duke General-Admiral read his memorandum, added various reservations, and then endorsed the proceedings in general. . . . There followed a speech on the breakdown of barriers between the estates, on reforms, and about purely Russian as opposed to foreign principles, and about the English constitution, and the zemstvo, and about how formerly the prospect of peasant liberation tormented the nobility, and so on. Prince Urusov, Drenteln, and Makov made short remarks that showed their lack of sympathy for concessions. There was no detailed discussion because the tsar had said at the outset that he merely had raised the question and wanted us to talk about it first among ourselves." According to Valuev, the heir to the throne said that nothing should be done since the summoned representatives of the social estates "will be petulant complainers, lawyers, etc.."[216] These words of the successor, Valuev noted, exerted a "visible influence" on Urusov and Makov.

The second session, chaired by Grand Duke Konstantin Nikolaevich, convened on 23 January in the Marble Palace. State Secretary Peretts, who attended the meeting, has left a detailed account. He recalled that, due to the absence of the heir to the throne, there were no "decisive judgments," merely a preliminary "rehearsal," in the Grand Duke's words. At the outset of the proceedings the Grand Duke raised the question of which reform project was preferable—his or Valuev's—assuming that one or the other eventually would be adopted. Valuev spoke first, summarizing in detail his opinion that social groups should be involved "to the fullest extent possible in discussion of all or at least the most important legislative issues." Valuev emphasized that he had just presented to the tsar a new memorandum "rather better developed than the first."[217] He added that he thought his project corresponded better to the demands of society than that of Grand Duke Konstantin Nikolaevich. Valuev concluded with these words: "I know that my ideas are not shared by Your Imperial Majesty, not by the tsarevich, not by my

respected colleagues [Valuev pointed to Urusov, Drenteln, and Makov].
Hence I can only *reserve* my opinions, that is, bow to the general disagreement with me, take back my project, retaining the right to revive
my proposals when there are better chances for adoption and implementation. I will not agree to any amendments. Over sixteen years I
have learned how to keep silent, and I will continue my silence just as
stubbornly, and perhaps I will live to see a time when my voice will be
heeded."[218]

The Grand Duke's project was now the sole proposal before the
meeting. The Grand Duke spoke about certain changes that he had made
in his project: first, instead of separate assemblies for the nobility and
zemstvo representatives he now wanted to establish a single assembly;
second, the basic purpose of the assembly should be preliminary discussion of new laws and not action on zemstvo or gentry petitions.

Urusov, Drenteln, and Makov then spoke. "After a short silence from
the members," wrote Peretts, "Prince S.N. Urusov said in a soft, ingra-
tiating voice: 'Your Imperial Highness, while not permitting myself to
delve into details concerning your proposals, which may be in essence
quite useful, I consider it only fair to point out that their publication
may be seen by society as a gift or a concession, and that hardly would
advance the interests of the government, especially in this time of tur-
moil. Will it not be said that the government was frightened by the
threat of the social-revolutionaries?'"[219]   Urusov clearly opposed the
Grand Duke's project. Chief of Gendarmes Drenteln expressed similar
sentiments. Without discussing the substance of the project, he argued
that it was not essentially a constitutional act, and therefore could not
satisfy the expectations of society. "In a word, it will create for the
government endless new difficulties." Makov spoke in the same spirit.
He observed that involving the public in discussions of legislative projects was unquestionably useful and desirable, but he then argued that
this involvement must be delayed because of the abnormal situation prevailing in Russia. He said that the complex circumstances had led to the
establishment of Governors-General and broadened the competence of
military tribunals. "In such circumstances, in view of the extreme difficulties facing certain Governors-General, one may confidently assert
that in these parts of the empire neither law nor properly structured administration exist."[220]   Makov thought it wise first to eliminate the
emergency laws and then to proceed to discuss reform.

The chairman concluded with a lengthy speech. Having said that he
fully recognized the difficulty of publishing his project on the tsar's
twenty-fifth jubilee (he had never really thought about this problem),

the Grand Duke attacked his opponents and offered a positive appraisal of his proposals. Thus, with the exception of the Grand Duke and Peretts, all participants of the 23 January meeting spoke against the reform project.[221]

The third session commenced at one o'clock on the afternoon of 23 January in the Marble Palace, this time with the heir to the throne present. Peretts also has left the best account of this meeting. Grand Duke Konstantin Nikolaevich, the chairman, made short introductory remarks. He said that his project was feasible, although its publication on 19 February would be unwise. He summarized: "The projected regulations, with a little elaboration, can be of use in the near future: not today, but tomorrow."[222]

At the end of Konstantin Nikolaevich's speech, the tsarevich took the floor and made clear his disapproval of the chairman's position. "In my opinion, this project should not be published today or tomorrow. It is in essence the beginning of a constitution, and a constitution will bring us no benefit, at least for a long time. They will elect as deputies empty windbag lawyers, who will deliver only orations, and there can be no good in this. In Western states constitutions bring only grief. . . . In my opinion, we ought to study not constitutional designs, but something completely different." To support this contention, the tsarevich cited the Danish ministers who had complained to him that thanks to "parliamentary windbags" it was difficult to govern in various jurisdictions. After this pointed address by the tsarevich the chairman tried to object that most elected officials would be "intelligent and useful individuals," not just lawyers. The tsarevich reiterated that his ideas were justified by the state of the municipal dumas and zemstvo assemblies, which were inactive because of public apathy.

Makov supported the tsarevich, but by asserting that actually "various areas of administration are incomparably better where there is no zemstvo."[223] Valuev also spoke at length, and even defended the tsarevich. First, on the basis of his prior experience as Minister of Internal Affairs, he agreed completely that the zemstvo assemblies and municipal dumas were really inactive. "These institutions have not secured for Russia the benefits that the government had anticipated. Hence to give the zemstvo assemblies new and broader powers would be imprudent." Second, he asked whether preliminary discussion of legislative projects by members of society would be advisable since "the central government stands above the local representatives in all relationships. . . . Therefore, it does not need examination of its proposals and views by inhabitants of small cities or districts, who are less educated and knowledgeable. I

would like to know what sort of advantage might accrue from the remarks of a deputy from Tsarevokoshaisk or Kozmodemiansk."[224] To
support his argument, Valuev alluded to use of experts by the State
Council during discussion of the Zemstvo Statute and the participation
of local representatives in the commission on labor legislation which
he had chaired.

Then Valuev joined the tsarevich's attack against the plan of Grand
Duke Konstantin Nikolaevich. "If the government should deem it proper and necessary to call society to participate in discussions of vital
legislative issues, it would not do well to proceed by mere development
and generalization of existing principles of legislative procedure; in such
crucial circumstances the government should adopt not suddenly, but
gradually, the general constitutional arrangements which are the achievement of the whole civilized world."[225]

Urusov also spoke in opposition to the Grand Duke's proposal. Thus
no one in this third meeting cared to support Konstantin Nikolaevich's
opinion. Finally, the chairman asked the tsarevich what he had meant
when he spoke of the need not for constitutional projects "but for
something entirely different." Alexander Alexandrovich answered: "My
idea is very simple. I think that we find ourselves in an almost impossible situation. There is no unity of government; saying nothing of the
Governors-General who are doing heaven knows what, I must say that
there is no unity even among the ministers. They act at cross purposes,
not thinking of a common tie. It is bad enough that some are more concerned with lining their own pocketbooks[226] than with the work entrusted to them. We must tell the tsar of the need for common policy
in government, and uphold one common system." Grand Duke Konstantin Nikolaevich stated his full solidarity with the tsarevich, and emphasized that he always had objected to the unaccountability of the
Governors-General because it was not permissible "to have in the state
several almost autonomous monarchs."[227] However, he indicated that
the tsarevich himself should speak personally to the tsar about common
policy since the meetings had not been called for this purpose.

Discussion of the projects of the Grand Duke and Valuev had ended
in the rejection of both. In his diary entry on 23 January, the tsarevich
wrote: "At 1:15 I went to Uncle Kostia's for a meeting, attended by
Valuev, Prince Urusov, Makov, Drenteln, and State Secretary Peretts.
At Papa's order we examined Uncle Kostia's and Valuev's memoranda
on reform of the State Council, and establishment of an assembly of
deputies drawn from the nobility, zemstvos, and cities. Both projects
were rejected unanimously for many reasons, which I will not recount

since they would take up several pages. The main reason for dissatisfaction with these measures was that they would further confuse our domestic affairs and also would be one of the first steps toward a constitution."[228]

Actually, the composition of the committee predetermined its findings. With the exception of Valuev, the remaining members were very limited individuals who thought that the only way to fight the revolutionary movement was to intensify repression. At the same time, the majority of the members understood that the steps taken by the government in the preceding two years to fight the revolutionary movement had not strengthened the government's authority, but had weakened it. The establishment of the Governors-General had led, as Grand Duke Konstantin Nikolaevich said, to the creation of a series of "almost autonomous monarchs." That the transition to emergency measures weakened the autocracy is sufficiently convincing evidence of the crisis facing the regime.

Let us return to the position of Valuev, which seems so contradictory. On one hand, he advocated involvement of "conservative elements"—that is, the nobility—in the examination of legislative projects by the State Council; on the other, he removed his own reform project from consideration. The reason for the latter action was that Valuev understood the inevitability of his project's defeat, and he therefore even spoke against the Grand Duke's plan. The argument that he used to attack the Grand Duke's project applied just as well to his own. Were not the delegates from Tsarevokoshaisk and Kozmodemiansk also the "conservative elements" that would enter the Congress of Elected Representatives? His phrase about the need to "adopt general constitutional arrangements" certainly did not help his own efforts. The implementation of Grand Duke Konstantin Nikolaevich's project certainly would have been the first step toward realization of his own plan to call a Congress of Elected Representatives. One is left to assume that Valuev was motivated in this instance by personal antipathy toward the Grand Duke.[229] Peretts wrote about Valuev's behavior: "I...have never considered Valuev a true statesman, nor even a knight of honor and conviction. He is, rather, a courtier, but the impropriety of his speech today surpassed all bounds."[230] Peretts' evaluation was not entirely just. Valuev was a courtier who wished to please everyone, yet here was not so much an attempt to satisfy the tsarevich as an expression of antipathy toward the Grand Duke. Within a year, in even more complex circumstances, Valuev would speak in defense of Loris-Melikov's project, knowing full well that the new tsar opposed it.

On 29 January the fourth and final session on "constitutional" projects convened at the Winter Palace. Alexander II served as chairman, and Court Minister Count Adlerberg also participated. "Yesterday," wrote Valuev in his diary on 30 January, "the idea of 1863 was interred again, probably for a long time. They cited against it the same objections that were made at earlier meetings."[231] Alexander II wrote in his memo book: "Meeting with Kostia and others, decided to do nothing."[232]

During the first stage of the crisis of the autocracy "constitutional" projects were rejected. If one closely analyzes these projects, nothing really constitutional is found in them. However, due to the difficult situation of the moment, their realization might have amounted to a tentative step toward a constitution. Everything depended on the actual alignment of political forces. The Estates General in France was not an agency that limited royal power, even though during the Revolution of 1789 it declared itself to be a National Assembly. Obviously many statesmen of the tsarist regime, including even the not very intelligent tsarevich, were aware instinctively of the danger.

This examination of government policy in the years 1878-1880 suggests a number of conclusions. The first certainly would be that this policy emanated from a regime in crisis. As I noted earlier, this crisis was a result of the reforms of 1861 which robbed the peasants. In the late 1870s the situation in the countryside was tense. Crop failures and attendant famine gripped several provinces; there were wide rumors about land partition and a certain increase in peasant disturbances—all this could not but concern the government. Against this background the revolutionary struggle of the Populists stirred great fear in ruling circles. The crisis of the autocracy was evident primarily in the transition from ordinary to emergency legislation, and secondly, in the realization that some sort of reform to broaden public support of the government was needed. Even so, during the initial stage of the crisis the government chose not the path of reform but rather a consistently reactionary policy in all aspects of national government.

The change to emergency laws, involving broader competence for military tribunals, a number of administrative and law enforcement measures, and above all the creation of the Governors-General, did not yield positive results for the government. On the contrary, despite these actions the revolutionary movement developed further. Although the Governors-General were supposed to fortify the autocracy, they weakened it. Establishing their own "state within the state," the Governors-General destroyed unity of action and the principle of organized administration. Such an institution could not help but diminish the autocratic emperor. Another symptom of the crisis was the belief of many government officials in the need to broaden public support of the regime by involving "conservative elements" in decisions on important issues. Others raised the question of reform of a state administration that had proven so weak in dealing with the revolutionary movement. It is important to notice that during the first period of the crisis of the autocracy neither socio-economic nor political concessions were made. Concessions were to be made only when the crisis grew more serious. A change in government policy awaited dramatic events, such as the bomb explosion in the very residence of the tsar—in the Winter Palace itself.

CHAPTER II

THE SUPREME ADMINISTRATIVE COMMISSION

The explosion in the Winter Palace set off by S.N. Khalturin on 5 February 1880 threw the government into complete disarray and made the crisis of the autocracy even more profound. Grand Duke Konstantin Nikolaevich wrote in his diary on 7 February 1880: "We are experiencing a time of terror like that of the French Revolution; the only difference is that Parisians in the revolution looked their enemies in the eye, whereas we do not see, do not know, do not have the slightest idea of their numbers . . . . Universal panic."[1] Several days later he wrote: "A week has passed since the horrible explosion, yet the residents of St. Petersburg have not recovered from the blow. The panic continues: finally they have all gone crazy, lost their heads, and the wild rumors are spreading more than ever."[2] A.A. Kireev, an adjutant to Grand Duke Konstantin Nikolaevich and a member of a conservative Slavophile circle, stated in his diary on 15 February: "The nihilists have started a general panic among all classes. Many have left the city. The most fantastic rumors about bombings circulate."[3]

One of the first measures taken by the government after the explosion was the attempt to bridle public opinion. Editors and publishers of Petersburg newspapers and journals were invited to the Ministry of Internal Affairs where Chief Press Supervisor Grigoriev announced new restrictions on the press. According to the editor of *Russkaia Starina,* M.I. Semevsky, who took notes on the meeting, Grigoriev presented to the editors "a most outrageous and fantastic demand not to publish articles concerning the educational system operating in our fatherland, or any educational establishment under the jurisdiction of the Ministry of Education." According to Semevsky, this demand was issued in the form of an "imperial command" over the signature of D.A. Tolstoy. Grigoriev also announced by order of the tsar that the press was prohibited from publishing articles concerning German foreign policy, in particular about Russo-German relations, "in order not to irritate Germany by careless criticisms of its policy."

The editors Polonsky (of the newspaper *Strana* [Land]) and Saltykov-Shchedrin (of the journal *Otechestvennye Zapiski* [Annals of the Fatherland]) rejoined that these decrees would create intolerable conditions for the press, since the press was in fact ordered not to write about anything at all. In summary, Semevsky observed: "And so the Ministry of Internal Affairs, with its customary short-sightedness and cruelty, has accosted the press, seizing it by the hair like some obscene whore, instead of requesting the press to support and defend the regime."[4] Nonetheless, in connection with Grigoriev's proposal of 6 February, the Main Press Administration published a special circular which, in accordance with the "imperial command," prohibited discussion in the periodical press of the educational system or the new project for university reform.[5]

The blast in the Winter Palace, which demonstrated the complete inability of the Third Section to guard the imperial family, prompted the government to institute a number of new measures to control the revolutionary movement. As early as 7 February Alexander II met with his son, the heir to the throne. "I spent this morning with papa," wrote the tsarevich in his diary for that day. "We spoke at length about steps that finally must be taken, very decisive and unusual steps. But today we arrived at no decision."[6]

According to P.A. Valuev, Alexander II called a meeting on 8 February at which the tsarevich, Valuev, Miliutin, Makov, Adlerberg, and Chief of Gendarmes Drenteln were present. The tsarevich "proposed an impossible supreme investigative commission with dictatorial powers over the whole of Russia. The commission would be tantamount not only to *de facto* abolition of the Third Section and the Chief of Gendarmes, but also of other authorities now governing Russia. Moreover, the chairman of the commission would become the *de jure* equal of the emperor himself so far as the exercise of dictatorial investigative power is concerned. Trepov, not the tsarevich, is the probable author of this scheme."[7] Alexander II rejected the plan, and the meeting adjourned without result.

The author of the scheme was not Trepov, but Katkov. In his editorial in the 7 February issue of *Moskovskie Vedomosti*, Katkov wrote: "The fight against organized sedition. . .must be waged by a single strong arm. It is essential that one government agency, possessing the full confidence of the tsar, should exercise dictatorial power in the struggle against evil. On it should rest all responsibility and it should be granted all available weapons to carry on the fight. Other agencies must assist it. Without interfering with the procedures or administration of other departments, the agency must enjoy complete freedom of action in political affairs. It should direct and coordinate the Governors-General; no procedural formality should hinder the use of its power."[8] Thus Katkov, who wielded influence over the tsarevich through Pobedonostsev, devised the plan to create a Supreme Administrative Commission.

On 9 February Alexander II changed his mind, and he announced the formation of a Supreme Administrative Commission under the chairmanship of Count Loris-Melikov. That day the tsar entered the following note in his memo book: "Meeting decided to name Loris-Melikov chairman of Supreme Admin. Com.."[9] Judging by this note, it might be assumed that the functions of the Commission were not yet sufficiently clear to the emperor. On the same day the Extraordinary Conference "For the Formulation of Measures to Defend Tranquility and Security in the Empire" was convened. The Conference heard a proposal to increase the police force in Petersburg, its suburbs, and other nearby cities, and to limit "to the extent possible" the number of those public assemblies "which serve as a meeting ground for unreliable persons in general, and for young students of both sexes in particular."[10]

It was recommended that the Ministry of Internal Affairs pay "special attention to the tendentious articles in our press which divert the suspicions and indignation of the public from the milieu that breeds malefactors and which arouse suspicion against persons and classes that have had no part in revolutionary crimes."[11] The Ministry also was asked to publish "in official reports" statistical information about those "who are involved in political crimes." Valuev presented these recommendations to the tsar later that day, and obtained Alexander II's complete approval.

Let us turn to the question of the Supreme Administrative Commission. According to Valuev, who cited Count Adlerberg as his authority, the Commission was the result of a letter from the tsarevich to Alexander II.[12] As chairman of the Committee of Ministers, Valuev formulated the functions of the Commission.[13] On the morning of 11 February, before the meeting to establish the functions of the Supreme Administrative Commission, Valuev sent to Alexander II a memorandum in which he wrote: "I did not share immediately and perhaps did not understand fully the ideas expressed by the tsarevich on 8 February. The words 'Investigative Commission' sounded ominous to me. It seems to me that centralization of investigative operations will complicate the work of the Commission to the extent that success will become impossible. Besides, I should like to comment on the appointment of Trepov. Despite his merits, it will be difficult for the current municipal governor and perhaps for the Chief of Gendarmes to get along with him."[14] Valuev went on to say that he had changed his mind about the Supreme Administrative Commission because of the appointment of Loris-Melikov as director, but he still thought it wise to give the Commission a certain form, and to grant it specific functions.

His program consisted of the following seven points: "(1) The Commission should not be a supreme investigative agency, but a supreme administrative agency, with jurisdiction over all crimes that are designed to subvert the governmental system and over revolutionary propaganda in general. "(2) The director of the Commission should not be hampered by the requirement to consult with other departments. Members drawn from other departments should be mere assistants to Loris-Melikov and should facilitate transfer of data from their departments."

The third point held that the director of the Supreme Administrative Commission must be allotted full power to maintain order in the capital and its suburbs. The city governor would be subordinate to the Commission director. According to Valuev, "without this proviso, I think it impossible to attain the unity required for the defense of His Majesty from assassination, for the attainment of public order, and for investigative searches in the capital."[15] The fourth through seventh points dealt with the grant of full police powers to Loris-Melikov. He would be empowered "to control and direct investigations of political cases" in the capital. All local authorities would be obliged to execute his orders and to supply him with necessary information. Other government departments also would be obliged to render every assistance.

If Katkov had conceived the idea of the Supreme Administrative Commission, it was Valuev who defined its character and converted the plan into reality. Valuev also drafted the decree on the creation of the Supreme Administrative Commission. According to Valuev, his draft underwent no fundamental changes, and it served as the basis of the decree of 12 February establishing the commission. Not counting the preamble, which expressed the desire "to end the uninterrupted series of attempts by brazen criminals to shake the government and social system in Russia,"[16] the decree consisted of eleven points. The first said that the Commission was intended to "preserve the government system and social peace; the second point discussed the composition of the Commission (the director and the members appointed at the director's "direct discretion"). The third and fourth points reported the nomination of Loris-Melikov as director and outlined the system of appointment for other members. Points five through eleven defined the functions of the Commission. The functions were limited to various means of struggle against the revolutionary movement. The director was granted authority over Petersburg and its environs—that is, he received authority "to control and direct investigations of state crimes in Petersburg and the Petersburg military district." The position of the Petersburg Governor-General was abolished. The Commission also was invested with the power of "supreme direction" of state criminal investigations in other areas of Russia. All agencies, including the military, were obliged to execute without question the orders of the Supreme Administrative

Commission "concerning the preservation of the governmental system and public order." The director was granted the right to "issue all orders and take the appropriate steps to preserve order and peace both in Petersburg and in other areas of the empire . . . ."[17]

The Supreme Administrative Commission was an executive body headed by a dictator. The decree said nothing about the rights of Commission members. The determination of the original composition of the Commission by the director himself indicated that the members of the Commission would do nothing but follow orders, as Valuev had foreseen. The prerogatives of the director were very extensive, though they were confined to the general area of struggle against the revolutionary movement.

In this same spirit the Extraordinary Conference formulated a resolution concerning the powers of temporary Governors-General, and their relationship to the Supreme Administrative Commission. This resolution, approved by Alexander II on 29 February, preserved the powers of the Governors-General, and also the principle of "direct subordination of provincial establishments of various agencies to the heads of those agencies."[18] All ministers and commanders-in-chief would be obliged to supply the director of the Supreme Administrative Commission and the Minister of Internal Affairs with all information relevant to "state crimes;" they also would have to obey the orders of these two individuals in the area of criminal investigations.

The powers of the Commission director ostensibly were limited to a single sphere of activity—the fight against the revolutionary movement. In reality, however, his powers were much broader. From the first days of the Supreme Administrative Commission its director interpreted his authority in a wider sense. Miliutin testified directly on this point in his diary following a conversation with Loris-Melikov on 10 February, the day after the tsar's public order creating the Commission and naming Loris-Melikov as director: "Count Loris-Melikov understood his role to be not only a chairman of an investigative commission, but a dictator to whom all ministers, all other officials were subordinate."[19] Valuev had a similar impression: "Count Loris-Melikov attended the committee meeting. Obviously, he has not taken his proper place, and sees himself in quite another role—as organizer of all fields of state administration."[20]

The creation of the Supreme Administrative Commission marked the beginning of a new stage in the crisis of the autocracy. If the assassination attempt by Soloviev in 1879 had set the government on the path of decentralization of power via the institution of the Governors-General, it now was headed in the opposite direction. The transfer of very considerable powers to Loris-Melikov suggested the creation of a personal dictatorship, and the centralization of power. The director of the Supreme Administrative Commission became a sort of sub-emperor. Both the creation of the Governors-General and the dictatorship of Loris-Melikov violated the principle of autocracy. Infringement of this principle was a certain indicator of the governmental crisis. The hesitation of Alexander II during the debate over the Commission, and his sudden decision to create the Commission despite his doubts, underlined the enormous confusion in governmental circles.

On 15 February, only three days after the Supreme Administrative Commission had begun to function, Loris-Melikov published his appeal "To the Inhabitants of the Capital," in which he asked for public support. "Without giving rise to exaggerated and premature expectations," he wrote, "I can make only one promise—to dedicate all my efforts and abilities so as not to permit even the slightest weakness and not to hesitate to use the strictest methods to punish criminals, while at the same time I also will strive to foster and protect legitimate interests. I am certain that all honorable individuals who are loyal to the tsar and who love their country will support me. I consider the support of society essential to the restoration of normalcy. . . . " Loris-Melikov asked the residents of Petersburg to be calm, and not to believe any insidious rumors. "If the people are rational and steadfast in the current distressing climate, this will be a solid guarantee of success in our effort to attain a most important goal."[21] Loris-Melikov's appeal stirred up a huge response in the press, and prompted a number of letters from various officials and anonymous citizens who had devised plans to fight against "the criminal gang of nihilists."

Loris-Melikov's dictatorial activity did not even arouse opposition in the Anichkov Palace.[22] However, the ministers were clearly upset over the Supreme Administrative Commission; they saw the director's actions as infringements of their own authority. On 25 February Pobedonostsev wrote to E.F. Tiutcheva: "Loris-Melikov has now been appointed, but his position is impossible unless he can clear himself a place. From the first the whole government, especially the ministers, have greeted him with silent opposition, and his central and most difficult struggle will be with these gentlemen. . . . If he manages to circumvent them at first, and then to vanquish and discard them, his purpose will have been accomplished. If not, then nothing will come of it, as the ministers now prophesy. So this month will be a time of decisive test."[23]

Let us briefly describe the personality of the director of the Supreme Administrative Commission. A prominent military leader, a fighting general who took part in a number of campaigns, Loris-Melikov was the commander in the Caucasus theater in 1877-1878. Decisive and courageous, he achieved several major successes in the war. During a long term of duty in the Caucasus he served as commander of Terskaia region, and was appointed *ataman* of the local Cossack infantry. After the war, in early 1879, he became temporary governor of Astrakhan, Samara, and Saratov provinces during the cholera outbreaks in Astrakhan; in mid-1879, after Soloviev's assassination attempt, he became the temporary Governor-General in Kharkov province. Intelligent, energetic, flexible as well as extraordinarily ambitious and insincere, Loris-Melikov acquired authority and achieved popularity among the liberal elements of society.[24]

In contrast to the other Governors-General, Loris-Melikov sought to win over the oppositional, or liberal, elements of society. The social base of governmental authority would be broadened, and Loris-Melikov thought this essential in the fight against revolution. Naturally, his view of the Governor-General's responsibility was broader, and thus much more dangerous to the revolutionary movement, than the policy of naked repression, exile, and hanging pursued, for instance, by the Odessa Governor-General, Totleben, and his assistant Paniutin.[25]

The extreme reactionaries of the Pobedonostsev and Katkov stripe, and the liberal bureaucrats like- Miliutin and Grand Duke Konstantin Nikolaevich, were very sympathetic to the creation of the Supreme Administrative Commission and to the appointment of Loris-Melikov as its director. On 11 March Katkov wrote to Alexander II concerning the appointment of Loris-Melikov: "May God help this valiant general. . . deliver us from sedition. He must fight against a most pernicious form of evil. It would be dangerous to delay the exposure and eradication of this evil, but a diagnosis that mistakes a superficial ailment for a chronic disease is equally dangerous. The idea of acting in unison with society is a wise idea, but to have society as a solid ally there must be agreement not so much of opinion as of interests. One must not trust public opinion, especially in such a difficult time as this. . . . History records many striking and horrifying examples of catastrophe caused by [premature] adaptation to public opinion."[26]

To summarize Katkov's view, one might say that he asserted the need for merciless struggle against the revolutionary movement without making any concessions whatsoever. The Slavophile Kireev formulated his own reaction to Loris-Melikov's appointment somewhat more simply:

"I have read the order about Loris-Melikov. A full dictatorship. Vice-emperor. If the present emperor does not deal successfully with the nihilists, then let someone else try. Probably His Majesty does not feel comfortable in the role of hangman."[27]

Konstantin Konstantinovich, the son of Grand Duke Konstantin Nikolaevich, reflected his father's opinion. In a diary entry about Loris-Melikov he wrote: "I like his [Loris-Melikov's] brand of thinking and the ideas with which I became acquainted last summer in Kharkov. . . . It seems to me that he will not be guided by the senseless proposition that universal censorship can stop intellectual ferment, or that threats and repression alone can quell an uprising."[28]

Conservative opinion coincided with the traditional policy of the government over the previous fifteen years. It involved the unceasing intensification of reaction, with the intention of limiting and emasculating the reforms of the early 1860s. Conservatives looked on repression as the only way to fight "sedition."

The second opinion, characteristic of the liberal bureaucracy, arose from recognition of the need to adopt further liberal reforms that would not, of course, infringe on the prerogatives of the autocracy. The liberal bureaucrats believed that repression would have to be intensified in the fight against revolution, but they thought that repression alone could not prevent revolution. Repression should be accompanied by certain reforms that would hinder the further propagation of revolutionary ideas. During the crisis of government policy, when authority was unable to "govern as before," the liberal opinion took definite shape. The appointment of Loris-Melikov as director of the Supreme Administrative Commission was considered by the liberal bureaucrats to be the beginning of an about-face in government policy.

Now let us turn to the press and its reaction to Loris-Melikov's dictatorship. The editor of *Moskovskie Vedomosti* was generally sympathetic to the appointment of Loris-Melikov, but warned him about attempting "to act in unison with society." The appeal "To the Inhabitants of the Capital" was criticized in *Moskovskie Vedomosti*. "One must not seek everyone's cooperation, everyone's assistance," said the editorial on 17 February 1880. "May God preserve us from other assistants. To try to please everyone, to satisfy all without discrimination, is a poor way to gain popularity."[29]

The legal liberal press greeted the creation of the Supreme Administrative Commission with greater emotion. "Thank God! We are relieved!" wrote *Golos*. "This imperial decree has brought to the Russian people the tranquility that we have needed for so long. . . . We needed an assurance that tomorrow would come, and assurance is not difficult to find in this decree." The article went on to discuss the Commission, its tasks, and especially the appointment of Loris-Melikov as director: "His name is itself capable of inspiring confidence."[30] *Golos* was delighted by Loris-Melikov's appeal to the residents of the capital. "There is a spirit somehow new, pacific, and unusual in the words [of the appeal]. Instead of the 'obligatory command' that one might have expected from a person entrusted with so much authority, we have an appeal 'To the Inhabitants of the Capital.' "[31]

Vestnik Evropy [Herald of Europe] was somewhat more restrained but it too reacted positively to the appointment of Loris-Melikov, and to his appeal to the Petersburg citizens. "We are confident that our society has heard this call for its support with the utmost gratitude. It will display its readiness to answer this appeal in the fashion that the government indicates," said the March issue.[32] Even *Otechestvennye Zapiski*, which stood on the left wing of the legal press, approved the establishment of the Supreme Administrative Commission. "As always, when emergency plenary powers are granted to one person, his name more or less clarifies the whole program of action. In the present case, when it became known that Loris-Melikov was to be director of the Supreme Administrative Commission, everyone was relieved because they were convinced that the enormous powers held by this man would serve not to aggravate society, but to calm and appease it."[33] However, Loris-Melikov's appeal for the cooperation of society provoked a certain skepticism, which revealed itself as early as the April issue of the journal.

The Geneva-based publication *Obshchee Delo* [Common Cause] voiced a different opinion regarding Loris-Melikov. An article by Dragomanov treated the appointment of Loris-Melikov as a sign of crisis in the regime. "There can be no doubt that the appointment in autocratic Russia of a legal co-equal to the emperor is the beginning of the dissolution of imperial autocracy."[34] In an open letter to Loris-Melikov, Dragomanov wrote: " . . . If you really want to eliminate from Russia that which you call 'the criminal actions that disgrace our fatherland,' then eliminate the autocracy and its companion—the tyranny of officials. Only then will one be able to speak of the future prosperity of the nation. Do you seriously believe what you have written? Do you really respect the 'public' to whom you appeal?"[35] Dragomanov then enumerated the steps which, in his opinion, represented a minimum program for Loris-Melikov: the abolition of emergency laws, the liquidation of the Third Section, the establishment of freedom of the press and assembly, and the convocation of a Zemsky Sobor [Assembly of the Land]. It is thus evident that liberal society, with the exception of its extreme left wing, reacted favorably to the establishment of Loris-Melikov's dictatorship.

The revolutionary press dealt repeatedly with Loris-Melikov. The editorial in the first issue of *Listok Narodnoi Voli* [Leaflet of the People's Will] noted ironically: "Determined to eradicate sedition, His Majesty again has rearranged the musicians in his quartet. General Gurko has fled in complete disgrace, and the salvation of Russia has been entrusted to Loris-Melikov with the Supreme Administrative Commission thrown into the bargain."[36] The second issue of the paper contained a special article about Loris-Melikov, written by N.K. Mikhailovsky. "They say that to the figures of Minin and Pozharsky will soon be added a statue of Loris-Melikov. They say that a grateful Russia pictures the Count in a General Adjutant's uniform, but with a wolf's snout in front and a fox's tail behind . . . . Many not only will excuse the Count's fox-tail, but even praise him for it . . . . However, this Asian diplomat is not only a clever man, but a cruel one as well."[37] The dictatorship of Loris-Melikov, according to *Narodnaia Volia*, was intended to "consolidate the forces of the government, to divide and weaken the opposition, to isolate the revolution, and to strangle all the government's enemies one by one . . . ."[38]

Another expression of the attitude of revolutionary circles toward Loris-Melikov was an attempt to assassinate him on 20 February, only eight days after his appointment. The would-be assassin, I.P. Mlodetsky, who had close connections with the Populists, was sentenced to death on 22 February by a military court[39] and executed. On the same day Alexander II wrote the following cynical note in his memo book: "Mlodetsky hanged at 11 A.M. in Semenovsky drill-ground. Everything in order."[40] The Executive Committee of *Narodnaia Volia* wrote in a proclamation dedicated to Mlodetsky: "The supreme judge in this case was Loris-Melikov, who ratified the death sentence because of a unsuccessful attempt on his life. The moral character of this dictator, the renovator of Russia, is base."[41] The proclamation mentioned that the assassination had been attempted without the permission of the Executive Committee. Mlodetsky had proferred his services to the Executive Committee, but had not received an answer to his proposal.

One of Loris-Melikov's first steps was to subject the Third Section to his control. On 26 February he sent Alexander II an official memorandum in which he asserted that "unity of command is the only sure way to attain success against sedition."[42] He also indicated that the uncoordinated actions of government agencies were among the chief reasons for the failure to suppress the revolutionary movement, and that every delay in creating unity of command was extremely dangerous. "If in the near future we must study the ways in which the population has become susceptible to revolutionary elements, our immediate task nevertheless must be to crush the anarchistic tendencies of the insurgents, to demonstrate the beneficial effects of government strength in preserving order, and thereby to expose the insidious false doctrines of the revolutionaries."[43] Loris-Melikov concluded by outlining measures that involved the complete subordination of the Third Section to the head of the Supreme Administrative Commission.

In accordance with this memo, which was approved by the tsar, the government issued a decree on 3 March that placed the Third Section under Loris-Melikov's temporary control.[44] The Chief of Gendarmes, General Drenteln, was dismissed from his post; his replacement was to be Major-General Cherevin, one of the tsarevich's closest friends. According to Miliutin's rather restrained description, Cherevin was a man "known for his inclination toward the gay life."[45] Clearly, Loris-Melikov saw the need to intensify repression against the revolutionaries as his immediate task.

Let us now consider the Supreme Administrative Commission itself. Besides Loris-Melikov, the Commission had nine members: Supreme Procurator of the Synod K.P. Pobedonostsev, commander of the Guards' Headquarters and of the Petersburg military district, General-Adjutant A.K. Imeretinsky, acting Chief of Gendarmes P.A. Cherevin, a secretary to the Committee of Ministers, M.S. Kakhanov, Senators M.E. Kovalevsky and I.I. Shamshin, Supreme Procurator of the Senate P.A. Markov, Superintendant of the Chancellery in the Ministry of Internal Affairs S.S. Perfiliev, and Major-General of the Suite M.I. Batiianov.[46] It should be noted that two members of the Commission, Pobedonostsev and Cherevin, were very close to the tsarevich. This is proof that Grand Duke Alexander Alexandrovich was not without influence in selecting the Commission's membership.

The rights and duties of Commission members were very ill-defined. Basically, they were to carry out the director's instructions. The role of the Commission itself was consequently very modest, and it was at best a consultative group. Judging by financial records, the salaried staff was very small. It consisted of five officers, assigned to different military units, and two officials from the Senate staff.[47] However, the number of people who worked with the Supreme Administrative Commission was actually much larger than this. In fact, twenty-one officials—including one Privy Counsellor and five State Counsellors—from the Senate, the State Chancellery, the Ministries of Internal Affairs, Justice, and other departments, were assigned to assist the Commission.[48] In addition, the Commission enlisted the services of Major-General R.A. Fadeev, General E.M. Bogdanovich, and Colonel N.M. Baranov,[49] whom Loris-Melikov sent abroad in April. Furthermore, the Supreme Administrative Commission possessed its own police force, consisting of thirty-two men: one secret agent, two police officers, nine gendarmes, eleven Cossacks, and eleven city policemen.[50]

The Commission's structure is not known, except for the Special Judicial-Political Department. In a memorandum of 10 November 1880 Loris-Melikov wrote that "this department consisted of Senator Shamshin, a colleague of the Supreme Procurator in the Criminal Appeals Department, one former provincial procurator, two secretaries of the Senate, several young officials assigned to this area, and the requisite number of lower chancellery officials."[51] This special department examined all cases of "state crimes" that came to the attention of the Supreme Administrative Commission, and it also worked out legislative proposals, such as the plan to extend the law of 19 May 1871 to cover regions of Siberia.[52]

On 4 March the Supreme Administrative Commission met for the first time. Speaking of the problems confronting the Commission, Loris-Melikov indicated that "the first among them is to adopt decisive measures to suppress the most outrageous actions of the anarchists; a second and more complex problem is to discover the means to cure the underlying causes of sedition." Loris-Melikov concentrated on those matters which, in his opinion, complicated the "government's struggle against sedition," and whose resolution would be the initial task of the Commission. He considered the basic prerequisites for victory over the revolutionary movement to be unity of action among all administrative and judicial agencies "involved in exposure and investigation of criminal plots and actions, and the discovery of ways to establish such unity."[53]

A second reason for the government's failure to fight subversion was "the extremely slow process of prosecution, even in cases of state offenses." The third and fourth problems for the government were the insufficient organization of administrative exile and of police supervision. According to Loris-Melikov, both administrative exile and police supervision were useful in dealing with politically unreliable persons, if exercised with "appropriate discretion." However, in reality, such discretion was not exercised. "One cannot help but notice that instances of administrative exile are so frequent that the arrangements for these exiles have become a state responsibility. As far as police supervision is concerned, what is basically a method of observing suspicious individuals has become the functional equivalent of a denial or limitation of legal rights: a person under police observation is limited in his choice of domicile, and is not trusted by his friends, who are forced to forego associations with him for fear of calling suspicion on themselves."[54] Loris-Melikov therefore thought it essential to regulate administrative exiles and police supervision. Loris-Melikov considered these four questions to require speedy resolution. Of them, the basic problem remained the lack of unity in the administrative-police and judicial systems.

There were four additional meetings of the Supreme Administrative Commission: on 11 and 24 March, 15 April, and 1 May. The session of 11 March examined a report that recommended steps to speed up prosecutions in "state offenses." It also considered a note by Supreme Procurator Markov dealing with conditions in the Petersburg jails that were visited by Markov, Shamshin, and Batiianov. Markov noted that the law of 1 September 1878 was not being enforced faithfully. "According to provisions of this statute, the use [of jails for political detention] should occur only in those cases where there is no legal evidence of state crimes that would require formal prosecution, but where there is evidence of political disloyalty. . . . The members of the Commission have looked into certain cases processed under the law of 1 September which turned out to be purely criminal cases involving prosecutions for offenses covered by the Statute on Punishments."[55] Loris-Melikov also reported to the session on various measures he had taken, specifically those to unify the actions of provincial agencies and gendarme officials, and on the Petersburg municipal governor's plan to increase the number of policemen.

On 24 March Loris-Melikov informed the Commission of an official memorandum dealing with changes in legal prosecution in cases of political crimes. The Commission also was acquainted with a new report on the organization of a secret search unit for political cases in Petersburg. The commissioners heard the report of Markov, who together with Shamshin and Batiianov had investigated the problem of political prisoners held in Petersburg, and who also had drafted a set of proposals to speed up prosecutions. The Commission approved these proposals and concluded that "the data compiled on cases processed in Petersburg under the law of 1 September 1878 shows repeated instances of incorrect application of these regulations, attended by the deprivation of freedom of those suspected of political disloyalty without sufficient justification. Such cases, in addition to the personal material and moral damage that they entail, have very harmful consequences for the government, create dissidents, cause annoyance, and thereby hinder the government's battle against criminal propaganda." The Commission pointed out that "not infrequently searches take place without the requisite circumspection and they yield no concrete results."

Other questions before the Commission concerned the subordination of prisons to various agencies and the problem of administrative exile. The Commission heard an estimate of the number of persons under police surveillance, and a report by Loris-Melikov on the situation of these individuals. This report raised the possibility of freeing those persons who had "corrected their behavior and their morals." Finally, Loris-Melikov read a circular calling for abolition of the death penalty "at the discretion of the emperor."[56]

The session of 15 April dealt with the activity of the Main Prison Administration and with the Petersburg House of Preliminary Detention. The Commission decided that all places of confinement should be subject to the Main Prison Administration. (Previously, the House of Preliminary Detention had been supervised by the municipal governor, while Vyshnevolotskaia and Mtsenskaia prisons had fallen under the local governor's control.) Prince Imeretinsky was asked to investigate conditions in the Moscow Deportation Prison, and in the Mtsenskaia and Vyshnevolotskaia prisons.

Imeretinsky delivered his report during the final session on 1 May. On the basis of his study of prisoners in administrative exile, Imeretinsky maintained that their cases could be divided into five categories. The first four categories included those persons deserving administrative exile. The cases of the remaining prisoners, who had been banished administratively, could be reviewed "with the goal of changing or reducing punishments and even seeing their complete abolition."[57] Imeretinsky also noted the inconsistency in the procedures adopted by prisons.

The Supreme Administrative Commission did not concur with all of Imeretinsky's ideas. "With reference to the conclusions of Prince Imeretinsky's report, it was argued that administrative exile was an essential tool for dealing with those persons against whom there was insufficient direct evidence to merit prosecution, but whose continued presence in these unusual political circumstances was recognized as harmful to social peace. Although the use of administrative exile might involve regrettable mistakes in some instances, the possibility of such errors alone did not justify a full-scale reexamination and investigation of all cases of exile by administrative order. A general review would call into question the meaning of orders by high local administrative agencies, and would undermine their authority. . . . "[58] The Commission rejected Imeretinsky's plan.

Such were the issues discussed by the Supreme Administrative Commission. In analyzing these discussions, it might be concluded initially that all of the most important questions connected with the Commission's main function, the fight against the revolutionary movement, were treated in these sessions. However, in my opinion, most of the discussions were simply *pro forma*, since the sessions were very brief. The first meeting of the Commission, at which its tasks were defined and its plan of action determined, lasted only two hours. The second session dealt with ten questions in two and one-half hours; the third session covered nine issues in three hours and the fourth—four questions in a little over two hours. Prince Imeretinsky's report on the condition of political prisons took up two hours at the fifth session.

The main questions which confronted the Supreme Administrative Commission in connection with its basic task included the following: (1) the unification of all police and judicial agencies in the fight against the revolutionary movement; (2) the acceleration of court proceedings in cases of political crime; and (3) the review of the existing organization of administrative exile and political surveillance. Regarding the first question, the key organization in the struggle with revolution was the Third Section. According to data collected in August 1880, the Third Section consisted of 72 persons, plus supernumeries and civilian staff.[59] The Third Section also employed a certain number of secret agents within the empire and abroad.[60] The Third Section comprised three offices and a newspaper unit, which earlier had played an important role. The first office handled questions of administrative exile, the general observation of political prisoners, and relations with provincial gendarme offices, plus other matters. It looked into cases involving "the pronunciation of impertinent words" in reference to the imperial family. The second office dealt with personnel problems of the Third Section, and analyzed requests for funding submitted to the tsar or directly to the Third Section.[61] It also issued various kinds of residence permits (i.e. passports) to women, who normally did not possess the right to hold such permits.[62] The third office acted as a secret political police force, and dealt with a whole complex of problems in the struggle against the revolutionary movement. The newspaper unit observed the press and conducted anti-revolutionary propaganda. It published various sorts of "patriotic" literature, and frequently issued bribes to the press. In 1871 a unit for legal consultation was added to these other sections under the authority of the head of the Third Section, the Chief of Gendarmes.

The activity of the Third Section recently had been broadened significantly in response to the growth of the revolutionary movement. The sharp rise in estimates for secret expenditures in the late 1870s and early 1880s testified to this expanded activity. In 1877 the allocation for secret expenses was 186,877 rubles; in 1878—251,877 rubles;[63] and in 1880—558,957 rubles. The account for secret expenses in 1880 was subdivided into the following categories:[64]

Item A: for police guard—52,000 rubles
Item B: for Petersburg municipal governor (secret service)—29,000
Item C: for Moscow Governor-General (secret service)—7,500
Item D: for the press abroad—21,000
Item E: for the domestic secret service—65,000
Item F: to counteract propaganda—300,000
Item G: for foreign agents—19,000
Item H: funds at the disposal of the Chief—58,377
Item I: for Kiev provincial gendarmerie (secret service)—7,080
Total: 558,957

Most of the secret appropriation was spent on bribery of journalists and on publication of anonymous brochures.[65]

The law of 9 September 1867 determined the organization of gendarme offices in Russia.[66] This law had abolished the old corps of gendarmes and established a new structure. The new corps comprised three police districts (in Warsaw, the Caucasus, and Siberia), the provincial gendarme administrations (in six northwestern provinces there were 50 district gendarmeries[67]), the gendarme police units for railroads, the gendarme divisions and mounted gendarme command. The staffs of these gendarme agencies were not large. The corps headquarters consisted of twelve officers and officials, one doctor, and twenty-three clerks. The staffs of provincial gendarme administrations included two officers—the director and his adjutant—plus two clerks.[68] Officers who worked in these agencies were required to serve for five years and to have a high school education, but the education requirement was not always enforced. The basic function of the provincial gendarme offices was "surveillance." Obviously, the net of agents was very thin, since the statute of 9 September 1867 allowed directors of provincial gendarme offices only 500 rubles for secret expenditures.[69]

In the late 1870s the personnel of the Corps of Gendarmes increased significantly. According to the annual report of its headquarters, the corps' staff included 521 officers and 6187 lower officials on 1 January 1880.[70] Nine officers and eleven soldiers worked in the three district gendarmeries; in provincial gendarme offices there were 328 officers and 2290 junior officers;[71] 126 officers and 2431 junior officers worked with the railroad police. Finally, in the gendarme divisions there were 53 officers and 1310 soldiers, and in the mounted commands five officers and 145 soldiers. The educational qualifications of officers in the provincial agencies and the railroad police were not very high. In the former group, only 4.56% had received higher education; among the latter, only 3.17%. The soldiers, or more precisely, the junior officers, were all literate.

Judging by the appropriations, the number of secret agents in provincial gendarme offices increased somewhat, but remained modest. According to information on expenses for the first six months of 1880, 50,481 rubles were spent on secret agents in the provincial and foreign units, but in Petersburg alone the city governor spent 90,000 annually.[72]

The gendarmes were not the only police agencies involved in the struggle against the revolutionary movement: there was also, for example, a police unit (border police, civil police, and investigators) in the Ministry of Internal Affairs. The disarticulation of police agencies was especially troublesome in Petersburg. In the capital there was a secret investigative unit attached to the Third Section, the civil police, and a "Secret Department for the Preservation of Social Order and Tranquility" under the municipal governor: all these agencies were involved in the suppression of the revolutionary movement[73]

Loris-Melikov adopted certain measures to coordinate the actions of the gendarmes and police in the capital. On 27 March he informed Minister of Internal Affairs Makov that "in order to attain greater success in the suppression of the anti-government movement in Petersburg, I have found it necessary to remove the authority to conduct secret surveillance from the Third Section and to entrust it to the municipal governor . . . . " However, this step did not mean that the Third Section ceased to participate in the "battle with sedition" in the capital. Even "after the transfer of direct surveillance powers in the city and the power of investigation to the city governor, the Third Section of His Majesty's Chancellery preserves its former authority to conduct surveillance of various strata of society to determine the general political atmosphere."[74]

To establish unity of action among provincial gendarme offices and local branches of the Ministry of Internal Affairs, Loris-Melikov sent a series of proposals to Alexander II, which the tsar confirmed on 10 March. Gendarmes were directed in all cases "relating to the organization of order in the state and social tranquility" to report to their supervisors, and to forward copies of these reports to local governors or to the Governor-General. The gendarmes were obliged also to act with the consent of the governors. The governors were obligated to tell the gendarmes of any reports concerning "the preservation of order."[75] As a rule, there was no coordination between the governors and gendarmes prior to the spring of 1880. This lack of coordination was confirmed by the governors' answers to a confidential letter from Makov on 6 May. The governors of Chernigov and Nizhny Novgorod provinces provided the most detailed descriptions of conditions in their jurisdictions. According to the Chernigov governor, " . . . the gendarmes have acted not only independently, but altogether separately from the provincial administration, and only rarely in cooperation with the executive police; the general direction of the gendarmes' activity and the results that they have achieved remain unknown to the high officials of the provinces . . . . Although the gendarmes act in most cases with the approval of the Third Section and the Ministry of Internal Affairs, sometimes there are no parallel orders from the departments, and not a few times instructions have been contradictory. The governors have not had access to secret information at the disposal of gendarme officials; yet sometimes the governors have received very important secret information concerning the results of investigations, and this data has not been communicated to the gendarmes. The governors' lists of persons under surveillance have been in complete disagreement with the lists held by the gendarmes." The governor maintained that only in those provinces where there were "good" personal relations was there communication among departments.[76]

The governor of Nizhny Novgorod wrote that in Nizhny Novgorod and Yaroslavl provinces there had been efforts to coordinate the actions of gendarmes and police officials, but these efforts would not be successful unless "officials in the corps of gendarmes were fully controlled by the governors."[77] As we shall see below, Loris-Melikov considered the subordination of the gendarmes to provincial governors essential for the final solution of the problem of coordination.

In order to make investigations more effective, Loris-Melikov proposed the organization of a permanent foreign *agentura*. To this end, he sent Colonel Baranov of the Supreme Administrative Commission abroad to Rumania, Switzerland, and France in April 1880; he also sent State Counsellor Yuzefovich to Germany.[78] According to Baranov's report to the Supreme Administrative Commission, he had accepted the following tasks: (1) to draw up a plan for creation of a secret political *agentura* abroad; (2) to collect information on the activity of the Russian emigration; (3) to enter an agreement with a certain

Meier and convince the latter to visit Petersburg; (4) to study the organization of the Paris police. This last task was the official part of Baranov's commission.

Baranov devoted most of his attention to the organization of an *agentura* in Paris, the city which served, in his words, as the "headquarters of sedition."[79] The *agentura* was set up within the Paris prefecture; its director was an official from the secret-surveillance unit named Mercier. The Parisian prefect, Andrier, assumed supervision and general direction of Mercier. All these arrangements were to remain strictly secret. "Andrier wishes that the character of the Russian *agentura* in Paris and his participation in it be known only by his Imperial Highness and the director of the Supreme Administrative Commission."[80] A law student at the Université de Paris, as well as a former judicial investigator, F. Murashko, was designated as Mercier's translator. However, Baranov admitted in one of his last communications to Loris-Melikov that this *agentura* did not prove itself worthwhile. In his report on 6 September Baranov noted: "In the course of four months Mercier has given me assorted information and the results of his surveillance two or three times a week; since he is not directed by anyone who knows the Russian language or the Russian life-style, he gathers material that is of little interest from our point of view."[81] As a consequence the alliance between the Third Section and the Paris prefecture did not develop further.

According to Loris-Melikov, success in the struggle against the revolutionary movement required the coordination of activity undertaken by gendarmes, police, and the judicial institutions, and an end to the constant wrangling between the Ministry of Justice and the Third Section. The basis of the wrangling was the increasingly assertive encroachment in the field of jurisprudence by the gendarmes, who acted in complete violation of the Judicial Statutes of 1864. The law of 19 May 1871 had initiated the process of encroachment. It gave the gendarmes the right to bring prosecutions in political cases, although representatives of the procurator's office were supposed to participate in the prosecutions.

As noted earlier, these regulations granted to officials in the corps of gendarmes, and in their absence, to police chiefs and district police officers, the right to arrest "persons suspected of committing state offenses, their accomplices, and persons belonging to anti-government associations."[82] These arrests took place without the consent of judicial agencies, including the procurator's office. The gendarmes interpreted the law so broadly that further criticism from the judicial agencies was inevitable. Soon after the formation of the Supreme Administrative Commission Loris-Melikov directed Kakhanov to acquaint himself with the conflict between the gendarmes and the judicial agencies, and to make recommendations to resolve it.

Kakhanov's report, presented on 23 March, gave a detailed summary of the situation at the local level and included his recommendations for change. Kakhanov noted that the matter under investigation "was very instructive since it was graphic evidence of the real rift between departments which should pursue the same goal of suppressing disorder. This rift is undoubtedly one of the most important reasons for the partial failure of previous programs, for the improper application of laws, for the failure of government forces, and it accounts in part for the difficult situation in which we find ourselves now."[83] In the quarrel between the Ministry of Justice and the Third Section, Kakhanov sided with the latter, although he did not deny that the gendarmes had applied improperly the law of 1 September 1878. The author blamed the judicial reform for causing the conflict between the departments. "The judicial reform, having assumed a more advanced set of laws and a higher level of development than actually existed in Russia, created an independent court and changed the significance of the procurator .... The new importance of the judicial officials placed them beyond the customary position of Russian officials. For this reason and because of a natural reaction against their former subordination, judicial officials understood their appointment as a call to reforming activity, and they sided not with the government but, if one may say so, with the opposition, with the dissenters. Procurators did not dissociate themselves from this judicial reaction, but, with few exceptions, zealously endorsed the goal of separating the judiciary from the influence of administrative departments."[84]

In Kakhanov's opinion, these tendencies were aggravated by the Ministry of Justice, which constantly tried to prevent administrative interference with the functions of the judiciary. Moreover, there was no system governing appointments to the judiciary. Consequently, there were many incompetent persons serving in the procurators' offices. " ... It is no accident that the procurators continually strengthen the ranks of anti-government lawyers." In conclusion, Kakhanov declared that although it was essential to limit the application of the law of 1 September 1878, that law should not be removed from the books until "the Ministry of Justice understands its responsibilities, and shows itself able to discharge those responsibilities."[85]

Loris-Melikov agreed whole-heartedly with Kakhanov. The numerous official memoranda in which Loris-Melikov raised the question of insufficient cooperation from the judicial department in the "fight against sedition" prove Loris-Melikov's concern about this problem. Loris-Melikov gave a copy of Kakhanov's report to the tsarevich, who replied on 2 April: "Very sensible, and unfortunately, accurate. It would be desirable to show this report to the emperor, in order to convince him of the heretofore abnormal and incorrect direction of the Ministry of Justice."[86]

However, Loris-Melikov did not succeed in solving this problem. Even such a powerful dictator as the director of the Supreme Administrative Commission could not act in violation of the judicial statutes, especially in such a period of crisis. The judicial establishment, set up by the reforms of 1864, naturally contradicted the general system of state power, which remained basically feudal. The departmental conflicts between the gendarmes agencies and the Ministry of Justice reflected the contradictory nature of the political superstructure itself. The progress toward bourgeois reform in various spheres of political life was far from uniform.

Let us turn to a second issue—prosecutions in cases of "state crimes." According to data from the Third Section and the Ministry of Justice, there were 1087 cases being prosecuted in Russia on 1 March:[87] Approximately half of these cases involved articles 246 and 248 of the Penal Code ("pronunciation of impertinent words" referring to the tsar or the imperial family).[88] In this category there were only a few cases that could be considered political, since many of them concerned mere slips of the tongue, or occurred when the defendants were drunk.[89] Loris-Melikov apparently had this in mind when he wrote to Alexander II in a report on 26 July that the number of cases involving state crimes in February 1880 was about five hundred.[90] However, this judgment may be disputed. While cases under articles 246 and 248 did not prove that people were active participants in the revolutionary struggle, they did illustrate popular disaffection from the existing system.

During the period when the Supreme Administrative Commission was active there was a reduction in the number of prosecutions for political crimes. As I indicated earlier, Kakhanov headed a newly-created Special Judicial-Political Department in the Chancellery of the Commission; this department was asked to look into 482 cases from 18 March to 21 June. It actually examined 453.[91] According to the Third Section, there was not a single case left to review by 1 July. Loris-Melikov's official memorandum for 26 July stated that in all of Russia there were only 65 cases of state crimes that still required examination.[92] Actually, the number of cases was much larger. According to the Third Section, there were 277 cases on 20 July still being processed by provincial gendarmes or the railroad police; the Ministry of Justice was working on 36 cases on 8 August.[93] If the national agencies—the Supreme Administrative Commission and the Third Section—dealt with fewer cases of state crime, the local gendarmes dealt with an almost constant number.[94]

Let us consider the third issue—the review of the administrative exile system and police surveillance. Administrative exile was carried out on the basis of four legal statutes. The first of these was the law of 5 December 1855. According to this law, promulgated by the Minister of Internal Affairs, the Governors-General had the right to banish "depraved persons" from a province. However, the Governors-General first were required to inform the Minister of Internal Affairs about this and to include "a detailed summary of the reasons for the banishment and those measures of punishment to which the persons previously had been subjected."[95] Ultimately, the issue of administrative exile was resolved jointly by the Minister of Internal Affairs and the Third Section.

In 1870, in connection with the strike at the Nevsky Cotton Factory, this law was broadened. According to a report of the Minister of Internal Affairs, Alexander II gave the governors "at the first news of a strike in any factory and without following the usual judicial procedure, [the right] to exile strike leaders to the provinces."[96] On 30 September 1871 the right to exile strikers was extended to all kinds of strikes.[97]

The second government statute that served as a legal justification for administrative exile was the law of 19 May 1871, which changed the rules of evidence in political cases. If the government possessed insufficient evidence to convict in a criminal trial, the Minister of Justice would have the right to petition jointly with the Chief of Gendarmes to obtain "an imperial decision to cease prosecution or to resolve the case through administrative channels,"[98] that is, to order administrative exile. The third relevant statute was the law of 1 September 1878, mentioned above. According to this law, the Minister of Internal Affairs and the Chief of Gendarmes could act together to exile politically disloyal persons. The last legal basis for administrative exile was the decree of 5 April 1879 creating the temporary Governors-General. This law permitted exile of those persons "whose presence in a certain place was considered harmful."[99] Thus the mere whim of the administration could be the basis for exile.

According to Senator Kovalevsky, a member of the Supreme Administrative Commission, there were approximately 1200 persons in administrative exile. Perhaps 230 of these were in Siberia (this includes those sentenced by a court), and about 1000 were exiled in various parts of European Russia. The temporary Governors-General had used the law of 5 April 1879 to exile 575 persons, including 130 sent to Siberia. From 1 April to mid-July 1880, 53 persons were subjected to administrative exile, including 16 sent to Siberia.[100]

According to the journal of the Supreme Administrative Commission, there were 6790 persons in Russia under police surveillance for political activity.[101] However, even members of the Commission doubted the reliability of that estimate.[102] If it is noted that in the same province a governor and a director of the police might make different estimates of the number of persons under surveillance, it is not surprising that the Commission's official estimate was not trustworthy.[103]

On 3 April Loris-Melikov sent to Alexander II an official memorandum in which he summarized the steps necessary to regulate the system of exile and surveillance. "Observation of politically unreliable persons, primarily concentrated in northern and northeastern provinces, seems impossible and inconceivable because of the inadequate number of police personnel and their unsatisfactory quality. The absence of real supervision enables prisoners to flee or hide from government authorities. The constant increases in the number of exiles without corresponding increases in the number and quality of police threatens to make the question of political exiles a problem of national significance." Among the exiles there were many students. There were also persons who "recognized their errors and whose subsequent behavior has met with the approval of police supervisors."[104] Therefore Loris-Melikov argued that cases of exile should be reviewed on the basis of official reports. Alexander II approved that suggestion.

Loris-Melikov entrusted the study of the administrative exile problem and the system of police surveillance to Senator Kovalevsky, who presented his report in the latter part of July. Kovalevsky thought it essential to limit the authority of the local administration in the field of administrative exile. "The experience of recent years shows that if administrative exile is to be used by the state it should be used only in cases of extreme need and within precisely defined limits; to implement this program without prejudice or partisanship, we need a group that includes other officials besides those who have initiated the process of exile."[105] To this end, Kovalevsky thought it wise to establish within the Supreme Administrative Commission a special bureau consisting of the director, the Ministers of Internal Affairs and Justice (or their assistants), two members of the State Council, and two senators. This measure was never adopted since the Supreme Administrative Commission soon was disbanded.

It must be said that some people were subjected to administrative exile with no justification whatsoever. In Petersburg itself there was extreme confusion on this point. As Baranov admitted in a report to Loris-Melikov, the guilt of individuals exiled from the capital was not always clear-cut: "In the majority of instances the opinion of the Third Section is very different from that of the Petersburg municipal governor. General Zurov might recommend that some persons be exiled to Eastern Siberia; yet the director of the Third Section might think that the same persons should remain at liberty in Petersburg even without police surveillance."[106]

Soon after the creation of the Supreme Administrative Commission the St. Petersburg city governor gave Loris-Melikov a list of 113 names of persons who were liable to be banished from the capital. Five of these individuals, including the well-known journalist N.F. Annensky and the democratically-minded progressive book publisher F.F. Pavlenkov, were exiled to Siberia. Thirty persons were told simply that they must leave St. Petersburg. In the other 78 cases the government decided to do nothing.[107]

Loris-Melikov was a strong opponent of government sanctions against persons whose guilt had not been proven clearly. In a report to the Petersburg municipal governor on 2 April 1880, Loris-Melikov wrote: "From the reports sent to me concerning crimes against the state, I find that both the police and the authors of denunciations often searched political suspects without sufficient justification, or that they conducted searches at the wrong times, and therefore turned up no incriminating evidence. Sometimes these reports lead me to suspect that the police actually have helped to conceal evidence of state crime by searches which arouse too early the suspicions of persons who are accessories to these crimes. Moreover, the operations of the agencies responsible for the conduct of searches, which always have a powerful influence on the person searched and on his associates, always must be based on justifiable pretexts and must follow a preliminary check that confirms investigators' beliefs that a thorough search is necessary."[108]

Having analyzed the steps taken by the Supreme Administrative Commission to fight directly the revolutionary movement (the coordination of police, gendarmes, and the judiciary, the organization of a more rapid review of state criminal cases, the review of the issues of administrative exile and police supervision, the end of unjustified arrests and searches), it is evident that all these measures had a common aim—to create a more efficient system of repression. Yet at the same time these actions doubtless helped weaken the system of police terror.

During the tenure of the Supreme Administrative Commission capital punishment still was employed. Mlodetsky, the would-be assassin of Loris-Melikov, I.I. Rozovsky, a student at Kiev University accused of possession and dissemination of illegal literature, Junior-Officer M.P. Lozinsky, who was convicted of disseminating illegal literature and of armed resistance to arrest,[109] and A.A. Kviatkovsky and A.K. Presniakov, who were members of the Executive Committee of *Narodnaia Volia*—all were executed by hanging. Loris-Melikov's role in this last case is clear from the coded telegram that he sent to Cherevin in Livadia, concerning the death sentence pronounced in the "trial of the sixteen." In this telegram, dated 31 October, he wrote: "I wish to inform His Majesty that simultaneous execution of all the condemned in the capital would produce a painful impression among government supporters in society."[110] Loris-Melikov recommended that only Kviatkovsky and Presniakov be hanged, and noted that commutation of the death sentence was widely expected by the public. The director of the Department of State Police, Baron Velio, argued that commutation of the death sentences would produce "favorable results." "I cannot hide the fact that this directive makes it difficult for me to speak with real certainty. As a man and a statesman I would be ready to associate myself with the majority opinion, which expects a reduction of the sentences for the condemned, especially since reduction of the sentences would accord with the signs of increasing political calm. On the other hand, I cannot help but imagine the unavoidable criticism of this step, even though this criticism would be made by a small minority. My position is the more difficult because I realize that in the event of new criminal activity, whether or not the death sentence is employed now, there will be immediate criticism of me, although the ultimate decision to apply punishment or withhold it lies outside my competence."[111] The responsibility for the hanging of Kviatkovsky rested squarely on Loris-Melikov.

If the basic purpose of the Supreme Administrative Commission was to combat the revolutionary movement, this was not its only *raison d'être*. According to Loris-Melikov, the Commission also should "discover means to eliminate the causes of sedition and its support." This second task was not so much a product of Loris-Melikov's personal opinion as the result of complex circumstances that made government in the old fashion untenable. Loris-Melikov, who stood far above Makov, Drenteln, Count Tolstoy, and his other colleagues in political acumen, understood these circumstances. This political sensitivity explains his appeal to the public and the various reform projects that were necessary in his opinion "to deprive the revolutionary movement of favorable soil."

On 5 March Loris-Melikov met with representatives of the Petersburg municipal government, including the mayor, Baron Korf, and four town councillors (Mitkov, Likhachev, Glazunov, and Kavos). The other participant was Kakhanov from the Supreme Administrative Commission. Loris-Melikov asked the city officials to express "with complete candor" their opinions about what caused the terrorist acts designed "to shake the governmental system and the social order," and to suggest measures that might help stop the terror. According to minutes of the meeting, "the reactions of the mayor and the town councillors concerned general steps to reduce the receptivity of various social elements to the revolutionary doctrines, and to preserve order in the capital."[112] Loris-Melikov devoted most of his attention to discussion of proposals "that could guarantee order" in Petersburg.

The opinions expressed on this problem can be summarized in six points. The first three involve administrative-police matters: the need to coordinate police activity, the need for swifter investigation of cases involving state offenses, and the need for a "more careful approach to preventive arrest and exile and for close examination of the degree of guilt or association to criminal activity, especially for students."[113] The next two points relate to improvements in the standard of living. One proposal involved "changing the hours of trade in the interests of the lower classes," and the other proposal dealt with assistance to needy students in finding work and renting apartments. The final point concerned landlords. According to the participants, the organization of police surveillance through landlords in the capital had not been of much help in the struggle against revolutionaries, and it was very expensive. At the end of the meeting Loris-Melikov announced that a number of these proposals had already been studied by the Supreme Administrative Commission, and he requested that data on sums expended for maintenance of landlord surveillance be sent to him. This meeting with city officials acquainted them with the attempts of the Supreme Administrative Commission to fight the revolutionary threat, but like the appeal to Petersburg residents the meeting had no real results.

Loris-Melikov's attempt to acquire popularity, and to win the sympathy of students in particular, forced him to adopt other measures that involved him in a strange kind of philanthropy. In early April 1880, shortly after his appointment as director of the Commission, Loris-Melikov "contributed" 2500 rubles toward the fees of 100 Petersburg university students. The university inspector drew up a list of 70 students who needed a stipend for their tuition.[114] This gesture was purely political in nature; it was intended to bolster Loris-Melikov's personal popularity.[115]

Other members of the Supreme Administrative Commission also understood the need to attract the "well-intentioned part of society" to the government's side in the fight against sedition. One memorandum by General Batiianov is interesting in this regard. The first section of this document discussed the struggle against the revolutionary movement in the capital and the participation of public leaders in this struggle. "The efforts of the government alone have been powerless to restore order in the capital and cleanse it of malignant elements. Therefore, one must act through the municipal government to involve the owners of apartment houses themselves, whose observation of their lodgers could be a great advantage since they are so close to the problem. The surveillance could be organized on the principle of mutual obligations—that is, one would be responsible not only for oneself but also for one's neighbor. This would guarantee that surveillance was not merely a formality, a fiction, but rather a serious activity because the landlords would control each others' vigilance."

Since the police "did not take advantage of the sympathy of society," Batiianov proposed creation of a group of district officials who would be elected by the city council and who would make use of the trustworthiness of landlords. "These elected city officials would explain to home owners the meaning of the mutual obligation, and would supervise the fulfillment of the owners' responsibility to observe lodgers; finally, they would collect whatever information that the owners did not wish to make available directly to the police."[116] These municipal officials would be something like master spies. Batiianov also touched on the issue of administrative exile "on a large scale," and he recommended the use of Sakhalin Island for this purpose.

In the second section of his memorandum Batiianov spoke of the need for a series of reforms aimed at "strengthening the shaken governmental system." However, he believed that reforms could succeed only "if experts were consulted and involved in their formulation." Batiianov thought that Loris-Melikov already had used "the experience of experts" successfully; he probably had in mind the meeting with city officials. Batiianov argued that the Supreme Administrative Commission should use this technique more often. After assuming that the most important issue of the day was the need for *public education*, Batiianov recommended "that citizens outstanding for their responsibility and loyalty should be summoned from university centers, the zemstvos, and the private sector. Professors, zemstvo officials, and eminent citizens—the older generation—could give the Commission a host of practical suggestions concerning the education of youth."[117] These steps, in Batiianov's opinion, would have a salutary side-effect: they would secure for the Supreme Administrative Commission the complete trust of the public.

The Batiianov memorandum achieved no concrete results. But like the proposals of Loris-Melikov, it testified to the government's efforts to broaden its social support, to attract to its side certain bourgeois elements. It was another manifestation of the crisis of government policy.

The crisis of the autocracy led to a definite consolidation of the forces in the government camp: both liberal bureaucrats and reactionaries placed great hopes in the Supreme Administrative Commission and its director, Loris-Melikov. If in 1879 the government's policy could be described as one of universal reaction, in 1880 both liberals and reactionaries understood "the impossibility of government in the old manner," and consequently the necessity for certain reforms. On the other hand, both camps strove to destroy "sedition" and to stop the terrorism of *Narodnaia Volia.*

Representatives of the two groups offered different reform projects. Not only liberals like Kakhanov, but even reactionaries like Generals Fadeev and Bogdanovich acted as advisors to Loris-Melikov. Major-General R.A. Fadeev had been ordered to assist the Supreme Administrative Commission, as noted above, playing the role of "expert consultant" to Loris-Melikov. Retired Major-General E.M. Bogdanovich, a man with a very dubious reputation, an adventurist and a rogue, had served many years in the Ministry of Internal Affairs as an unpaid consultant; he also acted in this capacity under Loris-Melikov.[118]

Loris-Melikov's appeal for cooperation from the "loyal part of society" evoked a stream of projects aimed at the "salvation of Russia." The overwhelming majority of these projects was proposed by an assortment of reactionaries: petty officials, landowners, and police functionaries. Many of them were submitted anonymously or over false signatures like "Peter Patriot." There were proposals for a "society of internal security," which was an organization of "loyal spies," a project for "a special investigative unit," a project for "a universal photographic passport system" by Titular Counsellor Angelov, and so on. Almost all of these proposals spoke of the need for reforms, and they assumed that police measures alone "cannot pacify the nation."[119]

Without analyzing all these projects for the "destruction of sedition," we can look at a few of the more interesting ones. On 7 April General Fadeev sent a memorandum to his superior, Loris-Melikov. In the past Fadeev had been one of the publishers of the reactionary paper *Russky Mir* [The Russian World], and the right-hand man of Field Marshal Prince A.I. Bariatinsky. In the early 1870s Fadeev had been an active opponent of reforms for the Russian army.[120] It is worth noting that Fadeev's memo did not demonstrate any profound comprehension of the reasons for the growth of the revolutionary movement in Russia. On this score he wrote: ". . . Doubtless Russia's present malaise, no matter how acute and obvious its outward symptoms, is merely the result of misunderstanding, and it will disappear on its own as soon as the accumulated misapprehensions are clarified." In his view, the very existence of a revolutionary party was based on misunderstanding, since the "juveniles who constitute its real strength are the victims of deception." The dissatisfaction of the majority of educated society was also a result of misunderstanding, since society "wanted nothing more than self-determination in our domestic affairs, without interfering with the age-old prerogatives of the regime."[121] (In this last point, Fadeev was probably correct.) According to Fadeev, the people were "completely loyal to the regime and complained only because of the imperfections in the tax system, which constituted a heavy burden on them." Russia's malaise was therefore a "passing and quite exceptional phenomenon."[122]

In another report entitled "Candid Thoughts on Russia's Present Condition," Fadeev stressed that it was impossible to eliminate sedition by repression alone. "The maximum that one can achieve through emergency measures is a temporary cessation of seditious activity." In presenting his positive program for change, Fadeev argued that the chief enemy was bureaucratism. "Much is required to return our country to full health, but to prevent a sudden revolution, to implement essential changes that will avert danger once and for all, very little is required. A single initial step will convince Russian opinion of the decisiveness of government power: to put an end to the decrepit bureaucratic tutelage. . . . This step will not only not undermine Russian autocracy, but will save it in the long run, returning to the regime its original significance."[123]

According to Fadeev, there was no need "even for the innocuous Zemsky Sobors of Tsar Alexei Mikhailovich."[124] He thought it would suffice to form provincial committees resembling those established in the late 1850s to work out the abolition of serfdom. Fadeev suggested a plan of action for these committees in this report, and in another entitled "Additional Observations," which was an addendum to a memorandum written on 4 January 1880 before the creation of the Supreme Administrative Commission.

In the first report Fadeev presented the committee program in five points. The first order of business would be to plan ways to fight "sedition" "through the combined efforts of social forces." The second point suggested "the improvement and rearrangement of rural life, which was now excessively difficult."[125] This point was made more concrete in the "Additional Observations." Fadeev recommended a reexamination of the existing fiscal system (the head tax, the passport system, the salt tax). He also called for review of corporate institutions at the district level—the communes and the communal tax obligations. The third point spoke of the need for agreement between the activity of the government and of the zemstvos, if only at the provincial level; the fourth point called for review of the zemstvo and municipal statutes, and of the judicial and educational systems. The fifth point of Fadeev's program involved definition of the relations of zemstvos among themselves, and with the national government. "If the real foundation of the Russian state one day will be the zemstvo and nothing else, the zemstvos must not interfere with the government which is trying to develop this foundation today."[126] It was the task of the provincial committees to examine this problem in detail. Fadeev's ideas were not expressed with great clarity, but one can understand their essence: if the zemstvos were reformed on a reactionary pattern, they could occupy an important place in the system of governmental institutions. Fadeev thought that before the provincial committees were convened it would be necessary to gather zemstvo representatives, or representatives from the provincial zemstvo councils, or specially-elected individuals.[127]

Fadeev maintained that the Russian state should develop along in the special path reserved to all Slavic peoples. "When the Moscow manufacturer, and the Nizhny Novgorod merchant, and almost all commercial farmers began more or less to recognize our natural direction, the politicians wrote a constitution for the liberation of Bulgaria by Russian blood. And what did they write? Instead of those institutions which arise naturally in every Slavic land—a sovereign ruler or prince and a brief *skupshchina* [assembly], the Russian government gave Bulgaria the very same constitution which the Frenchified conspirators of 14 December 1825 wanted to impose upon Russia, and which the government fortunately rejected with buckshot."[128]

Such was the basic content of Fadeev's reports. In analyzing them several conclusions may be drawn. First, Fadeev understood the need for certain concessions which, in his view, would facilitate the "struggle against sedition." The abolition of the head tax, of the excise tax on salt, the review of the passport system, decisions on the questions of the commune, communal tax burdens, and district corporate institutions, the organization of the peasantry—all these demands (with the exception of the last, which was intended to preserve gentry landowner-ship) were by their nature objectively bourgeois, and corresponded to the interests of Russian development. This whole section of Fadeev's program coincided completely with the demands of liberal society and its spokesmen in the government, the liberal bureaucrats. Fadeev saw the development of the Russian state system in a reactionary Slavophilic spirit. His plans for zemstvo and municipal reforms were objectively bourgeois. Fadeev's plan showed rather clearly the consolidation of the government camp in this complicated situation. The reactionaries moved to the left, and on certain questions the liberal bureaucrats moved to the right on the political scale.

Let us turn now to the memorandum of General E.B. Bogdanovich, dated 9 March 1880. Bogdanovich mentioned that in the last twenty years he had performed many jobs for the Ministry of Internal Affairs and had had several opportunities to travel throughout Russia. This experience made it possible for him to study various strata of the populace and to judge methods to "suppress sedition."[129] Discussing the struggle against revolution, he stressed that "false doctrines, in what-ever form they might appear, could only be dangerous to the existing order if society itself were receptive to such propaganda." In Bogdano-vich's opinion, such a receptive climate existed; consequently, it was necessary to create conditions which would make the further dissemi-nation of falsehoods impossible. "To achieve this end, it is not enough to annihilate sedition by hangings and other personal punishments of state criminals; one must organize conditions of life so as *to prevent any possibility of success for false doctrines in Russia* .... The force of the local police and the organs of political surveillance cannot do this alone."

Bogdanovich contended that repression must be accompanied by a policy that would make the atmosphere less conducive to sedition. He saw the greatest danger as coming from the *déclassé* element and the groups of working people close to this group. He included the long-shoremen on Volga wharves among these dangerous workers. This cate-gory of workers had appeared as a result of the exorbitantly high fiscal burdens on the peasantry, who had been forced to leave the country-side and to live as transients without passports. Bogdanovich had seen the counterparts of this Lumpenproletariat in other cities. "In Moscow there was the notorious 'gold squadron,' consisting of the dregs of all strata of society."[130] He also discussed the semi-criminal and criminal organizations like the "Jacks of Hearts" which existed not only in Moscow, but in Kiev and Odessa as well.

Later the General described another group that he considered dangerous: " . . . the currently peaceful, physically-developed and almost universally literate working class in the Ural region may, like the transients, turn into a terrifying destructive force if the government does not try to improve their lot." He added that the problem of the working class "is not without its dangers even in Petersburg . . . . Obviously, the existing living conditions cannot satisfy that class, and therefore there is a climate conducive to false doctrines, which promise 'a land flowing with milk and honey.' " Summarizing his analysis, Bogdanovich stressed that the primary sources of discontent were "factory workers, seasonal laborers, and transients."[131]

bogdanovich made proposals to help improve living standards for the people and to reduce the influence of revolutionary propaganda. He divided these proposals into seven points. The first task would be to give amnesty to transients without passports; these individuals thus would be transformed from the most dissatisfied group in society to "sedentary workers." The second task should be "guaranteed remuneration for the work of laborers." Bogdanovich thought it essential "to deprive swindlers of the opportunity to exploit workers in seasonal industries." The government also should guarantee the regularity of wage payments to workers, ask city councils to "supervise relations between management and labor," and assist in the establishment of workers' guilds.[132] The third and fourth points concerned the development of local industries and the organization of public work programs with the intention of guaranteeing wages to the unemployed. The fifth and sixth points (ideological issues) spoke of the need for public education and the arrangement of spiritual conferences—that is, of religious and moral encounters.

The final point touched on broader rights for local administration. Bogdanovich asserted that the central government should have the "power to initiate" in questions connected with popular welfare or the political loyalty of the people. But "local deputies of the central government should be given the right in proper circumstances to convene and chair meetings involving the marshals of the nobility, zemstvo officials, and city councillors. These meetings could deal with economic issues and might work out proposals to eliminate poverty. . . ." This step would "place the government in a living relationship with the people and would create a wholehearted trust in the government. . . ."[133]

Like Fadeev, Bogdanovich understood the need for certain reforms to avert the further spread of revolutionary propaganda. But unlike Fadeev, Bogdanovich devoted attention to describing the problems of those groups that were most dangerous to the government. He was worried primarily about the Lumpenproletariat and the more literate groups in the working class. One can see this last point clearly in the part of his program calling for improvement of the workers' lot. Bogdanovich almost never mentioned the peasants' problems. His comment on those without passports touched the peasantry only indirectly. Bogdanovich did not propose any general program of reforms, but he and Fadeev shared a recognition that repression alone was insufficient and that certain reforms were needed.[134]

Let us turn to the proposals of liberal bureaucrats, beginning with the March memorandum of Privy Counsellor Rembelinsky, who then served as State Secretary to the State Council. Rembelinsky suggested that the basic problem was to "find the causes of the malady," otherwise the government's decisions would be ineffective. According to Rembelinsky, such an inquiry was impossible without the participation of the press. "Without free access for all to publish, we cannot reach our goal. By allowing real freedom to criticize, the government can benefit from its critics. Open dissatisfaction is always less dangerous than concealed dissatisfaction. In our time the press has acquired an enormous moral power. Governments can limit the use of this power only by exercising judicious influence." Rembelinsky added that zemstvo and municipal institutions should be enlisted in the attempt "to search out the causes of the spread of fantastic false doctrines." The regime should promote further development of zemstvo and municipal self-government and "induce public figures to offer their ideas on government policies in some form or another. . . . "[135] Rembelinsky did not list the concrete measures that he wished to be taken. However, his suggestion to induce liberal elements to discuss government policy was quite bold for a liberal bureaucrat. P. Viskovatov, a professor at Derpt University, entertained similar ideas in his report on the need for a free press.

The fullest and most detailed summary of the liberal bureaucrats' viewpoint may be found in the anonymous pamphlet "Report on the Chief Causes for the Spread of Revolutionary Propaganda in Russia and Measures to Stop It." After handwriting and content analysis, it is clear that A. V. Golovnin, the former Minister of Education, wrote the pamphlet. Golovnin also discussed the reasons for the growth of the revolutionary movement. Among them was the imperfection of the administrative apparatus: "the absence in Russia of a well-defined general administrative system and a consequent disunity and disharmony in the actions of individual government agencies."[136] The main cause was the peasant reform, which had not given land to the peasantry. The insufficiency of allotments, the disproportion of redemption payments to the cost of land, and the tax burden, particularly the salt duty, led in his words to the appearance of a rural proletariat—that is, to the ruin of the countryside. However, he also spoke about the destruction of the gentry, and about the appearance of a "gentry proletariat." Golovnin also blamed the inadequate system of education for the growth of the revolutionary movement. He had in mind the reform of the high schools in the early 1870s. He deplored the moral and material condition of the Orthodox Church, "particularly that of our white clergy."

Golovnin divided his solutions into two categories: police measures and "organic measures." He did not spell out the police measures except to say that all police agencies should be unified and subordinated to the Supreme Administrative Commission. Among the organic measures he included the establishment of a unified system of state administration—that is, the foundation of a super-governmental agency that would coordinate the actions of all other state institutions. According to Golovnin, there was no need for a completely new agency; it would be enough to reorganize the Council of Ministers, "making it into a cabinet responsible to the emperor.[137]

Golovnin presented his proposals to ameliorate the peasant problem in still greater detail.[138] He included in his discussion: reform of the wine excise tax, which was leading to the closure of most home-based distillation; the abolition of the salt tax; a program for the resettlement of peasants; the creation of loan institutions to help the peasants purchase land; and finally, the reform of the head tax system. "We set this step after the others for two reasons: (1) reform of the poll tax would reduce the total of peasant tax payments by a very small fraction; and (2) before one levies a tax, one has to know the tax base. Without a judicious solution to the peasant land problem no new tax levy can have a correct and solid foundation. A change in the existing disposition of peasant lands is now more important than any conceivable reform in the state financial system: *without reforms that will eliminate the existing basic inadequacies in rural relations, it is pointless to dream about the possible advantages of a correctly-designed head tax.*"[139] The basic problem was to provide the peasantry with sufficient land; this would be accomplished by resettlement of peasants and the foundation of loan institutions.

The next point in Golovnin's program was reform of the educational system. "The organization of a correctly-functioning school system in Russia" required the schools to play a stronger role in moral education (vospytanie). According to Golovnin, the school not only must impart knowledge, but moral principles as well. Speaking about the reform of primary and secondary schools, he made an extremely reactionary demand: to subject the primary schools to the Church's authority—that is, to create a system of clerical schools. Obviously the crisis of the autocracy and the growth of the revolutionary movement were behind the evolution of Golovnin's view on this subject, since in 1862 as Minister of Education he had protested against the proposal of the Synod to subject all primary schools to the Church's control. Golovnin also asked for a review of the 1871 statute on secondary schools and for the development of professional training programs. He concluded his discussion by raising the question of how to "strengthen the moral authority of the clergy and improve its material position."[140]

Analyzing the Golovnin program one sees that, unlike the authors of other reform projects, he correctly understood the reasons behind the growth of the revolutionary movement; he blamed the peasant reform of 1861 which had not provided the peasantry with sufficient land. Hence he devoted most of his attention to the solution of the land question, although he did not propose to do away completely with gentry land ownership. Therefore, the Golovnin program, however interesting, would not have yielded tangible results in the end.

A review of all the reform projects submitted by government officials confirms the proposition that I argued earlier: the crisis of the autocracy led to a consolidation of forces in the government's camp. The majority of officials saw the need for certain reforms, and everyone demanded more decisive steps against the revolutionary movement. One such step was the Golovnin proposal to transform elementary schools into clerical schools.

Let us now turn to the reform proposals made by the liberal opposition. The fondest hopes of the liberals were expressed in the memorandum called "On the Domestic Situation in Russia," forwarded to Loris-Melikov in 1880 by a group of public figures in Moscow. Over twenty people signed the memorandum, including S.A. Muromtsev, A.I. Chuprov, and V.Yu. Skalon.[141] Most of the memorandum was devoted to explanation of the growth of the revolutionary movement, but its concluding section presented measures intended to promote "a meeting of the minds."

The first section of the memorandum argued that "the root cause of the unhealthy form which opposition to the government has taken is the absence of proper and free channels for the expression of discontent with government policy." The memorandum pointed to the difficult position of the press, which was deprived of the opportunity to express public opinion since it was limited to the discussion of measures proposed by the government; if the press should ever be too critical of the government, it would face severe repression. "The only alternatives are to be silent, to be hypocritical, or to use the language of allegory," said the authors of the memorandum. "However, such language corrupts literature, and often mistakenly incites public opinion. When the press discusses government policy within the narrow permissible limits, the reader searches between the lines for hidden criticisms. When the press praises the government, the reader attaches no credence to its utterances, considering them to be hypocritical."[142]

The second section of the memorandum suggested that "it is impossible to eradicate evil by repression. Repressive measures are not only ineffectual solutions to existing problems, but breed new difficulties. Repression is inevitably attended by arbitrariness. Arbitrariness soon leads those in power to conclude that 'He who is not with us is against us.' This formula is particularly dangerous when pronounced by the police, since it labels as enemies of the fatherland useful and pacific individuals who happen not to agree with some facet of official policy." The liberals noted that recently the government had begun a campaign against the intelligentsia, "which alone contitutes the thinking element of the Russian people."[143] The second section concluded with the assertion that no repression could inhibit the free development of critical thought.

The third and longest section attempted to explain the causes of the extreme dissatisfaction, which had engendered the "current troubled situation." The first cause was the unsatisfied need for public participation in government. Administrators had placed every sort of obstacle in the way of attempts to participate in governmental affairs. "Heedless of the consequences, the government tells society that a state as vast as Russia may be run almost exclusively by bureaucrats. The zemstvo has been suppressed systematically even though every year, by virtue of the natural law of historical development, zemstvo institutions have turned out more and more capable public servants."[144] The memorandum cited examples of the government's attempt to inhibit the development of zemstvo activities, and of the government's desire to change the zemstvo from an independent organ of local self-government into an institution completely subordinate to provincial and district authorities.

Thus the "unsatisfied need for public participation in government" was, in the opinion of the liberals, a consequence of the government's policy toward the zemstvo. The second cause of public dissatisfaction was the absence of effective guarantees of personal inviolability. The memorandum argued that the independence of the court system, the strict observance of all statutes of the Judicial Code of 20 November 1864, and the avoidance of unwarranted arrests and police searches were elementary precautions for the existence of a civilized society. "Civilized society is incompatible with any kind of administrative limitations on the court system. Administrative constraints always express arbitrariness; they show that the government itself does not wish to be bound by those common laws which are its own creations, that the government is looking for the chance to encroach upon the independence of the courts, and on the rights of individuals who come into contact with the courts. No rationalizations can ever justify this conduct of the government in the eyes of society, and therefore such conduct always serves to undermine the authority of the government itself." [145] Special attention was paid to the system of administrative exile, which could be used without trial or investigation, and to which the government frequently resorted.

Other causes for public disenchantment, in the liberals' view, included the state of self-government, the courts, the press, and also secondary and higher educational institutions. They pointed to the constant reductions of the rights of the zemstvo and the courts, and to the systematic campaign against the press, depriving it of the most elementary freedom. The liberals took this as proof that the government had "something to hide from the public." Summarizing their ideas on the condition of the press, they wrote: "The stifling of the impulse to speak openly and loudly is an important source of the current dissatisfaction; by their very nature, educated people desire to exchange ideas and discuss their convictions. Conflict is quite natural in the world of ideas. To eliminate this conflict is to eliminate thought itself. No limitation on the freedom to protest can weaken the power of thought. On the contrary, limitation concentrates thought, and under circumstances which make the struggle of ideas impossible, such limitation will create political and social struggle." [146]

Turning to the issue of secondary schools, the authors of the memorandum announced that they did not intend to discuss the merits of the classical system of education. In their view the main problem was that the classical system had been imposed by force. They asserted that the arbitrariness of supervisors and extreme formalism of instruction dominated in the classrooms. As a result, pupils were receiving neither the necessary intellectual nor moral education. The main problem in higher education was that the Ministry of Education violated the Statute of 1863, which the liberals considered to be a solid basis for the development of higher education in Russia.

Thus the liberals ended their recital of the reasons for social discontent. They dealt primarily with legal norms, and completely ignored economic problems. The robbery of the peasantry through the reform of 1861 and the consequent preservation of certain vestiges of serfdom in the economy—these economic conditions made possible the violation of elementary principles of bourgeois law.

Let us examine the positive program of the memorandum. It may be formulated briefly in the following way. In order to succeed in the struggle against the revolutionary movement, it was necessary to return to the policies of the early 1860s, to abolish all reactionary measures, which had circumscribed, narrowed, and in some cases eliminated the "reforms of the beginning of Alexander II's reign." However, the liberals also made another demand, elucidated in the final section of the memorandum. "The discontent which pervades the whole of Russian society and which has arisen because of the incorrect direction of the government's domestic policies can be ameliorated only through general measures. The government is not strong enough to implement them alone. The whole of society must cooperate. One need only cast a cursory glance over the condition of our country to come to the conclusion that the time has come to attract all of Russia's healthy forces to action."[147]

After this assertion the memorandum referred to the urgent problems of the state, including the ominous financial situation, the scarcity "of the productive forces of the people," food allocation, the incipient economic depression and others. All of these problems necessitated the application of a collective effort by the state and society. The conclusion noted that "Russia was no less ready for free institutions than Bulgaria."[148] The demand for "zemstvo representation" was nothing other than a demand for a constitution, which was hardly original. It reflected the hopes of a great many liberals, hopes that were expressed in numerous zemstvo petitions.

In an official memorandum dated 11 April but approved even earlier by the Crown Prince, Loris-Melikov spelled out his program in detail.

He began by analyzing the situation prevailing in Russia up to February 1880—that is, up to the foundation of the Supreme Administrative Commission. "I could not help but recognize that affairs had pushed us to the precipice. The tsar of the Russian lands, the sovereign of 90 million subjects, could no longer consider himself safe in his own home . . . . " In Loris-Melikov's view such a situation demanded special measures. "The very uniqueness of the situation indicated that traditional policies could not solve our problems. Firmly convinced that close cooperation with right-thinking individuals was a prerequisite for success, I addressed an appeal for support to the citizens of the capital on the first day after assumption of my new responsibilities."[149] Loris-Melikov therefore thought it essential to attract "right-thinking" people to the government's side—in other words, to broaden the government's social base of support.

In the next section of the memorandum Loris-Melikov summarized the actions taken by the Supreme Administrative Commission. "I worked for two months to unify and strengthen the police force, while at the same time I tried to elucidate in the greatest possible detail the various causes which led us to our present troubled state, to explain the mood of the public, and to work out a program that might help us attain our goal—the restoration of order."[150] As evidence of his attempt to strengthen the police Loris-Melikov pointed to the new coordination of the gendarmes and the police, the swifter processing of political cases by the police, the new orders dealing with administrative exiles, and the review of cases involving persons under political observation.[151]

Then he turned to the second question—to the elucidation of the causes of discontent, and the development of the revolutionary movement. Loris-Melikov saw one cause for the shortcomings of the administrative system, which had been incapable of adapting to new conditions. "The new initiatives (of the 1860s) created in many areas of administration a new situation for administrators and demanded of them new knowledge, different methods of operation, different talents. This fact was not understood clearly and many administrative agencies failed to discharge properly their responsibilities."[152]

According to Loris-Melikov this lack of administrative flexibility had made the implementation of the peasant reforms and the establishment of the new court system unsatisfactory. The clergy continued "to stagnate in ignorance," the significance of the nobility had declined, the value of the ruble had dropped, and taxes had increased. Another contributory factor was the position of the zemstvo. "The zemstvos, which from the beginning attracted the finest elements of the local population, could not for long maintain their high level of effectiveness given the lack of resources for a broader attack on local problems, and the lack of vigorous government support for their efforts."[153] Loris-Melikov believed that the entire tragedy stemmed from the shortcomings of the governmental apparatus. This analysis of the situation in Russia and the causes of the growth in the revolutionary movement was unoriginal, indeed almost typical of official thinking in the higher bureaucracy.

Before presenting his positive program, Loris-Melikov tried to summarize briefly the goals of Russian society and what society expected from the government. "There are expectations for certain minor improvements or adjustments; desires that the government make a concerted effort to correct the inadequacies in various spheres of administration; convictions that it is essential to abandon extraordinary measures and return to traditional methods of government as soon as possible; and one encounters the opinion that now is the time to make radical changes in the central institutions of government authority." He went on to mention the complaints of the people about the burden of the salt tax, and the mutual responsibility rule. He discussed dissatisfaction with the clergy and the "universal criticism levelled against the current direction of the school system."[154] These criticisms came from every layer in the population, beginning with government officials and the nobility and ending with zemstvo and municipal officials. "Finally, there are proposals for the foundation of popular representation patterned on Western models, or on the basis of old Russian institutions, or on the basis of zemstvo participation in the State Council."

The head of the Supreme Administrative Commission declared himself categorically opposed to these latest proposals. "It is my deep conviction that no reforms in the spirit of these proposals are now needed, and that such reforms would be harmful if instituted because they are absolutely ill-timed." According to Loris-Melikov, the people in general were not thinking about representative institutions and would not understand them in any case. "Such a step (as the granting of representative institutions) would appear to observers at home and abroad as a concession made under duress."[155]

Thus Loris-Melikov spoke out decisively against any concessions in the area of representative government, considering such concessions untimely. At the same time he argued that in order to extricate Russia from its crisis a series of reforms should be adopted. There followed measures needed "for the preservation of the government system and social tranquility." This program consisted of five points. The first point dealt with the need to "continue the pursuit of the revolutionaries while not confusing them with people guilty of crimes not directly connected with the socialist-revolutionary disturbances."[156] The second dealt with the coordination of all government agencies in the fight against "false and criminal doctrines." This point addressed not only the issue of police cooperation, but also coordination of judicial bodies with the police. The third point spoke about the need for gradual return "from extreme measures to traditional legal procedures."

The fourth and fifth points presented the program of reforms. It was necessary "to awaken governmental institutions and officials to a greater awareness of the vital needs of the populace and its representatives. It would be wrong not to view with favor the desires of the clergy, the activity of the zemstvo, and the requirements of the cities. We should implement those proposals of crucial import which were drafted long ago and which have been tied up in all sorts of offices and commissions."

"These proposals include, among others, raising the moral level of the clergy, reform of the head tax, the granting of rights to Old Believers, review of the passport system, facilitating peasant resettlement outside of crowded districts, the reform of provincial administrative institutions, regulation of labor-management relations, and change in the management of the periodical press, which has a unique role in Russia. In Western Europe the press is merely the expression of public opinion, while in Russia the press influences the formation of that opinion. It is useful, in my view, and indeed necessary if we wish to pacify aroused minds through practical assignments, to attract the nobility, the zemstvos and the cities to participate in the solution of issues connected with local needs. Participants in this process should not be elected from the institutions involved; instead the government can always select from among the most informed and loyal elements those persons whose work and knowledge would certainly yield positive results in the solution of economic, managerial, and financial questions, but whose contributions would fit within the limits of the government's policy."[157]

Finally, Loris-Melikov dealt with the Ministry of Education, or more precisely, with its supervision. He wanted "to reestablish the trust formerly offered by all classes and strata of society, but without radical changes in the basis of the educational system." Loris-Melikov continued: "I bluntly declare to Your Majesty that the essential changes in the staff of the Educational Department will be greeted enthusiastically by the whole of Russia. Without such changes the success of our new program will be impeded by entrenched bureaucrats, whose presence clouds the present and threatens the future of our country."[158]

Loris-Melikov's program was quite moderate. With the exception of one proposal to change policy with respect to zemstvos and municipal governments—a proposal presented in the memorandum in a very lapidary and rather vague manner—all of the reforms suggested by Loris-Melikov had been discussed for many years in various commissions and agencies. The selection of "informed and loyal persons" for deliberations on political questions was also unoriginal. Informed persons had been invited from the nobility to participate in the Editing Commissions in the late 1850s; representatives of the zemstvos and cities had discussed the Statute on Military Obligation in 1874. The issue of changes in the staff of the Ministry of Education amounted to a call for the replacement of Minister D.A. Tolstoy "without making radical changes in the basis of the educational system." Despite the limitations in Loris-Melikov's program, the very fact that he believed police methods alone to be insufficient, and thought certain reforms to be essential, was itself significant, and testified to the crisis in government policy. The very existence of the crisis, manifested by the inability of the government to rule as before, created the need for definite concessions, and for an extension of the social base of the government. On the other hand, the intensification of the class struggle prompted an intensification of repression and direct encroachment on the independence of the courts hindered the struggle with the revolutionary movement, or more accurately, the punishment of revolutionary leaders.

One additional point of interest was raised in the memorandum of 11 April. After enumerating his suggestions for reform, Loris-Melikov wrote: "The Supreme Administrative Commission was summoned at the command of Your Majesty for the preservation of the governmental system and social tranquility. In such a large and complicated task it cannot and must not be limited to the drafting and implementation of police measures alone. The establishment of immediate order and a firm guarantee of domestic tranquility can be effected only through the program spelled out above. The elaboration of these proposals will require the attentions of the concerned ministers and other government agencies. But the Supreme Administrative Commission must be allowed the authority to raise issues related to those outlined in my program for the preservation of the governmental system and social tranquility, and to discuss the proper time for their execution. The head of the Supreme Administrative Commission must be responsible for coordinating work in the concerned ministries on these issues, and when necessary, he must solicit the opinions of Your Majesty."[159]

Thus Loris-Melikov asked that the functions of the Supreme Administrative Commission be broadened significantly with respect to those laid out in the decree of 12 February. Formerly the intervention of Loris-Melikov in all fields of government activity, although sanctioned by the government, had no legal basis; now he asked for a legal formulation of his powers. The official memorandum of Loris-Melikov was approved by Alexander II, and consequently the dictatorship of Loris-Melikov was legalized.[160]

The Crown Prince was extremely enthusiastic about this memorandum. In a letter dated 12 April he wrote to Loris-Melikov: "Thank God. I cannot tell you how glad I am that His Majesty accepted your memo so graciously and with such trust. I read with great satisfaction and joy all the marginal notes of His Majesty, and now one may go bravely forward and confidently and unhesitatingly execute your program to *the happiness of our dear motherland* and the unhappiness ?? of the ministers, who must be very upset over this program and His Majesty's decision."[161]

The implementation of the second part of Loris-Melikov's program, summarized in his report on 11 April, began with the removal of Count Tolstoy from the post of Minister of Education. Count D.A. Tolstoy, the very personification of reaction, was extremely unpopular among broad elements of liberal and liberal-minded society, including high-ranking officials. Therefore Loris-Melikov calculated that Tolstoy's dismissal would be greeted with enthusiasm and considered a symbol of change in government policy. This naturally would tend also to strengthen the popularity of the head of the Supreme Administrative Commission.

In Loris-Melikov's view, Tolstoy's actions had contributed significantly to the public's dissatisfaction with government policy, and this dissatisfaction had been conducive to the growth in the revolutionary movement. In October 1881 Loris-Melikov wrote to his former secretary, A.A. Skalkovsky: "If nihilism, accidentally imported into Russia, has assumed such loathsome forms, surely the man most responsible for this development is Count Tolstoy. By cruel, arrogant, and inept policies he has managed to arouse against himself the wrath of students, teachers, and the family itself."[162] In the first few days after the creation of the Supreme Administrative Commission Loris-Melikov made his first steps toward dismissal of Tolstoy. This is indirectly suggested by a letter from M.N. Katkov to Alexander II, dated 11 March, wherein Katkov voiced concern over the possible dismissal of Tolstoy. "Your Majesty, I speak before You, as before God. Whatever his personal qualities, Count Tolstoy has served You honestly and loyally, and has distinguished himself by actions that will place his name in the glorious history of Your reign. The storm which rages against him was not aroused by his personal defects nor by administrative errors, but rather by the steadfastness and loyalty with which he has exercized his responsibilities."[163] Katkov went on to advocate the swift implementation of Tolstoy's project for university reform."Through the successful execution of this reform the spirit of rebellion will be choked out of one of its main sources."[164] Katkov's defense of Tolstoy apparently had a definite impact.[165] It would have seemed that Alexander II's approval of Loris-Melikov's memorandum, raising the issue of Tolstoy's ouster, should have settled Tolstoy's fate. However, given the indecisiveness of the emperor, who was able to hold simultaneously two diametrically-opposed opinions, Loris-Melikov decided to involve the tsarevich in the decision on Tolstoy. On 16 April the head of the Supreme Administrative Commission wrote to Grand Duke Alexander Alexandrovich: "Due to changed circumstances, I have the honor to request humbly that Your Excellency delay for a short while your discussion with His Majesty about Count Tolstoy. I shall drop by and personally explain the reason for this two-day delay . . . ."[166]

A.A. Saburov, the former trustee of the Derpt educational district, replaced Tolstoy as Minister of Education. K.P. Pobedonostsev, the intimate friend and tutor of the tsarevich, took Tolstoy's place as Supreme Procurator of the Synod. Thus the assistance of the tsarevich in the ouster of Tolstoy was duly acknowledged.[167] Tolstoy's ouster was greeted very enthusiastically, except by the reactionary camp. "The mindless, wild exultation of the blind crowd over Tolstoy's fall continues," noted A.A. Kireev in his diary on 25 April 1880.[168] Tolstoy's dismissal was a great victory for Loris-Melikov, one not easily achieved. He himself confessed: "After two months of effort I finally achieved the ouster of Tolstoy, that evil genius of the Russian earth. There was general rejoicing in the government. Everyone remembers how people kissed each other at Matins, and greeted one another with the words: 'Tolstoy has fallen, truly fallen.'"[169] Even part of the upper bureaucracy was pleased by Tolstoy's dismissal. N.K. Mikhailovsky wrote in *Listok Narodnoi Voli* that "the dismissal of that Minister of Obscurantism is a real service of the dictator."[170]

Loris-Melikov also effected other changes in the government: the liberally-inclined N.S. Abaza became director of the Main Press Administration, and Kiev University professor N.Kh. Bunge became deputy Minister of Finance. Bunge was appointed without the knowledge of Minister of Finance Greig. A.A. Abaza, who with Minister of War D.A. Miliutin had very close relations with Loris-Melikov, probably inspired the elevation of Bunge.

At this time Loris-Melikov also pushed his program for extension of zemstvo rights. Loris-Melikov ascribed to zemstvo activities an enormous significance, seeing in them the best means to oppose constitutionalism. He wrote to A.A. Skalkovsky in the letter previously cited: "The more firmly and clearly is posed the question of the all-class zemstvo, adapted to the contemporary conditions of our life, and the more quickly zemstvo institutions are introduced into the remaining provinces, the less susceptible we will be to the attempts of the notorious but very small part of society trying to introduce a constitutional system, so ill-suited to Russia."[171]

The zemstvo program of Loris-Melikov has been preserved in a project-letter from Loris-Melikov to Minister of Internal Affairs Makov. At the beginning of this letter Loris-Melikov wrote: "I have arrived at the positive conviction that repression alone is insufficient to extricate Russia from its current serious and painful crisis. Simultaneously with the resolute⸱ and systematic prosecution of the subversives, we must adopt measures which indicate a concerned and positive attitude on the part of the government toward the needs of the people, classes, and public institutions, and which will strengthen the trust of the public in the government, and will prompt social forces to a more active support of the government in its struggle against pernicious false social doctrines."

Loris-Melikov believed that among those public elements that might facilitate the "enforcement of legal order" the zemstvo occupied a prominent place. "It must be admitted that due to an unfavorable turn of events, the zemstvo, which originally had attracted the very best of the local citizenry, did not long maintain itself at this high level. A certain vagueness in the Zemstvo Statute concerning the jurisdiction of these institutions led to misunderstandings on their part, to separate restrictions on zemstvo activity, and to the government's own suspicious attitude toward the zemstvo."[172] One solution for this problem was the stimulation of zemstvo activity, the involvement of the zemstvo in the discussion of certain questions "affecting local needs." Loris-Melikov wished to make a series of additions to the Zemstvo Statute. "However, since a review by me of the Statute as a whole might have certain disadvantages in that it would raise false hopes in zemstvo circles, it would seem more proper for the Ministry of Internal Affairs and other responsible agencies to undertake to raise the question of changing various sections of the Zemstvo Statute."[173] According to Loris-Melikov these proposed changes could be passed on to zemstvo assemblies for discussion. Final discussion would take place in a special commission under the Ministry of Internal Affairs, where zemstvo chairmen could participate.

Among the issues which might be raised "without undesirable consequences" Loris-Melikov included the following: to give to zemstvos of contiguous provinces the right to discuss and adopt measures to fight epidemics and agricultural blights; to work out more equitable distribution of the food resources of the empire; to define more exactly the competence of the zemstvo in education, not confining this activity to agricultural education; to set time limits forcing the governors to turn over zemstvo petitions to the appropriate ministries; to broaden the rights of the zemstvo "to assist social classes and to fulfill class responsibilities," particularly to pay a *per diem* subsistence allowance to zemstvo members and jurors; to prohibit the election to zemstvo membership of village and district officials; to "increase the significance of zemstvo chairmen and members by explaining that it is not within the competence of the administration to decide on the political disloyalty of zemstvo personnel or to banish them without stating the cause . . . . " Loris-Melikov also spoke about giving provincial and district zemstvo assemblies the right to invite to their sessions non-members, just as municipal councils did, and about forbidding zemstvo chairmen and members to accept contracts and supplies "for the rudiments of zemstvo operation."[174]

Loris-Melikov's zemstvo program, however moderate its character, certainly would have facilitated work in the zemstvo, and would have broadened its field of activity. His plan signalled a change in the government's previous attitude toward the zemstvo, an attitude expressed in the undeviating desire to reduce the zemstvo's sphere of activity. Increasing the zemstvo's competence was one concession which Loris-Melikov was willing to make in order to preserve unshaken the governmental system of autocratic monarchy. At this time the zemstvo played the same role that it had played in the 1860s: a diversion from a constitution. Especially important in this connection was the one point of Loris-Melikov's project which considered abolition of the administration's right not to confirm politically unreliable zemstvo members in their posts. According to the rules of 1866, medical workers, insurance agents, and other persons serving in the zemstvo had to obtain approval from the provincial administration. In 1879 the Minister of Internal Affairs had introduced a proposal to the Council of Ministers that might have extended this rule to deputies of zemstvos and municipal administrations.

On the basis of Loris-Melikov's remarks in August 1880 Minister of Internal Affairs Makov revived his proposal on this subject before the

Committee of Ministers, but its intent was clearly the opposite of the 1879 plan. Makov now wrote that after the publication of his 1879 order "there had not been a single case where the rule was applied to elected officials." He added that this "law produced a demoralizing effect not only among those working in the zemstvo, but also among those who elected zemstvo officials."[175] In accordance with Makov's new position the Committee of Ministers decided that elected zemstvo personnel need not be confirmed by the governor, and that the governor did not have the right to dismiss them from office.

Loris-Melikov also took practical steps to broaden the functions of the zemstvo, and to involve the zemstvo in the discussion of questions touching local government agencies. For example, in 1880 it became clear that changes would have to be made in the Statute on District Peasant Institutions. Minister of Internal Affairs Makov thought that these changes should be discussed by the provincial offices of peasant affairs in joint sessions with the provincial zemstvo councils. However, Loris-Melikov agreed with the chairman of the Chief Committee on Rural Affairs, Grand Duke Konstanin Nikolaevich, that this form of zemstvo participation was unsatisfactory. The Grand Duke insisted that this issue be discussed by the zemstvos in separate sessions of the provincial assemblies, not the provincial councils. He also advocated preliminary discussions by district zemstvo assemblies.[176]

In other fields of state administration Loris-Melikov also attempted to involve certain segments of the populace in discussions of various reform projects. Minister of State Domains Baron Liven sent to Loris-Melikov a plan to convoke district agricultural congresses, and an all-Russian agricultural congress under the ministry's authority. Having endorsed this proposal, Loris-Melikov wrote to Baron Liven: "In order to fulfill the tasks laid upon me by His Majesty's order to preserve the governmental system and social tranquility, I deeply believe that among other things the government must be more attentive to the urgently expressed demands of society and its representatives. In order to do this, and at the same time to quiet by proper exertions those aroused minds which are greedy for action, I find it very useful to involve representatives of the nobility, the zemstvo, and cities in the discussion of issues concerning their local needs."[177] In conclusion, Loris-Melikov noted again the urgent need for Liven's program, while indicating that the agricultural congresses should proceed by a strictly defined agenda and under the control of the administration.

This shows convincingly enough that the government's policy toward the zemstvo had changed. While the Ministry of Internal Affairs did not dare to challenge Loris-Melikov's new course in zemstvo policy,[178] certain bureaucrats treated the new policy with skepticism. Speaking about Loris-Melikov, Valuev wrote in his diary on 27 May: "He has been taken in by the wiles of the zemstvo representatives and the related temptation for cheap popularity."[179] The other questions raised in Loris-Melikov's report of 11 April were dealt with later, after the Supreme Administrative Commission had ceased to exist.

During the spring and summer the Supreme Administrative Commission continued to work on the agenda of issues set out by Loris-Melikov in the session on 4 March. Commission member Senator I.I. Shamshin inspected the Third Section, looking into cases involving exile for political disloyalty. In his diary State Secretary E.A. Peretts recorded the words of Shamshin that the inspection had disclosed many cases of exile without any justifiable grounds, and that the activity of the Third Section had left an extremely negative impression on the senator.[180] "According to Shamshin, the affairs of the Third Section were in great disorder. Very often, extremely important documents, which had served as the basis of action, could not be located in the files. When he asked for these documents, frequently he was answered that they did not exist; when he insisted on seeing the papers, particularly when he threatened to complain to Count Loris-Melikov, searches were carried out and the missing papers often turned up. Sometimes the documents were found at the homes of officials, sometimes in boxes at the chancellery office. On one occasion an important document turned up on the floor behind a bookcase."[181]

However, the Supreme Administrative Commission never met in full session after 4 March; from the beginning of the summer until the Commission's abolition there was not a single meeting, although the work of the Commission was very intensive. The head of the Commission, who was then at the zenith of his power, ruled the governmental life of the nation as he had earlier. This situation fully corresponded to the intent of those who created the Commission as a consultative body under a dictator. Individual members of the Commission labored according to the directions of Loris-Melikov, who obviously felt no need to call business meetings of the Commission.[182]

During this period Loris-Melikov raised the question of the abolition of the Supreme Administrative Commission with Alexander II. On 26 July Loris-Melikov sent the tsar a memorandum on this subject. The introduction of the memorandum analyzed the work of the Commission in coordinating police and gendarmes, and in streamlining the trial procedure in political crimes.[183] It also discussed the new procedures for administrative exile, and for dealing with persons under police surveillance.

"In adopting these and other related measures, the Commission has striven constantly to eradicate the problems which have prompted society to look so apathetically at the violation of the old order. In order to attain this goal I have not missed a single chance to strengthen the inborn loyalty felt by the Russian people toward Your Majesty, to fortify the trust of the public in the government's actions and intentions, which are designed to create by peaceful methods an environment conducive to the further development of the domestic welfare of Russia . . . . "[184] The head of the Supreme Administrative Commission then recounted the steps he had taken to achieve this goal. One step was the directive to Governors-General that explained that the right to grant clemency to prisoners condemned to death was the prerogative "of the Monarch's compassion."[185] Describing the existing situation, Loris-Melikov wrote: "I am far from convinced that the criminal activity of the socialist-revolutionary Party has ceased, yet at the same time I cannot attribute exclusively to the efforts of the Commission the appearance in society of certain hopeful signs that testify to a definite easing of public anxiety."[186] "Not indulging in self-deception," he continued, "I am, on the contrary, convinced that subversive social doctrines cannot be neutralized in a short period of time; this will require the continued and concerted efforts of the government and the public."[187]

Elaborating this point, Loris-Melikov emphasized the primary importance of taking away from subversives the soil on which to develop revolutionary ideas, and stressed that this could only be done through the combined efforts of government and society. Turning to the advisability of maintaining the Supreme Administrative Commission, Loris-Melikov asserted that it "must not be that permanent agency in the governmental structure that has the responsibility not only to create, but to maintain long-term unity among governmental forces in the fight against subversion . . . . Its activity, like that of every executive agency, must not be continuous; otherwise, inevitably it will break the normal course of state administration, interfere unproductively in the spheres of competence of other state institutions, and give a false impression of the state of affairs in Russia to our own citizens and to foreign observers."[188]

Loris-Melikov argued that the time had come to abolish the Supreme Administrative Commission, which had achieved its immediate objectives, and also to unify police investigations under one agency. This agency would be, of course, the Ministry of Internal Affairs, which would have concentrated in its offices the power "to direct all the police forces of the state." Loris-Melikov thought it essential to abolish the Third Section, and to transfer its functions to the Ministry of Internal Affairs. He went on to say that "if the powers of the ministry became too extensive" it was possible without particular damage to remove from the ministry the Postal Department, Telegraph Department, and the Department of Spiritual Affairs. "These changes, by concentrating the control of all police forces in the state, both general and political, in the hands of the Minister of Internal Affairs, and thereby giving him control over municipal and zemstvo affairs, and the press, would provide the minister with the means and the opportunity to rule with a strong hand, assuming of course the friendship and goodwill of other governmental agencies."[189] Actually, this plan would have given the Ministry of Internal Affairs full power, and the minister himself would become *de facto* a kind of prime minister, and in certain circumstances, a dictator.

Alexander II approved the Melikov memorandum and on 6 August signed a decree abolishing the Supreme Administrative Commission. "Having followed from the inception of the Commission the activities of its director, We are convinced that the Commission's immediate goal —the coordination of governmental forces in the struggle against sedition —has been achieved due to the program of General-Adjutant Count Loris-Melikov; Our further decrees for the preservation of the governmental system and public order can be executed through the old legally-established procedures, with a few minor increases in the jurisdictional authority of the Ministry of Internal Affairs." Consequently, the Third Section was abolished and its functions transferred to a newly-created Department of State Police "in anticipation of complete unification of police supervision in one agency of the above-mentioned ministry."[190] The Minister of Internal Affairs was simultaneously designated Chief of Gendarmes, and thus devolved on him all the functions of the director of the Supreme Administrative Commission—namely, "supreme control over all investigations of crimes against the state."[191] The Departments of Post and Telegraph, as well as Spiritual Affairs were removed from the competence of the Ministry of Internal Affairs.

Loris-Melikov was appointed Minister of Internal Affairs and Chief of Gendarmes, and Kakhanov and Cherevin were made his assistants; Makov became Minister of Post and Telegraph and director of the Department of Spiritual Affairs.[192] Initially, Loris-Melikov had proposed to raise the question of abolishing the Supreme Administrative Commission later, sometime in the fall, but certain circumstances forced him to raise it sooner. According to the testimony of Peretts, the reason was that Loris-Melikov "feared an increase in the powers of Valuev and Makov, who, desiring to win over public opinion, had renounced their old retrograde policies and had requested the tsar's permission to review in a liberal spirit the Zemstvo Statutes and the laws on the press."[193] In order to forestall their influence, Loris-Melikov also was forced to present his plan for the abolition of the Supreme Administrative Commission more quickly than he had intended. Polovtsov also discussed this matter in his diary. "Bypassing Loris-Melikov, (Makov) requested an imperial command to create a commission to discuss press laws, and a committee with zemstvo participants to discuss the Zemstvo Statutes. This last step was simply dangerous. . . . It forced Loris-Melikov to take steps that he had sought to delay until year's end upon his return from Livadia."[194] There was further confirmation of this motivation in a letter from Loris-Melikov to the tsarevich on 31 July. ". . .It would have been far preferable to present my memorandum upon your return from Gapsal, but certain accidental circumstances prompted me to accelerate my program in order to obtain consent from His Majesty before His trip to Livadia."[195]

Loris-Melikov painted the abolition of the Supreme Administrative Commission as a voluntary attempt to reject dictatorship and his own position as favorite.[196] Most of the government camp accepted this explanation at face value. Cherevin told Polovtsov that "it is extremely rash from Melikov's standpoint to turn himself from an all-powerful leader into an ordinary minister, whose power will be paralyzed by other ministers."[197] Kireev praised Loris-Melikov's step, but saw in it something which Cherevin did not notice. "Loris-Melikov displays great tact. He himself has stepped down from his dictatorial position and has transformed himself into a prime minister. Essentially his power has not decreased, for he pursues now the political maneuvers begun earlier. The Third Section is under his control, but the dictatorship has ended. The Third Section has been destroyed, everything looks 'liberal'."[198] Kireev was closer to the truth than Cherevin, but even he did not fully understand the significance of the abolition of the Supreme Administrative Commission. Loris-Melikov's dictatorship had been preserved; it merely had assumed different forms.

Let us summarize. The Supreme Administrative Commission was founded as a result of the crisis of the autocracy, and it signified the impossibility of governing by earlier methods. S.N. Khalturin's terrorist act was a great jolt to the government and provoked panic within its ranks. This event heralded the beginning of a new stage in the crisis of the autocracy. The first stage of the crisis had witnessed the change from old methods of rule to emergency measures—the creation of the provisional Governors-General, the transfer of state crimes to military tribunals, reactionary measures in education and zemstvo affairs. Now these steps were insufficient. The new stage of crisis called not only for repression, but for certain concessions.

Moreover, the government now abandoned its attempts at limited decentralization of power in favor of centralization of authority in the hands of one man. Loris-Melikov's program corresponded fully to the needs of the government in the new stage of crisis; even though its first priority was the intensification of repression, it had another goal as well —to broaden the social base of support for the government and to implement reforms that might stem the tide of discontent within Russia.

Even though the decree of 12 February strictly circumscribed the functions of the Supreme Administrative Commission, the Commission's jurisdiction—or more precisely that of its director—was so broad that its creation signified the establishment of a personal distatorship. The Commission itself played a modest role, and its members, as Valuev had foreseen, were mere deputies of the director.

The memorandum of 11 April legally expanded the sphere of activity of the Commission, but again its practical effects touched only Loris-Melikov. Therefore, the political course pursued by Loris-Melikov and formulated explicitly in this memorandum was a direct consequence of the bomb explosion in the Winter Palace that had caused universal confusion in government circles. ". . . Thanks to this struggle, and only thanks to it," wrote V.I. Lenin, having in mind the heroic struggle of the Populists against the government, "the situation was changed again, and the government again was forced to make concessions. . . ."[199] It was the revolutionary struggle of the Populists that forced the government to soften the reign of police terror, and to transform Loris-Melikov himself into a unique kind of liberal bureaucrat.

The further development of the governmental crisis brought in its wake a consolidation of the government's forces—unified on one hand by hatred of the revolutionary movement, and on the other by an understanding of the need to make concessions to keep the governmental structure intact. One such concession, foreseen by leading public figures and by Loris-Melikov himself, was the revitalization of the zemstvo. The government's zemstvo program was implemented only partially during the existence of the Commission. Further steps occurred during the ministerial tenure of Loris-Melikov.

The abolition of the Supreme Administrative Commission certainly did not mean the end of Loris-Melikov's dictatorship. It meant instead that a temporary emergency dictatorship was made into a permanent one. Likewise, the abolition of the generally-detested Third Section did not signify a relaxation of political surveillance. On the contrary, it led to the centralization of police agencies under the auspicies of the Ministry of Internal Affairs, and it gave the minister himself much greater power.

CHAPTER III

THE MINISTRY OF M.T. LORIS-MELIKOV

The abolition of the Supreme Administrative Commission did not diminish the authority of Loris-Melikov. On the contrary. He became Minister of Internal Affairs and Chief of Gendarmes after having eliminated a series of potential threats to his personal influence. The police, the press, local administration, the zemstvo, and municipal administrations were all subject to his control as Minister of Internal Affairs. In fact, his sphere of action was now even broader than before; it encompassed every field of policy-making save one—foreign policy. Foreign policy was directed in practice by War Minister Miliutin, who was very close to Loris-Melikov.[1] Melikov's influence spread even to education and finance. As before, his recommendation brought the appointment or dismissal of ministers and other high officials.

Loris-Melikov's closest political allies were Miliutin and A.A. Abaza, soon to be Minister of Finance. Loris-Melikov sought out their opinions on important issues. D.A. Miliutin noted in his diary on 11 October 1880: "Again I had a prolonged discussion with Count Loris-Melikov, who again asked my views about various personnel changes at high-level positions. Apparently, he has managed to incline His Majesty toward the replacement of Greig, to raise the question of the abolition of the head tax, to revitalize the zemstvo, and much more; just a few months ago one could not even talk about these matters. The Ministry of Finance was offered to Abaza. . . . "[2] The appointment of A.A. Abaza,[3] chairman of the Department of State Economy of the State Council, was a great achievement for Loris-Melikov.[4] The crucial field of finance was now fully within his sphere of influence. By political conviction Abaza belonged to the liberal bureaucrats, and was an advocate of further bourgeois reforms.

On the influence of Miliutin and Abaza over Loris-Melikov there is the testimony of E.M. Feoktistov about conversations with his colleague Yuzefovich, a council member of the Main Press Administration and one of Loris-Melikov's intimate associates. On 21 October 1881 Feoktistov wrote in his diary: "From my conversations with Yuzefovich I am convinced that to some extent the supposition of many people is true— that is, although Loris-Melikov was given almost dictatorial power, his actions were far from independent. According to Yuzefovich, in every case when an important issue came up, or when an important decision had to be reached, Loris-Melikov hurried to confer with Abaza and D.A. Miliutin."[5] Abaza and Miliutin, clearly, were Melikov's closest advisers and allies. The colorless Minister of Education, Saburov, was also completely under Loris-Melikov's influence and that of his allies. The chairman of the State Council, Grand Duke Konstantin Nikolaevich, and State Secretary E.A. Peretts also supported the Minister of Internal Affairs.

Initially, the tsarevich was exceedingly well-disposed toward Loris-Melikov. In his diary on 9 August 1880 he wrote: "Today we read in the papers about the appointment of Count Loris-Melikov as Minister of Internal Affairs. This is a vital step, long-awaited by all."[6] The tsarevich participated in the organization of the senatorial inspection carried out by Loris-Melikov, and the latter, in turn, exerted every effort to facilitate the appointment of the tsarevich's tutor Pobedonostsev as member of the Committee of Ministers. On 15 April he wrote the tsarevich about the advantages of including Pobedonostsev in the Committee of Ministers. ". . . His constant participation in the deliberations of the Committee is not only desirable, but will be very valuable. The Committee often concerns itself with matters affecting education. Starting from the premise that only a close tie between school and Church can guarantee the future advancement of popular education based on strong religious elements, I find that the presence of the Supreme Procurator of the Synod in discussions of such matters would facilitate an impartial and thoroughgoing solution."[7]

Certainly, Loris-Melikov wrote in this fashion not so much because he thought the presence of Pobedonostsev a crucial necessity, but rather because he sought to oblige the tsarevich. However, it should be noted that the words about "a close tie between school and Church," that is, lending the elementary schools a clerical character, expressed Loris-Melikov's own position. At the end of the letter Loris-Melikov indicated that it was awkward for him to raise this question with the emperor since it did not come under his proper jurisdiction. Yet in late October he spoke about it with Alexander II, and he secured the tsar's consent to the appointment. It was mentioned earlier that Loris-Melikov and Pobedonostsev accompanied the tsarevich on the trip to the Crimea. By the end of the year, however, Melikov's relations with the tsarevich had cooled.[8]

In my opinion, one reason for this cooling of relations was the influence of Pobedonostsev over the tsarevich. Pobedonostsev had been antagonized by Loris-Melikov's efforts to implement reformist plans. A second reason was the extremely friendly relationship of Loris-Melikov with the morganatic wife of the emperor, Princess Yurievskaia,[9] relations which were not easily accepted by Grand Duke Alexander Alexandrovich as the emperor's son. In fact, this second reason was probably the more important. On 18 December Polovtsov noted in his diary: "The tsarevich is angry with him [Loris-Melikov] because he is courting the favor of Princess Yurievskaia."[10] The princess herself admitted to close friendship with Loris-Melikov. In the Laferté volume, essentially Yurievskaia's memoirs, she writes: "This outstanding minister [Loris-Melikov] understood what a loyal and valuable ally the princess was as the wife of the tsar."[11] Evidently, Loris-Melikov often exploited Yurievskaia's favorable disposition in order to exert pressure on the weak-willed emperor. Slow and uneducated, Yurievskaia nevertheless possessed a much stronger character than her morganatic spouse. Deeply in love with his young wife, the aged Alexander II humbly acceded to her wishes. D.A. Miliutin wrote in his diary in 1881: "The late tsar was completely in the hands of Princess Yurievskaia. . . ."[12]

Let us return to the problem of Loris-Melikov's relations with officials in the upper bureaucracy. It was quite natural that the former Minister of Internal Affairs should have been antagonistic toward Loris-Melikov. The chairman of the Committee of Ministers, Valuev, had a rather complicated relationship with Loris-Melikov. Valuev looked on his successor as a rival, and assumed that Loris-Melikov desired to augment his power by taking the chairmanship of the Committee of Ministers. Loris-Melikov's position on the zemstvo question annoyed Valuev, as did his toying with the press. However, on one of the basic tenets of of Loris-Melikov's political policy—the need to involve public figures in the drafting of various reform projects—Valuev was in sympathy with the Minister of Internal Affairs. Yet even here the views of the two men were not quite identical. Such was the constellation of forces in the government during the second period of Loris-Melikov's dictatorship.

In early September Loris-Melikov spelled out his program to the editors of the largest newspapers and journals in Petersburg. The editors had been invited by the Minister of Internal Affairs to be admonished about certain recently-published articles. In an official memorandum to Alexander II dated 20 September, Loris-Melikov wrote: "Prompted by articles that recently appeared in certain periodical publications, I took it upon myself to invite the editors of the most significant newspapers and journals for a detailed discussion and strict admonition."[13]

Actually, according to the published announcement about the meeting which was printed in the September issue of *Otechestvennye Zapiski*, Loris-Melikov summoned the editors "especially in order to make clear to them that they should not arouse public opinion by insisting on the need for public participation in legislation and administration, either in the Western European manner or on the model of the old Zemsky Sobors, since nothing 'of the sort was being considered." Furthermore, according to the announcement, the Minister of Internal Affairs told the editors that he found "such idle twaddle" most unpleasant since it was connected with his name. He told the editors that, as minister, he had received no special powers [to carry through democratic reforms] and had no intention of doing so. "He was firmly convinced that at present the most necessary work, and that to which he had turned all his attentions and efforts, was to endow new institutions with the requisite authority, and to bring into harmony with them older institutions, changing the latter as much as was needed to achieve this end."[14]

Thus Loris-Melikov saw his task not in the drafting of a new form of representative government but in the assertion, or more precisely, establishment of the rights of "new institutions," that is, of the zemstvo and municipal administrations, and the new judicial agencies; he wanted to establish close ties between these new agencies and the older institutions of government. In his opinion, the realization of this program "might" require five to seven years.

This immediate program was outlined in five points. The first concerned the zemstvo and other public and estate agencies. The problem was to create conditions suitable for the normal functioning of these institutions, and to broaden their rights "in those cases when in practice their legal authority, so necessary for the correct operation and the economic improvement of local areas, turns out to be insufficient." The second point dealt with the police. The government would have to "coordinate" the police, that is, to unify the police and the gendarmes and "to set them in harmony with the new institutions, as well as to guarantee the observance of proper legal safeguards." The third point concerned powers that ought to be granted to provincial and local institutions in order to solve a number of problems. The next point dealt with the forthcoming senatorial inspections, designed to "explore the desires, needs, and living conditions of the inhabitants of various provinces," and "when possible, to satisfy those desires and needs." The fifth point concerned the press. The minister proposed to allow the press to "discuss various steps, orders, and instructions of the government on the condition that it [the press] not confuse or needlessly arouse public opinion by the above-mentioned idle illusions."[15] This program was very moderate. It did not hold any scheme to involve representatives of the public in law-making, and it contained nothing new in comparison with Loris-Melikov's April memorandum.

Neither the democratic nor the moderate liberal elements were satisfied with Loris-Melikov's plan. In the October and December issues of *Yuridichesky Vestnik* [Judicial Herald], in the column called "Miscellany," S.A. Muromtsov wrote two articles, which were far from enthusiastic about Loris-Melikov's program. "Seven years is far too long a time to give the zemstvo and other public and estate institutions the chance to exercise fully those rights which they already possess by law. One needs only a firm resolve to observe the law and to abolish all secret and non-secret circulars and other instructions which restrain the exercise of those rights. . . . The abolition of all orders which restrain the freedom of the press, and at minimum the return to the system that existed in 1865 could be accomplished by the stroke of a pen. Given good faith, five to seven years are not necessary to enforce fully article one of the criminal code, which prohibits punishment if a sentence is not pronounced in accordance with judicial statutes. True freedom of the press and revitalization of the zemstvo is impossible while administrative arrest and exile still exist. It is very surprising that, in the program of the minister, not a single word has been spoken about this subject."[16]

On 20 September M.E. Saltykov-Shchedrin wrote to P.V. Annenkov: "You probably know that Loris-Melikov summoned all the editors and read them a speech in which he announced that it was useless to think about a constitution, and that to spread constitutional ideas was to spread confusion among the public. There you have liberalism explained. But one can write about illegal police activity and can advocate that the zemstvos not be impeded in the exercise of all their legal rights."[17]

One of Loris-Melikov's first steps after the abolition of the Supreme Administrative Commission was to schedule senatorial inspections, a subject he had mentioned to Alexander II in the memorandum of 11 August. In that document he argued that senatorial inspections long had been a reliable way to identify local needs and that they provided the government with precious information about the condition in the provinces. Besides, "if the inspectors themselves are carefully selected, these inspections will serve to make intelligible the various opinions current outside the capital centers, and to complete information now in the hands of the Ministry of Internal Affairs and the Chief of Gendarmes about many crucial questions."[18] Among these questions he included the proposed reforms of provincial administrative institutions, "methods for the unification of police agencies," the determination of the causes for the spread of revolutionary propaganda, and the study of the effect of administrative exile, repression, and other government programs. "The present time would be highly favorable for senatorial audits in six or seven areas of the empire. These inspections would be extremely useful not only to the directors of the Ministry of Internal Affairs, but also doubtless to other agencies. . . . The very scheduling of the inspections cannot fail, in my opinion, to have a calming effect since it would be proof of Your Majesty's care for the welfare of the people."[19]

In accordance with this memorandum inspections were scheduled in the following provinces: Samara and Saratov—Senator I.I. Shamshin; Kiev and Chernigov—Senator A.A. Polovtsov; Voronezh and Tambov—Senator S.A. Mordvinov; Kostroma, Kazan, and later Orenburg and Ufa —Senator M.E. Kovalevsky. All provinces named for inspection were agricultural rather than industrial; Kostroma alone was a non-blacksoil province. The selection of these particular provinces revealed to some extent which problems most worried the government. It should be noted that in the majority of the provinces slated for inspection (Kostroma and Ufa being the exceptions), peasant landholdings were very inadequate: about half or more of all former serfs in these provinces held less than three desiatins of land.

Saratov	49.3%	Kiev	82.0%	Voronezh	70.1%
Samara	44.3	Chernigov	46.7	Tambov	80.6
Orenburg	61.8	Kazan	47.8[20]		

It must be said that in these provinces Populist propaganda was very widespread. Not one of these provinces was industrialized. This proves that not much attention was paid to the worker question at this time. In attributing such great import to the forthcoming inspections, Loris-Melikov certainly had in mind more than gaining a better acquaintance with the activities of these provinces.

The precise instructions for the inspections were drafted by various agencies and were sent by the Minister of Justice and the General Procurator of the Senate to Alexander II for confirmation. In fact, however, all this was orchestrated by Loris-Melikov. He, and not the General Procurator of the Senate, read instructions to the departing senators. This seemingly insignificant incident clearly demonstrated that Loris-Melikov functioned as a kind of prime minister.[21] In late August Loris-Melikov delivered the following speech to the senators: "Your inspection will not be just another senatorial inspection. The problem is not how to bring to justice and dismiss from office corrupt officials. No, here you must examine how to ameliorate the general shortcomings of our provincial governmental system, and decide how to unite and harmonize elements that recently perhaps have not always tended to function together smoothly. Having become Minister of Internal Affairs, I see now that the minister has to sign a colossal stack of papers, and that he is surrounded by a stable full of bureaucrats. Why do I need them all? Would they not be more useful if they would expend their energies on provincial administration?"

Loris-Melikov emphasized the problem of government centralization, which forced even issues of secondary importance to be decided in Petersburg. "Petersburg holds the whole nation in its grasp." Having acquainted himself with the condition of the local administrative system, Loris-Melikov recommended analysis of the problem of how to reduce the number of officials in various provincial agencies and "unify government in a single assembly, even if it means the participation of elected representatives."

Then Loris-Melikov turned to the zemstvo problem. He stated that while in his former post as Kharkov Governor-General he had formed a negative impression of the zemstvo. "The people are dissatisfied with the zemstvo, which costs so much in taxes and does so little. Yet from Petersburg I see that high officials are contemptuous of the zemstvo. . . ." Did the zemstvo deserve such a reputation, he asked, and could its activity be made more fruitful? "I know that there are people dreaming about parliaments, about a central zemstvo duma, but I am not one of them. This matter is one for our sons and grandsons, and we can only prepare the soil for them."[22]

In conclusion, the minister stressed that the issues he had raised did not exhaust the list of problems to be examined by the senators, nor did it restrict their inquiry. "Each senator will ask whatever questions he deems important and propose whatever solutions he thinks appropriate." Loris-Melikov ended by praising Alexander II, "who, despite the length of his reign, has continued to work for the welfare of Russia."[23]

The printed instructions given the departing senators dealt mostly with issues relevant to the interests of the Ministry of Internal Affairs. "Pay attention to those aspects of local life which are somehow connected with the spread of seditious doctrines, and with the favorable reception of those doctrines. Give the fullest possible description of the provinces you are inspecting, and indicate, where possible, measures that might weaken the influence of seditious doctrines."[24] Another point in the instruction asked the senators to describe the effects of various forms of repression on the local intellectual atmosphere. A special section of the instruction was devoted to the need to analyze the "attitude" of the peasantry, particularly concerning the rumors about a "black partition [land redistribution]." The senators were asked to collect detailed information on the economic position of the peasantry, on the causes "of decline in the standard of living and public morals," and to recommend solutions to these problems. In particular, they were requested to consider how to facilitate "acquisition of land by peasants as private property, and the regulation of internal migration. . . ."[25] The inspectors were to acquaint themselves in detail with the condition of peasant communal government, and with local offices of peasant affairs.

Much attention was allotted to the zemstvo. "Since the results achieved by the zemstvo did not justify the initial expectations of the government and society, the senators should analyze the causes of this failure and seek ways to stimulate zemstvo operations and make the zemstvo equal to other local institutions, without arousing hopes for a central representative zemstvo assembly."[26] Senators must also study municipal government institutions and become familar with sanitary conditions in the cities. The instruction also spoke about the need to analyze local governmental agencies with the view of reorganizing and uniting various departments, and to reduce the number of institutions and bureaux. Moreover, ways must be found to coordinate the actions of various police agencies, including the gendarme offices.

The final points in the instruction included by the Ministry of Internal Affairs dealt with the Jewish problem and the Old Believers. The senators should investigate the condition of the Old Believer communities and decide how urgent it might be to "lessen the existing restrictions affecting the schismatics." Concerning the Jewish question, the senators were to "pay attention to the nature of the influence exerted by the Jews and to the practical operation of legislation affecting the Jews."[27]

The judicial department asked the senators to review the operations of crown and village judicial institutions. Attention should be devoted to the procuratorial office, and to the activity of sworn witnesses in the courts; jails should be inspected. The relationship of judicial officials and the police must be studied also.

Much attention was to be devoted to problems under the jurisdiction of the Ministry of Finance. It was essential to investigate the problem of the head tax, the abolition of which, judging by Loris-Melikov's official memorandum of 11 August, had been approved already by Alexander II. The senators were to review the reasons for the accumulation of arrears and to discover ways of avoiding this; they were also to discover to what extent the passport system hindered the free movement of the popula- ⟩ tion. Further, the inspectors must determine to what extent the excise tax on salt prevented the use of salt in cattle feeding, and how much the price of salt would drop were the excise tax to be eliminated. In addition, the activity of rural banks and savings institutions and their influence on the decline of usery in the countryside deserved study. Finally, the manufacturing and commercial activity of Jews should be scrutinized with a view to drafting new legislation on the subject. The repeated reference to the Jewish question suggests an interest by the government in introducing amendments to existing legislation. It was thought necessary also to study the conditions of craftsmen and factory workers in order to determine whether there should be a new law to limit the working day, as well as the age of workers. In addition, the problem of demand for technical personnel was mentioned. The inclusion of these points in the instruction suggests inspection of an industrial province but, as we have seen, this was not the case here. Apparently these latter points were not really of vital importance.

A significant section in the instruction was reserved for the Ministry of State Domains. Senators were requested to acquaint themselves with the activity of local agencies of the ministry and to consider the effects of mergers with provincial authorities; they were to gather data on the rent of taxable utilities, on the condition of local agricultural schools subject to the ministry's control, and on the contribution of these schools to agriculture. They were to inspect tree nurseries in steppe provinces; to study the supply of charcoal in their assigned provinces; and to examine the problem of peasant relocation. The senators were asked to consider the possibility of cooperation between the ministry and the zemstvo on agricultural matters. The senators were instructed to study the relations between farmers and their hired help and to recommend measures to normalize these relations. Finally, the last four points of the instruction required the senators to study the condition of schools.

I have summarized fully all 46 points of the instruction because all the questions raised in it are extremely important if we are to understand the tasks which Loris-Melikov had set himself. They amounted, in the first place, to steps toward the "pacification" of the peasantry. Naturally they were all palliatives, and failed to touch the basic problem— how to provide land to the peasantry at the expense of the gentry. A considerable role was allotted to the reorganization of local provincial and district institutions, the revitalization of the zemstvo and the merger of zemstvos with governmental agencies. The unification of all police agencies and their coordination with judicial bodies were also important.

Loris-Melikov took special care to strengthen and set in order the police system. On 10 November he presented an official memorandum on "The Complete Merger of Police Command in One Institution—the Ministry of Internal Affairs." This memorandum addressed the issue of combining the Department of State Police [the former Third Section] with the Department of Executive Police. The substantive question already had been resolved in August by Loris-Melikov's memorandum, according to which the Department of State Police had been created "preliminary to the complete unification of the directorship of all Russia's police under the Ministry of Internal Affairs."[28]

Loris-Melikov began by asserting that, having studied carefully the operation of the Department of Executive Police, he had concluded that the merger of agencies should take place immediately. He considered it essential that "the new institution should deal exclusively with cases directly relating to internal security, to the enforcement of law and order and the prevention of crime. Only under this proviso will the new institution be able wholeheartedly to dedicate its efforts to the execution of its primary and most vital task." Other business should be transferred from the Department of Executive Police to other branches of the ministry. Loris-Melikov proposed that some matters, originally handled by the Third Section, now should fall to the Department of General Affairs or the minister himself. He had in mind such matters as the Old Believers, violations of the Statute on Military Obligations, and petitions by private individuals for relief.

Loris-Melikov proposed to limit the staff of the Department of State Police to 52 officials (instead of the 128 who staffed the Third Section and the Department of Executive Police). "Such reduction will make it possible for experienced and competent officials, who have demonstrated their zeal and knowledge, to conduct departmental business. As a result, and in view of the attraction of this agency to loyal senior officials, it will be necessary to permit certain deviations from the ministry's norm in classification of officials and in salary levels."[29] The director of the department would belong to the third class instead of the fourth, the vice-director to the fourth class instead of the fifth, and so on. Salaries would also be increased: the director would receive ten thousand rubles instead of seven thousand; the vice-director, five thousand instead of four.[30]

Alexander II assented to this plan on 15 November.[31] As early as August the director of the Department of Post and Telegraph, Baron

Velio, had been named director of the Department of State Police.[32] In mid-November Yuzefovich was named vice-director.[33] The Department of State Police carried the following responsibilities: "(1) the prediction and prevention of crimes and the preservation of public safety and order; (2) cases of offenses against the state; (3) the organization and supervision of the operation of police agencies; (4) protection of the borders and border communications; (5) granting of passports to Russian citizens, residence permits to foreigners, deportation of foreigners from Russia, repatriation of Russians accused of crimes on foreign soil, and supervision of law enforcement in cases involving residence rights of Jews; (6) supervision of the production, storage, trade, and transport of weapons and explosive materials; (7) supervision of all forms of cultural and educational activity and of many matters of secondary importance."[34] The functions of the department were very extensive.

There were three offices within the department—administrative, legislative, and secret. The first of these dealt with general police business, including financial problems. The second dealt with the organization of police institutions in Russia and with the drafting of legislation in this field. The secret office served the function of political police—that is, it carried on the struggle with the revolutionary movement.

Along with this first memorandum Loris-Melikov submitted another calling for the creation within the Ministry of Internal Affairs of a special judicial unit to replace the abolished juridical unit of the Third Section. This unit would be charged with "drafting and legal preparation in cases involving state crimes," and with execution of ministerial directives "in matters relating to the judicial department."[35] The judicial unit was to have a modest staff of five persons. This second memorandum was approved by the emperor on 15 November. The Supreme Procurator of the First Department of the Senate, Rychkov, was named head of the special judicial unit.

In addition to these steps, Loris-Melikov attempted to strengthen administrative authority at the local level. On 10 November he presented an official memorandum "On Increases in Salary for Governors and Municipal Governors." "The significance of governors and municipal governors as the highest representatives of the regime in the provinces and urban areas demands that their service position correspond in every particular to the degree of influence that they must have in the proper government of localities." He went on to indicate that, despite their importance, governors received a modest salary of 5,432 rubles (without living or travel allowances). The minister proposed to raise salaries to seven or eight thousand per annum depending on the province. For example, the Petersburg and Odessa municipal governors would receive eight thousand but the Kerch and Taganrog governors only five thousand.[36] Alexander II also approved this plan.[37]

Intending to eliminate completely the autonomy of the gendarmerie, the Minister of Internal Affairs proposed in a secret circular that captains of the gendarmes report directly to provincial governors rather than to the Department of State Police. "Since within a short period there will occur a complete merger and unification of police within a single institution, I find it necessary that henceforth all captains of the gendarmes should submit all information about political cases under their jurisdiction to the governors in summarized form, in duplicate. Upon receipt of such reports, and in all instances involving state offenses, the governors will communicate directly with the Department of State Police."[38] The circular ended by stating that governors must deal personally with matters "under the jurisdiction of gendarme officials," and not pass this responsibility to subordinates. This circular was a definite step toward the complete subjugation of the gendarmes to gubernatorial authority.[39]

In early 1881 N.K. Grot, one of the reformers of the sixties, was appointed head of the Department of Prisons. Apparently Loris-Melikov was dissatisfied with Galkin-Vrassky, the head of the Main Prison Administration. Technically, Loris-Melikov did not have the power to dismiss Galkin-Vrassky; therefore, while the man was allowed to remain at his post, Loris-Melikov made Grot his superior. On 21 January 1881 the Minister of Internal Affairs reported to the Committee of Ministers that he proposed to appoint Grot head of the Prisons Department with responsibility for drafting a plan of prison reforms. The Committee of Ministers concurred on 27 January.

The Committee of Ministers' directive stated that the Minister of Internal Affairs retained his overall control of the Prisons Department. A second point in the directive granted "temporarily to State Secretary Grot the rights and duties of the Minister of Internal Affairs in his capacity as President of the Trustees of Prisons and as the superior of the Main Prison Administration."[40] Grot also received the right to participate and vote in meetings on prison affairs and to represent the Minister of Internal Affairs in the Senate and in all dealings connected with prisons."[41]

The government naturally was concerned about the economic condition of the population. The most intelligent statesmen understood that the standard of living was correlated directly to the growth of "sedition." Consequently, Loris-Melikov devoted much attention to this issue, attention reflected both in the practical measures adopted by the government and his projects for governmental reforms proposed in the memorandum of 28 January 1881.

An extremely interesting analysis of the economic position of the people can be found in the report by Assistant Minister of Finance Bunge, who submitted it to Alexander II in late September shortly after his appointment. Bunge analyzed the situation of the peasantry and recommended ways of improving it. He argued that while most peasants, with a few regional exceptions, had received allotments corresponding in size "to His Majesty's stipulations," "over the course of time, where population increased, and especially where allotments were comparatively small or of bad quality, these land allotments had proven inadequate to feed the peasants and to enable them to meet tax and redemption payments. When this problem was compounded by a bad harvest due to climatic factors or harmful insects, and by cattle disease, peasants in whole districts and even provinces were impoverished."

Bunge indicated that the payment of taxes and redemption dues in certain regions had ceased and the government had been forced to send food aid. In Smolensk province the arrears on redemption payments exceeded twice the annual fee; in Novgorod province arrears were one and a half times greater than the annual installment, and in various districts of Chernigov province they were three to five times larger. "These misfortunes are sadder still since it takes longer than one or two good years to improve the welfare of peasants who have lost cattle and become impoverished; even then, on a small allotment the improvement in material conditions cannot last for long."[42] Bunge's report devoted much space to suggestions for improvement of the financial picture and therefore of the living standard of the populace, particularly of the peasantry. Bunge considered first a program of resettlement that would supply land to the peasantry. ". . . The chief means of improving the situation of the rural population in areas where improvement is deemed necessary is resettlement of the excess population unable to feed itself."[43] He strongly recommended that distribution of treasury land in European Russia and in peripheral areas be terminated. This source of land henceforth would be reserved for transient peasants.

Turning to financial matters, Bunge pointed to the urgency of abolishing two taxes—the head tax and the salt tax. He was concerned especially by the disadvantages of the head tax. "Remissions and levies calculated on a per capita basis bind the people to the land since the taxation level is fixed not by the income from an allotment, but by the number of souls and their income. From this flows the need for the passport system and the mutual responsibility rule, which obliges the more competent peasants to pay for the poor." Bunge recommended "reform of the head tax system" by differentiation on a regional basis according to land fertility.[44] The salt tax, which brought fourteen million rubles annually in revenue, was also "extremely inequitable as a tax payed proportionately not to income, but to the number of souls in a family."[45] Bunge advocated the abolition of the salt tax in order to ease the plight of the needy and to improve cattle raising. (The tax decreased the likelihood of salt usage in cattle feeding). The government would compensate for lost revenues by instituting a number of other taxes (a land tax on persons of previously non-taxable groups, an income tax from various groups, a tax on capital).

Bunge's report as a whole corresponded closely to the liberal program that was spelled out in various periodicals and in economic publications.[46] The evident intent of this program was, first, to dampen the land hunger of the peasantry without infringing on gentry land, and second, to transfer from feudal methods of taxation to bourgeois methods—from the head tax to the income tax. This aspiration of Bunge was fully shared, as we will see later, by all representatives of the liberal bureaucracy, whose views Loris-Melikov shared at this time.[47]

One of the Minister of Internal Affairs' first moves in the financial and economic area was to abolish the salt tax. In early October during his stay in Livadia Loris-Melikov wrote Alexander II about the need to eliminate the salt tax, but he did not win the tsar's approval at that time. Returning to Petersburg, he again insisted on abolition in a letter dated 14 October. In the beginning of this letter Loris-Melikov admitted that the abolition of the tax might not achieve all the economic results expected. "Yet in the abolition of the salt tax, whatever the monetary results, there are considerations of a higher order, before which all else is insignificant. The Russian people find the salt excise one of the most detestable of taxes. Therefore, its abolition will satisfy so many expectations and will correspond so well to the people's desire that the moral impression of abolition alone will more than offset the temporary financial losses in the government's budget." The minister emphasized that the emperor, who had freed the people from serfdom, also must approve the abolition of the salt tax. "Such new generosity from the heights of the throne will be greeted sincerely with unrestrained enthusiasm by all estates and groups and will strengthen the union of the tsar with the people."[48]

Loris-Melikov looked on this move primarily as a political step affecting the battle against "sedition." He insisted that the salt tax be abolished forthwith in order that the Ministry of Finance would have time to find sources "to make up budgetary losses" in the way described by Bunge. In order to untie his hands in decisions on economic matters Loris-Melikov obtained the dismissal of Finance Minister S.A. Greig in late October, and engineered the appointment of A.A. Abaza as replacement. With his appointment Abaza received instructions as to how he was to direct financial affairs. These instructions stated that the improvement of the "financial system" of the empire "must take precedence over all other matters and proposals, whatever their import."[49] We do not know who wrote these instructions, communicated to Abaza in the tsar's name, but one cannot exclude the possibility that their author was Loris-Melikov.

After assuming his ministerial post Abaza sent Alexander II a letter in which he laid out the conditions essential to the execution of "His Majesty's instructions." "In elaboration of this basic idea, I consider it my sacred duty most loyally to suggest certain measures, without which all the efforts of the Minister of Finance cannot, in my opinion, achieve the goal set by Your Majesty. To achieve this goal, I think it essential: (1) to assure the Minister of Finance that, in strict adherence to imperially-approved budgetary rules, no expenditure not shown in the budget will be permitted without the knowledge of the State Council, and (2) to return to formulation of a normal budget for the War and Naval Ministries . . . . " Here Abaza indicated that the demands of the Army and Navy would have to be adjusted to the resources of the treasury. (3) In connection with financial needs pursuant to foreign policy it was necessary to define "according to the express instructions of Your Majesty the future relationship between the Ministers of Foreign Affairs and Finance." (4) Since the Ministries of State Domains and Communications have such crucial significance in national economic policy, "it is essential for the harmonious economic development of the nation that there be not only full unanimity of all departments with the Ministry of Finance, but a certain dependence in financial relations as well."[50] These were the conditions set down by Abaza. In conclusion, he wrote: "In most loyally requesting Your Majesty's concurrence with the above-mentioned points, I am unable to promise quick improvement in the economy; on the contrary, I foresee in the immediate future an intensification of the economic crisis, further decline in the value of the ruble, and the inevitability of budgetary deficits."[51]

The appointment of Abaza gave Loris-Melikov the opportunity to realize his most solemn dreams. Loris-Melikov presented to Alexander II a decree abolishing the salt tax, which was signed on 23 November. "Desiring in this grave hour of food scarcity . . . to manifest to Our divine trust, Our people, a new proof of Our concern for their welfare, We have found it proper to abolish the excise levied on salt effective 1 January 1881, and to reduce the customs tariff on imported salt."[52] The decree concluded by expressing the hope that the abolition of the salt tax not only would lessen the burdens of certain Russians, but would assist the development of the cattle industry, agriculture, and other branches of the economy as well. Valuev described this decree in his diary with his usual sarcasm: "A decree, sounding like a manifesto, marked by illiteracy in the phrase calling for divine blessings 'on these commissioned efforts,' and with a strange mixture of God, the pauperized classes, and cattle raising."[53]

The abolition of the salt tax was instituted without the usual formalities. Neither the State Council nor the Committee of Ministers discussed the question.[54] This prompted hard feelings in high bureaucratic circles, and as State Secretary E.A. Peretts pointed out, the abolition cost the state not a little revenue. In a diary entry on 5 December he wrote: "In the fine print of the imperial order on this question there is one oversight that costs the treasury seven million rubles, and threatens to ruin small salt entrepreneurs to boot. The excise duty on salt, recently collected, will be returned by the treasury to the wrong parties. The big salt entrepreneurs, like the merchant Blinov, will receive a windfall of one to one and a half million rubles; besides what they paid into the treasury, they already have received an excise from smaller-scale salt traders on salt already mined. The situation of these latter [smaller-scale traders] is critical."[55] Other financial questions raised by Loris-Melikov himself and by Bunge were not resolved during Loris-Melikov's ministry. The issues were set out in general form in Loris-Melikov's well-known memorandum to the emperor on 28 January 1881.

The other issue which really worried the Minister of Internal Affairs was the food-supply problem. In 1880 a whole series of provinces suffered a bad harvest, as a result of which the food-supply situation was tense. Loris-Melikov's memorandum to the tsar reflected this tension. On 20 September he wrote: "Concerning food supply, although current information cannot be considered particularly worrisome, we nevertheless continue to receive petitions from officials in various areas of Russia for loans [of seed] for spring sowing and [of food grain] for consumption. This matter cannot but concern me since in some provinces bad harvests have repeated several years in a row, and in case of a new scarcity of breads the situation could be complicated. This might affect adversely tax collections and the new harvest, and with incitement from disloyal elements might lead to disorder among the peasantry."[56] Naturally, this could not fail to concern a Minister of Internal Affairs.

Loris-Melikov then asserted that future government aid in the form of food and loans would be insufficient, and that public works—the construction of railroads, highways, canals, and other improvements—would have to be organized. He mentioned this matter again in a memorandum on 25 April. In this document he noted that the universal increase in bread prices had the "unfortunate result that they give disloyal persons a pretext to arouse the fears of the populace by the spread of nasty rumors."[57] In addition, Loris-Melikov said that the nation's bread supply was adequate, but that it was being held in reserve in anticipation of further price increases. He expressed special concern over the situation in the capital where bread prices had risen swiftly to five kopecks per pound of baked black bread in mid-October. As early as September Loris-Melikov had called in the mayor, municipal electors, and city governor to discuss "prevention of further price increases on articles of primary necessity."[58] In his October memorandum the minister advocated decisive steps to lower prices of baked rye bread. He announced an agreement with the Chief Intendant of the War Ministry that permitted a bread loan to the city of 35,000 sacks of rye flour for eight months.

Loris-Melikov actually succeeded in lowering bread prices in Petersburg. Peretts gives us a detailed account of this in his diary on 2 November. "When bread and flour prices were extraordinarily high—partly because of secret collusion among the large traders, Loris invited them to his office and asked them to lower prices. The merchants objected, citing crop failures in many provinces and other unfavorable conditions. They also argued that bread and flour prices were not set by law and that they could not be forced to lower prices. Then Loris announced to them that he had spoken before as Minister of Internal Affairs, who was obliged to concern himself with the national food supply, but if the merchants did not want to accept his rational arguments, then he would speak to them as Chief of Gendarmes, whose duties he recently had begun to discharge. The current, extremely high bread prices, which were not at all necessary, might provoke popular uprisings, which he was obliged to prevent. Therefore, he told all the bread merchants that if they did not lower bread prices within 24 hours, they would be banished from the capital by administrative order. The merchants were not pleased by this speech, but it had its intended effect. The next morning newspapers carried an announcement that because some people were malnourished, certain merchants (Dukhinov, Polezhaev, and others) were cutting bread prices so many kopecks."[59]

The crop failure that affected the nation was substantial. In a memorandum to Alexander II, Makov wrote about his tour through the mid-Volga provinces in May and June 1880. "Periodic crop failures in southeastern Russia, the disastrous and unprecedented insect plague which ravaged grain in the south, have created a problem requiring immediate attention."[60] In the fall of 1880 the food-supply problem grew even worse. In late October Loris-Melikov brought the matter before the Committee of Ministers. According to his statement, demands for food loans now exceeded the supply of food capital.[61] Loris-Melikov did indicate that the Ministry of Internal Affairs did not possess exact data because of the lack of statistics. ". . . Not only do government institutions lack sufficiently reliable data on the size of the harvest and the magnitude of the food assistance needed, but even zemstvo, municipal and other agencies, who are responsible for the collection of this information, lack precise data on the amount of bread held in warehouses or shipped to other localities."[62] It is understandable that the available statistics gave a very unclear picture of the food supply problem. At Loris-Melikov's prompting, the Committee of Ministers created a Special Committee on Food Supply, consisting of the Ministries of Internal Affairs, Finances, Communications, and State Domains.[63] The Special Committee dealt with the distribution of food loans[64] and made a number of policy recommendations (collection of grain statistics, methods to fight drought, and bread beetles).

One method of assisting peasants was to permit them to rent crown lands at favorable rates. This plan, drafted by the Ministry of State Domains, proposed "as support for peasant communities, shaken in certain localities by a series of bad harvests and other unfavorable circumstances,"[65] to permit peasants to rent crown lands "regardless of the distance between these lands and the peasant settlements." However, this plan could not change the situation in the countryside to any extent since the government had ignored utterly the main problem—the social and economic factors that shaped peasant life. Loris-Melikov managed to achieve more tangible results in Petersburg. It was more important to insure tranquility in the capital.

The zemstvo policy of the Minister of Internal Affairs did not change much under Loris-Melikov inasmuch as his predecessor, Makov, had followed the master plan established by the head of the Supreme Administrative Commission. Loris-Melikov's position was spelled out for Makov in a letter in May 1880.[66]

As minister Loris-Melikov strove to broaden the sphere of zemstvo activity, and to involve zemstvo agencies in the discussion of many economic problems. On 22 December the Zemstvo Section of the Ministry of Internal Affairs, in accordance with a decision of the Main Committee on the Improvement of Agriculture, sent out a circular instructing provincial governors to permit discussion of various reforms affecting the local committees on peasant affairs created by the law of 27 June 1874. These discussions would take place in local zemstvos and in the provincial bureaus on peasant affairs. The circular listed the issues recommended for discussion[67] and contained a detailed collation of zemstvo petitions on the issue. The circular concluded by proposing "to make clear to peasant bureaus and the zemstvos that, regardless of the opinions set out in the collation of petitions, other generalizations about different plans to restructure local institutions of peasant affairs might be made if the zemstvos or peasant bureaus thought it useful to do so."[68] The zemstvos intrepreted this circular very broadly, and found it possible to discuss issues far beyond the framework of the law of 27 July 1874.[69]

The newspaper *Zemstvo* played a large role in stimulating zemstvo activity; it began publication on 3 December 1880. V.Yu. Skalon, the chairman of the Moscow district zemstvo board, was the editor, and the well-known zemstvo activist A.I. Koshelev was the publisher. The editorial in the first issue stated that "the future of our country rests in local self-government: within its tight confines Russian society is growing accustomed to creative and rational direction of its own affairs while therein the forces at work in society are aroused and exercised, and its most urgent demands are made clear."[70]

Despite these steps designed to stimulate zemstvo activity, Loris-Melikov moved in zemstvo policy with due caution, attempting in every way to restrain zemstvo groups from what he saw as superfluous activity. Of interest in this regard was a Committee of Ministers discussion of a Kherson zemstvo petition calling for inter-provincial zemstvo congresses, in particular, to coordinate the fight against the bread beetle. In his speech to the Committee, Loris-Melikov said: "The Kherson zemstvo petition to permit the projected congresses of zemstvo representatives for the mutual exchange of ideas and to adopt a common plan to deal with the beetles in the stricken provinces deserves attention, it would seem, because of the special circumstances. I have found, however: (a) that it is now premature to raise the question of congresses, as the Kherson zemstvo requests, and that it is enough to limit ourselves to the experience of this year; (b) to achieve the goal set out by the zemstvo it is unnecessary to select representatives through elections in zemstvo assemblies. It would be more cautious and altogether more expedient for zemstvo councils to pick directly two or three persons from each province. These council meetings would be held in the usual place, so that they can be chaired by the provincial governor. . . ."[71]

Loris-Melikov not only rejected the option of zemstvo congresses in general, but even opposed the assembly of elected zemstvo representatives on the question of bread beetles. However, in conversations with zemstvo leaders he portrayed himself as an advocate of everything save an all-Russian zemstvo duma. A.I. Koshelev wrote about his conversations with Loris-Melikov during approximately the period when the zemstvo congress issue surfaced before the Committee of Ministers. "From him I learned much of interest. He never expected the tsar to consent to the convocation of a zemstvo duma; yet he intended to gather a general, rather large commission from the zemstvos. In non-zemstvo provinces the government would appoint representatives to this commission."[72]

The press policy of the Ministry of Internal Affairs had been defined in early September in Loris-Melikov's announcement to the newspaper editors of Petersburg. The new policy had extended the rights of the press to some degree; now various government measures, orders, and instructions could be discussed so long as the problem of representative institutions was not broached. In fact, the yoke of censorship was not as restrictive during Loris-Melikov's dictatorship as before. In 1880 and early 1881 a whole series of liberal publications appeared: the newspapers *Zemstvo, Strana, Odessky Listok, Glasnost, Poriadok,* and *Ulei*; the old slavophile paper *Rus* began to publish again. A number of liberal journals which carried articles by members of the democratic intelligentsia also began publication: *Russkaia Mysl, Zemskaia Shkola, Novoe Obozrenie.* This development suggested a new vigor in journalism.

In comparison with the preceding years, repression of the press was reduced significantly.[73] In the fall of 1880 Loris-Melikov got his close associate Kakhanov appointed to the Special Committee for the Review of Criminal Statutes on the Press, chaired by Valuev.[74] The basic purpose of the review of press regulations was to transfer the supervision of the press to judicial agencies. On 24 October Valuev noted in his diary: "Yesterday I had a preliminary meeting on the press issue. Count Loris-Melikov, N. Abaza, and Kakhanov participated. It is difficult to imagine the aplomb and arrogance of Loris-Melikov in combination with his half-naive incompetence. At whatever price, he has begun to want himself out of the business of press supervision: under cover of legislation he wants the whole thing transferred to the Ministry of Justice and subordinated to judicial review, although he has not a single correct idea or clear concept concerning the form that a trial might take. He obviously whistles Abaza's tune, although he imagines himself to be the author of the melody, and executes it like a clever performer."[75] In view of Valuev's antagonism to Loris-Melikov, much of his commentary cannot be taken seriously; however, the factual information cited here is undoubtedly correct.

The Committee held its first meeting on 30 October. This session considered 'a report by N.S. Abaza summarizing the principles of the proposed reform. "The thesis of judicial investigation and the Ministry of Internal Affairs' refusal of the unpleasant responsibility to restrain the press were presented in such a way as immediately to gain the upper hand," noted Valuev. "This time I refrained from arguing, and merely summarized in my introductory remarks developments since 1861. Prince Urusov and Pobedonostsev understand what is at issue and are horrified, but they either are unable or unwilling to resist. Makov is bound by his own unsuccessful past, and by the delicate nature of the current situation. Frisch cannot help but speak for [the Ministry of] Justice, while Kakhanov and Saburov echo the Minister of Internal Affairs."[76]

Therefore the disposition of forces in the Committee favored Loris-Melikov. The proposals to prohibit administrative agencies from interference with the press were of undeniable positive significance, and society greeted the proposals with approval. On 5 November the Committee invited representatives of the Petersburg periodical press to participate in discussions: M.M. Stasiulevich, A.A. Kraevsky, M.E. Saltykov-Shchedrin, N.P. Giliarov-Platonov, A.S. Suvorin, V.A. Poletika, and V.V. Komarov. According to Valuev, they were invited "to hear *gravamini et desiderata.*"[77] Stasiulevich gave a long speech.[78] Its basic content amounted to the assertion that only the liberation of the press from administrative arbitrariness and its governance by law could guarantee the press its rightful position in society. "There is only one way to achieve an independent press—namely, the law and the courts must stand between the censor and the press; the censor must be allowed to supervise, but not to judge or to punish. No other paths to the establishment of order in the press are open...."[79] Stasiulevich concluded by expressing the hope that the draft of new regulations would be shown to representatives of the press before final approval.

After the invited journalists departed the Committee adopted Valuev's proposal to create a commission to write the new press regulations. Valuev was also the chairman of this commission. "I am moving much differently now than I had expected to in July. Apparently, under these circumstances freedom of the press is a foregone conclusion. It remains to find ways and means to make it less dangerous. Yesterday the Minister of Internal Affairs said something to the effect that 'the press is as necessary as the air,' and, under the new laws with the help of the courts, journalists will sit quite prettily indeed. The new Minister of Finance spoke about 'society' and the law just as a journalist would. The head of the Press Administration is at one with the journalists. Kakhanov is Loris-Melikov's lieutenant, but he is sensible and careful. Saburov leans in the same direction. Pobedonostsev is inscrutable. Prince Urusov sees the value of 'admonitions' to the press, but he cannot oppose the new regulations. Makov, Frisch, and I are left. With differentials."[80] Of course, Valuev's allusion to "complete freedom of the press" was unjustified; what is of interest is his opinion. On this question he was more conservative than his colleagues on the Special Committee.

It would be unfair to suppose that Loris-Melikov thought new press regulations necessary merely to lighten the censorship. While he certainly wanted to reject administrative supervision of the press, it does not follow that he wanted to give the press complete liberty. Of interest here is a letter from Valuev to the head of the Press Administration, N.S. Abaza, on 8 December. "Your Excellency is aware that in the opinion of the Minister of Internal Affairs, an opinion which you share, Petersburg newspapers abound with articles that do not correspond to the interests of this government or this form of government, but that under the current legislation on the press the government is not empowered to eliminate or even reduce this unfortunate problem. With this in mind, there is proposed a transfer from a mixed system of administrative and judicial review to a stricter system, wholly under judicial control."[81]

On 5 November the Special Committee established a subcommission to draft guiding principles for a review of criminal law, forecasting proposed changes and new criminal sanctions in cases involving the press. This subcommission consisted of the chairman Valuev, Prince Urusov, Frisch, and N.S. Abaza. Serious disagreements were heard in the subcommission over rules guiding the investigation of censorship violations. All three members considered it necessary, in accordance with the existing statute, to try cases involving the press in judicial chambers. They cited the acquittal of employees of *Sovremennik* [Contemporary] in 1866 as an example of correct procedure.[82] They thought judicial review at three levels "undesirable, because the appearance of a pre-trial article might produce a negative impression on the public, and if this were to result in the transfer of the case from one reviewer to another, then more intense public scrutiny might prejudice the inquiry." Therefore, Urusov, Abaza, and Frisch thought it unwise to retain the existing system of review when the censors and procurators disagreed. They thought such cases should be entrusted to the First Department of the Senate and to the Ministry of Internal Affairs.

On the issue of trial jurisdiction, Valuev had another, objectively progressive, position. He thought that "crimes and violations by the press should be subject to the general system of criminal proceedings, since a deviation from the general rules of procedure is hardly desirable and convenient at this time."[83] In view of the complex circumstances, Valuev wanted to return to the original system, established by the judicial statutes: to try cases involving the press in district courts.[84]

In the event of disagreement between the Ministries of Internal Affairs and Justice, Valuev proposed to retain the old system. On the other issues the subcommission agreed unanimously, and it drafted new regulations for review of the press law. This draft has been preserved in the Valuev papers in the form of four memoranda: (1) "On the Rights of Administrative Agencies Dealing with the Affairs of the Press;" (2) "Basic Positions on the Review of Criminal Law Involving the Press;" (3) "A Checklist of Proposed Reforms and Additions to Penal Regulations on the Press;" (4) "Basic Regulations for Administrative Oversight of Existing Instructions on Censorship and the Press." According to the first memorandum, administrative units retained the following rights in relation to the press: (1) licensing of periodical publications and approval of responsible editors; (2) prohibition (with justification for each instance to be submitted to the Committee of Ministers) of publication or discussion of various issues in the press; (3) seizure of a publication before distribution has begun; (4) referral of cases to judicial authorities in cases of legal violations; (5) receipt of mandatory copies of every publication before distribution.

The report went on to say that all violations of press statutes would fall under judicial auspices. "The present recourse to administrative punishment is abolished; delay and seizure of periodical publications and the destruction of the offending articles now may be accomplished solely by judicial order."[85] The matter of jurisdiction was treated in two separate variants from the two points of view indicated earlier.

The second memorandum spoke of the need "without delaying the general review of the code of punishments to make changes and additions to those articles of the code dealing with crimes and violations of press laws; these changes and additions are crucial to guarantee proper prosecution of abusers of the printed word."[86] It was considered necessary to define precisely the maximum length of confinement: three years in prison, five years under guard, with a maximum fine of three thousand rubles. The law would have provisions for reducing these penalties in the presence of mitigating circumstances. However, this section concluded by defining the punishment for provoking judicial prosecution involving periodical publications as six months in prison. Other violations merited one year.

The "Checklist" memorandum consisted of 19 points. Among them were points dealing with blasphemy and mockery of the Christian religion, and of other non-Christian religions that prevailed in states recognized by the Russian government. Other items concerned printing of insulting references to the imperial family[87] and the heads of foreign governments, insulting remarks about laws existing in Russia, and so on. Of interest was the twelfth point of the Checklist, citing the punishments for "arousing enmity between estates, tribes, and in general between separate units or classes of the population . . . or between workers and managers, and for arousing workers to organize strikes." The fourth report summarized basic rules for administrative oversight of current press regulations. The first point stated that "both presently-existing systems of censorship, preliminary and punitive, will remain in force until experience dictates otherwise."[88] The Minister of Internal Affairs received the right to introduce the punitive system gradually into those areas where the judicial statutes were operating. At the wish of editors all periodical publications in the capitals and other cities, where the new punitive system would operate, were freed from preliminary censorship. The only exceptions were "publications for popular consumption."

Publications freed from preliminary censorship had to pay a fee of from five to eight thousand rubles in the capitals, and from 2500 to 4000 in the provinces. The minimum for publications of uncensored original material was lowered to five pages and for translations to ten pages. Publications of a scientific, technical or economic nature were allowed to publish without preliminary censorship on the same scale as hitherto. Religious censorship was combined with the general censorship by including representatives of the Spiritual Department on the censorship board. Censorship of foreign periodicals and books essentially remained as before. Such was the project drafted by Valuev's subcommission. Analysis of it shows that with the exception of the introduction of a single system of prosecution for press law violations—that is, the judicial procedure—no other substantive changes were made. Moreover, it should be said that the punishment for violations was increased. The abolition of administrative interference in the affairs of the press was a positive development in that it would tend to diminish government arbitrariness. The Special Committee discussed the Valuev project for the final time on 28 February, on the very eve of 1 March. In a diary entry dated 31 December 1881, P.A. Valuev characterized the work of the Committee in the following manner. "The entire agenda in the commission on the press was set by Count Loris-Melikov's system, and reflected the strange peculiarities of the contemporary official milieu . . . . Among commission members Minister of Finance Abaza was at one with Count Loris-Melikov and spoke the language of *Golos* [Voice] and *Novoe Vremia* [New Times]. Kakhanov was the lieutenant, but restrained and cautious. The Minister of Justice and his colleague scarcely could reject the new legislative honor being preferred to or forced upon the judicial agency. Prince Urusov wavered. Pobedonostsev was horrified and protested, but his protests were not vigorous at all. Makov was perfunctory; Abaza, the chief of the Main Press Administration, played the hypocrite and practiced that fine bureaucratic art in order to mask his innermost thoughts from his patrons. After the second session in the presence of journalists I thought it impossible to bring matters to a satisfactory conclusion, but Count Loris-Melikov and N. Abaza had convinced themselves that they could neither avoid me nor persuade me to drop my opposition. After that the discussion continued on its own inertia but no one expected success, and after 1 March no one mentioned it again."[89]

Valuev's description is correct on the whole if the attribution of motives to explain the actions of Committee members is set aside. This evaluation of motives is far from objective. However, one thing is certain: the Special Committee consisted of a group of individuals with very different ambitions. If one adds that the emperor and his camarilla strove for the universal bridling of the press, it is clear how difficult it would have been to unite these diverse elements. As a result, no really substantial changes in the law could have been made. Yet, taking all this into account, it must be emphasized that the status of the press in 1880 and early 1881 was better than it had been in previous years.

While in Livadia in the fall of 1880 the Ministers of War and Education, Miliutin and Saburov, presented to Alexander II a report on the conditions in post-secondary schools and on needed changes in the university statute. Judging by the report, the initiative behind this discussion must have come from Alexander himself. Changes in the university statute had been part of Loris-Melikov's program of reforms as summarized in his memorandum of 11 April 1880. The immediate pretext for consideration of the issue on October was the student uprisings which occurred at this time.

The report began by analyzing the situation in the universities. "In our opinion, the current situation is scarcely satisfactory. Coming from all parts of Russia, living in an alien milieu, and without any means of material support, young people seek friendship and support in comradely circles. Yet the existing university regulations are intended to prevent fraternization of students and even to destroy their links to the university itself." The authors then stated that existing rules prohibited student organizations from assisting indigent students, and even forbade meetings connected with this problem. "Despite the prohibition, meetings take place and funds are collected—but in secret, and therefore without any control or supervision."

In the opinion of the ministers there was a great hidden danger here. Students with "ill intent," that is, revolutionary-minded students, "might become masters of the university at any time" despite their small numbers.[90] The majority of students, "the best and most sensible ones" in the report's terminology, could not counteract the minority because they were not organized. "Thus, the government deprives itself of a powerful and unique method of reducing the importance of the bad students by rejecting the beneficial influence of the best students on their comrades. The student inspectorate and administration lose the opportunity of exerting moral influence on the young since they must deal with an inchoate mass and cannot depend on a few outstanding personalities among the students who might influence their fellows." The authors of the report treated the problem of student organizations very narrowly—from the point of view of how best to fight the spread of revolutionary ideas among students.

The report then stated that the prohibition of student meetings and consequently the absence of the right to call them meant that "every meeting is a disorderly cabal of all students of the university, and for this reason alone meetings are always turbulent and ready to disperse rapidly into mobs." According to Miliutin and Saburov, the legalization of meetings would mean that students would gather under different circumstances, and the meetings would be very modest in size, since they would be called by autonomous groups. One result of the absence of corporate student organizations was the destruction of fraternal feelings among students, which in the past had been "a powerful means of inculcation in them of honesty and general moral qualities."[91] Corporative fraternal spirit, which played such an immense role in the officer corps, was very much needed by students, particularly at the time. The authors supported this assertion by arguing that most students "come from a virtually uneducated milieu, and that the moral outlook acquired from their families loses all authority over them [in universities]. Since university life, after the destruction of fraternal ties, cannot inculcate in them any moral ideals, these students are left without firm principles, and in this way is created the type of people who have acquired the notorious reputation of nihilists."[92]

According to Miliutin and Saburov, therefore, the absence of corporative ties and fraternal spirit led to the spread of revolutionary ideology. What were the solutions to this problem? The authors thought of two possibilities. The first solution was to turn universities into lecture halls open without limitation to all interested persons. Under this plan university courses would become a series of public lectures, and students would be the public. The police would be responsible for keeping order. In the authors' opinion such a reform naturally would lower the level of teaching from the scholarly to the popular. Moreover, the admission of a large number of people without limitations might lead to a "disturbance" that the police could not handle. This solution would mean, in their opinion, the end of higher education in Russia.

"If the first solution is impossible, then it must be recognized without argument that students have common interests and affairs, a common life, and a common intellectual outlook. Therefore, it is more correct and wise to permit openly what students do now in secret. In essence, student activism has a single cause: their terrible poverty and their desire to help their poor comrades. This is why they set up money funds, dining rooms, organized assistance, and so on. Most meetings are called to discuss these problems, or in order to establish courts of honor to judge colleagues who have besmirched the dignity of students."[93] Therefore the authors proposed to recognize the existence of student corporative organizations, particularly since such organizations already enjoyed official recognition at two Russian universities.[94] More concretely, they thought students should be allowed to organize monetary funds for needy fellows, to open inexpensive dining halls, to organize job placement centers, and take other steps to assist those in need. They also proposed establishment of student courts of honor.

Miliutin and Saburov also proposed to allow students "to assemble for election of persons to run the above-mentioned organizations, and to discuss questions arising in connection with these organizations, as well as general academic problems placed on the agenda by the university administration." Student meetings were to be permitted but they would be limited to corporate and academic issues. Moreover, "to assure order and discipline in these meetings," each university would draw up special rules. These rules might allow meetings only on university premises by course or group, and might limit their number.

The authors thought that these reforms should be implemented gradually, with due caution. They preferred not to issue a general order on the matter, but instead to permit each local trustee to introduce the new system "in whatever degree, and with whatever safeguards might be deemed necessary." Then the report considered whether it would be advantageous to introduce a student uniform; trustees of education districts would have to be able to express their opinions on this issue. Miliutin and Saburov thought that student uniforms would be quite beneficial since they felt that "in most student disturbances, as it later became clear, the leaders were from outside the university and unconnected with it; student uniforms would separate the students to some extent from these agitators."[95] Thus, uniforms were supposed to prevent outside elements from infiltrating the university. In addition, the introduction of uniforms might facilitate "the establishment of contacts and friendship among students and a feeling of honor and pride in the university uniform."[96] The ministers concluded by stating that their proposal could be implemented only after the end of student disturbances.

Analyzing the report and its proposals, it is clear that it was inspired directly by the student disturbances of the fall of 1880 and represented a certain concession to student demands. This concession also presupposed that the government's position would be strengthened. The authors believed that their proposals would satisfy the academic demands of students while hindering the spread of revolutionary propaganda in the universities. In actuality, the implementation of these proposals would have facilitated a certain democratization of student life and would have had a positive effect on Russia life. Alexander II approved the report, but no practical steps in this field were made.

In late 1880 university councils presented their opinions on the need for a review of student regulations. Their views had been invited on 25 June 1880 by Saburov, who had proposed that university administrations discuss the student regulations confirmed in late 1879. On the basis of these reactions the Ministry of Education drafted a special report "On Proposals Concerning Review of Student Regulations Compiled from Reactions by University Councils."[97] "In order to assure students the opportunity to study without disturbance," stated this document, "they must be placed in a normal situation on university grounds where they gather because of common goals and desires to be educated." This lead to the question of the extent to which the existing regime in the universities guaranteed students a normal life, and whether it contributed to the outbreak of student uprisings. Moreover, it was said that police actions were not effective, so long as the basic causes of student disturbances were not eliminated.

"The main cause of repeated disorders is the shortcomings in student life within the walls of the university . . . . The existing regulations on university students are based on the assumption that students do not constitute a special corporation. Consequently, these rules do not permit any sort of social intercourse among students. Students are not allowed any collective activity whatsoever. Hence, existing university rules are intended to prevent any congregation of students, to limit their association with the university to attendance of lectures and completion of various formalities of a police character."[98] The report noted that the universities admitted that these rules were not observed in practice.

The Council of St. Petersburg University wrote the following: "It is inconceivable that young persons who earlier sat for several years in the same auditorium, heard the same lecturers, worked in the same laboratories, studies, and library, would not feel a spiritual affinity among themselves, would not have questions that intimately concerned them all, and aroused and disturbed their impressionable and sensitive natures." As a result, the existing student regulations were not observed and corporate organizations—in particular, monetary funds to help needy students—existed in spite of the rules. The Council of Moscow University stated frankly that "auxiliary monetary funds" had operated for more than ten years, were properly organized, and disposed of very large funds of money. The report went on to say that such a situation had a negative impact on the moral development of the young, "who were accustomed to various secret artifices, unauthorized meetings, and other essentially illegal actions."[99]

The universities thus advocated the abolition of the existing limitations, which caused student dissatisfaction, and they stated the need to review current regulations. However, as the report emphasized, this did not signify recognition of a corporate student organization. "The basic element of the 1879 student regulations—that students do not constitute a special organization—must remain in force in the future. Students need only belong to some kind of fraternal group capable of assisting the needy . . . and have the right to assemble to discuss the operation of student institutions and other academic matters."[100] The universities' general position amounted to an advocacy of student institutions and organizations dedicated to help needy comrades. These organizations included financial funds, inexpensive dining halls, and job placement centers. It was thought expedient to allow literary evenings, concerts, plays, and also scholarly circles "for the cooperative study of science, literature, and the arts." The universities did not recommend the publication of special rules to control the form of these organizations. They wished to leave this matter to university councils. The right to organize student organizations naturally would mean permission for student meetings to discuss the business of these organizations (the election of officers, discussion of their actions, and so on).

The report considered in detail the conditions under which a meeting might be called. Assemblies could be convoked only with the permission of the university administration. So that meetings "might not transgress the limit on subjects open for discussion," the universities recommended the presence of a member of the administration. Only recognized associations, circles, academic groups, or students from a particular region might ask for permission to hold meetings. "Meetings of entire departments or of the whole university will not be permitted under any circumstances."[101] The report concluded by discussing the advantages of student courts of honor, with very limited powers. The university councils' program fully corresponded with the proposals of Miliutin and Saburov.

On 29 December 1880 Minister of Education Saburov wrote another memorandum to Alexander II about the need for swift examination of student regulations. He argued that "since the second half of the academic year is the best time for changes in university rules, it is advisable now, before the lectures start again, to define the order in which the proposed measures will be introduced in the universities."[102] Since the reform program would affect all institutions of higher education, Saburov thought a special committee should discuss "the order and stages in which Your Majesty's directives will be implemented, and the conditions which would serve to assure tranquility in institutions of higher education."[103]

On 5 January 1881 a conference on the university question was convened under the chairmanship of Miliutin. The participants were: the Ministers of Internal Affairs—Count Loris Melikov; Finance—Abaza; Education—Saburov; Communications—Posiet; State Domains—Prince Liven; the Supreme Procurator of the Synod Pobedonostsev; Assistant Minister of Finance Bunge; member of the State Council Delianov; and the chief of the Main Administration of Military Academies, Isakov.

According to Miliutin's diary, "the meeting began with a long oral presentation by Saburov. He developed very well the rationale that we think justifies a change in university regulations .... Then I said a few words .... Loris-Melikov also made a few comments in support of our proposals .... Bunge confined himself to several brief observations on the content of Saburov's report, but Isakov, very unexpectedly, opposed the new measures. And then the other participants, one after the other, spoke against them in various ways. Most critical were Delianov and Pobedonostsev, but this could have been predicted. Seeing that it would be impossible to reconcile these contradictory positions, I proposed to delay further discussion until another time."[104] By Miliutin's testimony the only supporter of the project, besides himself and Saburov, was Loris-Melikov.

Pobedonostsev also wrote a detailed account of this meeting in a letter to E.F. Tiutcheva on 9 January. "The first meeting was on the eve of the Epiphany, at the very hour when the waters were consecrated; it was long, tiring, and irritating. We talked about the wild, insipid, illiterate projects of Saburov on the organization of student meetings. A thing which did not even merit mention because of its absurdity was subjected to serious discussion. This alone was bad enough .... In October he and Miliutin had presented this plan to the tsar, and the tsar had approved it. They gathered us to discuss a *fait accompli*. Loris-Melikov with his native volubility immediately endorsed the project. He probably did not expect everyone else to oppose it. Bunge, Abaza, Delianov, Liven, and Posiet all expressed opposition in more or less soft and deferential tones. To my surprise, N.V. Isakov, obviously prepared in advance, spoke very eloquently and cleverly against the plan. Of course, I also opposed it, and more decisively than the rest."[105] Pobedonostsev then noted that on the eve of the meeting Bunge, Abaza, and Isakov had been inclined to support the Saburov proposals, but F.M. Dmitriev, who had been invited to Petersburg by Saburov to become trustee of the Petersburg educational district, had dissuaded them. Analysis of Pobedonostsev's account shows that its presentation of factual details differed little from Miliutin's account.

Sometime later on 10 January Miliutin held a second session on this question. This time "by previous agreement with Saburov and Loris-Melikov and several others, we restricted the debate to the proposed reform of student inspection and its subjection to the rector's and administration's control. However, even on such a minor issue we were unable to avoid prolonged and heated debate, if only because certain members desired to vent their spleens at the new Minister of Education.

Again Pobedonostsev and Delianov distinguished themselves by their
virulent speeches. To everyone's surprise, Isakov joined those two pessi-
mists, in whose eyes students are nothing but a rabble of outcasts and
bums, who cannot be improved .... After all this outpouring of gall
everyone but Delianov announced with certain reservations their agreement with the proposal. They even were forced to admit that it was
impossible to oblige the university administrations to enforce strictly
all the provisos of the former draconian law against student dining halls,
reading halls, and so on."[106] Despite bitter argument the committee
approved not only a reform of student inspections, but in essence the
Miliutin-Saburov proposals for a change in student regulations.

In his diary Miliutin blamed the disagreements that arose in the committee on the presence of D.A. Tolstoy's adherents in the committee,
and on the "weakness and naivete" of Saburov. In fact, the arguments
were not so much a manifestation of personal sympathy or antipathy
as they were reflections of differing political views. On one side were
the representatives of reaction: Pobedonostsev and Delianov; on the
other side, the liberal bureaucrats. Both parties had the same goal: the
pacification of students, and the termination of disturbances in higher
educational institutions. The means to this end were different. According to Miliutin, the meeting showed the precarious position of the Minister of Education, who could retain his post "only through the presently all-powerful support of Count Loris-Melikov."[107]

Having concurred with the Miliutin-Saburov plan, the committee introduced several amendments. In letters to E.F. Tiutcheva, Pobedonostsev mentioned the further work of the committee on two occasions. On
14 January he wrote: "There was another meeting with Saburov, just
as absurd as the last. It is awful to think that the Minister of Education
is an ass! It is even worse that many people do not understand this,
or do not want to understand it and seriously agree with him."[108] Pobedonostsev returned to this issue on 26 January, this time in more detail. "So we met again on student affairs—a disgusting meeting. The ass
Saburov and War Minister Miliutin, a man without ideological principles, agreed with monstrous absurdity to give students some sort of
absurd constitution, the right of assembly and elections. Saburov reads
a most absurd speech, and they support him, although far from everyone [supports him] .... Count Loris-Melikov stands on Saburov's
side. He says himself that Saburov is a fool, but adds: what can be
done? Dismiss Saburov?"[109] These letters showed clearly enough Pobedonostsev's position on the university question.

Thus, the arguments reflected two lines of government policy—liberal and reactionary. Each camp recommended its own solutions to the

crisis of the autocracy. On this occasion the liberal policy prevailed. Repression alone could not effectively deal with the student problem. On 18 February Alexander II confirmed the special committee's decisions in accordance with the majority platform.[110]

On 31 January, even before Alexander II's final confirmation of the special committee's decisions, Saburov made a report to the State Council about university inspection, and justified it by the emperor's orders for swift review of this section of the university statute. "To arrange expeditiously student university inspections, it seems desirable to base the new statute on two main principles: (1) inspection, as an integral part of university governance, must not be separated from direct supervision by the university staff; and (2) the personnel chosen as inspectors and their activity in fulfilling the duty to supervise students must meet such requirements as would guarantee the independence, firmness, and generally the propriety of their inspections."[111]

Guided by these principles, the Minister of Education wished to subordinate inspection to the university rector and administration in accordance with the statute of 1863. Appointment of inspectors would be handled in a different fashion than was envisioned by the 1863 law. "To appoint as inspectors all members of university councils would be most inconvenient." According to Saburov the inspector, who functioned pretty much as a policeman, should possess a number of personal qualities, "the careful and reliable checking of which would be possible only after the closest acquaintance . . . . The selection of dozens of individuals is absolutely impossible."[112] To obviate this difficulty Saburov proposed to allow rectors to recommend candidates for the job of inspector to the trustees of educational districts, with final confirmation to be made by the Minister of Education.

Here Saburov deviated from the 1863 statute, and this was not the only time he did so. For example, he advocated that the instructions to be followed by inspectors be written and confirmed not by the university council, but by the administration—including the rector, prorectors, and faculty deans—with the approval of the district trustee. A more important deviation from the 1863 statute was Saburov's attempt to increase the powers of the inspector. "This augmentation is essential in order to concentrate in his hands the supervision of all student affairs, and with the close relations between rector and inspector, to process these matters swiftly."[113] In the new plan the functions of the university court were narrowed in comparison with the functions outlined in the 1863 statute. Most student disciplinary offenses not under an inspector's jurisdiction would be handled by the university administration, and only matters of "particular importance" in the judgment of the district inspector would be treated by the university court. Furthermore, the university administration was to examine cases "of student confrontations inside the university and outside it," and also actions "not in accord with the concept of student honor and dignity."

Such were the contents of Saburov's presentation to the State Council. His plan broadened significantly the duties of the inspector, and made him independent of the university council. The rights of the administration (the rector and other high officials) were extended at the expense of the university council and university court. The Saburov plan was a sort of middle road between the 1863 statute and the temporary instructions drafted by Tolstóy. Probably, to be more precise, Saburov's plan was closer to the temporary instructions than the 1863 law.

The plan, which had been distributed to members of the State Council, was opposed seriously only by Baron Nikolai.[114] Most members declined to reply. Loris-Melikov made no substantive comments, but remarked that "there are no obstacles to submission of this plan for the consideration of the State Council."[115] The head of the Third Section, Prince Urusov, concurred with the project as a whole, but added some amendments. He proposed that the inspector be selected by the university administration, but that the inspector's instructions be written by the university council.

The comments of Baron Nikolai were more significant. First, he objected to the appointment of the inspector, and insisted on elections. In his opinion, the inconvenience of electing an inspector by a large collegial gathering certainly had to be recognized; however, "this truth applies to all elections, and just as easily could be applied to the election of any official .... " Therefore, he proposed a compromise: to give the university council the right to elect an inspector from among three candidates chosen by the administration. Secondly, he objected against the subordination of the inspector to the rector, rather than to the university council. "For any action by the rector to succeed on the basis of moral suasion over students it is essential that the rector never act alone, but only as an expression of the accumulated moral authority of all university personnel, and he must rely in all cases on the strength of that authority. As soon as he becomes an autonomous high police functionary, the strength of his authority is shaken .... He will be looked upon not as the head of academic self-government, but as a senior policemaster ...."

Nikolai also objected to the limitation of the functions of the university court. "It is awkward to permit a trustee to define the competence of a university court .... "[116] Finally, he was decidely opposed to the plan that would allow the university administration to deal with student disruptions in and out of the university, or with actions not consonant with student honor or dignity. He said that this plan contradicted the "spirit of the 1863 statute."

The only serious opposition to Saburov's project came from Baron Nikolai. An interdepartmental discussion (the Departments of Law, and Civil and Spiritual Affairs) of the Saburov plan began on 23 February and ended on 2 May—that is, after Saburov's retirement and his replacement by Baron Nikolai.[117] The State Council abolished the 1879 instructions, and adopted the provisions for supervision of students outlined in the 1863 statute. The new emperor approved the decision of the State Council on 29 May.

The cancellation of the 1879 instructions by the State Council and the approval of the emperor showed first, the power of the student movement that had called a new strike in the spring of 1881, and second, the magnitude of the government's political crisis. After 1 March, and even after the publication of the Manifesto of 29 April on the strengthening of the autocracy, the government dared not hold to the program that it had adopted in 1879.

On 28 January 1881 Loris-Melikov presented to Alexander II an official memorandum containing a detailed summary of his planned reforms. He began by speaking about the tasks set by the emperor when he was appointed Minister of Internal Affairs. He stressed that these tasks involved "not only strict prosecution of the harmful manifestations of social doctrines and the resolute consolidation of the government's power, shaken temporarily by the deplorable events of recent years, but above all the utmost possible satisfaction of legal requirements and the needs of the people."[118]

In contrast to his earlier memoranda, Loris-Melikov now saw his task not so much as the introduction of repressive police measures as the implementation of a program designed to reduce the basis for the spread of revolutionary ideas. He argued that the first step taken in this direction already had yielded results. "The gradual return of national life to its proper course satisfies in large measure the desires of right-thinking society, and fortifies the temporarily-shaken faith in the strength and solidity of government authority in Russia."

The memorandum enumerated Loris-Melikov's actions in all areas of domestic politics, beginning with the abolition of the Third Section and ending with the abolition of the salt tax and the change in zemstvo policy. All these actions, in Loris-Melikov's opinion, "exerted and are exerting a beneficial influence on society by pacifying its troubled condition and by arousing loyal preparedness to serve You, Your Majesty, with all its strength to complete the great deed of state reforms."[119]

On what data did Loris-Melikov base such an optimistic judgment of the public's mood? This question deserves a detailed answer. If one has in mind the liberal element of society, the Minister of Internal Affairs was correct. Loris-Melikov's policy, which amounted to a softening of the former reactionary course in state administration, was viewed favorably by liberals. The disposition of "right-thinking" society—that is, of representatives of the ruling class—could not have justified a statement about the incipient "pacification of minds." Loris-Melikov understood this perfectly well, and he had different, weightier reasons behind his judgments. From February 1880 to late January 1881, a period of eleven months, the Executive Committee of *Narodnaia Volia* had not carried out a single terrorist act.[120] Moreover, the Third Section and later the Department of Police had no direct indications of preparations for further political assassination attempts. In 1880 the mass movement had shown no tendency to grow; on the contrary, it was on the decline. While in 1879 there had been a certain increase in peasant disturbances, the number in 1880 had been very small. It must be said, however, that the situation in the countryside was still tense, since rumors about a "black partition" circulated as before.[121] The activity of the worker movement also showed a certain decline in comparison to 1879. Furthermore, its magnitude in this period was not significant. All this, but chiefly the absence of terrorist acts, justified Loris-Melikov's optimistic evaluation. However, the Executive Committee of *Narodnaia Volia* had not abandoned the struggle, and preparations for an attack on Alexander II continued.[122]

It must be noted that the government was poorly informed about the activity of the Executive Committee. For example, in an official memorandum on 20 September Loris-Melikov informed Alexander II that the center of the revolutionary movement was Moscow. "A long conference with local [Moscow] authorities strengthened my previous convictions, communicated earlier to Your Majesty, that Moscow is now the center of propaganda."[123] This statement was, of course, inaccurate. The reason for such poor information about the activities of revolutionary organizations largely involved the heroic activity of an agent of the Executive Committee, N.V. Kletochnikov, who had become an official in the Third Section, and later in the Department of State Police. Kletochnikov had informed the Executive Committee about potential dangers.[124] It was also significant that the revolutionaries arrested after Goldenberg did not provide detailed information, and this also complicated police searches. For this reason Loris-Melikov had not even the faintest idea about the activity of *Narodnaia Volia.*

After describing the domestic situation in these glowing terms, Loris-Melikov argued that this situation should be used to advantage "in the further development of order." To this end he advocated the implementation of steps designed to complete the "great reforms." He also noted that many proposals under consideration had been worked out to some extent in central institutions, and that the senatorial inspections, having gathered the necessary data on local conditions, also would be of assistance in preparing the reforms. But "even this data, after it is finally analyzed, certainly will not be sufficient without the practical knowledge of persons closely acquainted with local conditions and requirements." Loris-Melikov thought it proper to involve representatives of local society in discussions of the draft reform projects. He stressed that the participation "of precisely this group of individuals would be necessary in the future struggle against sedition."

"It is extremely important," Loris wrote, "to find ways to involve society in the preparation of these reforms." Yet, as he had in his official memorandum on 11 April 1880, Loris-Melikov argued that "for Russia any kind of organization for popular representation in forms borrowed from the West is inconceivable. Not only are these forms alien to the Russian people, they would shake their basic political outlook and introduce complete confusion, the results of which are difficult to foresee." He also rejected the convocation of a Zemsky Sobor, or zemstvo duma, by arguing that "the simple revival of ancient representation would be difficult to implement and, in any event, a dangerous experiment of returning to the past."[125] He nevertheless proposed to involve representatives of the cities, nobility, and zemstvo in the drafting of various reforms.

In contrast to its predecessor, this memorandum explored the issue concretely and precisely. Loris-Melikov thought it necessary to create temporary preparatory commissions, "like the Editorial Commissions organized in 1858," so that zemstvo and municipal delegates could participate in the discussions. The government would appoint the staffs of these commissions from representatives of government departments; the emperor would add "informed and loyal officials and others known for their competence in science or their experience in various areas of government administration or national life."[126] It was proposed also to appoint inspectors from the Senate on the staff. The commissions would be chaired by high government officials. The creation of two commissions—administrative and financial—was proposed. Each would be subdivided into special subcommissions or sections. The administrative commission would deal with questions of interest to the Ministry of Internal Affairs: (1) the reform of local provincial administration; (2) drafting of legal projects supplementing the Statute of 19 February 1861; (3) study of methods to abolish the status of temporary obligation—that is, to shift peasants to obligatory redemption and to lower redemption payments in areas where they were especially heavy; (4) review of the zemstvo and municipal statutes in order to make additions and amendments "in the light of past experience;" (5) questions connected with the organization of a system of national food supply, particularly with the creation of food reserves; (6) preparation of necessary steps "to guard the cattle industry." The responsibilities of the administrative commission essentially concerned two tasks: (1) the reform of local administration, including the statutes on public organizations; (2) the drafting of legislation covering the peasantry in order to improve the Statute of 19 February 1861 so as to generate further capitalist development in agriculture.

The financial commission's responsibilities were vaguely described. It would draft legislation on the head tax, the passport system, and other problems. Loris-Melikov said that this matter would be decided later by the tsar on the basis of an official memorandum from the Minister of Finance.

These commissions would elaborate legislative projects "within the limits set by His Majesty's will."[127] Consequently, the commissions' activity would be strictly regimented, and no legislative projects might be prepared without "His Majesty's order." These modest proposals might have led, under certain conditions, to more serious concessions by the government. According to V.I. Lenin, "the realization of the Melikov project *might* under certain conditions have been a step toward a constitution, but it also might not have been: everything depended on what would be stronger—the pressure of the revolutionary party and of liberal society, or the resistance of the very powerful, coherent, and unscrupulous party of unwavering adherents of the autocracy."[128]

For consideration of the legislation drafted by the two commissions mentioned above, Loris-Melikov advocated the creation of a general commission. Chaired by an appointee of the emperor, this commission would consist of the members of the preparatory commissions. In addition, it would include elected representatives from provinces in which the zemstvo statute operated, and from certain large cities (two representatives per province or city). In order to involve "the most valuable and informed individuals," the provincial zemstvos and municipal councils would be permitted to choose not only among deputies, but among other persons residing in the city or province.[129] In non-zemstvo provinces, representatives would be picked by local officials—that is, appointed. This affected primarily the national border areas. The commission would deliberate no longer than two months.

After the general commission had approved a legislative project it would be submitted to the State Council, together with the recommendations of the minister under whose jurisdiction the project fell. "In order to lighten the workload of the State Council in this area, perhaps Your Majesty will decide to add ten to fifteen new voting members, representatives of public organizations who possess special knowledge, experience and outstanding talents."[130] It was unclear whether these representatives would be added to the State Council by appointment or by election. Fearing that the emperor would take this proposal as a constitutional project, Loris-Melikov emphasized that the work of the preparatory and the general commissions would be advisory only. "This system of preliminary analysis of crucial questions connected with the national interest has proven itself already in practice, and has nothing in common with Western constitutional forms. The sovereign retains universally and exclusively the right to raise legislative questions, and the right to set limits on solutions in whatever ways he sees fit." Furthermore, "the invitation to members elected by public institutions will be preceded by the composition of the legislative project in preparatory commissions of government officials, plus a few non-officials well-known to the regime."[131] Hence, a piece of legislation would have to be put together by government bureaucrats, and only later submitted to discussion by public representatives.

Loris-Melikov recommended the preparation of relevant materials already available to central governmental agencies, and that this work be completed before the end of the senatorial inspections. The respective agencies were to transmit this material to the preparatory commissions "in the form of legislative proposals." The minister assumed that the preparatory commissions might begin work by the autumn of 1881, and that the general commission could be appointed by early 1882. Loris-Melikov wrote in conclusion: "I will allow myself to state before You, Your Majesty, my deep conviction that failure to satisfy the above-mentioned expectations at the present time unavoidably will lead, if not to public disillusionment, then to apathy in civic affairs; as the sad experience of recent years has shown, this apathy constitutes the best soil for anarchist propaganda."[132]

If this program is compared to its predecessor, the memorandum of 11 April 1880, it is not difficult to discover substantial differences. While the sphere of reforms is similar, the issue of how to involve public representatives in their preparation is resolved differently. In the 11 April memorandum Loris-Melikov treated the problem of representation very cautiously; he advocated that representatives be selected not by election, but by appointment on the recommendation of local officials. In the latter document he was much bolder. While the method of selecting public representatives to the State Council was not specified—one might even assume that this would be done by appointment—the representatives to the general commission would be elected.

Why in January 1881 did Loris-Melikov promote a more radical program? There had been not a single terrorist act; the number of peasant demonstrations and also the number of strikes had declined. What was the reason? It would seem that the reason lay in the general state of tension prevailing in Russia. Despite the lack of new assassinations, the government, mortally frightened by the past, had recognized gradually the need for concessions.[133] This factor was reflected in Loris-Melikov's memorandum.

Juxtaposing Loris-Melikov's proposals to those of Grand Duke Konstantin Nikolaevich and Valuev, much similarity is evident. Loris-Melikov's plan was less moderate than the Grand Duke's. It was very close to that of Valuev. The general commission projected by Loris-Melikov was nothing other than Valuev's Congress of State Deputies. The two plans resolved in almost identical fashion the issue of how to involve public representatives in the State Council. All the same, one must emphasize the very moderate nature of Loris-Melikov's proposals, which in no way threatened the principles of autocratic authority. Yet, as noted before and as V.I. Lenin justly observed, under certain conditions these proposals might have been a step toward a constitution—a frail constitution that nevertheless might have promoted a certain invigoration of Russian political life and, eventually, the formation of bourgeois political parties. This project of state constitutionalism looks very anemic beside M.M. Speransky's plan of state reform, which would have involved broad segments of the ruling elite in public life.

Loris-Melikov's official memorandum underwent discussion in high government circles. On 3 February 1881 Valuev wrote in his diary: "On the third, Michel 1er dropped in on me. Especially courteous. ... This must have meant something. Sure enough: it seems that His Majesty would have me participate in a meeting. . . on Loris-Melikov's report. The good boyar sent it to me yesterday, a monument of intellectual and moral mediocrity. Together with naively cynical boasting, course flattery of the tsar, and a vulgar presentation of various lies, there is the earlier idea about some sort of editing commissions composed of selected experts."[133] Such was Valuev's evaluation of Loris-Melikov's plan. However, as we will see, it was an evaluation for Valuev's personal consumption only, since he never spoke against the plan. Most likely, the evaluation was merely more of the "original and ornate prose" that Valuev so loved to write.

Loris-Melikov's proposals first were discussed on 5 February at a meeting in Alexander II's presence. The participants included the tsarevich, Grand Duke Konstantin Nikolaevich, Count Adlerberg, Count Loris-Melikov, Prince Urusov, Abaza, Valuev, and Nabokov. Loris-Melikov read his memorandum at the meeting. According to Valuev, it was approved on the whole. "Business ended with general approval of the Minister of Internal Affairs' proposals, and the usual vague reservations about 'caution in working out details.' Consideration of these 'details' was entrusted to a committee of the same individuals without the tsar, under my chairmanship. Michel 1[er] asked me in a loud voice if it would be possible to add Solsky as an editor; I was very glad because this will reduce my workload considerably."[135] Hence the State Controller was included in the Special Committee.

Judging by entries in Valuev's diary, the Special Committee met in the Anichkov Palace on 9 and 14 February. Concerning the first session, Valuev wrote: "The meeting was a sorry affair, but innocuous. Only Abaza grasped the situation *en grand*. Count Loris-Melikov has yet to comprehend it, although he has contrived and whistled a certain tune for the others in a certain key, but he doesn't remember the key in which he whistled. No rational decision was possible. The framework, concepts, formulae, are all provisional. You cannot buy the truth for three kopecks."[136]

The minutes of this meeting were copied on 16 February and forwarded to the emperor. During its deliberations the Special Committee approved with certain amendments the creation of preparatory and general commissions. The Committee thought it unwise to decide in advance the number of preparatory commissions, and wrong to include members of the preparatory commissions on the staff of the general commission. "Turning to other proposals on the staff of the general commission, the Committee finds that the election of an identical number (two) of representatives from each province and large city would not correspond to the sharp distinctions in the areas, and especially in the population density, of our provinces and cities. It would be preferable to take one or two delegates from provincial zemstvo assemblies, two from municipal councils in the capitals, and one delegate from other large cities."[137]   The Special Committee left open the issue of representation for Siberia and the national peripheries (the Caucasus, and the Kingdom of Poland). It did not propose to establish a fixed term for the general commission's operations.

These were the Special Committee's amendments to Loris-Melikov's program. However, the Committee did not concur in the most important point in his plan, the inclusion of ten to fifteen new representatives from public institutions in the State Council—that is, of representatives from the zemstvo and city governments. Apparently this point disturbed Alexander II himself, since he wrote a question mark next to it in the margin of Loris-Melikov's memorandum.

Among the various people who urged the tsar not to accept these reforms, not the least important was the German emperor, who attempted to influence his nephew. According to Alexander III, Wilhelm I having caught wind of the proposed political reforms, "begged him (Alexander II) in a personal letter not to adopt them; if things had gone so far that concessions could not be avoided and popular representation had become a political necessity, the German emperor advised him to give popular representation as modest a role as possible, to give representation as little influence as he could, and to preserve real power for the government."[138]

The Committee thus concurred in that part of the memorandum which introduced no real changes in state organization. The involvement of well-known public figures in political discussions had occurred earlier, although to a more limited degree, in the Editorial Commissions, during the drafting of the Military Obligations Statute, and of the Law on Employment of Workers. On 17 February Alexander II approved the minutes of the Special Committee.[139]   In late February a governmental communiqué was written on the basis of the approved minutes. The communiqué began with a summary history of the Supreme Administrative Commission, which was intended not only to fight sedition, but to discover "ways in which government life could be returned to its proper and legal course."[140] The communiqué then discussed Loris-Melikov's memorandum of 28 January and the tasks it set.

"His Majesty the Emperor, desiring to make a new sign of his trust in his people. . .has consented to the basic idea that it is timely and advantageous to involve local officials in an advisory capacity in consideration of various legislation which His Majesty deems deserving of solution to develop further and to perfect the imperial reform program."[141] Then the communiqué mentioned the meeting in Petersburg of the temporary preparatory commissions and the forthcoming discussion of their decisions in the general commission with the participation of zemstvo and municipal representatives. The communiqué concluded with a detailed description of the composition of these commissions and their rights as stated in the Special Committee's decision.

On the morning of 1 March Alexander II summoned Valuev to the Winter Palace and handed him the draft of the government communiqué; the tsar asked for Valuev's opinion. According to Valuev's "Report of 1 March," "if I had no objections, I [was] to call the Council of Ministers together on Wednesday, 4 March."[142] It is clear that immediately after his return from the palace Valuev studied the proposed project and wrote an official report in which he said that, in his view, the project was "very well" put together.[143] He then informed Alexander II that the Council of Ministers would meet on 4 March at 1:30 in the afternoon. However, the bomb thrown by Grinevitsky changed all events to follow.

The policy of Loris-Melikov while Minister of Internal Affairs remained the same as that which he pursued during the first period of his dictatorship. Under the influence of the revolutionary movement the government had been forced to make certain concessions. These concessions were reflected both in police-administrative measures (although this certainly did not imply an end to repression) and in policy toward the press, higher education, and the zemstvo. Even so it must be said that Loris-Melikov adopted very stringent measures against revolutionaries. For example, in a Ministry of Internal Affairs circular to the Main Prison Administration on 8 October it was proposed to send "state criminals" to Siberia bound in handcuffs and, in accordance with the Statute on Exiles, to shave half their heads.[144] On 2 April 1881 the Main Prison Administration sent out another special top-secret circular which said that, according to the Governor-General of Eastern Siberia, this requirement was not being met and that "such deviations" should be eliminated.[145]

In fall 1880 Loris-Melikov established an extremely severe regime for political exiles at the colony in Nerchinsky district.[146] In a note to the Governor-General of Eastern Siberia on 20 September Loris-Melikov summarized these new rules on political exiles. They were to be in chains at all times, and kept in cells at night. According to point 17 of these rules: "In cases of open resistance or plotting, since no reasonable measures will prove sufficient, the warden may use cold weapons or in extreme cases firearms, without having to answer for wounded or slain prisoners."[147] Wives and others who accompany prisoners to their place of exile would be allowed a visit only every other day. The most severe step in these rules was the prohibition of any correspondence.[148]

Despite the dictatorship, which by no means ended with the abolition of the Supreme Administrative Commission, "extreme measures" and other forms of repression were employed less frequently than in the late 1870s. This reflected a new phase in the crisis of government, for the regime no longer could "rule as before" through naked force. If, during the first stage of the crisis prior to February 1880, the government relied solely on intensified repression, during the second stage of the crisis this no longer was sufficient. The government was forced to make certain concessions in order to win the support of "right-thinking" (i.e.–liberal) society, and to institute certain economic reforms. Moreover, repression took what one might call a "legal" form. The uncontrolled authority of governors-general and other officials, which had weakened autocratic power, now was limited.

This created limited possibilities for a more relaxed atmosphere in public life. Even people who were far from apologists for Loris-Melikov admitted that the situation had improved. For example, M.E. Saltykov-Shchedrin, analyzing the situation in Russia in summer 1880, wrote to A.N. Ostrovsky: "The censorship is now more relaxed; in fact, everything has relaxed. Loris-Melikov has shown the wisdom of a true biblical serpent. Imagine, we have heard nothing about him, and we are even beginning to imagine ourselves to be out of danger. Last year it was impossible even to contemplate nightfall without fear."[149]

Another witness was Vera Nikolaevna Figner, who discussed this matter in her autobiography. Concerning the conditions of revolutionary work in the capital in 1880 and early 1881 she wrote: "In Petersburg itself propaganda, agitation and organization were conducted very extensively. The absence of police chicanery and abuses by the gendarmes was very propitious for work among students and workers. This was a time of universal activity and hope. Yet the demand for regicide loudly resounded, because Count Loris-Melikov's policy did not fool anyone. The essence of the government's attitude toward society, the people, and the party had not changed in the slightest. The count transformed the most heavy-handed and severe forms into milder ones, but he took back with one hand what he gave with the other. For example, having undertaken the widely-heralded return of administrative exiles, he himself employed administrative exile in Petersburg. The instruction of 15 December 1880 made the lot of exiles even worse; this instruction deprived them of such a valued right as correspondence with their families. Therefore, public opinion in the revolutionary world demanded a continuation of terror and the death of the tsar himself, as well as that of his hypocritical-liberal favorite." [150]

On the whole this is a fair evaluation of Loris-Melikov's regime, but at the same time it must be noted that the populists ignored the concessions which the government had made under the direct influence of the revolutionary struggle. V.I. Lenin wrote: "Revolutionaries will never, of course, reject the struggle for reforms, or fail to take advantage of even the most unimportant and minor concessions, *if* by so doing they can strengthen their attack and facilitate complete victory." [151] That *Narodnaia Volia,* in the *absence of a mass revolutionary struggle*, did not alter its tactics in response to Loris-Melikov's reforming activity proves that they had not understood fully the changed circumstances following the reforms. The decision to involve the popular masses in the revolutionary struggle against the government made by the Executive Committee and presented in "The Preparatory Work of the Party" [152] could have been carried out more successfully under Loris-Melikov's regime, which was a by-product of their heroic struggle.

The plan of state reforms advanced by the Minister of Internal Affairs, in contrast to his early memoranda, contained a rather broad program of economic as well as administrative changes. The intention to involve public figures in the preparation of the reforms signalled an attempt by the government to broaden its social base of support. However, even this modest step encountered opposition among the elite and was approved by the tsar only in a diluted form. It must be noted that the reforms adopted and projected which touched on reorganization of the government were bourgeois in nature. They were designed to increase centralization and to soften the feudal features of the system of state administration.

Emperor Alexander II was killed by the bomb of I.I. Grinevitsky, an agent of the Executive Committee of *Narodnaia Volia*, and his son Alexander III succeeded to the throne. As G.V. Plekhanov had predicted at the Voronezh congress of *Zemlia i Volia* [Land and Liberty], one more check was added after the letter "A". Alexander III was a man of very limited mental capacity; indeed, he was poorly educated and largely ignorant. Even the apologist S.Yu. Witte, analyzing his beloved monarch, wrote that Alexander III was a man "comparatively little-educated—one might say, he was a man of ordinary education . . . . Emperor Alexander III had a modest intelligence, but an enormous, outstanding heart."[1]

In contrast to his weak-willed father, Alexander III held a definite set of opinions. These views were decidedly primitive. They did not extend beyond Uvarov's triadic formula: "Orthodoxy, Autocracy, and Nationality." To guard the purity of "our father's faith," the unshakeable principle of autocracy, and to develop the Russian nationality in the patriarchal-reactionary sense of that word—these were the basic tasks which the new emperor set himself. One must be fair to him: he fought most persistently for these ideals with all the intolerance inherent in his limited mind. One must admit also that in certain foreign policy matters he showed good judgment. However, even unintelligent people can acquire a pragmatic streak. In contrast to his father who had bowed before his royal uncle Wilhelm I, Alexander III sharply altered Russian foreign policy. In this field he compared favorably to his father, who not infrequently had forgotten the national interests of the country which he ruled. The foreign policy of the new emperor was far from pro-German. However, this became clear only later, after Alexander III had recovered from the tragedy of 1 March, after he had learned that hostile forces did not represent a direct danger to his own life.

The assassination of Alexander II provoked immediate panic and complete confusion in the government. Valuev wrote in his diary: "At first one expected street demonstrations. The army would have to be employed to preserve order. I insisted on this; but there were no commanders or staff officers. Directives were issued, but they were unconnected."[2] However, these fears proved unfounded. There were no anti-government outbursts. On the contrary. According to D.A. Miliutin and A.A. Bobrinsky, the crowd in Palace Square tried to revenge themselves on a certain young man who somewhat resembled a nihilist.[3] According to Valuev, "the streets were full until 10 P.M., but then they emptied. When I went to Anichkov Palace at 11 P.M. with the draft manifesto, Nevsky Prospect looked like it usually does late at night."[4]

However, despite the absence of anti-government disturbances and revolutionary announcements, the young emperor and the government authorities were lost in confusion. In addition to the act of 1 March there were other causes of confusion. On 2 March during his interrogation Zheliabov stated that "the succession to the throne of His Imperial Highness Alexander Alexandrovich scarcely will satisfy the expectations of the party, which will meet this obstacle without hesitation and will attack the new emperor too."[5] This statement from a party leader could not fail to have had a pronounced effect.[6] Zheliabov's statement acquired greater weight after the discovery of the conspiratorial apartment on Telezhnaia Street on 3 March,[7] and of the tunnel under Malaia Sadovaia Street on 4 March.[8] Finally, on 10 March the Executive Committee of *Narodnaia Volia* sent the new emperor a letter, which was a kind of ultimatum.[9] In this document, speaking of the current situation in Russia, the Executive Committee wrote: "From this position there are but two exits: either revolution, which is inevitable and cannot be averted by criminal sanctions, or voluntary devolution of sovereign power to the people."[10] Since Alexander III did not intend to pursue the course of "voluntary devolution," the alternative depicted by the secret and feared Executive Committee could not but create still greater confusion.

This forced the government to avoid a quick trial of Alexander II's assassins. On 5 March Loris-Melikov presented an official memorandum that withdrew his earlier plan of a trial in the military district court in favor of a trial before a Special Commission of the Senate, which would begin its functions after the burial of Alexander II."[11] Advocating the Senate trial, the Minister of Internal Affairs wrote: "One cannot ignore the fact that the execution of the criminals might provoke their co-conspirators, who are still at large and emboldened by one success, to attempt further attacks on the person whose life constitutes the firmest assurance that Russia will live through this difficult year without organic change. Meanwhile the forthcoming burial of the deceased emperor will pose special problems of security for the new monarch."[12]

In an analysis of the moods prevailing in government circles, one letter from K.P. Pobedonostsev to Alexander III is particularly interesting. In this letter, dated 11 March, Pobedonostsev admonished his former pupil about the security precautions the latter must take in order to guard his "sacred person." Pobedonostsev's advice consisted of five points. "When you decide to sleep, lock the doors behind you, not only in your bedroom, but in all the adjoining rooms and including the outside exit. A trustworthy person should check all the locks, and make sure that the internal bolts on folding doors are locked in place."[13] The second point concerned the need to check alarm bells before sleep, since a lead wire might have been cut. The next point recommended an evening search of the tsar's apartments to see that no one had gotten inside during the day and hidden under the furniture. The final two points addressed the need for an adjutant to sleep in a nearby room, and for a check of all persons close to the tsar, and immediate dismissal of anyone who aroused the least suspicion.

Pobedonostsev's fears of another possible assassination were shared by others. Miliutin wrote in his diary on 3 March: "I agreed to go with Count Loris-Melikov and Count Valuev to meet His Majesty and persuade him not to expose himself or the empress to attack during continual trips from the Anichkov Palace to the Winter Palace and back."[14] However, as Miliutin noted later, he did not succeed in meeting Alexander III, and they decided to send Loris-Melikov alone. Apparently Valuev had this same incident in mind in a diary entry on 5 March: "Yesterday, 4 March, I wrote Loris-Melikov about the dangers facing His Majesty during journeys from palace to palace, and I mentioned, just in case, the establishment of an order of regency."[15] Moving in the company of powerful officials, the adjutant to Grand Duke Konstantin Nikolaevich, General Kireev, described the atmosphere prevailing there. "In the minds of Petersburgers there is nonsense, in their hearts confusion and paralyzing fear. They have started to say that you won't be able to conquer the nihilists, and in fact the nihilists' rule would be better, so let them grant a constitution."[16] Such "constitutional" inclinations were not widespread, but their very existence suggests a definite fear and confusion.

Fear for the fate of Russia's ruling dynasty extended beyond the borders. As Schweinitz noted in his memoirs, after Alexander II's assassination Bismarck ordered him to telegraph twice a day about the situation in Petersburg. "If I do not receive a telegram at regular intervals, I will assume that the telegraph is not working anymore."[17]

On 8 March Major-General Baranov, a man close to the new emperor, was made St. Petersburg municipal governor.[18] He was unintelligent, a bully, and an accomplished liar who now made a career of "fighting sedition in the capital." This appointment can be traced to the direct initiative of Pobedonostsev, who proposed Baranov to Alexander III. In a letter to the young tsar on 6 March Pobedonostsev wrote about the need to replace high government officials with new people: "Here in Petersburg people turn up accidentally. Yesterday Baranov arrived; may I say again that this man may render great service to your Majesty, and I hold moral authority over him."[19] Even earlier, on 3 March, Pobedonostsev had written about the same issue: "May I once again remind Your Majesty about Baranov. This is a man devoted to You— I know—and he knows how to act when it is necessary."[20]

It should be noted that Baranov served to heighten fear and confusion in government circles with his stories about newly-uncovered plots. Analyzing the "frenetic" activity of Baranov, Pobedonostsev wrote his friend E.F. Tiutcheva on 15 March: "Baranov showed up barely able to stand. Since his appointment he has not rested day or night. His main work is done at night. Tomorrow, he says, will be a terrible day . . . . There is an attack on the tsar and the Prussian prince planned at four places on the road; at one point on Nevsky people dressed like cabbies will gather in order to open up a cross fire. He already has in hand the blueprint of these plans . . . . 'Of 48 people who were to participate, I have 19 in my hands. I am going to make arrests. Tonight,' he concluded, 'what else I shall discover is unknown.'" Naturally, all of this was merely the fruit of Baranov's lively imagination, yet it helps to feed the anxiety which gripped the autocrat of all the Russias. "Imagine the position of the poor tsar," wrote Pobedonostsev in this letter; "He had to travel to the fortress today, knowing that at each step death awaited him." Pobedonostsev went on to tell Tiutcheva that in front of the Winter Palace, opposite the Saltykov Gate, they had dug a trench at Baranov's orders "where they found 17 lead wires for mines."[21] Thus the unrestrained talk of the new municipal governor did much to increase panic in St. Petersburg.

At Baranov's initiative a kind of "Committee of Public Safety" was created under his aegis. Loris-Melikov wrote to Baranov: "In view of the series of insidious plots intended to shake the governmental system and culminating in the events of 1 March, His Majesty the Emperor has made a firm decision to set a limit to the further development of seditious criminal activity, to give to the inhabitants (of the capital) genuine tranquility." It was proposed "to summon the aid of delegates from the city's citizenry, who would form under the aegis of the municipal governor a temporary council . . . ." The municipal governor was to propose to this council "measures that he considers necessary to guard public order." All measures approved by the council would acquire "legal force" and would be implemented immediately if they did not require "His Majesty's approval." Proposals not approved by the majority of council members would not be enforced.

Then Loris-Melikov described the system of selection for council members. Not everyone would have the right to vote for these delegates; only homeowners and "persons renting in their own names apartments in privately or state-owned buildings,"[22] and also owners of industrial and commercial enterprises, including small street stands, could elect one delegate. The electoral system would be the following: each elector would submit a nomination recommending his favorite candidate. "Consideration of these nominations would take place in special commissions in each ward."[23] The commissions would consist of a police officer, the city council delegate, and two officials or civil officials appointed by the municipal governor. Election was by simple majority of votes in each ward. The elected delegates from wards then would meet in the municipal governor's office and select from among themselves 25 representatives to serve on the council. These elections took place practically overnight. Loris-Melikov's note was delivered to the municipal governor on 18 March, and on the next day delegates were already being picked from the wards.

Analyzing the introduction of the elections, the newspaper *Golos* wrote: "The celerity of the elections, and the misunderstandings inevitably connected with this celerity, naturally . . . had unfortunate results. The lack of preparation of the voters manifested itself in several curious cases. So the commissions collecting ballots explained to the voters that they could cast their ballots only for someone who lived in their ward, not for a nonresident."[24] As *Golos* indicated, electors often announced that they did not know for whom to vote. Then commission members recommended a vote for the candidate approved by the police. Consequently, as *Golos* confirmed, "the elections violated the elementary rules of electoral systems."[25]

The "elected" were summoned on the next day to a general meeting where Baranov advocated two measures "to establish order in Petersburg." One concerned the organization of searches of those entering the city; the second involved observation of passengers on the railroad. This latter idea involved a regulation that passengers arriving in Petersburg would have to apply for a cab "through the police." The police would write down the number of the driver, and the driver would be obliged to inform the police of the passenger's address.[26] Analyzing

Baranov's speech before the delegates and his recommendations, Miliutin wrote in his diary on 21 March: "The speech went ungracefully even before, but Baranov's two ideas were so obviously impractical that one began to doubt his sanity. At least the description of Baranov's reception of the delegates published in the current issue of *Golos* ridicules the municipal governor and reminds one of the comic stories of Shchedrin."[27]

After the approval of Baranov's program, delegates to the Temporary Council were selected. Obviously these delegates were not elected properly since a list of recommendations was submitted to the electors by the police. Peretts wrote in his diary: "Obviously the whole thing was a farce, in which the members of the council were predetermined by the municipal governor."[28] On 23 March the members of the Temporary Council were presented to Alexander III. The overwhelming majority of members were from the ranks of the upper and middle bureaucracy.[29] Among the members, particularly among the candidates, were a number of representatives of the industrial and commercial bourgeoisie. However, the candidates and members also included rather well-known representatives of the Petersburg intelligentsia: the university rector, Beketov, the lawyer Potekhin, the historian Semevsky, the journalists Kraevsky and Eliseev. The former Municipal Governor-General Trepov received the highest number of votes (176 out of 228).[30] The composition of the council, or as contemporaries called it "The Parliament of Sheep," satisfied the desires of liberal society. The newspaper *Strana* wrote: "The establishment of the council under the municipal governor by means of elections has resulted in a membership that can only be called satisfactory."[31] *Golos* also reacted favorably to the council membership.

On 22 March the council began its activity. Originally it had been decided that the council would meet every day until April. However, this plan was not followed since only six meetings had occurred before mid-April.[32] According to P.E. Shchegolev in his article "After 1 March 1881,"[33] the work of the council amounted to drafting of several projects and instructions.[34] At first the council's business was conducted in its two subcommittees: the first, under the chairmanship of Count Vorontsov-Dashkov, for the organization "of a bodyguard for His Majesty's person," and the second for the creation of an organization of house porters. According to Semevsky, there were other special committees "For Measures Against Landmines," and "To Define the Responsibilities of the Police and House Porters in External Surveillance of Homes."[35] One of the first problems discussed in the council was the protection of the tsar while Alexander II's body was being transported to the Peter and Paul Fortress. Each of the council's members was made responsible for the observation of one house along the procession route.[36]

In order to clarify the work of the Temporary Council, I shall cite an account of one meeting. At the sixth session, held 17 April, the following problems were discussed: (1) "security regulations for the railroad leading to the tsar's residence;" (2) "measures for material improvement in the situation of students in higher educational institutions;" and (3) numerous projects to guarantee security in the capital. All these projects were silly, and some of them simply absurd. For example, there was the proposal of the merchant Karpov to establish residence committees consisting of the proprietor and delegated tenants. These committees would watch new residents and give them "residence tickets" containing a physical description. The police were given the right to search without warning, "to make a rollcall of residents, and to compare the physical descriptions written on the residence tickets with the appearance of the actual resident."[37]

Apparently, certain members of the Council assumed that the activity of the Council had enormous national significance. At the 26 April meeting one member, a well-known adventurist and humbug named General Bogdanovich, introduced a proposal to share the Petersburg "experience" with other cities in the empire. "In view of the tremendous benefits" of the Council, he recommended that "we petition the emperor to create similar councils in every provincial capital of the empire."[38] However, this "clever" proposal was not supported, and the government did not intend to adopt it. The activity of the Parliament of Sheep was fruitless, and it was disbanded in early summer.

The creation of this "Committee of Public Safety" is of great interest as evidence of the confusion and panic that had seized the government and the emperor himself in March 1881. The appeal "to society" itself revealed the weakness of the government, its inability to weather the storm without assistance. Still another point deserves mention: the Temporary Council was the predecessor of the Holy Retinue. Particularly noteworthy was the subcommittee chaired by Vorontsov-Dashkov and designed to guard the tsar's life. Analyzing the situation in Petersburg, Valuev wrote in his diary on 23 March: "The erratic course of affairs continues, and the drama is now turning into comedy. They are entrenching the palaces, it is prohibited to walk along their footpaths; the Temporary Council under the municipal governor imagines that it has been summoned to control the police and the municipal governor himself. The Minister of Internal Affairs is seldom seen and does not even participate in the preservation or establishment of security in the capital. The ball rolls swiftly on an inclined plane, and shatters. One has to be prepared for anything. May God's will be done."[39]

On 27 March Alexander III abandoned his capital without warning and took up residence in Gatchina. Pobedonostsev wrote Tiutcheva about his regrets: "He is nevertheless in Gatchina. The tsar does not show himself to the people, he hides, sets off for Gatchina almost secretly. How sad! How heavily it must weigh on the people."[40] Speaking of the impressions which the Gatchina journey produced on St. Petersburg society (the bureaucratic world was what he had in mind), Polovtsov wrote on 27 March: "In the city they are saying: C'est [la] fuite de Varenne . . . ."[41] It is regretted that instead of Gatchina the tsar did not pick Troitskaia Lavra, where he might have gone to fast for national enlightenment. In Gatchina he will be even more isolated than in Petersburg—that is, he will listen only to Pobedonostsev and Baranov, whose charlatanism has aroused universal opposition."[42] Alexander III's exit to Gatchina was evidence of his overpowering fear of the revolutionaries. Even there, in Gatchina, the tsar felt himself secure only "behind seven locks."

After visiting Gatchina on 29 March to see the emperor, Polovtsov described security precautions in this way: "In Gatchina I took a coach and headed toward the palace, which was surrounded on all sides by sentries, uniformed horsemen and plainclothes police. The same thing inside the palace."[43] So strong was the fear gripping Alexander III and his circle that the autocrat of all the Russia's voluntarily had transformed himself into a prisoner inside the Gatchina Palace!

It is possible that the Gatchina trip was inspired by Baranov, who wished to gain even more influence over the emperor. On 31 March this notion shone through a letter from Pobedonostsev to Tiutcheva. "Fog. Nothing can be seen. Even Baranov is enshrouded by fog. I *do not know* what he is doing or what he is thinking, but in my soul I have no trust. He must not be left alone without someone to control him, and now no one restrains him. He goes alone to see the tsar and tells him what he wants. What he has told me on brief and rare occasions I do not like, and my hope is not inspired by his words. I am afraid that there is something going on here. To frighten a young tsar[44] and get him in your power. I am afraid that the Gatchina trip may be connected with this idea, to isolate the tsar. It is difficult even to get near Gatchina. It is not the same as Tsarskoe Selo."[45]

The flight to Gatchina illustrated the young emperor's paralyzing fear of revolutionaries and demonstrated the confusion and panic prevailing in government circles. The creation of the Temporary Council under the municipal governor was also proof of this panic. The crisis of the autocracy now had reached its zenith.

On 27 March the Minister of Internal Affairs sent a secret circular letter to the governors. He emphasized the need to strengthen faith in the tsar by whatever means necessary. The contents of the letter and the advice to act "with extreme caution" also symbolized the confusion in government circles. The beginning of the circular indicated that the assassination of Alexander II had led "not to inevitable disorders all over Russia, but to universal mourning and expressions of sincere loyalty" to the new emperor. Loris-Melikov stressed that it was "the most sacred duty of loyal citizens and especially of government officials to uphold this saving national faith."[46]

The next lines in the circular spoke about popular rumors concerning the assassination of Alexander II; the people held that nobles, who were unhappy over the abolition of serfdom, supposedly had assassinated Alexander. It was rumored also that the new tsar would reestablish serfdom. The Minister of Internal Affairs displayed great concern over the situation in the countryside, and he instructed the governors to take a series of preventive measures to preserve order in the empire. "You must act with extreme caution in order not to arouse the popular imagination, but use every opportunity to explain that royal kindness and His Majesty's enduring love for the people always will characterize the Russian sovereign's actions." In conclusion, Loris-Melikov asked the governors to "pay most careful attention to each rumor and every violation of order, to establish truth by appropriate explanations, and to meet disorder with the necessary prudent steps . . . . I am certain Your Excellency will devote to matters of this nature all the requisite attention, care and vigilance, while acting in cooperation with the numerous loyal elements of Russian society."[47]

Despite the element of bravura in the letter—the assertion that the people and the tsar were united—the letter was permeated with anxiety and fear of popular disturbances. In my opinion, this explains why Loris-Melikov did not talk about repressive measures, but instead urged provincial administrators to be calm, careful, and cautious.

The only repression in March 1881 involved censorship of the press, and this was carefully limited. While in 1880 the number of government actions against the press was insignificant, and in early 1880 dropped to zero, government censors did have a definite role to play in March 1881. On 4 March Loris-Melikov sent to Alexander III a memorandum about warnings administered to the newspapers *Strana* and *Golos* for editorials "explaining the hideous recently-committed crime [the assassination] as a product of the reactionary system and attributing responsibility for Russia's recent misfortune to those tsarist advisors who ruled by reactionary measures."[48] On 12 March a judicial prosecution was launched against the newspaper *St. Peterburgskie Vedomosti* [St. Petersburg News] for an editorial containing "a wholesale and impermissibly vicious accusation against our administration, that we did nothing but rob the treasury on a colossal scale."[49]

Again on 16 March the Minister of Foreign Affairs sent Alexander III a memorandum about the press. "On my return today with the official memorandum, I learned that tomorrow several newspapers will publish articles that are harmful in the present troubled time. Therefore, although I discussed with Your Majesty the disadvantages of closing simultaneously three newspapers—*St. Peterburgskie Vedomosti, Molva* [Talk], and *Russky Kurier*—that had permitted publication of sharply critical articles, I now think it wise not to delay punishment any further. Today I intended to halt publication of *Molva* and *St. Peterburgskie Vedomosti* for one month, since they are both extremist publications. The first is extremely liberal, and the second reactionary."[50] In the case of *Russky Kurier*, Loris-Melikov thought "personal punishment" might suffice.[51]

On 24 March Loris-Melikov submitted two official memoranda: one concerning prohibition of retail sales of the newspaper *Poriadok* [Order], and the second about an eight-month suspension of the newspaper *Smolensky Vestnik*.[52] The number of actions against the press in this period was large, considering that from the moment Loris-Melikov had become minister (that is, from August 1880 until March 1881) there had been only two warnings administered to newspapers. The new repressions evidenced the deep anxiety of government officials. During the first month after Alexander II's death, the government found itself in complete confusion and fear. This mood was reflected not only in the Parliament of Sheep and other measures, but primarily in the inability of the tsar himself to set a political course. Consequently, there was much political infighting in the first two months after the assassination.[53]

The assassination received wide coverage in the Russian press. In an editorial on 3 March *Moskovskie Vedomosti* called for universal support for government authority. "Freedom and a truly human life in society are possible only if there exists a unified and unquestioned authority above all others. Its diminution inevitably breeds trouble. To the degree that the sovereign power shows weakness, primitive and beastly forces grow. Social decay sets in, violence commences, the foundations of all morality are shaken, the spirit of corruption overcomes everyone's minds. . . ." The newspaper also expressed confidence that the new reign would be a "time to live by reason and be oneself."[54]

Liberal papers took a different position. The newspaper *Strana* was the most radical. On 3 March the editorial began with a rather explicit discussion of the pointlessness of reactionary measures systematically introduced by the government since 1866. In the newspaper's opinion, the politics of reaction had not proven effective. What was the solution? "The solution is nothing less than to reduce the responsibilities of the head of state, and in so doing to reduce the danger which threatens him from malefactors and fanatics." How might this goal be achieved? Here *Strana* spoke radically. "It is necessary to establish in any proper social and political system a lightning rod for the head of state. Representatives of the Russian land should decide the basic features of domestic policy; therefore, responsibility for policy should rest with them. Henceforth, the Russian tsar would serve only as the worldly, universally respected symbol of our national unity, power, and the future enlightenment of Russia."[55] In order to guarantee the tsar's safety, *Strana* wished to transform him into a "symbol," that is, to deprive him of real power, and give him rights analogous to those of the English monarchs. The tsar would reign, but not govern.

Like *Strana, Golos* tried to prove that reactionary measures would not have positive effects, and spoke about "sharing responsibility." Addressing the tasks before the government, *Golos* wrote in an editorial on 4 March: "In our view, the path is clear. We must orient ourselves according to the goals of the slain emperor."[56] In other words, *Golos* wished to implement the reforms which Loris-Melikov had advocated to Alexander II.

Other liberal newspapers, however, did not treat the need for reform so radically as did *Strana*. The newspaper *Zemstvo,* analyzing the situation in Russia since the assassination, spoke about the need to summon zemstvo representatives to a meeting where they might discuss possible solutions to the nation's difficulties. "The questions posed by the present cannot be resolved by the usual bureaucratic methods; they require the participation and cooperation of society."[57]

All liberal newspapers considered it essential to involve representatives of society in deliberations about solutions to current problems, and the more radical papers raised the issue of limiting autocratic power. The exception in this regard was the Slavophilic *Rus*, which stood on the right wing of the liberal movement, or more precisely, on conservative-liberal tenets. *Rus* wrote: "It is not a question of liberalism or reaction at the present terrible moment, but simply of good sense and civic honesty. It is necessary to display firm, severe, energetic, threatening, and *intelligent* authority."[58] *Rus* emphasized that any action that could be interpreted as a concession was inappropriate.

Zemstvo assemblies also reacted to the events of 1 March. A number of zemstvos sent the tsar addresses expressing their sympathy and full support of the tsar and the government, and their readiness "to go forth to battle with sedition."[59] Several of these addresses called for unity of the tsar and the people—that is, for summoning "the representatives of the land."[60]

The assassination of Alexander II also stimulated a flood of projects for the "salvation" of Russia. In early March the famous activist B.N. Chicherin presented a long memorandum entitled "Tasks of the New Reign." He began by trying to prove that the growth of the revolution-ary movement was by no means a result of reactionary policy. "Many people attribute the sad condition of Russian society to those reaction-ary designs which dominated the last half of the preceding reign and seemed to lead to a mutilation of the reforms (of the 'sixties). This re-proach shows only an extremely superficial understanding of the situa-tion."

In Chicherin's view, the cause lay much deeper; it was the result of the speed with which the reforms of the 1860s had been realized. Chi-cherin tried to prove this proposition by citing the examples of two other countries, particularly that of France. "Every society, suddenly thrown out of its usual rut and forced to operate under completely new conditions, loses its equilibrium and wanders for a time without direc-tion."[61] In Chicherin's opinion, this led to intellectual uncertainty. The second section of his project was devoted to criticism of the liberal pro-gram. He thought that the appropriate "medicine" was not the establish-ment of a free press, which had given birth to the "Chernyshevskys, Dobroliubovs, and Pisarevs," not satisfaction of student demands, not the return of political exiles, the abolition of emergency measures, or the reestablishment of legal order. Chicherin even spoke against the abo-lition of emergency laws; true, he also rejected administrative arbitrari-ness, and complimented Loris-Melikov. He spoke of gratitude "to that statesman, who, looking more soberly at things, had found it necessary to show more caution, more humanity, and more indulgence toward our lost young people."[62]

Chicherin also rejected the need for administrative reform as well as measures to improve the peasantry's position. In his opinion, no increase in allotment size through resettlement, no tax relief, no equalization of duties could improve the situation in the countryside. In his conception, the peasant question did not even exist. It was nothing more than a myth, "created by the imaginations of Petersburg liberals, and not without significant socialist influence." He believed that the causes of peasant poverty were the poor cultivation of the soil, the exploitative organization of farming, drunkenness and family divisions. The main causes were the existence of communes and the mutual responsibility rule. These reasons, with the exception of the latter, typically were cited by certain privileged intellectuals who supposed that peasant poverty was not a result of feudal vestiges in the economy, particularly of gentry landholding, but rather a result "of laziness and drunkenness."

Next Chicherin turned to the problem of political reforms. Could one now insist on "the completion of the structure [of Alexander II's reforms] ?" "At present only the adherents of nihilism, or those who are in no condition to think or understand, can talk about finishing the structure. Now any limitation of authority would be fatal."[63] Chicherin then asserted that the first order of business was to fight against socialism, "the evil of the day." He said that the fight was easier in Russia than abroad, since Russian socialism had not spread among the masses. Chicherin emphasized that the government should fight decisively against socialism using any means. "Any weakening would be fatal: any pretension to adhere to legal means would be a sign of weakness."

Thus Chicherin advocated a pitiless attack against socialism, regardless of legal practice. Yet repressive measures alone were insufficient; according to him, it was necessary to arouse "healthy elements and to restrain those who abet destructive forces." By involvement of healthy elements Chicherin did not allude to the creation of a parliament since, in his opinion, the Russian people were not ready for it. He had other, more modest things in mind. "This goal could be attained by adding delegates from the nobility and the zemstvo to the State Council. Of course, such an institution would be inadequate for constitutional government, but through it the Russian people will acquire what they need."

The rest of the memorandum was devoted to the elaboration of this position. According to Chicherin, there should be one noble representative and two zemstvo delegates from each province. He thought that this would satisfy both conservatives and liberals. For the former, this move would consolidate "conservative forces" in the State Council, and give them a majority; for the latter, a summons of delegates would be "an expression of nascent political freedom."[64] Chicherin also noted that merely to invite experts to the State Council, but not to give them the right to vote in it, would satisfy no one. In conclusion, Chicherin asserted that "Russia was fated to set out on the constitutional path,"[65] but this would occur only when the sovereign decided that a constitution was essential.

Chicherin's project was contradictory in content. The project's basic recommendation was to apply all means available to the fight against the revolutionary movement, regardless of legal standards. On one hand the author rejected the liberal social and economic reform program; on the other he criticized the commune and the mutual responsibility rule— that is, he showed himself to be a partisan of capitalism in agriculture. While he opposed Western European political forms and any reduction in autocratic power, Chicherin also went farther than Loris-Melikov in his desire to involve elected representatives in the State Council. He proposed to add over 100 new members to that legislative-consultative body. He discussed an attempt to consolidate conservative forces in the State Council, and to create thereby a kind of right-wing opposition. The fact that Chicherin forwarded his project to Alexander III through Pobedonostsev reflected his sympathy for conservative elements. All this suggests that under the influence of the revolutionary movement Chicherin moved from a modest liberalism to liberal-conservatism.

Let us turn to the ideas of L.D. Gradovsky, a staff member on the liberal *Golos*. His project, sent to Loris-Melikov, is a brilliant illustration of the confusion among liberals after 1 March. Basically, Gradovsky advocated a central investigative commission to study the causes of the growing revolutionary movement. He did not propose a concrete program. In his opinion, neither repression nor partial reforms could achieve desirable results. "The government must study the causes of the trouble before it can take decisive steps in either direction. This study must be done now, since time is short, and disaster approaches from all quarters. It approaches from the revolutionary party. . . . It approaches from the people, who do not comprehend the true reasons for the trouble, but understand it in their own way, blaming everything on the upper classes and preparing to eradicate these classes. What will happen when both currents are combined? What will happen if this *Pugachevshchina* begins?"[66]

Let us briefly examine a number of projects submitted by spokesmen for aristocratic circles. The first among them was A.A. Bobrinsky's proposal, dated 10 March. Bobrinsky basically ruled out any concessions, while advocating some sort of representation. Bobrinsky tried to prove that repression alone could not accomplish anything. "In my opinion, the time has come when Russia must be involved in consultation. The historical issue of what kind of representation is needed must now be answered."[67] The main problem with which elected representatives would deal was the struggle against sedition. "To summon the whole country to fight against the regicides is not a concession. To make the best people responsible for revenging the disgrace and scar of 1 March is not a weakness."[68] Bobrinsky did not define what forms of representation he had in mind. His project argued, on one hand, the need to struggle against the revolutionary movement; on the other, Bobrinsky recognized that repression alone would solve nothing. Bobrinsky wanted to involve conservative groups in the fight against sedition, and thus to increase the government's social support.

The project of Count P.P. Shuvalov[69] was written in May 1881. This plan was more lengthy than Bobrinsky's plan. Its basic ideas may be formulated as follows: at present repression alone cannot succeed against the revolutionaries; one must involve representatives of society—zemstvo representatives—in government affairs. Shuvalov thought that these representatives should be added to the State Council. Like Chicherin he rejected an invitation to experts on particular issues. In contrast to the first Shuvalov project, studied earlier in this book, the May plan did not refer to a bicameral system of representation. However, the original plan dealt with the introduction of representative government abstractly, while the second was more specific.[70]

Despite their differences, all these projects had much in common. First, they all reflected the anxiety and confusion produced in high government circles by the assassination of Alexander II. Secondly, they raised the problem of how to involve representatives of society—specifically, zemstvo representatives—in national government, and above all in the fight against the revolutionary movement.

As noted earlier, several hours before his death Alexander II summoned Valuev and asked him to review the planned announcement about convocation of the temporary preparatory commissions in Petersburg and the subsequent discussion of their decisions in a special commission with zemstvo and municipal representatives. Valuev had approved the announcement and set a meeting of the Council of Ministers on 4 March. Naturally the assassination upset these plans.

On 6 March Loris-Melikov gave Alexander III an official memorandum calling for a meeting of the Council of Ministers. Simultaneously he drew up a new draft announcement. This new project differed from its predecessor. The second variant had a rather briefer introduction, and it did not refer at all to the activity of the Supreme Administrative Commission. There were no changes in the body of the announcement.[71] The final section of the project was rewritten. It referred to the assassination, to "universal mourning," and to the firm resolve of the new emperor "to execute precisely his father's will." "Based on this decision, His Imperial Majesty deigns to order the precise execution of the sacred will of his sovereign father . . . . His Majesty finds it advantageous to instruct the Minister of Internal Affairs that the promulgation of His Majesty's commands on this subject will be the same as that determined by the deceased emperor, Alexander II."[72] Alexander III approved this new draft without setting a date for the Council of Ministers to meet.[73] It would seem that the young tsar again had demonstrated his favorable attitude toward Loris-Melikov's project "constitution," a plan he originally had approved in February at a Special Committee session.

However, this was not actually so. Alexander III always had opposed any kind of plan to involve public figures in decision-making, since he viewed this as a threat to the autocracy. The emperor's closest advisor, the Supreme-Procurator of the Synod, had oriented him in this anti-constitutional direction. On 6 March Pobedonostsev wrote Alexander III a very long letter in which he explained his own political ideas in detail. "If they sing to You the old sirens' song that there is no need to worry, that You should continue in the liberal course, that You must bow before so-called public opinion—for God's sake, Your Majesty, don't believe them; don't listen. This would be disaster, disaster for You and for Russia. This is as clear to me as the day. This will not make you safer, rather it will increase Your danger. The mindless malefactors who killed Your father will not be satisfied by any concessions, they will become merely more cruel. Once the evil seed has been sown, one cannot destroy it except by iron and blood."

He then spoke about the wrath and awakening of the people (in the reactionary sense). According to Pobedonostsev, the people suspected treachery, and accused the slain emperor's close advisors of it. Therefore, these advisors could not be left at their posts. "Pardon my frankness. Do not leave Loris-Melikov. I do not trust him. He is a trickster and may still play his *double game*. If You surrender Yourself into his hands, he will lead You and Russia to disaster. He only knows how to introduce liberal projects and conduct intrigues. He is not a Russian patriot. For God's sake, Your Majesty, watch out that he does not win Your favor, and don't waste time."[74] Pobedonostsev recommended that the young tsar choose the reactionary path firmly and unequivocally, and not yield to the entreaties of the Minister of Internal Affairs.

Pobedonostsev was not alone in his reactionary plans. He found support among members of the imperial family. In a letter to Tiutcheva on 6 March he wrote: "I left the church with Sergei and Pavel [the tsar's brothers] who had just arrived[75] depressed, confused, and fearful . . . . Sergei told me that he was horrified by what Loris-Melikov had done and planned to do . . . . and told me that His Majesty might go along with Loris-Melikov."[76]

The Emperor Wilhelm I, an uncle of Alexander III, also gave some advice to his nephew. In contrast to Pobedonostsev and others, Wilhelm did not deny the advantages of summoning popular representatives; he did advise extreme caution. He did not advocate the introduction of universal suffrage, nor that parliament be given the actual power to rule the state. Simultaneously Wilhelm I warned against unlimited freedom of the press, and thought it possible merely to create religious equality.[77]

On 7 March Alexander III decided to call the Council of Ministers to discuss Loris-Melikov's proposals on the next day—Sunday. Many accounts of this meeting have been preserved, so that one can reconstruct its course rather precisely.[78] The meeting commenced at 2:15 P.M., and lasted until 4:30. There were 24 persons present: the emperor, Grand Dukes Konstantin and Mikhail Nikolaevich, Vladimir Alexandrovich, Chairman of the Committee of Ministers Valuev, Ministers Loris-Melikov, Miliutin, Saburov, Adlerberg, Posiet, Liven, A.A. Abaza, Nabokov, Makov, Supreme-Procurator of the Synod Pobedonostsev, head of the Second Section of His Majesty's Chancellery, Urusov, State Counsellor Solsky, head of the Naval Ministry, Peshchurov, Assistant Minister of Foreign Affairs Giers, members of the State Council Count Baranov, Count Stroganov, Mansurov, Prince Oldenburgsky, and Peretts.[79]

Alexander III opened the meeting, briefly summarizing the history of the issue. He ended his remarks with the following words: "I give you advance notice that the question has not been decided yet, since my deceased father also wanted the Council of Ministers to examine these proposals before their final confirmation."[80] This statement gave the participants an open field for discussion. Then the tsar proposed that Loris-Melikov read through his proposals—that is, the memorandum of 28 January, and also both drafts of the governmental communiqué (written before and after 1 March). During the reading of the memorandum, which summarized the successes achieved by concessions,

Alexander III interrupted Loris-Melikov, saying: "Apparently we got lost." Loris-Melikov told Bilbasov that the reading of these documents lasted more than an hour.

Count Stroganov opened the debate. Addressing Alexander III, he said: "The measures that have been proposed are in my opinion not only untimely, given the current situation which demands so much of the government's attention, but harmful. This measure is harmful because its adoption means the transfer of power from the monarch, who is absolutely essential to Russia now, to the hands of various good-for-nothings, who dream not about the general welfare, but about their own personal gain." Stroganov's speech was interrupted by rejoinders from Loris-Melikov. Stroganov ended with the words: "This road leads to a constitution, which I do not desire for You (the tsar) or for Russia. . . ." At this the emperor replied: "I am also afraid that this is the first step toward a constitution."[81]

Valuev spoke next, stating that he did not share this fear. "The proposed measure is very far from a constitution. It is intended to take into account the opinions and views of people who know more than we residents of Petersburg about the true needs of the nation and of the people. . . ."[82] Valuev then addressed the history of the proposal in detail, indicating that he once had made a similar proposal, though in different form, in 1863. This time Valuev threw his full support behind Loris-Melikov's plan. Miliutin also spoke in a similar vein. "The proposal submitted to Your Majesty, in my opinion, is needed now. At the beginning of each reign the new monarch must show to the people his intentions and future course." Miliutin gave a careful analysis of the domestic policies of the preceding reign, and emphasized the need to adopt Loris-Melikov's proposals. "Your Majesty, we are not talking about a constitution. Not in the least. We propose merely to set on proper foundations that which already exists. . . . Before us there is an important legislative task at the end of the senatorial inspections. Naturally success can come only if we consider this matter from all angles—that is, not only from the chancellery's or bureaucrat's point of view. With this in mind, permit me to support whole-heartedly Count Loris-Melikov's proposals."[83]

After Miliutin the Minister of Post and Telegraph, Makov, an opponent of Loris-Melikov, spoke. He said that Loris-Melikov's plan had been read to him for the first time only now, so that he had not yet analyzed it. "But so far as I understood the Minister of Internal Affair's speech, its basic idea is limitation of the autocracy. I declare frankly that I am irreconcilably opposed to such limitation. It would lead Russia to disaster. Besides, I am bound in conscience to say that now is not the time to be studying plans to limit power and to change our system of government."[84] Abaza followed, and spent most of his time refuting Makov. Abaza concluded by noting that "Loris-Melikov's plan seems to me, as Minister of Finance, to be absolutely essential. . . . "[85] Loris-Melikov added an argument that his plan was desirable to calm down society, and that it must not be delayed.

Pobedonostsev made a very long speech. "Your Majesty, I am bound by oath and conscience to tell You what is in my heart. I find myself not only in confusion, but in despair. As in former times, before the fall of Poland, they said *'finis Polonia,'* we are also almost compelled to say *'finis Russiae.'* Thinking about the plan proposed for Your approval makes one's heart sick. The plan sounds deceitful; I will say more—it breathes deceit. . . ." Like Stroganov and Makov, Pobedonostsev argued that Loris-Melikov's plan meant the introduction of a Western European constitution. "The constitutions which exist there give rise to every injustice, every intrigue." He then developed his idea that Russia was strong because of the autocracy, symbolized by the unbreakable union of tsar and people. Pobedonostsev mercilessly censured the reforms adopted in the early 1860s, particularly the zemstvo and new judicial statutes. "And when, Your Majesty, do they propose that You found on foreign models a new parliament? Now, only a few days after that nefarious deed when on the other side of the Neva the remains of the benevolent Russian tsar, so harried during his life, are not yet interred. . . . At such a terrible time, Your Majesty, one should not think about founding a new parliament, in which new corrupting speeches will be pronounced, rather one should think about action. You must act."[86]

This speech had a stirring effect on all the participants, especially upon the tsar himself. On this point every account of the meeting agreed. According to Miliutin's diary: "Everything said by Stroganov, Makov, and Posiet was pale and insignificant in comparison with Pobedonostsev's long jesuitical speech. This was not a mere refutation of the proposals, rather a direct, wholesale rejection of everything that had been done in the last reign. He dared to call the Great Reforms of Emperor Alexander II a criminal mistake. Pobedonostsev's speech, delivered with rhetorical pathos, was animated by a vague Slavophilism; it was a denial of everything that constitutes the basis of European civilization. Many of us could not conceal our nervous annoyance at certain phrases of that fanatic reactionary."[87]

After Pobedonostsev's discourse, Abaza again took the floor and stated that the Supreme Procurator's speech was an "indictment of everything that had been done in the last quarter century." The Minister of Finance argued that the assassination of Alexander II was not the result of reforms, but the consequence of the development of socialist ideas that had arisen not only on Russian soil. In conclusion, Abaza defended past and future financial reforms, and advocated again that representatives "of the educated classes" be involved in the discussion of certain reform projects.

State Controller Solsky gave a long speech in a conciliatory tone. He said that there were not substantive disagreements between Pobedonostsev and the majority of council members, since no one wanted to limit autocratic power or introduce a constitution. "We need now neither a limitation of power nor a constitution, but a strong, energetic, unfettered executive power like that we have always had in Russia. In a word, we need the autocracy. Yet autocratic power must be used responsibly, and must be based on an awareness of real popular needs."[88] The State Controller defended Loris-Melikov. He insisted that the fears expressed by Council members were unfounded, since the government always could exercise influence over the people involved in policy discussions; he thought that these people would be of moderate persuasion and hence susceptible to the government's pressure. "Empty fears are not new to us." He concluded by returning to the remarks of Pobedonostsev, who had upset everyone by painting the situation in very dark colors and had not made a single proposal himself. "At the end of his speech Konstantin Petrovich justly observed that in times like these one must act. A plan of action has been proposed to us. If it is not a good plan, then we should replace it with another. But we cannot afford to confine ourselves to criticism and remain motionless."[89]

According to Peretts, Posiet, the Minister of Communications, gave a clever speech[90] which dismissed Loris-Melikov's plan as untimely, and asserted that the revolutionaries would mistake it for a concession. The chairman of the Department of Laws, Prince Urusov, spoke very ambiguously. On one hand he seemed to endorse Loris-Melikov's program. He emphasized that the government must "seek support in the cooperation of public representatives. . . , " by which he meant representatives of "the best people" in the nation. On the other hand, he stated that "one need not infer from the proposed project that representatives from the cities and the zemstvos are necessarily the best people."[91] Urusov recommended that the Committee of Ministers reexamine Loris-Melikov's plan.

Saburov and Nabokov also defended Loris-Melikov's plan.[92] Prince Oldenburgsky and the head of the Ministry of State Domains, Prince Liven, supported Prince Urusov's plan to refer the Melikov proposals to the Committee of Ministers. At the end of the meeting the Grand Dukes gave their opinions in response to Alexander III's prompting. Grand Duke Konstantin Nikolaevich made a long speech in support of Loris-Melikov's plan. According to Peretts, the Grand Duke joined Urusov and Oldenburgsky in recommending further study by the Committee of Ministers, since the deliberations of that day had shown "various opinions."[93] Grand Duke Vladimir Alexandrovich said that ". . .the current proposals are impossible. They must be abandoned. One must either take a step forward or a step backward. I am convinced that we must not move backward; therefore, we must take a step forward. On this we must agree. While there have been objections against Loris-Melikov's proposals, these objections have concerned details and not the basic idea of the plan."[94] Therefore, he thought it possible to reexamine the project. However, it should not be rejected. Grand Duke Mikhail Nikolaevich declined to evaluate the plan, since he said he had still not acquainted himself with it.

Before the close of the session Count Stroganov told the tsar that he would also not oppose discussion of the project in the Committee of Ministers. Prince Urusov, making his suggestion more precise, said that the project should be examined first by a small commission and then by the Committee of Ministers. The emperor agreed, proposing that Count Stroganov form such a commission. However, Stroganov refused, and no concrete decision on the calling of a commission was reached. With this the meeting ended, and Alexander III thanked everyone for participating.

The majority of the speakers—nine persons in all (Abaza, Valuev, Loris-Melikov, Miliutin, Nabokov, Solsky, Saburov, Grand Duke Konstantin Nikolaevich, and Vladimir Alexandrovich)—had defended the proposed reforms. Four persons (Stroganov, Pobedonostsev, Posiet, and Makov) had been opposed. Prince Urusov, Oldenburgsky, and Liven had not given precise opinions, and had asked for further discussion.

What was the result of this Council of Ministers' meeting? The participants were divided in their assessments. Valuev was silent and left no relevant diary entries. This would suggest that Valuev believed nothing important to have been decided. Miliutin and Peretts saw things differently. Miliutin wrote: "And so the tsar decided to reexamine the proposals of Count Loris-Melikov, first in a small committee, and later in the Committee of Ministers. This course of affairs has given us more confidence than we had after Pobedonostsev's frightening, thunderous speech. Nevertheless, we left the meeting in a depressed and irritable mood."[95] E.A. Peretts gave a similar, but more optimistic account. On 9

March he wrote in his diary: "Loris-Melikov is very unhappy over the outcome of yesterday's session. In my view, he is mistaken: things turned out very well and the goal has almost been reached. Of course, things did not come off perfectly, but how can such serious matters be decided in one meeting?"[96] Peretts then indicated that Grand Duke Konstantin Nikolaevich was pleased with the results of the meeting, and had said that Grand Duke Vladimir Alexandrovich would be appointed chairman of the commission to reexamine Loris-Melikov's plan. In fact, no decision of this kind was made. The proposal to create a new commission to consider Loris-Melikov's plan suggests a desire to delay decision for an indefinite period.

How did Alexander III view the proposals? As we have seen, he did not express his own judgments, but circumstantial evidence allows us to determine his opinion. Alexander III was opposed secretly to the proposals of Loris-Melikov. There were several factors besides the general *Weltanschauung* of the young tsar which pointed to his opposition. First, the invitation of the two most active opponents of the reform—Pobedonostsev and Stroganov—to participate in the Council of Ministers' meeting.[97] Second, the tsar's behavior during the meeting, particularly his comments (like the one in which he expressed fear that "the proposed measure is a step toward a constitution"). The fact that the meeting ended with a decision did not mean that its chairman lacked an opinion. The tsar was doubtless on the side of Pobedonostsev and Stroganov,[98] but he could not express his point of view. He was too frightened of the future. He did not have a clear view of the forces ranged against him, or of his supporters. Finally, he was terrified by the events of 1 March. These circumstances explain why, despite his opposition to Loris-Melikov's plan, he did not make a decision. Analyzing the prevailing situation, V.I. Lenin wrote: "If we speak not about what could have been, but about what actually happened, then we must cite the indisputable fact of the *wavering* of the government. Some stood for decisive battle against liberalism, and others for concessions."[99]

After the meeting of 8 March the situation remained fluid for a long time. In high government circles two opposing forces finally had crystallized: the liberal bureaucratic group—Loris-Melikov, Abaza, and Miliutin[100]—and the reactionary group headed by Pobedonostsev. At the same time it must be said that the influence of Loris-Melikov was on the wane and that of Pobedonostsev and his group on the ascendant. The Austro-Hungarian ambassador wrote in a confidential dispatch to Minister of Internal Affairs Hamerlei on 9/21 April 1881 about the position of Loris-Melikov: "Not long ago the omnipotent Count Loris-Melikov, famous for his cleverness, had enjoyed the faith of all Russia, and also of Europe; although he is still Minister of Internal Affairs, he has had the rug pulled out from under him. Everyone knows that very soon he must fall, and they turn their backs on him. He has lost authority, and this paralyzes the functioning of that vital institution, the Ministry of Internal Affairs, where nothing has been done for several weeks."[101]

Pobedonostsev's influence grew and grew. Without talking about meetings with the tsar (unfortunately, the number of his meetings with the tsar could not be determined), one sees clear signs of his new-found power. He communicated with Alexander III in writing more often than before. It should be noted that in only one letter did he touch questions directly relevant to his agency.[102] The influence of new individuals also grew quickly. Besides Baranov, who had exercised much influence over the young emperor thanks to stories about a successful war against "subversives," new faces appeared on the scene: Count N.P. Ignatiev and I.I. Vorontsov-Dashkov.

Formerly an important diplomat, and now as before an unabashed liar, Ignatiev began to play on the confusion of the tsar. Without exception, all contemporaries of every political persuasion characterized Ignatiev as an incorrigible liar, and their descriptions were absolutely accurate. In his memoirs E.M. Feoktistov wrote: "What Russian does not know about this regrettable trait of his character—the unrestrained and somehow insatiable need to lie? He lies to satisfy the demands of his own nature, as the bird sings, the dog barks; he lies at every turn without the slightest reason or need, even when it harms himself."[103] Ignatiev's nature was close in its qualities to the character of the Gogolian hero Nozdrev or Baron Munchhausen.

After the signing of the San Stefano peace treaty, Ignatiev had held a rather modest post as temporary Governor-General in Nizhny Novgorod, where he arranged provincial fairs. Finding himself in Petersburg at the beginning of the new reign, he began to acquire influence in high spheres thanks to Pobedonostsev. In a letter to Alexander III on 6 March, Pobedonostsev wrote about various bureaucrats of his acquaintance. "Your Majesty, I see and know them all, and they are worthless. Out of all the names I can suggest to you Count Nikolai Pavlovich Ignatiev. He still has sound instincts and a Russian soul, and his name is still good in the healthy part of Russian society, among the common people. Take him for now, but you will have to find someone reliable soon."[104]

Ignatiev's influence was already tangible in mid-March. On 16 March Miliutin wrote in his diary a report of a conversation with Loris-Melikov: "He [Loris-Melikov] expressed serious fears about the reactionary party, which is beginning to form around Pobedonostsev. Everyone who wants to swim with the new current is crawling to the reactionary group. Surprisingly, Count Nikolai Pavlovich Ignatiev is among them."[105] Polovtsov discussed the authority of Ignatiev in the eyes of the emperor. On 19 March he recorded Abaza's words that it had been decided to give the first vacant ministerial portfolio to Ignatiev.[106]

In my opinion, the reason that this representative of "healthy instincts" rose so fast was that his outlook coincided with that of the tsar. Among the Ignatiev papers is a memorandum, dated 12 March, in which Ignatiev presented his program of government activity. The contents of this memorandum coincided very closely with the opinions of Pobedonostsev and Alexander III. "Everyone recognizes how important is the current period: the first steps of a new reign, which has begun so unusually, have a decisive moral significance. . . . The current situation is intolerable; one must find a way out of it." Then Ignatiev argued explicitly that no concessions were permissible. "Reforms, or changes that can be interpreted as concessions prompted by the martyrdom of the tsar-liberator, are undesirable." According to Ignatiev, steps now should be taken to protect the royal family. "The influence of the government must be bolstered through the proper appointment of officials and the firm supervision of their activity."[107] Ignatiev thought it necessary: (a) to practice extreme frugality in spending; (b) besides the scheduled meetings with zemstvo representatives on financial and administrative reforms, "one must ask the zemstvo's opinion on the most crucial social question—whether the zemstvo people are willing to act more decisively concerning the fight against sedition than did the former tsarist advisors. . . . "[108] This idea amounted to a proposal to put the fight with sedition on a "popular" basis, by widespread solicitation of denunciations.

The memorandum discussed this matter directly. "The majority of the peaceful population is not disposed to have any relations with the police or to inform authorities about planned crimes or dangerous persons. One should use the present period of indignation to change this inconvenient and dangerous view of society. Obviously, to correct the danger we must change the law on informers. . . . We should create every opportunity to provide the necessary information without the informer being subject to investigation or suit. An even greater contribution can be expected from the public's own desire to preserve our governmental system . . . through the vigorous participation of citizens, through elected elders and sentries, who will guard order and observe the residents in their wards."[109] Here Ignatiev recommended the establishment of an enormous army of informers and provocateurs.

However, this was not the quintessence of Ignatiev's program. He thought that the government could be successful only if it could be rid of certain features of public life which had ruined "the fine beginnings" of Alexander II's reign. "In Petersburg there is a large Polish-Yiddish group that controls banks, the stock exchange, the legal system, much of the press, and other public agencies. By many legal and illegal means they have attained enormous influence on the bureaucracy and on the course of government business. Separate sections of this group are connected with the systematic plunder of the treasury and with sedition .... Favoring the blind imitation of Europe, these people, cleverly preserving their neutrality, very greedily have exploited the extreme actions of the terrorist groups and embezzled funds. They recommend the broadest rights to Poles and Jews, and representative institutions on the Western model. Every honest voice in the Russian land is zealously drowned out by the Polish-Yiddish cries, which assert that one should listen only to the intelligentsia and that Russian demands should be rejected as backward and unenlightened."[110]

This reactionary-chauvinistic conception, which opposed bourgeois forms of political organization to the "genuine Russian" patriarchal elements that had grown out of the seigneurial mentality of the feudal period, complemented the views of the young tsar and his ideological mentor, Pobedonostsev. In the short-term, Ignatiev recommended that the tsar travel to Moscow or its environs and convoke there editorial commissions to draft legislation on local institutions and finance. "The beginning of the reign in Moscow under the guardianship of loyal people and discussions with zemstvo representatives would leave an indelible mark on the whole new reign."[111]

Analyzing the contents of this memorandum as a whole, the following conclusions are reached. First, the whole memorandum, permeated by a reactionary-chauvinistic spirit, was directed against Loris-Melikov and his political policy. It accorded completely with the views of the reactionary group headed by Pobedonostsev. Secondly, it is not difficult to discern in the memorandum the Slavophile ideas of the Aksakov circle, which called for the resurrection of ancient forms of communication between the tsar and "the land" such as Zemsky Sobors. The question arises: why did Ignatiev write this memorandum? It seems indisputable that it was tailored to the young tsar. There is no evidence available to prove that Alexander III read the memorandum. However, there is indirect evidence that Alexander III was acquainted with Ignatiev's views. In Valuev's diary in the entry for 21 April 1881 there is the following phrase: "The tsar said about Count Ignatiev that it was

good that he is in the government because he 'is a real native Russian.' "[112] This phrase can scarcely be restricted to its literal sense. Consequently, Ignatiev was appointed Minister of State Domains on 20
March. According to Peretts, the Ignatiev appointment was recommended, ironically enough, by Loris-Melikov himself.[113]

Another rising star was Count I.I. Vorontsov-Dashkov, who had been
an intimate of Alexander III in the past. He was the head of the subcommittee to guard the tsar in the Temporary Council of the municipal
governor, and in late April he became the chief of the imperial security
entourage. This foreordained his appointment as Minister of the Imperial Court. Evaluating Vorontsov-Dashkov's position in the court, the
Austro-Hungarian ambassador wrote in a dispatch to his Minister of
Foreign Affairs on 2/21 April: "Count Vorontsov-Dashkov uses the great
personal grief of the tsar and his position as a trusted person to prepare
his road to replace Count Adlerberg; however, he will not occupy this
place for long. Count Vorontsov will be as loyal a servant to His Majesty as Count Adlerberg was to the last emperor."[114]

Such was the constellation of forces in the government in March-
April 1881. It is essential to point out that in this period Pobedonostsev
exercised the greatest influence over Alexander III.

While the role of Loris-Melikov had been reduced and his dictatorship
had ended on 1 March, it would be inaccurate to suppose that he became a minister who exercised no power or influence of any sort. As
before, Loris-Melikov *de facto* fulfilled the role of prime minister. He
still played a role in organizational realignments in the government. For
example, in late March the Ministry of Post and Telegraph and Non-
Orthodox Religions was abolished and absorbed into the Ministry of
Internal Affairs; Loris-Melikov was not without influence in this process.[115] One must not forget that the Minister of Internal Affairs possessed a serious political weapon—the perlustration of letters.

Literally within a few days the Ministers of Education and State Domains were dismissed. According to Peretts, these changes also showed
Loris-Melikov's hand.[116] However, according to a confidential letter from
Loris-Melikov to Miliutin, the initiative in the dismissal of Saburov belonged to Pobedonostsev.[117] Saburov was in any event a man of very
limited ability, but he had been compromised when a student, Papy
Podbelsky had struck him publicly in the Petersburg University auditorium.[118] Miliutin reported Loris-Melikov as saying that Alexander III
wanted to appoint Delianov Minister of Education on Pobedonostsev's
recommendation, but that Loris-Melikov had dissuaded the tsar. Baron

Nikolai was named to replace Saburov; Pobedonostsev also had mentioned the baron's name to the tsar.[119] In accordance with the tsar's directive, Loris-Melikov informed Saburov about the "imperial" decision that he should resign, contacted the head of the First Section of His Majesty's Chancellery to prepare a directive to this effect, and an announcement of Baron Nikolai's appointment. These actions went beyond the normal jurisdiction of the Minister of Internal Affairs.

At the recommendation of Loris-Melikov in early April the Procurator of the Petersburg Judiciary, V.K. Plehve, was named to replace Baron Velio as director of the Department of State Police. In his recommendation the Minister of Internal Affairs wrote: "The service record and moral qualities of V.K. Plehve serve as sufficient assurance that he will bring to his new post the same energy and rationality that characterized his service in the procuracy."[120] Loris-Melikov then noted that Kakhanov and Chicherin approved Plehve's candidacy. As I noted earlier, Loris-Melikov also played a role in Ignatiev's appointment as Minister of State Domains.[121]

Finally, there were other changes in the government which had nothing to do with Loris-Melikov's maneuvers, but can be attributed to his opponents' influence. The best example was the retirement of Grand Duke Konstantin Nikolaevich from the State Council chairmanship and other positions. Moreover, Loris-Melikov's protégé N.S. Abaza, the head of the Main Press Administration, was dismissed and replaced by Prince P.P. Viazemsky. These personnel changes in the upper bureaucracy occurred in the first weeks after Alexander III's succession to the throne.

Even after 1 March Loris-Melikov played a definite role in government appointments, although this role was less significant that it had been earlier. The fact that orders on changes and appointments of ministers were passed on through Loris-Melikov demonstrates that he was seen as something more than a mere Minister of Internal Affairs. The tsar gave him ticklish assignments which were altogether outside his jurisdiction. For example, in early April Alexander III asked him to speak with Yurievskaia about leaving the Winter Palace, and also about the three million rubles given to her by Alexander II—money that she had decided to place in the State Bank in the names of her children.[122] Loris-Melikov did not retain definite influence and power because Alexander III liked him. Loris-Melikov was rather the beneficiary of the delaying tactics that the young tsar was forced to pursue in his fear and confusion.

The uncertainty of the future also conditioned the behavior of the contending bureaucratic circles. On 16 March Miliutin wrote in his diary: "Having discussed the current situation in absolute secrecy, Loris-Melikov and I have decided that we should both adopt a waiting posture until it becomes clear which of the two contrary paths the emperor will choose."[123] Miliutin then indicated that in the event of victory by Pobedonostsev's party, neither he nor Loris-Melikov would remain in the government.[124] Despite the political uncertainties, Loris-Melikov did not deviate from the course which he had set in the 28 January memorandum, and had defended on 8 March.

In this connection there was an important conversation between Loris-Melikov and Polovtsov, recorded by the latter in his diary. The conversation took place on 26 March, and according to Polovtsov, was prolonged. Summarizing Loris-Melikov's ideas, he wrote: "Above all, there should be a unified ministry, but such a ministry can do nothing without elected representatives. Taking a blank sheet of paper, Loris made this note:

Unified Ministry

1. assertion of authority
2. reform of the schools
3. law on the press
4. reduction of redemption payments
5. reform of the tax system
6. elected officials.[125]

The ministers and the elected officials must find some way to resolve the five issues which are listed in order of importance."[126]

Thus, the first priority was to form a unified ministry. However, the tsar took no steps, choosing to leave his future political course undefined. In late March Pobedonostsev had an audience with Alexander III at Gatchina and conducted a rather frank conversation with him. "I am accustomed to speak the truth to You, and so I consider it my duty to inform Your Majesty that our enemies have a program and a definite plan of action, but the government has nothing similar .... It is essential that the people gathered around You, Your Highness, be people agreed in their views; people who could set into action a prepared plan, if You should grant approval." In response, the young emperor said nothing of substance. He said only that up to now the ministers had not been worth consulting. "In summary," wrote Pobedonostsev, "this conversation had a very disheartening effect on me .... It is obvious that he [the tsar] is lost in indecision ...."[127]

The sole step taken toward realization of Loris-Melikov's program was discussion of the plan to reduce redemption payments. Minister of Finance Abaza introduced this issue in the State Council in late March, and the Main Committee on the Improvement of Agriculture had discussed it as early as November 1880. At this session Abaza had said that it was necessary to lower redemption payments in the non-black-soil provinces where the payments "do not correspond at all in their magnitude to the insignificant value of land."[128] The problem was especially pronounced in Smolensk, Pskov, and in certain districts of Vladimir, Tambov, and Chernigov provinces. The Minister of Finance said that the problem was that obligations were determined "not only by reference to land prices, but also take into account the private income of the peasant; still, the difference between the payment and the actual value of the land has become greater with each year."[129]

The question had not been resolved by the Main Committee, and in early 1881 Abaza had created a special subcommittee under the chairmanship of Senator K.I. Domontovich to examine it.[130] In February and March the subcommittee had investigated carefully the areas where payments would have to be lowered, and tried to decide the size of reductions. The subcommittee's plan would have affected 13 provinces: Vladimir, Vologda, Kaluga, Kostroma, Pskov, Mogilev, Moscow, Novgorod, Olonets, Petersburg, Smolensk, Tver, Yaroslavl, and in the non-blacksoil regions of Viatka, Kazan, Nizhny Novgorod, Orel, Penza, Perm, Riazan, Tambov, Tula, and Chernigov. Reductions of 40 to 56 percent would apply in Olonets, Smolensk, Novgorod, Chernigov, Moscow, Petersburg, and Tver; reductions of 21 to 23 percent would apply in Kazan, Yaroslavl, Vologda, and Perm. In individual districts the reductions could be still greater. Thus, in Varnavinsky district in Novgorod the reductions were from 60 to 65 percent. In other districts (Rybinsky in Iaroslavl and Bolkhovsky in Orel) the reductions were only 7.5 to 10 percent. The average drop in payments was 35 percent.[131]

On 30 March Abaza raised this issue in the State Council. In his presentation the Minister of Finance announced that he agreed with the subcommittee's views. He also touched the question of obligatory redemption of peasant allotments in non-blacksoil areas. "Turning to the question of obligatory redemption of peasant allotments in non-blacksoil areas, the Minister of Finance believes that he should explain that the need for this measure is related to the proposed reduction of redemption payments. To leave temporarily-obligated peasants, who in 1881 number 837,500 souls, with high quitrent payments and redemption obligations two or three times higher than the new projected levels for peasant proprietors surrounding their settlements, would lead to misunderstandings and dissension among the obligated peasants."

In Abaza's opinion there was only one solution that could avoid this problem: to accomplish the redemption of temporarily-obligated peasant allotments in the shortest possible time—that is, before 1 January 1883.

The minister also proposed to extend this measure to those temporarily-obligated peasants "who live on valuable allotments in districts where the soil quality is varied and in the vicinity of peasants who work low-quality non-blacksoil land and whose redemption payments have been reduced. This would avoid misunderstanding on their part in case they were left with obligations to gentry landowners."[132] With relation to peasants in blacksoil provinces, Abaza also thought it necessary to raise the issue of obligatory redemption, setting the exact period of time as no later than five years—that is, 1886. Thus, Abaza's plan was designed to bring redemption payments into line with land prices, and to transfer peasants to obligatory redemption. Its clear purpose was to reduce feudal vestiges in the economy.

Loris-Melikov approved the Minister of Finance's proposal, and stressed its great political impact. "Local officials report that among the people there are already absurd, perhaps even deliberately seditious rumors circulating to the effect that rights granted during the last reign are to be taken away. It is essential to dampen this speculation and strengthen popular confidence in the continuation of monarchical interest in the public welfare."[133]

Loris-Melikov also proposed a number of substantive additions. First, he thought that redemption payments also should be reduced in five steppe provinces (Orenburg, Ufa, Samara, Astrakhan, and Stavropol). Second, he thought that the change to mandatory redemption for all temporarily-obligated peasants should be introduced simultaneously across the nation. Loris-Melikov made several other proposals as well. They involved providing poor peasants with additional acreage (by giving credit toward purchase of land, rents of treasury-owned land, and organization of peasant resettlement), and easing peasant departures from the commune. Loris-Melikov also called for new legislation on the following issues: (a) to allow agricultural societies to give up ownership of land that they had redeemed and to transfer it to the treasury; (b) to reduce or to abolish the mutual responsibility burden; (c) to abolish rules restricting peasant departures from the commune.[134]

In analyzing Loris-Melikov's additions to the Abaza plan, we see that they constituted an attempt to facilitate the growth of capitalism in the countryside. These proposals corresponded to the liberal program, which was designed to make certain improvements in the peasantry's position.[135] In fact, the proposals certainly would have been a step forward down the path of bourgeois agrarian development, even though gentry landownership would not have been assailed.

On 6, 7, and 20 April Abaza's report was discussed at joint sessions of the Department of Laws and State Economy and the Main Committee on the Improvement of Agriculture. The joint committee approved Abaza's plan together with Loris-Melikov's additions on the introduction of mandatory redemption throughout Russia after 1 January 1883. Moreover, it was found necessary to discuss and implement the other proposals of the Minister of Internal Affairs. For example, the joint committee recommended that the Ministries of Internal Affairs and Finance work with other agencies and submit to the State Council "as soon as possible" plans on the following issues: (1) how to simplify current regulations on peasant departures from communes, and to make it easier for a peasant to join a commune or to transfer from one commune to another; (2) to abolish restrictions on peasant exit from communes; (3) to abolish or diminish the mutual responsibility burden without violating the bases of communal ownership, where it exists; (4) to allow rural societies to surrender land that they had redeemed and give it to the treasury; (5) to simplify bureaucratic procedure and overcome restrictions on the completion of deeds in peasant land purchases; (6) to define conditions when unoccupied treasury-owned land might be given to land-poor peasants, and to facilitate peasant settlement on treasury-owned land; (7) to facilitate credit arrangements for peasant land purchases."[136]

All of Loris-Melikov's emendations were accepted in their entirety. Only one point, which concerned the reduction or abolition of mutual responsibility, was slightly altered: a phrase was added about the need to preserve "the foundations of communal ownership." According to Peretts' diary, Loris-Melikov emphasized, as Abaza had earlier, the political significance of reduced redemption payments. The Minister of Internal Affairs said that it would be "desirable to publicize the proposed statute as soon as possible, since in various places—in Bezhetsky and Vesiegonsky districts in Tver—agitators are spreading rumors among the peasants that the new tsar will enserf everybody again at the instigation of the gentry."[137] He also said that already there had been cases of peasant assaults on gentry landowners.

On 27 April a Plenary Session of the State Council considered reduction of redemption payments. None of the other proposals approved in the earlier joint committee meetings aroused any controversy, except the secondary issue of the magnitude of the reduction. On this question the former Minister of Internal Affairs, A.E. Timashev, said that gentry landowners should receive redemption payments equivalent to the quitrent,[138] since otherwise the principle of private property would be violated. "Let posterity not say that no one in the State Council spoke in defense of property. . . ."[139] However, Timashev's suggestion was not adopted. Timashev also ardently defended the abolition of the mutual responsibility rule, and advocated liquidation of the communal system. "What is communal cultivation of land? It is the immovable obstacle to any progress toward the peasants' material welfare. . . . Communal ownership is an obstacle to proper forms of cultivation."[140]

The Plenary Session confirmed the slate of proposals without change. However, the impression that matters were easily disposed of is illusory. In fact, there was an influential group, consisting of Pobedonostsev, Ignatiev, and Ostrovsky, that opposed the Abaza plan. It is clear from the Ignatiev-Pobedonostsev correspondence that Pobedonostsev had intended to speak at the Plenary Session and present his own opinion. Ignatiev and Ostrovsky associated themselves with Pobedonostsev. Yet on 27 April Pobedonostsev was absent from the Plenary Session since he had gone to see the tsar at Gatchina. On that same day Ignatiev wrote to Pobedonostsev: "The business was ruined by your absence and by Timashev's speech. . . . It disappeared under water. It was announced that you wished to speak, and the chairman loudly called you, and asked why you had not shown up. It seemed to me that nothing ought to stop you from submitting your opinion in writing, and having it read into the journal for His Majesty's benefit. If you do decide to do this, then I shall gladly send on your memorandum to be incorporated into the journal.[141] Ostrovsky, Stroganov, and I waited in vain for a chance to speak."[142] Obviously, Pobedonostsev was the leader of the opposition, and he was supposed to begin the attack, but his unavoidable absence[143] ruined the opposition's plans.

In a visit to Peretts on 28 April Pobedonostsev explained that his proposal would have been "to adopt mandatory redemption now, and the main elements of the reduced-redemption plan later. The latter issue might be referred to the ministries for further consideration by the experts."[144]

The period of infighting between the two government groups may be subdivided into two stages: the first from the beginning of March until the beginning of April, and the second from the beginning of April until the end of that month. The first period was characterized by a complete rupture in relations between members of the two groups, starting with the meeting on 8 March. The second period showed evidence of seeming reconciliation which was most clearly expressed at the meeting of 21 April.

After 8 March relations were cut off between Loris-Melikov, Abaza, and Miliutin on the one hand, and Pobedonostsev on the other.[145]

Analyzing the relationship, Peretts wrote in his diary: "Because of the 8 March meeting, Loris and Abaza will not shake hands with Pobedonostsev and Makov and will barely speak with them. In my opinion, they are wrong. One should not consider one's potential adversaries to be enemies. One might not sympathize with their views, or love them, but it is necessary to observe the rules of courtesy and propriety!"[146] Peretts stood closer in his politics to Loris-Melikov and Abaza than he did to Pobedonostsev. His diary entry and a letter from the Supreme Procurator of the Synod to Loris-Melikov suggest that the liberals were the ones who initiated the break in relations between the two groups.

In the first half of April the situation changed somewhat. Loris-Melikov met with Pobedonostsev and had a long talk with him. It is hard to say who initiated this meeting, since each party tried to attribute the initiative to the other. Miliutin said that Pobedonostsev took the first step. "Despite his influence at court, Pobedonostsev senses the awkwardness of his position; he came to Loris-Melikov with explanations, and assured him that his role in the 8 March meeting had been misinterpreted."[147]

Pobedonostsev remembered differently. In a letter to Tiutcheva on 10 April in which he analyzed his relationship to the "triumvirate," Pobedonostsev wrote: "Believe me, dear one, I have the feeling that I am living with mad men. And they think I am an idiot. Since 8 March Loris-Melikov, Abaza, and Miliutin will not speak to me, they avoid me like the plague. I hear their opinions that it is impossible to talk to me, that I am a man not of the nineteenth, but of the sixteenth century. It is an impossible situation. However, with Loris-Melikov the silence was broken on Wednesday.[148] Baranov was a factor; he came to me and said that Loris implored me to see him and offer an explanation. I talked with Loris all evening and naturally he left the same man, and so did I. Nevertheless, ministers should somehow confer together about the situation and what is to be done." Then Pobedonostsev reported that Alexander III had decided to summon all the ministers on Tuesday[149] "so that we can analyze our misunderstandings and disagreements in his presence and establish a common policy."[150] In the final analysis, it was of little import who had started the process of reconciliation, particularly since that step was influenced by circumstances, which suggested to both sides the need to act. Probably the issue of ministerial cooperation was raised by the tsar himself, who gradually was losing the fear that had gripped him the whole month of March.[151] This was confirmed by Loris-Melikov's memorandum to the tsar in which the former explained the aims of the government. In the beginning of the memorandum, dated 12 April, Loris-Melikov discussed the tsar's desire "to summon quickly a special conference to establish the government's future program, and to decide what should be done and how to do it."[152]

Let us examine this extremely interesting memorandum. It dealt with almost the same issues raised in the memorandum of 28 January, and listed by Loris-Melikov in his conversation with Polovtsov in March. However, here the old issues were presented in more detail, and several new issues were raised as well. Turning to the government's aims, Loris-Melikov mentioned nine points relevant to various facets of state administration. The first, second, and sixth points dealt with administrative reforms. In the first, Loris-Melikov said that in order to create "a strong and durable authority" at the local level, the government should unify the police and gendarmes in the provinces under the governor's control. He would have made junior officers in the gendarmes into village police sergeants.

The second point concerned reform of local administration. To simplify and make less expensive the local apparatus, Loris-Melikov proposed "to coordinate, when possible, the actions of various administrative agencies and to eliminate conflicts between them." He advocated reduction in the number of bureaucratic offices and hence of bureaucrats, and "to strengthen the authority of local administration for the final decision of ordinary current business. . . ."[153] He also thought it necessary to define the relationship of administrative agencies to judicial and public organizations. The sixth point called for reexamination of the Statute of 27 June 1874 on the organization of institutions governing peasants, and it recommended reform "of peasant communal government." Point five also fell in this group of questions, since it dealt with the zemstvo and municipal statutes. Loris-Melikov wanted "to create among various classes of the population a more equitable method of government in zemstvo and municipal institutions and to guarantee a proper system of election." He then advocated an extension of the activity of these institutions "in local economic affairs," and recommended definition of zemstvo and municipal relationships with administrative agencies.[154]

Three points—the seventh, eighth, and ninth—dealt with the peasantry. The first was entitled: "Measures to Prevent the Economic Dislocation of the Peasants." It contained proposals which were in complete accord with Loris-Melikov's plan presented earlier in his additions to the Abaza memorandum on reduction of redemption payments. The eighth point dealt with the national food supply. It proposed to replenish Russia's depleted food reserves in order to avoid huge monetary expenditures like that which had occurred in 1880 and 1881. Point nine discussed reform of the taxation and passport systems. "To abolish the head tax and reexamine its connection with the passport system. To organize new taxes on all classes and hence on a more equitable basis."[155]

Two points—the third and fourth—dealt with education and the press. Point three presented a detailed reform program for higher as well as elementary and secondary schools. All of the proposals for reform were intended to reinforce political stability. For example, the memorandum would have given universities a system "that will satisfy scholarly and pedagogical purposes, but also serve the interests of the social order." The plan discussed financial assistance for students, and the need for a more equal distribution of students among the university campuses "to prevent the unnecessary crowding of students in the capital." In secondary education, the gymnasium curriculum would be reexamined to bring it into conformity with the abilities of students "in order to decrease the number of dropouts who are so harmful to themselves and society." (The target of criticism was the classical system which Loris-Melikov resolutely opposed). Convinced that the existing system of secondary education was "too burdensome for poor parents," Loris-Melikov advocated a new type of school that would require six to seven years and provide finished professional training. The memorandum discussed the development of literary skills and the preparation of teachers to promote it. Loris-Melikov insisted that elementary education be broadened significantly. Point three concluded by mentioning the advantages of subordinating schools to one agency, and the need to define the relationship of public organizations (zemstvo and municipal agencies) to the schools.

The fourth point addressed "legal regulation of the press." Here it was proposed to solve "immediately and with finality" the problem of the press and to end the existing "unsatisfactory system." Loris-Melikov wanted to define by law the rights and responsibilities of the press, "to guarantee it a voice and the right of level-headed discussion of public issues, but to prevent unnecessary arousal of passions and the slander of personalities that is practiced so wantonly by certain publications."[156] With a small exception, all these aims were objectively bourgeois in character, and their realization would have been another step in the transformation of Russia into a bourgeois monarchy.

Having described the tasks that stood before the government, Loris-Melikov wrote the second part of his memorandum: "Preconditions for the Execution of the Government's Agenda." According to the Minister of Internal Affairs, there were two preconditions: first, "unity of government and unity of policy;" second, "involvement of public representatives in the preparation and execution of reforms. . . ." Speaking about the first precondition, Loris-Melikov pointed to the absence of unity in the actions of individual ministers, and in the government's agenda. "Given the contradictions of the central government, it is impossible to hope to establish order at the local level, and the split between ministers serves as fuel for the anti-government opposition." He therefore called for a united government. "The ministers must agree on the most crucial issues and establish a common program in domestic politics, a program binding on each of them. A minister has the right to his private convictions, but deviation from the program that might complicate the government's functioning cannot be permitted." In important cases, questions could be examined by the Council of Ministers, which had the right to demand explanations from agency heads. Loris-Melikov stressed that this program needed the confirmation of the tsar, who would introduce necessary changes or replace "ministers with new men, who also share the government's goals."[157]

The second precondition was involvement of "elected representatives of public institutions" in the preparation of reforms. Loris-Melikov noted that not all issues required the participation of these elected representatives. For example, reforms of the police and press could be discussed without them, and other questions would demand only "limited" participation. "I will not decide in advance the questions to be discussed by public representatives, nor the extent and form of their participation. This must be a part of the general political program, and must be set by His Majesty; it is possible to say now that the central bureaucracy will not be able to deal with many vital issues, particularly economic ones, without consultation and the participation of people who know more intimately national needs and variations in local conditions."[158] Then Loris-Melikov enumerated issues that, thanks to a lack of representative participation, had not been resolved for many years (passports, peasant resettlement).

Loris-Melikov stressed that the involvement of public representatives in no way limited the principle of autocracy, since representatives would have advisory powers only. Speaking of the current system, he noted that many measures were adopted under the pressure of public opinion (expressed in newspapers, in memoranda from private citizens, and in decisions of individual zemstvo assemblies). However, such opinions were "isolated and accidental," and the laws adopted under their influence were not always beneficial. "A proper recognition of public representatives would give the government the chance before publication of a law to test actual public opinion and extract from it important changes in legislation; society would be safe from legislative surprises, and by satisfying its ambition for public service, it would be stimulated to support the government and to assume moral responsibility for published laws."

The memorandum concluded by recommending the extensive involvement of public institutions in implementation of certain local reforms, such as the organization of resettlement, of credit, and other peasant-oriented measures. In Loris-Melikov's opinion, this would make possible a reduction of local bureaucracies, and might "give society joint responsibility with the government for the course of reforms."[159]

Such was the content of the 12 April memorandum. It included a more detailed program of reforms than earlier memoranda, and mentioned reorganization of police agencies in the provinces for the first time. It was the first really explicit comment on the need for government unity. Obviously the experience of the past one and one-half months, so full of political infighting, made this comment necessary. The issue of public representation was presented in more general terms. However, the need for elections was stressed more categorically than before.[160] On the whole, the 12 April memorandum was a further elaboration of Loris-Melikov's political program.[161] It must be reemphasized that Loris-Melikov's plans did not infringe upon the principle of autocracy, although their realization would have been a progressive step and, as V.I. Lenin indicated, might have been a step toward constitutional reforms. Both the reorganization of educational institutions and the proposed peasant reforms were part of a bourgeois program and would have accelerated the development of capitalism. Despite the circumstances which had changed so drastically after 1 March, Loris-Melikov was still trying to secure adoption of his program.

Loris-Melikov did not present his memorandum to the tsar secretly. According to Peretts' diary on 16 April: "In the city there are rumors that Loris-Melikov has raised the question of the need for government unity. While he does not propose to appoint ministers of only one political persuasion, . . . he does have in mind at least consultation among ministers before any important measures are proposed to the tsar."[162] Independently of this, early in April rumors circulated in Petersburg concerning publication of a manifesto on constitutional reforms. Pobedonostsev informed Alexander III about this in a letter on 23 April: "Many people were convinced on the fifteenth and then on the seventeenth of the month that something unusual was happening. The rumors about representation cropped up again . . . ."[163]

Pobedonostsev's information was not just a pretext designed to frighten the tsar. The Austro-Hungarian ambassador mentioned the rumor in a despatch on 9/21 April: "The last few days everyone has been saying that on Easter, which falls this Sunday [12 April], there should be a manifesto to the Russian people in which the tsar will promise solemnly immediate reforms in administration and other fields."[164]

We do not know how Alexander III reacted to Loris-Melikov's memorandum, but obviously the decision to convene the ministers on 21 April was a direct result of the memorandum. At any rate, on 17 April Loris-Melikov conveyed to Miliutin Alexander III's decision on the meeting and its participants. The participants would be Loris-Melikov, Abaza, Miliutin, Ignatiev, Nikolai, Pobedonostsev, and Grand Duke Vladimir Alexandrovich. According to Miliutin, the tsar flatly refused Loris-Melikov's request to invite Valuev and Urusov.[165] "The proposed meeting was prompted by very serious talks between the tsar and Loris-Melikov in which the latter explained the need to end the current uncertainty and secrecy in one way or another."[166] Pobedonostsev, who had a long conversation with Loris-Melikov on the subject, also insisted on the meeting. On 15 April Pobedonostsev wrote to the tsar: "Yesterday I spent the whole evening talking to Loris-Melikov, and I am happy that I could finally speak with him. Today he will again inform Your Majesty of the need to determine the tenets that will guide the new government agenda."[167]

Let us turn to the composition of the meeting. Who influenced the tsar in this case? One cannot give an exhaustive reply to this question. However, it is clear that Pobedonostsev was involved. At least Minister of Justice Nabokov was invited at Pobedonostsev's insistence. He requested this invitation in a letter to Alexander III. "Since Nabokov remains Minister of Justice and continues to send memoranda to Your Majesty, his moral position, if excluded from the meeting, would become untenable, and *most important*, his authority *vis-à-vis* subordinates *would be undermined*; this would harm an entire agency that is vital in the general governmental mechanism." Emphasizing the need to invite Nabokov, Pobedonostsev continued: "I know that Count Loris-Melikov also finds himself confused about the situation, but he has decided not to trouble Your Majesty with another proposal."[168]

Analyzing this letter or, more precisely, the final sentence, one can infer that Loris-Melikov made the initial proposal of participants for the meeting. From his list Valuev, Urusov and Nabokov were excluded. It is also possible to conclude that Loris-Melikov and Pobedonostsev jointly presented a list of participants on 14 April. There is weighty evidence for this second interpretation. Loris-Melikov would not have spent a whole evening talking with Pobedonostsev about the meeting of the ministers without some clear motive. Moreover, it should be noted that the two men came to complete agreement on this question; Pobedonostsev's letter to the tsar supported Loris-Melikov's petition for the meeting. Also it was not accidental that Pobedonostsev was informed about the rejection of Nabokov's candidacy.

Despite Loris-Melikov's agreement with Pobedonostsev, the significance and results of the agreement were unclear for the liberals. Therefore they prepared very carefully for 21 April. According to Miliutin, he and Loris-Melikov visited Abaza on the 20th to decide on a line of attack. Miliutin wrote: "Count Loris-Melikov is very depressed; he does not foresee anything good from the meeting. Abaza advises not to discuss specific issues tomorrow, but to try to establish a proper situation and atmosphere for ministerial activity. Abaza asserts that strong authority, so necessary under present circumstances, can only be exerted effectively if the tsar will surround himself with ministers whom he trusts completely and through whom he can act without any mediating influence. Obviously, he (Abaza) has in mind the insidious influence of Pobedonostsev and other people behind the scenes. For my part, I added that besides the personal confidence of the tsar there must be another prerequisite: that the ministry be unified . . . . Yet these ideas may wind up in the ashes if the meeting takes a different direction and specific questions of the day are broached."[169] Miliutin was right; the discussion of a concrete question could destroy immediately everything that had been achieved in reconciling the two warring groups. Reconciliation was more apparent than real.

Pobedonostsev tried to recruit Ignatiev as an ally before the meeting. On the eve of the meeting (20 April) Pobedonostsev wrote Ignatiev: "They will call us to Gatchina tomorrow, and I do not know what we will say there. Loris-Melikov would have liked a conference, but he has changed his mind. He would like to consult with you."[170] Then Pobedonostsev said that he would be home all evening, and he invited Ignatiev to visit. Thus the two sides prepared themselves for the Gatchina confrontation.

Miliutin's memorandum, "Thoughts on a New Conference," is of interest in analyzing his opinions on problems of domestic politics. In this memorandum the author analyzed government policy over the last twenty years, tried to define the essence of nihilism and the reasons for its spread, and presented a program of government measures which would facilitate progress in Russia and lead to "intellectual pacification."

Concerning the first issue, Miliutin wrote: "The chief evil of the day is, of course, the revolutionary underground movement—so-called nihilism. The struggle against this dangerous infection has been the primary concern of the government for many years—almost 20 years. During this difficult period every conceivable method has been attempted to halt and eradicate the infection. One cannot claim that the government has been limited in any way in its use of extreme measures . . . . We have had a constant state of siege. The government's hands never have been tied. Our government has unrestricted power; all the weapons are in its hands. The local administration is omnipotent . . . . Administrative exile has been employed often; then there are arrests, civil trials, military trials, special tribunals, and finally hanging."[171] However, these measures had achieved nothing; on the contrary, they had led to 1 March. Therefore, this repressive policy had been a failure.

Miliutin tried to describe the essence of "the underground movement" and compared it to West European socialist movements. In his opinion, there were substantial differences between the Russian and West European movements. The differences were: "(1) In Europe socialism had taken the form of political, almost scholarly, doctrine, and in Russia it was a wild, insane desire to destroy everything in existence; (2) In Europe the social movement had caught up the mass of the working population, led by an educated *avant-garde*; in Russia it consisted of gangs of young, half-educated students, radicalized and led around by a few hot heads." While Miliutin's analysis of Western European socialism was more or less accurate, his portrait of the Russian revolutionary movement was ill-conceived and simplistic. However, he had to admit that these "gangs of half-educated students" were supported by broad elements of society which did not sympathize with the existing governmental system.

What had caused this situation and how could it be changed? According to Miliutin, "the only solution is decisive movement forward, through improvement of the political and economic structure of the state."[172] Reforms were the only way to save Russia from the revolutionary movement. This point of view fully corresponded to the liberal outlook, expressed primarily in newspapers. Turning to reforms, Miliutin gave the peasant question highest priority. In his opinion, twenty years after the abolition of serfdom the position of the peasantry had not improved "as much as one had a right to hope," but instead had gotten much worse. Second, Miliutin argued for zemstvo reform because the government had put the zemstvo in a weakened and subordinate position. He said that currently the people were dissatisfied with every agency of the government. The Ministry of Education got the worst complaints. Summarizing, Miliutin observed that "the whole government structure needs immediate renovation," and stressed that "there can be no question of any constitution or anything resembling limitation of the autocracy." It was merely necessary to establish trust in the government and respect toward authority.

In conclusion, he spelled out a concrete plan for the government: "(1) to raise the zemstvo, to involve it in cooperation with government agencies, to unite it with local and central authorities. Certain forms of zemstvo participation in legislative deliberations, falling short of popular representation, might guarantee a more sympathetic popular response to government regulations, and might decrease complaints and criticism; and (2) serious reforms of central and local government agencies."[173]

Miliutin considered these issues "primary" and "organic". Simultaneously he advocated the formation of a special "college" where zemstvo representatives would deal with the peasant question in all its facets. After these issues had been solved, there was a series of others which have to be analyzed initially in special commissions with zemstvo participation and debated in the State Council, also with zemstvo representatives taking part. Miliutin noted that his proposals were in full accord with Loris-Melikov's plan and had been approved by Alexander II.[174] In a kind of general resumé the memorandum declared that "after the terrible event of 1 March and the beginning of the new reign it became necessary to act more decisively than one realized before, and in a broader framework."[175] Thus Miliutin believed that the assassination of Alexander II should not serve as an obstacle to the adoption of reforms; on the contrary, the reforms should be made more extensive. This idea was not original for it was current in the liberal press.

The Miliutin memorandum is very important for analysis of the author's political outlook after 1 March, and it is the more valuable since the author was one of the liberal triumvirs. The memorandum illustrated the complete coincidence of Miliutin's views with those of Loris-Melikov.

Both memoirs and epistolary sources illuminate the course of the 21 April meeting. The memoirs include the diaries of Miliutin, Peretts, and Valuev; the letters include a note from Pobedonostsev to Tiutcheva on 27 April. Miliutin's account of the meeting is the most valuable since he was a direct participant, while Peretts actually reported second-hand from Abaza's testimony. The merit of Peretts' account, in comparison with Miliutin's, is its completeness. Valuev's account also was based on Abaza's retelling and it has a more general form. Pobedonostsev also gave a rather lengthy account of the meeting in his letter to Tiutcheva. Since the most reliable accounts are Miliutin's and Pobedonostsev's, a summary of the meeting may be based on them.

The participants of the meeting were Alexander III, Loris-Melikov, Abaza, Miliutin, Ignatiev, Nikolai, Nabokov, Pobedonostsev and Grand Duke Vladimir Alexandrovich. They rode from Petersburg to Gatchina in one train car, but according to Pobedonostsev "everyone sat in a corner. My adversaries did not speak to me, nor I to them; they talked amongst themselves."[176]

Alexander III opened the meeting by announcing his "desire to hear our opinions on what measures should be taken and what program for future action should be adopted."[177] According to Miliutin and Pobedonostsev, Loris-Melikov spoke first;[178] his speech insisted on a series of reforms. Miliutin also argued for reforms. Afterwards Ignatiev, Abaza, Nabokov, and Nikolai supported the Ministers of Internal Affairs and War. Pobedonostsev spoke last. Miliutin wrote: "To our surprise, he spoke a completely different language than at the memorable meeting of 8 March; he even began to say that he shared the expressed opinions on the need for further improvements in the state structure. Then he started his moralizing, and delivered a sermon about truth, honesty, responsibility, and so on."[179] In general, however, Pobedonostsev's speech was not aggressive. The Supreme-Procurator's discourse did provoke objections from the participants. At the end of the meeting Grand Duke Vladimir Alexandrovich proposed to create a central investigative commission "on state crimes," but a decision on this issue was deferred.

Alexander III expressed the desire that the ministers meet when necessary to discuss questions of government policy in order to achieve comity and unity of action. The tsar proposed that the ministers discuss in the immediate future the most urgent issues, so that a final decision might be reached in a later meeting under his chairmanship.

The liberal group considered the results of the meeting to be positive. Miliutin wrote: ". . . Today's meeting turned out better than we expected. There was an absolutely unprecedented unanimity of opinion among the ministers: even Pobedonostsev wanted to make every effort to smooth over the sharp division between himself and his colleagues. . . . In any case, one can hope that this meeting will have a positive influence on the direction of the young emperor's thinking."[180] Abaza's assessment was even more gushing. According to Peretts, "Abaza thinks that this was complete victory for Loris and himself." In Abaza's opinion, Pobedonostsev had been destroyed, "ground into powder."[181] On the way back, according to Abaza, Pobedonostsev came up to him and Loris-Melikov and expressed regret for the misunderstandings after 8 March.

Pobedonostsev himself did not deny the improvement in relations between the ministers, but he depicted it somewhat differently. "As soon as we came out of the room everyone became happy. A sudden thaw had occurred among the ministers. Abaza almost embraced me. He was so glad that the misunderstandings had ended. It was exactly like a name-day holiday. We went to have lunch, and they started to tell anecdotes."[182]

The Supreme Procurator assessed the results of the meeting somewhat differently than Abaza had. "They went in fear of dismissal, and returned in unimagined triumph and began to say that they had achieved a brilliant victory. Over whom? Over me or over the tsar? According to them, I was wounded and their victory had been gained over me."[183]

Thus Pobedonostsev did not acknowledge his defeat. Moreover he was very well informed about the moods of his adversaries. In his letter to Tiutcheva he described the moods in high-society parlours and the Minister of Internal Affairs' interpretation of the meeting's results. "Loris had scarcely gotten home when women (0 these women!) sitting in drawing rooms had asked him with trepidation: 'What happened?' Elizaveta Pavlovna, née Euler, writes him: 'We know you have no time, but tell us—did you win out?' He writes: 'Yes,' and passes the note back."[184] So Loris-Melikov and his associates celebrated victory.

However, not everyone saw the results of the meeting in such optimistic terms. For example, Valuev, who had not attended the meeting, listened to Abaza's account and drew different conclusions. He wrote: "From all this it appears to me that we have only entered into new misunderstandings. . . . The tsar does not have a clear idea of what was desired and what was decided."[185] Actually the situation was not quite what Valuev imagined. True, Alexander III had made no objections to Loris-Melikov and his associates, but one should not conclude from this that the direction of internal policy was still unclear to the tsar.

The emperor found the meeting of 21 April an unpleasant experience. On the same day he wrote about this to Pobedonostsev. "Today's meeting made a sad impression on me. Loris, Miliutin, and Abaza resolutely continue the same policy and they want, one way or another, to lead us to representative government. Until I am convinced that this is necessary for Russia's welfare, it will not happen; I will not permit it." Later in the letter Alexander's attitude toward "representation" was made more concrete. "It is strange to listen to intelligent people, who can talk *seriously* about a representative element in Russia, and recite the formulas that they read in our scandal sheets and hear from bureaucratic liberals." Alexander ended the letter by emphasizing happily that his brother Vladimir also was opposed to a "representative element." The tsar again criticized his ministers, "who are deceiving themselves." [186]

This letter, which was not without grammatical errors, left no doubt about the tsar's position. The emperor not only defined for himself his path in domestic policy, but informed the leader of the reactionary group about his opinions. On 21 April the fate of Loris-Melikov, Miliutin, and Abaza was quite different from what they themselves imagined it would be. Yu. V. Gotie quite justly observed that in Alexander's letter to Pobedonostsev "one could see the first step toward the 29 April manifesto."[187]

How can one explain Alexander III's departure from the complete indecision that had seized him on 1 March? The absence of new terrorist acts and of mass demonstrations certainly helped to calm the young emperor. The awesome force that had propelled him to the throne no longer seemed so powerful or pervasive. There was an interesting diary entry by Miliutin on 9 April, containing Loris-Melikov's account of the interrogations of the newly-arrested Populists. "Their testimonies support the proposition that there was much conceit and exaggeration in the speeches of Zheliabov and his associates. This was a so-called 'terrorist' party with very few members or monetary resources; its force lay in the character and energy of a few leaders."[188] For our purposes an appraisal of Loris-Melikov's words is unnecessary, although on the whole Loris-Melikov was certainly correct. Doubtless the Minister of Internal Affairs sent accounts of these interrogations to the tsar, and they could not have failed to influence him. In late April Alexander III recovered somewhat from the fear that had gripped him since his father's murder. The young tsar's political outlook was very well-defined, and as soon as the fear began to pass, he began to clarify his position.

Let us turn to Pobedonostsev. First of all, it should be said that his policy of reconciliation did not signify a retreat from his reactionary opinions. It is clear that this retreat was a tactical maneuver, and only a maneuver. Reconciliation with Loris-Melikov and loyal behavior at the meeting of 21 April seemed essential to Pobedonostsev. It is possible that the Supreme Procurator of the Synod wanted to show that he could make concessions, and disorient his opponents by doing so. Alexander III's letter naturally caused Pobedonostsev to try to take immediate advantage of the tsar's attitude; however, he still proceeded with caution. On 23 April Pobedonostsev sent the tsar a long note in which he discussed the meeting of 21 April and the reconciliation that had occurred.

Only in the middle of the letter did he touch on his real subject: "Your Imperial Majesty, I dare to think that to produce tranquility at the present it will be necessary to send to the people an unambiguous and firm proclamation in Your name. This would embolden all loyal and well-intentioned citizens. The first manifesto was too short and vague."[189] Then Pobedonostsev advised the tsar to come to St. Petersburg, since the seclusion at Gatchina had given rise to various "outlandish" rumors. There was no direct attack against Loris-Melikov or his program here. Pobedonostsev moved very cautiously; he did not recommend to the tsar a plan of action, and limited himself to advice about a new manifesto. The contents of the manifesto were not mentioned.

On 25 April Pobedonostsev sent Alexander another letter, apparently written the night before.[190] In this letter the Supreme Procurator dealt directly with Loris-Melikov; he expressed his concern over meetings being held among representatives of the liberal bureaucracy. He recounted with anxiety Loris-Melikov's attempts to influence Grand Duke Vladimir Alexandrovich. He mentioned that all the "mindless" people who expected a constitution had cursed him—Pobedonostsev—for his opposition. Only at the end of the letter did he mention the issue that interested him. "Yesterday I wrote Your Majesty about a manifesto and I have not abandoned that idea. The state of indecision cannot continue; this would be fatal. If You make a decision, You must speak out. I sit for the second day trying to draft a manifesto with the advice of Count S.G. Stroganov, and I shall send it for Your perusal. May God bless Your decision."[191] In this letter Pobedonostsev was bolder in trying to bind Alexander III to his designs. The last phrase of the excerpt cited above is interesting in this connection; Pobedonostsev praised the tsar for his decision—meaning publication of the manifesto.[192]

Finally on 26 April Pobedonostsev sent the tsar the draft manifesto with a long accompanying note. Here was a direct approach to the emperor. "I hasten to send Your Majesty my draft of the manifesto, in which I have weighed every word. In my opinion, this draft meets the needs of the present time. Russia awaits this manifesto and will accept it with delight, excepting of course the mindless people who expect a constitution. Please notice that the manifesto deliberately expresses a firm resolve to preserve autocratic power; this is very necessary to silence rumors that a constitution will appear today or tomorrow. . . ."[193] Pobedonostsev noted that Count Stroganov was in complete agreement with the text. Furthermore, Pobedonostsev recommended that the tsar not show the manifesto to anyone else. "The matter is self-explanatory." Anyone invited to discuss the manifesto with the tsar would, according to Pobedonostsev, try to dissuade him from publication.

The Supreme Procurator of the Synod addressed his former pupil rather categorically. "If Your Majesty really has the firm intention not to permit the creation of institutions that are senseless and damaging to Russia, then I pray You not to hesitate to announce Your intention publically."[194] Everything in this letter was clear. While Pobedonostsev had been cautious in the first two letters, he now gambled all out, and . . . won. At noon the next day, 27 April, Alexander III sent the Supreme Procurator of the Synod the following telegram: "I approve wholeheartedly the draft manifesto. Meet me tomorrow at 2 P.M. to talk in more detail."[195]

Pobedonostsev celebrated his victory. Having received the telegram, he did not wait until the next day. He rushed straight to Gatchina, despite a plenary session of the State Council to discuss lower redemption payments. As I noted earlier, Pobedonostsev was supposed to speak against the decision of the Joint Committee on redemption payments; however, his joy was so great that he ignored the debate. Before leaving Petersburg he wrote Ignatiev a note about his departure to Gatchina, "where the tsar wishes today[196] to hear from me an explanation of a matter of interest to him in my agency."[197] Here Pobedonostsev contrived to lie twice: first, because no one had invited him to Gatchina on the 27th, and second, the invitation had nothing to do with his agency, the Holy Synod.

The Gatchina meeting was successful. The next day Peretts visited Pobedonostsev, who apologized again for his absence from the plenary session. Concerning his visit and reception by Pobedonostsev, Peretts wrote: "Although Konstantin Petrovich was generally attentive and polite to me today as he is always, nevertheless I noticed something in his character today that I had not seen before—a certain importance and feeling of accomplishment."[198] Obviously Pobedonostsev was brimming with happiness and pride. The most difficult problem was that he could say nothing about his success; he was "mute as a stone."

Having received the draft manifesto, Alexander showed it to Court Minister Adlerberg and sent it to his brother Grand Duke Vladimir Alexandrovich. "I have thought a long time about this, but the ministers promise to make the manifestos superfluous by their actions. Yet since I have not succeeded in getting any decisive action from them, and the hesitation continues, I resolved to ask K.P. Pobedonostsev to write me a draft manifesto [199] in which it was made clear that I would never permit limitation of autocratic power, so beneficial and necessary for Russia."[200]

While Pobedonostsev celebrated his triumph, his antagonists were still under the influence of their "successes" on 21 April. According to

Peretts' diary, Peretts had visited Pobedonostsev and then gone to speak with Abaza to share with Abaza his suspicions about the Supreme Procurator's open ill will toward Loris-Melikov, and the possible relation of Pobedonostsev's attitude to the Gatchina trip. Peretts' suspicion had been aroused when Pobedonostsev had thrown out a sentence about the need to replace Loris-Melikov. (Obviously, he had not held back). However, the Minister of Finance attached no importance to this. Abaza said: "Not yet a week has passed since the meeting. Then Pobedonostsev was defeated, and if the tsar conferred with him yesterday, it was certainly about some governmental issue."[201] This was the situation and the mood of the two sides on the eve of 29 April.

On the evening of 28 April there was a meeting on the Fontanka in Loris-Melikov's office; it was a conference of ministers (a sort of "cabinet" distinguished from the Committee of Ministers) including Loris-Melikov, Miliutin, Abaza, Ignatiev, Nabokov, Pobedonostsev and Grand Duke Vladimir Alexandrovich—that is, all the people who had attended the Gatchina meeting of 21 April. Four issues were discussed.[202] The first was Grand Duke Vladimir Alexandrovich's proposal to create a central investigative commission, a proposal mentioned first at Gatchina. According to Miliutin, "this proposal was destroyed by the criticisms of Count Loris-Melikov and Nabokov: they both pointed to the distressing results of similar commissions in the past, and [argued that] such a commission was unnecessary given the unification of police agencies and the end of the former antagonisms between police and judicial institutions."[203] The second issue was the function of the Department of State Police "in connection with a proposal to form a special unit to prevent crime."[204] According to Miliutin, this proposal was approved with a few amendments. The third issue was a review of various sections in the statute on zemstvos and municipal institutions; the fourth dealt with zemstvo petitions on the peasantry.

These last questions provoked the most spirited debates. Yet even here agreement was reached on the zemstvo and municipal institutions statute, and on legislative work on improvements in the position of the peasantry. Even the "ticklish" issue of participation by zemstvo representatives in legislative work was decided affirmatively in a general form. The only hold-out was Pobedonostsev, who "again began to demonstrate the harm of an elective element, and generally, the danger of involving 'local forces,' and he would only permit the government to handpick experts."[205] Since Pobedonostsev's opinion differed so sharply from everyone else's, Grand Duke Vladimir Alexandrovich proposed a compromise: "on the first occasion" invitations would be made "only to competent and loyal persons known to the government,"[206] and these persons would then discuss zemstvo participation on important legislative projects. This formula was accepted.[207] The meeting ended in the small hours of the morning.[208]

After the meeting the Minister of Justice informed everyone about the manifesto to be published the next day. According to Miliutin, "such unexpected news struck like lightning. What manifesto? Who prepared it? With whom had the emperor conferred? An embarrassed Pobedonostsev confessed that it was the work of his pen .... "[209] The secret was out. Loris-Melikov, Miliutin, and Abaza were indignant, especially after the Gatchina meeting where the tsar announced the need "for complete agreement and unity" among ministers, and had asked the ministers to agree among themselves on the vital issues. According to Miliutin, "Count Loris-Melikov and A.A. Abaza vigorously expressed their dissatisfaction, and said directly that they could not remain ministers. I associated myself with their opinion. Nabokov, Ignatiev, and Baron Nikolai, although more restrained, also expressed their surprise. A pale and embarrassed Pobedonostsev stood in guilty silence before his judges."[210] Obviously Pobedonostsev did not feel very comfortable at that moment. He wrote about this in a note on the meeting: "A dramatic moment. I managed to leave. It is curious that after this many people were upset with me and would not shake my hand."[211] The politics of reconciliation, whose initiator had been Pobedonostsev, now yielded its results. However, the manifesto had not appeared due to "the strategy" of the Supreme Procurator of the Synod. There were other, more serious factors, of which Pobedonostsev had taken successful advantage.

Let us turn to the contents of the manifesto. The first part mentioned the circumstances surrounding the succession and analyzed the policies of Alexander II. The second section defined the government's domestic program. "In the midst of Our great grief the voice of God bids Us to stand staunchly for government relying on God's design, with faith in the truth of autocratic power, which We are called to affirm and preserve in the national interest. . . ." [212] The basic aim of the new reign would be to preserve the purity of the principles of autocratic power. Every hope of representative participation in legislative institutions was dashed, even though such participation would not have violated the autocratic principle. In conclusion, the manifesto appealed to "all loyal subjects to serve Us and the state through faith and truth, by eradicating pernicious sedition, which has disgraced the Russian land, by affirming faith and morals, by the proper education of children, by the elimination of falsehood and exploitation, and by putting order and truth in the actions of institutions given to Russia by that benefactor, beloved by Our parents."[213]

This manifesto, written in the phraseology of the Orthodox Church, triumphantly proclaimed that the autocracy would make no concessions. That was its essence. The absence of a mass movement and of new terrorist acts, and the weakness of the liberal opposition enabled Alexander III to proclaim a reactionary course in domestic politics. In Miliutin's telling phrase, the program of the manifesto was reaction "under the mask of nationality and orthodoxy."[214] Even casual observers read the manifesto thus. On 30 April the German ambassador, Schweinitz, wrote in his memoirs about the possible foundation of a "Special Security Commission" (*Allgemeine Sicherheit-Kommission*) and of a reactionary ministry headed by someone like Peter Shuvalov."[215] However, the announcement of the program did not mean immediate reaction. This could only occur when the government had finally recovered from 1 March.

The publication of the manifesto provoked a storm of delight in reactionary circles. In its editorial on 30 April *Moskovskie Vedomosti* wrote: "Now we can breathe freely. The end of pusillanimity; the end of confusion. Before this unwavering, this so very firm, so decisive word of the monarch the many-headed hydra of deception must perish. Popular sentiment awaited this imperial declaration like manna from the heavens. In it is our deliverance; it returns to the Russian people the autocratic Russian tsar."[216]

The liberal press put on a happy countenance in the face of sad news, ignoring the reactionary part of the manifesto and emphasizing words that might create the illusion that Alexander III's regime would not deviate from introduction of future reforms. "With proper gratitude Russia will hear and read the manifesto in which the sovereign gives us courage and hope during these sad days of trial," said an editorial in *Poriadok*. "Now Russia knows the future: there will be 'order and truth' in the actions of institutions granted us by the deceased emperor, and this in itself will help us reach the other goals outlined in the manifesto. It should be remembered that the deceased emperor achieved the great work of his reign 'not so much by the strict commands of government, as by goodness and kindness.'"[217] The newspaper *Strana* wrote in the same spirit, expressing even more definite hope in the reformist activity of Alexander III: "Of course, the sovereign will not renounce new reforms that are considered necessary. The reforms proposed by the deceased tsar and illumined by his memory must continue."[218] In this case, if liberals did not engage in self-deception, they certainly failed to comprehend the essence of the manifesto.

The publication of the manifesto provoked a swift change in the government. On 29 April Loris-Melikov asked the tsar to accept his resignation, and Abaza followed suit on the 30th. Both resignations were accepted immediately. According to Valuev, Alexander III wrote on Valuev's request: "I regret that you did not find a more courteous pretext."[219]   P.N. Ignatiev became the new Minister of Internal Affairs. In Valuev's picturesque expression, Ignatiev had been clever enough to keep "one foot in each camp."[220] Bunge, who had been Assistant Minister of Finance, took Abaza's post. On 1 May Miliutin wrote in his diary: "I have decided to step down, but my friends advise me that it would be improper to connect my resignation with the manifesto."[221]   On 12 May Miliutin sent his request for resignation, and it was accepted. Miliutin's successor was the unintelligent and little-educated General Vannovsky, who during the Russo-Turkish war had been Staff Captain in the Rushchuksky division, commanded by the future emperor.[222]

On 1 March the crisis of the autocracy had reached its zenith, sowing confusion and complete disorientation in ruling circles. However, the assassination of Alexander II, which had required a colossal effort by the entire *Narodnaia Volia* party, and had distracted that party from its efforts in other fields, had not resulted in any political reforms. Preparation for the assassination deprived the party of the chance to take advantage of the relaxation of police terror, which had been caused by the party's actions. Despite certain achievements of the party among the factory workers of the capital and the creation of a battle organization, the Populists could not use these forces to good effect after 1 March. They did not have the strength to continue the terrorist campaign after the assassination of Alexander II. Even before 1 March, and especially after the regicide, the Executive Committee of *Narodnaia Volia* seemed completely helpless.

While the assassination did not lead to political reforms, fear and disorientation were so powerful that the new monarch was unable to set his political policy for two months after his succession. This indecision provoked infighting between government factions in March and April. The absence of subsequent terrorist acts and mass demonstrations, and the extreme timidity of liberal society enabled Alexander III with Pobedonostsev's help to publish a manifesto affirming the autocracy. "With 1 March the revolutionaries exhausted themselves," wrote V.I. Lenin. "In the working class there was no broad movement, no hard organization. This time liberal society turned out to be so politically under-developed that it confined itself to petitions after the assassination of Alexander II."[223]

However, the 29 April Manifesto did not mean the final establishment of reaction. Even under these circumstances the government could not force through such a program. Alexander III had rejected decisively any political reforms and had resolved to preserve the autocracy without change. The hour of reaction would come, but it would have to be preceded by a period of transition.

CHAPTER V

THE MINISTRY OF N.P. IGNATIEV

At the beginning of May Count N.P. Ignatiev became Minister of Internal Affairs. In his analysis of the situation V.I. Lenin wrote: "... The government of Alexander III, even after the manifesto affirming the autocracy, did not immediately show all its claws, but instead considered it essential to deceive 'society' for some time."[1] The government continued to fear its seen and unseen enemies, including the revolutionary populists and the mass movement, given the tense situation in the countryside.[2] The situation did not permit the government to embrace reaction immediately. N.P. Ignatiev was the most suitable statesman for this transition period. He was a demagogue and liar, and his rather absurd opinions inclined him toward the reactionary camp. Consequently, Ignatiev was a successful candidate for the post of Minister of Internal Affairs. According to contemporaries, the "dictatorship of the heart" was succeeded by the "dictatorship of smiles."

Ignatiev's views were generally primitive. For example, he did not understand at all the causes of the revolutionary movement in Russia. In a discussion with the Austro-Hungarian ambassador, Kalnoky, he explained matters in the following fashion: "I shall tell you something that I do not like to tell everyone. Would you like to know what is the basis for the nihilists' secret organization? It is the Poles and the Jews,"[3] he solemnly intoned. Moreover, the Minister of Internal Affairs was simply dishonest in the most common affairs, according to many contemporaries.[4]

We do not have any evidence that will permit us to decide who first suggested Ignatiev for the ministerial post. Probably the initiative was taken by Alexander III himself with Pobedonostsev's concurrence. Judging by Pobedonostsev's letter to the tsar on 4 March, the tsar had solicited advice concerning the appointment.[5] Even if Pobedonostsev was not the first to suggest Ignatiev's candidacy, Ignatiev was under Pobedonostsev's influence from the very outset of his ministry. The Supreme-Procurator literally dictated to Ignatiev on the most diverse issues facing him as minister. Ignatiev sent numerous projects to Pobedonostsev, and the latter acted as the minister's tutor for a time. In a letter dated 26 June 1881 Pobedonostsev prophesied: "There is great work ahead. Believe me, so that it will not be in vain, one thing is essential: the bright sun of truth. Without it the fog will not disperse. Fog does not disperse fog. In the Bible's words, it is necessary *to hate evil with one's whole heart*. There must be no mixture of light and darkness, Christ and Satan, yes-yes and no-no. You should possess the spirit shown by the biblical Elias to the false prophets, when he gave Christ a whip to drive the moneychangers from the temple."[6]

During Ignatiev's ministerial tenure, Pobedonostsev wrote him 79 letters concerned in one way or another with the activity of the Ministry of Internal Affairs. Ignatiev began to grow closer to Pobedonostsev in late April due to identical views on the reduction of redemption payments. This intimacy continued virtually until Ignatiev's retirement. The Minister of Internal Affairs also had connections with other colleagues—for example, with Ostrovksy, the Minister of State Domains. During almost his entire tenure as minister Ignatiev enjoyed the uninterrupted support of Alexander III. With Pobedonostsev's help, Ignatiev managed in late 1881 to win a battle with Cherevin, a friend of the tsar, who had tried to gain control over the Department of Police and the Corps of Gendarmes through his capacity as head of the Imperial Okhrana.[7] This incident showed the influence and strength of the Minister of Internal Affairs.

It should be emphasized that much of Ignatiev's influence and strength depended on Pobedonostsev's friendly attitude. During the period from May 1881 until mid-1882, Pobedonostsev's authority was enormous.[8] When Ignatiev obeyed Pobedonostsev, he was indomitable. While Pobedonostsev supported Ignatiev, he was not always pleased with the minister. For example, on 20 December 1881 the Supreme-Procurator of the Synod wrote in a letter to Tiutcheva: "It is our misfortune that Count Ignatiev has his weaknesses. He is full of intrigue, and he lies, and runs off at the mouth. Would you believe that there is no substitute for him at the present time? If you remove his name from the picture there is nothing but obscurity; people even mention Count P.A. Shuvalov. That would be final disaster. Therefore, you have to be satisfied with Ignatiev, a liar who can never be believed. I sense that this is not a man from whom you can expect truth, but I sense disaster if he departs."[9]

Ignatiev's ministry was characterized by the spread of every sort of provocation, denunciation, and treachery. During this period Gendarme Colonel Sudeikin carried out his police searches in Petersburg.[10] Commenting on the atmosphere at this time, Golovnin wrote to Miliutin in January 1882: "The mania of denunciations has spread in all levels of society. I am receiving anonymous letters with denunciations of my servants, who alledgedly speak badly of me."[11] This was no accident. It was the result of the Ignatiev-inspired system of provocation and widespread espionage.

One aspect of Ignatiev's program was his plan for political amnesty. It would have forgiven "the crimes and mistakes of all persons who, attracted by false and seditious doctrines, had been subjected to police investigation, and who had hidden themselves either abroad or at home by means of assumed names and forged documents."[12] Only direct participants in the assassination of Alexander II would have been ineligible for amnesty under this plan.[13] This wholesale provocation was not actually carried through because Pobedonostsev opposed it. Pobedonostsev had mistaken it for a sincere gesture, and feared that such a gesture was premature. "This plan I consider to be *mistaken, harmful, and dangerous*," he wrote.[14]

Another of Ignatiev's proposals, entitled "On the Chief Bases of Internal Security," was designed to create a massive army of spies.[15] This plan envisioned the organization of "artels" under state supervision and with treasury funding. An artel [cooperative work unit] would consist of apartment managers and doormen. Their sphere of action would include "generally all private living quarters or state-owned residences placed under observation."[16] To join an artel, a person would have to pay a fee or secure a recommendation. Only artel members could be employed as doormen or apartment managers. This army of spies would be supervised by a group of superspies [*obershpiony*] called inspectors and subsidized by the state. These plans reflected the Minister of Internal Affairs' aspirations to create a climate of mass provocation and espionage, a climate in which he felt as comfortable as a fish in water.

After notification of his appointment to the ministry, but before his actual appointment, Ignatiev composed a special memorandum outlining his basic orientation in domestic politics. Late in the evening on 3 May he presented this memorandum to Pobedonostsev. The next day the Supreme Procurator made a series of comments on the document— that is, he edited Ignatiev's proposals. Pobedonostsev offered much substantive advice. "I think the most proper form would be a circular from the Minister of Internal Affairs to the governors. A directive from all the ministers would be unprecedented and is hardly a proper way to proceed. An unsigned announcement in *Pravitelstvenny Vestnik* [Government Herald] would also entail disadvantages for the contents would have to be analyzed more thoroughly and more definite directives given."[17]

This was the origin of the famous Ignatiev circular to the governors on 6 May. In this circular, published in all newspapers, the aims of the government were enunciated in accordance with the 29 April Manifesto. The tone of the circular was lofty and demagogic. "Summoned to administer the Ministry of Internal Affairs at this difficult time, I consider it my duty to inform you of the government's views on the current domestic situation. The imperial Manifesto of 29 April suggested the way in which the government, with the cooperation of the entire nation, will attain its single high goal—the greatness and welfare of Russia."

Next there was a rather detailed explanation of the development of the revolutionary movement up to the murder of Alexander II. According to Ignatiev, the regicide could not be explained by mere reference to the conspirators' evil intentions; there must be taken into account the system of education, the rejection of religious and moral tenets, the inaction of the government, neglect of the "common welfare shown by government and public figures," and their greedy attitude "toward government and public possessions."[18] Ignatiev's list included none of the real causes of the revolutionary movement. As an analyst he was less competent than Loris-Melikov, who himself was far from a complete apprehension of these causes.[19]

Turning to the tasks facing the government, Ignatiev put highest priority on the "eradication of sedition," with the cooperation of the rest of the nation. He mentioned the anti-Jewish disorders and ascribed them to revolutionary influence. "The movement against the Jews which broke out in the South provided a sad illustration of how people, who are loyal to the throne and the fatherland, fall into arrogant disobedience and self-righteousness and unwittingly act according to the designs of the revolutionaries.[20] Such violations of order must not only be strictly prosecuted, but carefully prevented."

A second governmental task was formulated more generally; it had to do with moral and ethical questions. Ignatiev spoke about "the condescending attitude of society toward illegal means of gaining profit." Alluding to the manifesto, Ignatiev wrote: "The tsar's words call for immediate elimination of these cases .... Graft must be eliminated and prosecuted everywhere .... "[21] Ignatiev's interpretation of the Manifesto of 29 April was not literal since it did not refer explicitly to government corruption. Again rather vaguely, Ignatiev mentioned the idea of "introducing order and truth in the institutions founded by Alexander II." He had in mind zemstvo and municipal agencies. Ignatiev declared that difficulties would be overcome "given the friendly cooperation of government and society." Ignatiev also mentioned the "disinterested" role of the nobility, especially in zemstvo activity.

The concluding section of the circular contained a very explicit promise that the rights "granted" to the zemstvo and municipal classes would not be infringed. There was also a general statement on the peasant question. "The peasantry must not pay heed to harmful rumors; it must be completely confident that the freedom and rights granted earlier will be preserved; but that the government is anxious to lighten the peasants' burdens and improve their social status and economic condition." Finally, the circular spoke about the government's attempt to "establish proper methods to guarantee the utmost success to the utmost success to the vigorous participation of local activists" in the solution of local problems. Such were the contents of this officiously-worded, sententious circular, intended to achieve the broadest publicity. There was nothing concrete in it. The government's program was presented vaguely, so that one could not determine Ignatiev's future policies. This vagueness was surely deliberate.[22]

In general, the press reacted favorably to the circular. The reactionary and liberal newspapers read into the circular whatever they wanted to hear. On 7 May *Moskovskie Vedomosti* wrote: "Reading this circular, we feel ourselves at home, among family, amidst the Russian people . . . . We shall be Russians above all, true to the spirit and history of our fatherland, and we shall reject wild experiments in governmental affairs."[23] According to Katkov, a "native milieu" meant the unshakeable nature of the autocratic model of government and a decisive rejection of constitutional systems, which he called "wild experiments."

The liberal *Poriadok* stressed that the circular proved that the "government admits the need not only to preserve, but to develop the rights granted to the people, and that . . . public activity, public participation in the nation's affairs will be granted an appropriate role."[24] *Zemstvo* also supposed that the task set out in the circular "is close to that set during the ministry of Loris-Melikov."[25] The newspaper added that the circular left unanswered "most of the public's questions,"[26] and left undefined the government's future policy. The newspaper *Golos* evaluated the Ignatiev circular very cautiously. It observed that the memo's "substantive content alludes to and elaborates upon the basic tenets expressed in the imperial Manifesto of 29 April."[27]

It is possible to analyze Ignatiev's ministerial activity by studying his memoranda. They are valuable because, in contrast to the circular of 6 May, they were never intended for publication. Unfortunately, one aspect of Ignatiev's policy was not discussed in these memos: the struggle against the revolutionary movement. The memos can be dated to the second half of 1881.

Let us turn to one of these documents, which presented Ignatiev's program in full. Ignatiev began with the inadequacies of the government apparatus. "There is no doubt that *embezzlement of state property* goes on in many agencies." He thought that "joint efforts" were needed to solve this abuse. He mentioned involvement of "local elected officials" in deliberations over this matter. A second abuse was "the dilatoriness in the solution of problems, especially those under the jurisdiction of several agencies."[28] Therefore, Ignatiev saw corruption and bureaucratism, especially prevalent in inter-ministerial problems, as the primary shortcomings of the government machine.

He then mentioned "informed persons," whose involvement in the solution of many issues had produced good results in the past. He thought that this method should be used in the future. The next and longest section of this memorandum dealt with education. "Many nihilists are working as educators in *higher educational institutions. We must change the conditions which caused this sad state of affairs.*" Ignatiev called, first, for a review of personnel in higher educational institutions; second, for increased supervision over students; and third, for "elimination of those incentives (such as government stipends, and civil service privileges for university graduates) which artificially attract young people to college." Ignatiev also spoke about reforms in elementary and secondary schools that would lead to male and female professional schools in the countryside.

The final section dealt with economic questions. "The highest goal of the state is to raise and improve standards of living."[29] Analyzing the economic situation in Russia, Ignatiev noted: *"Industry is in a sorry state, artisans' skills are not being perfected, the factories* are placed under improper conditions and *suffer much from the theory of free trade and the accidental protection of individual enterprises."* The economic program was as follows: (1) create "normal" conditions for different industrial enterprises, and savings banks; (2) change railroad and customs tariffs to "give an advantage to domestic producers over foreign;"[30] (3) "stimulate native Russian production;" (4) organize small short-term loans to peasant agriculture by creating a network of agricultural banks under the general control of the government. Finally, Ignatiev advocated the preservation of the commune.

Most of the Ignatiev program was objectively bourgeois in nature. For example, the creation of professional schools in the cities and grammar schools in the countryside, and the economic program were bourgeois measures. However, Ignatiev also desired to preserve the commune, and this would not have facilitated the development of capitalism. Special attention should be devoted to the question of the "informed persons." The involvement of "informed persons" appointed by the government was a demagogic ploy designed to disarm the zemstvo leaders, who wished to participate in policy decisions.

Ignatiev's next three circulars, in contrast with the May circular, were business-like documents dedicated to the peasant question. The second circular, dated 23 May, had the most general contents. It proposed that governors tour their respective provinces in order to dampen "intellectual ferment." The circular said: "You must pay most attention to dangerous rumors on the partition of land, additional allotments, the 'black' partition, and so on." It emphasized that "a repetition of the disorders like those in the southern provinces during the pogroms must not be tolerated, and must be prevented by the adoption of timely and appropriate measures."[31] The Minister of Internal Affairs recommended against publication of any appeals to peasants, since such publications, as experience had shown, lent themselves to "incorrect and unfortunate" interpretations.

The first circular, dated 22 May, dealt with the sale of peasant cattle for arrears. "The bad harvests and decline of the recent past have reduced significantly the number of peasant cattle. Further reductions inevitably would harm agriculture and the very means of existence of the peasant family, particularly of children. . . . The government has decided temporarily, pending improvements in agricultural and monetary conditions, to exempt peasant cattle from sale to meet treasury arrears and old debts."[32] The circular announced that the sale of cattle could occur in exceptional cases only with the sanction of the district bureau on peasant affairs, when this would not lead to further disintegration of the peasant economy. That Ignatiev was forced to issue three circulars on peasant affairs in his first month of office certainly proved that the situation in the countryside was tense.

In confirmation there is a letter to Ignatiev from the Orel Governor, Boborykin, dated summer 1881: "I asked, given our current social and class forces, given the present structure of administrative, class, and peasant institutions, and given the present position of the clergy among the peasantry, whether the marshals of the nobility hoped to succeed in the struggle against people who are the enemies of our current governmental system, people, who would use any means to confuse and arouse the population. I also asked if the marshals thought it possible to quiet the people, end their land hunger, and all expectations of new charities from the tsar in the form of land, cancelled payments, an end to quitrent, and so on. All the marshals answered that the present tools for battle with revolutionaries are insufficient. The age-old belief of the people in a land partition is a result of their difficult economic situation, a situation that leads peasants to anxious agitation and belief in false rumors."[33] Other factors also suggested considerable tension in the countryside.

The third circular, dated 26 May, dealt with the transfer of peasants to redemption. It explained that, in connection with the State Council's decision about transfer of the remaining temporarily-obligated peasants to mandatory redemption, rumors had spread to the public and that there might arise attempts to forestall the government's plan by transferring peasants to a one-quarter-size free allotment. "The experience of the past has shown that most peasants who have transferred to a free allotment have become so poor that the zemstvo has been forced to give them yearly subsidies for food, and the peasants themselves have petitioned to be resettled on treasury land with a subsidy from the government." The Minister of Internal Affairs emphasized that on the eve of transfer to mandatory redemption such "frivolous disenfranchisement of the peasants" was especially undesirable.[34] This was evidence, albeit indirect, of the tension in the countryside and of the government's desire to avoid any excesses.

On 3 June a secret circular to the governors announced that because of petitions to leave soldiers in local quarters during the summer and "to prevent powerful disorders," Ignatiev and the Minister of War had obtained the tsar's agreement to a proposal that would have permitted infantry commanders, at the insistence of the provincial governor, to suspend normal summer military exercises. Ignatiev asked the governors not to abuse this plan, since summer exercises were important to military preparedness. The Minister of Internal Affairs thought exercises might be cancelled "if all previous attempts to prevent disorders have failed."

In conclusion, Ignatiev asked the governors, in agreement with the Church hierarchy, the provincial marshals of the nobility, and zemstvo representatives, "to exercise a rational influence on the rural population through the parish clergy and other responsible people, and also through influential nobles, zemstvo activists, and landowners in order to counteract the spread of the not infrequently negative judgments about governmental life in general, and about proposed changes in land relations in particular."[35]

This was definite evidence of a tense situation in the countryside. What was the cause of this tension? In my opinion, besides the general conditions that had engendered the peasant movement, the succession to the throne of Alexander III had a certain impact. Faith in the tsar, a feature of peasant ideology, combined with the special hope for "tsarist charities" at the beginning of the new reign. The same thing had occurred at the successions of Nicholas I and Alexander II. It also had been observed earlier in history. It would be unfair to conclude that after the Manifesto of 29 April the government felt completely certain of itself.

In a memorandum to the tsar on 15 March 1882, Ignatiev described the situation in the countryside: "There is no doubt that among peasants there circulate rumors about the division of land and a generally-undefined expectation of charities, independent of their own efforts and work; one cannot deny the dangers of such expectations, but in order not to exaggerate their importance, it should be borne in mind that they first appeared long ago and by themselves do not constitute a serious danger." He then pointed out that in the last ten months there had been no "violations of order" except in Voronezh and Tambov provinces where difficulties had occurred at harvest time as a result of "unfortunate rumors." He continued: "In response to the circular of 23 May, other governors sent comforting answers."[36] Ignatiev wrote in this self-assured vein in spring 1882, but in mid-1881 the situation had seemed different, which is why he devoted so much attention to the rural situation.

Ignatiev was very much concerned to strengthen the administrative and police apparatus, and to preserve the existing political regime, the autocracy. This facet of Ignatiev's activity displayed better than any other the government's gradual transition to reaction.

One of the Minister of Internal Affairs first steps was to propose to purge the state apparatus of various oppositional "liberal elements," who permitted themselves to criticize the government. Soon after his appointment Ignatiev sent to Alexander III a report concerning the anti-government attitudes which had become rife in the bureaucracy.[37] He began by referring to the "critical" attitude that gripped Russian society.[38] "Over time the slander and ridicule of government actions and statesmen became a universal criticism of all governmental actions, all statesmen, and the criticism began to undermine the governmental mystique and respect toward authority."[39]

The criticism was evidence of the unpopularity of the government's policy and of the people who executed that policy. During the crisis of the autocracy the public's critical attitude became more pervasive. "Unfortunately, it must be said that the leaders of those who had directed heavy blows against the authority of the government were all bureaucrats, with the exception of the ministers during their tenure in office."

Ignatiev then said that this "political poison" from the salons of the upper bureaucracy had affected deeply the younger generation of bureaucrats. "An inclination toward extreme judgments and political dissoluteness on the part of the fathers always has nourished radical convictions among the sons." According to Ignatiev, "it is a rare contemporary Russian bureaucrat who does not condemn the government and the elite, and he is rare if he does not consider himself justified in acting on these convictions." Initially, Ignatiev was correct. There was widespread dissatisfaction with the government's actions, and this caused the oppositional attitude within the bureaucracy. However, Ignatiev was wrong about the second issue. There may have been persons among the bureaucrats who desired to act "according to their personal convictions," but these were the exceptions. For most bureaucrats, as for most lackeys, another attitude was characteristic: curse the masters behind their backs, but unfailingly do their bidding. Reasoning by his false logic, Ignatiev said that one had to view most bureaucrats "as nothing other than active instigators of the revolutionary movement."[40] He then asserted that a successful struggle against the revolutionary movement would be impossible until this "bureaucratic sedition" was eliminated.

The Minister of Internal Affairs proposed to publish a special manifesto against bureaucratic sedition. Since "the disarray of the administration and distrust of authority began with the bureaucrats in Petersburg and later reached into the provinces, we must apply the cure for this illness, which saps our strength and reason, in Petersburg." The author supposed that measures to bridle the upper bureaucracy would "be approved by all Russia, with the exception of the Petersburg [read: "liberal"–P.A.Z.] press." "The dismissal from service of several bureaucrats subsequent to unrestrained conversations and condemnations of the government would be sufficient to produce a striking effect on all governmental servants."[41] Ignatiev reasoned that most officials were critical mainly because it was fashionable in high society to behave that way. This assumption was absurd. The opposition movement, one manifestation of which was the bureaucratic fronde, was, like every social movement, a result of the dissatisfaction of certain classes or class groups with aspects of the governmental system or with the system as a whole. In conclusion, Ignatiev proposed to delegate supervision "over political attitudes" of all civil servants in Russia to the Ministry of Internal Affairs. He believed that the "infectious verbal criticisms" should be stopped.

Ignatiev's draft decree on the purge of disloyal officials from the government also was written at the same time.[42] The preamble of this project merely summarized in different words the contents of the earlier report. The first point stated that within three months all state institutions, beginning with central and ending with district agencies, should be purged of all disloyal elements. The second point defined the criteria of disloyalty. "No official, regardless of rank, may be retained in the civil service, if he: (a) permits himself to criticize or analyze governmental directives at a place or time not sanctioned by law; (b) is found to be politically disloyal; (c) tries to change the essence of laws or decrees according to personal convictions not in agreement with the existing statutes and directives of the respective supervisor." The third point dealt with responsibility for dismissing bureaucrats. This was a matter for the personal choice of the ministers, governors, and the supervisors of central and provincial institutions.

The next points elaborated on the preceding ones. Points six and seven, which dealt with officials in the judiciary, were of independent interest. The sixth point proposed that the Ministers of Internal Affairs and Justice prepare for the Senate "a plan for relations that might be established between governors and procurators, with the proviso that procurators will not be removed from the governors' political supervision."[43] The plan called for the *de facto* subordination of all procuratorial officials to the administrative authority of governors. The seventh point dealt with judges, or more precisely, with supervision of the actions of judicial officials. "Without infringing on the law concerning judicial freedom from dismissal," the Minister of Justice would have to keep open his option to dismiss a recalcitrant judge. In cases where "certain individuals did not answer the government's requirements." the minister might request a judge to change his methods, or dismiss him. In special instances the judge himself could be placed on trial. This project did not actually contradict the statute giving judges freedom from dismissal, although it certainly represented an infringement on the independence of the judiciary, since a suit against a bureaucrat accused of official crimes could take place without the participation of sworn witnesses.

This plan was a result of Ignatiev's desire to broaden administrative discretion, which in turn reflected the general reactionary tendencies of the government. The adoption of this project would have made the Ministry of Internal Affairs into a police warden over all other agencies, and would have increased the administrative control of those in supervisory positions generally. However, the project could not have been adopted since it would have constituted a public admission of the unreliability of the state apparatus. Even Alexander III could not go that far. That is why he approved Ignatiev's report, but nevertheless considered it unwise to put Ignatiev's plan into action.

The spread of opposition within the bureaucracy at all levels characterized not only this particular crisis of government politics, but the deep organic defects of the old regime as well. The sad condition of the government machine was one element in the inevitable deterioration of the political structure in Russia.

Let us turn to the condition of police agencies. In May 1881 under the chairmanship of General Cherevin there was formed a commission for the reform of the police; however, after three months of work it had failed to reach any positive conclusions.[44] Despite this failure, Ignatiev did take certain steps in this area. In contrast to Loris-Melikov, he did not want to place the gendarmerie under the governors' authority. On 9 June 1881 a circular was published that abolished Loris-Melikov's old system prohibiting local gendarme offices from communicating directly with the Department of State Police.[45] This circular proposed that the heads of these agencies "report directly to the Department of State Police about all substantial violations of public order and tranquility, in addition to any oral or written reports on these events to provincial supervisors, local police chiefs, and municipal governors."[46] This circular held great significance. It established the independence of the gendarmerie *vis-à-vis* provincial governors, who were the highest representatives of the Ministry of Internal Affairs. Ignatiev pursued this measure very insistently. Thus, in an October circular, whose contents reiterated the initial circular, Ignatiev wrote: "Meanwhile, even now in some areas people continue to send reports to the governors rather than directly to the Department of State Police."[47] Ignatiev stressed that Loris-Melikov's directive in this sphere had been cancelled.

Ignatiev presented his opinion on the organization and mutual relations of the gendarmerie and police in a report now preserved in his personal archieve.[48] ". . . Although the police are subordinate to one person, they are still split into two sections—the gendarmes and the regular police." Then he developed a notion that was mentioned in the circular: it would be unwise to unite the police and the corps of gendarmes from below. "It would be awkward to begin unification at the local level since a unified local police force would have two directors—the Corps of Gendarmes and the Department of Police."[49] According to Ignatiev, this unification should begin from the top. "Information about possible violations of the peace must flow to a single center, and this center should direct all the government's attempts to prevent and stop criminal acts. Only such a procedure can give sufficient force to administrative action."[50] While recognizing the need for unification of the police and the gendarmerie, Ignatiev also violated that principle. He wanted to win popularity among the gendarmes, who were very unhappy about their subordination to gubernatorial authority.

In late 1881 there arose the issue of removing the Department of State Police and the Corps of Gendarmes from the jurisdiction of the Ministry of Internal Affairs. This was quite a surprise for Ignatiev. The issue arose in connection with General Cherevin's appointment as head of the Imperial Okhrana.[51] Cherevin submitted a project to the tsar that would have placed both agencies under his *de facto* control. The tsar evidently gave his preliminary approval. In a report on this project, Ignatiev wrote: "The sense of the proposal is that the Department of State Police and the Corps of Gendarmes will remain in the Ministry of Internal Affairs, but will answer to the head of the Okhrana, who is not subordinate to the Minister of Internal Affairs. If this plan is adopted, it will be tantamount to the reestablishment of the abolished Third Section, but in a much worse form."[52]

In connection with the appearance of this plan, it is possible to argue a certain hypothesis. It would seem that the idea of transferring the two police agencies to direct control of the head of the Okhrana belonged to the newly-appointed Court Minister, Count Vorontsov-Dashkov. The latter was not only Cherevin's immediate superior, but also his close friend. Moreover, Vorontsov-Dashkov was one of the leaders of the "Holy Retinue."[53] Therefore, the police and the gendarmes would have fallen under the *de facto* control of this "voluntary organization."

Naturally Ignatiev opposed this plan, which would have deprived the Minister of Internal Affairs of real authority. Ignatiev's opponents responded to his rejection of this plan by trying to engineer his ouster. In November rumors about his dismissal circulated in Petersburg. On November 20 Pobedonostsev mentioned them in a letter to the tsar: "For three days the rumors have persisted stubbornly and spread that there soon will be a change at the Ministry of Internal Affairs, and that Count Ignatiev is leaving. On the third day they discussed this in the salons, and they have made up a whole story about the dissatisfaction which You supposedly expressed to Count Ignatiev. Yesterday and today the ministers have talked seriously about this. The news has gotten to the stock exchange and caused extreme confusion there. . . . It would seem that there is something soft and unsteady in the position of statesmen when the Minister of Internal Affairs and head of the state police feels himself threatened by rumors that have sprung up from God knows where."[54] This rumor did not, of course, appear from nowhere; it was spread by the friends of Vorontsov-Dashkov and Cherevin.

In mid-September the tsar evidently had agreed to Cherevin's project and had written a note to Ignatiev about it. In answer, Ignatiev sent the tsar a letter and a report in which he demonstrated the inexpediency and potential harm of Cherevin's plan. "The only justification for the restoration of the Third Section. . . is that you have more trust in the head of the Okhrana than in the minister. If that is true, it would be simpler to appoint as minister a person who has the good fortune of enjoying Your Majesty's trust."[55] Ignatiev asked the tsar to preserve the existing system, and to change the minister, if necessary. Ignatiev gambled. This time he won. Pobedonostsev acted as mediator; judging by his letter to Ignatiev, he conferred with the tsar the same day.[56] Ignatiev's victory was complete. On 21 December he received a note of gratitude from the tsar. The evidence does not enable one to say what forced Alexander III to change his mind. Certainly the reason was Pobedonostsev's intervention. Apparently, he proved to the tsar that Cherevin's plan was dangerous. Cherevin's project was defeated, and the old system remained intact.

Let us examine the steps taken to "preserve" the existing political regime. The largest was the "Statute on Measures to Preserve State Security and Public Order." In the second half of May a special commission met under Kakhanov to discuss this legislation. Its membership included Cherevin, Plehve, Kazem-Bek, Zurov, Petersburg Municipal Governor Baranov, and the Moscow Police Chief, Kozlov.

On 30 July the Minister of Internal Affairs submitted the commission's draft of legislation to the Committee of Ministers. In his presentation Ignatiev stated that the assassination of Alexander II "could not fail to provoke a special effort to eradicate the causes for the government's partial failure to eliminate sedition."[57] He argued that one important cause was "the absence of proper unity of command in emergency measures against the socialist-revolutionary movement." He then elaborated on this hypothesis by analyzing the unrestricted power given the Governors-General in the decree of 5 April 1879. At the same time, he noted that central agencies had no such unrestricted authority. Ignatiev believed that the absence of such power in central agencies limited the effectiveness of officials, so that they frequently were forced to transgress the limits of their rights. "This certainly demoralized the police officials themselves. . .and the citizens who were constant witnesses of violations of the law by government agencies." Moreover, the lack of agreement in government decrees against the revolutionary movement, according to Ignatiev, was symptomatic "of the vascillation of the government in the choice of methods to fight sedition. This created complex, and not always efficient ways of administration."[58]

Therefore, it was resolved to reexamine and harmonize all existing legislation in order to: (1) compose rules broadening the discretion of the police in the struggle against the revolutionary movement; and (2) write a statute of emergency measures "to safeguard the government and the public order." Ignatiev stated that he approved the commission's project, but he had made a series of changes and editorial amendments.[59,] Judging by Plehve's letter, the Department of State Police was very desirous of a swift confirmation of the proposed statute. On 17 July Plehve wrote to Ignatiev: "In my opinion, certain sections of the new statute should be in effect by 1 September, and it is most essential to hurry its confirmation."[60]

On 4 August the project for a strengthened security force was considered in the Committee of Ministers. In a session lasting three and a half hours the Committee approved the project with certain amendments. Judging by a letter from Pobedonostsev to Ignatiev, most of the amendments were inspired by Minister of Justice Nabokov, and concerned the rights of administrators to dismiss unsuitable officials. "Yesterday I received from Mansurov [Executive Secretary of the Committee of Ministers] a new version of the articles of the security statute. I am very unhappy with them . . . . You will see that they were written on the basis of Nabokov's commentary . . . . In my opinion, this is *nonsense* and contradicts the sense of the whole statute."[61]

The Committee of Ministers confirmed Ignatiev's plan, but only for a three-year period. The Committee reasoned that "certain sections of the Statute on Emergency Measures require [full] legislative confirmation." Therefore, the plan was adopted as "a temporary measure." Simultaneously, the Committee made it possible for the Minister of Internal Affairs to introduce, "as experience dictates, separate legislative proposals on certain special subjects such as strengthening the rights of the police at the local level and changing the existing system of administrative exile."[62] In fact, however, this was a deception. By its nature and significance this issue demanded legislative consideration as a whole—that is, by the State Council. Debate should not have been limited to "certain sections." The government feared opposition in the State Council and decided to discuss the matter in the Committee of Ministers, a smaller and more pliant group. The Committee of Ministers also was empowered to extend the term of the statute.

Let us now consider the contents of the statute, which was published on 8 September. The statute proposed to declare "emergencies" in certain areas of the empire, and to broaden the rights of police agencies. A state of intensified security might be introduced when "public order in a given locality is violated by criminal attacks against the existing system of government, or against persons and property, or by the preparation of such attacks, when the application of existing legislation would be insufficient to preserve order ...". [63] A full-blown emergency would be declared if "the populace of a given area is disturbed by such attacks and emergency measures are necessary to restore order." [64] Thus, the reasons for a declaration of emergency were formulated in such a fashion as to leave much room for interpretation of the law. There were no concrete definitions in the statute. The Minister of Internal Affairs was to have the right to declare a state of intensified security, and the Governors-General also were to enjoy that privilege in their respective provinces. The power to declare a full-blown emergency was reserved to the Committee of Ministers, subject to the tsar's approval. Such declarations of emergency were to be effective during the calendar year when originally enacted, plus six months. Declarations might be extended by the Committee of Ministers if the Minister of Internal Affairs so proposed.

It was therefore rather simple to declare an emergency. The state of intensified security was particularly easy to invoke. Not only the Minister of Internal Affairs, but individual Governors-General could enact this provision of the statute. Such power weakened the principle of centralized authority, and bolstered the independence of administrative officials. The Governors-General, or in their absence, governors and municipal governors might issue mandatory directives "on subjects relating to prevention of violations against public order and state security." [65] Violators of these directives were liable to summary administrative judgment: a fine of up to 500 rubles, or arrest for up to three months. Moreover, these administrators held the right "to prohibit any popular, public, or private assembly, . . . to decree the close of any commercial and industrial enterprise for a temporary period, or until the expiration of the emergency statute, . . . to prohibit individuals from staying in areas affected by the statute." [66]

The Minister of Internal Affairs and the Governors-General enjoyed the right to transfer cases "of crimes covered by the general criminal code to military tribunals just as in wartime when they thought such transfer necessary to preserve public order and tranquility." [67] They could demand a trial *in camera*. Despite the principles of judicial independence, these officials could demand that the procuracy produce "for inspection, in less than two weeks, any separate investigative results or findings not already submitted to judicial purview."[68] This rule gave administrative agencies the right to pressure and influence the course of an investigation and its decision, since Governors-General already had the right to confirm sentences. Finally, governors and municipal governors were to confirm all candidates for positions in the zemstvo and municipal agencies and the courts,[69] and to dismiss employees of these institutions for disloyalty.[70]

Police captains and gendarme directors would have the right to detain for up to two weeks "all persons who inspire reasonable suspicion of having committee state crimes or of having had connections with such crimes, or of having been members of any illegal society."[71] These officials might decide "at any time" to search "in any premises, factory, or manufactory" and to seize any property that they thought necessary. This was the list of rights granted to local administrators under emergency situations under the Statute on Intensified Security. An analysis of these powers reveals that they restored prerogatives of the temporary Governors-General which had been somewhat reduced after the explosion in the Winter Palace. The statute certainly weakened central authority, and strengthened administrative arbitrariness.

The rules in the Statute on Emergency Security deserve attention. First of all, it should be noted that the Statute on Intensified Security remained in force during a real emergency situation. The Governor-General, or in his absence the commander appointed by the tsar, had a number of additional powers. He could (a) arbitrarily fine an individual up to 3000 rubles, or confine him to prison for three months; (b) dismiss any civil servants, including judges and procurators,[72] and also elected officials in estate, municipal, and zemstvo institutions; (c) halt periodical publications during the emergency period; (d) close educational institutions for up to one month; (e) stop or close regular assemblies of estate, municipal, and zemstvo institutions, or when necessary, call emergency sessions of these institutions. Thus Governors-General or plenipotentiaries of the tsar shared enormous powers, which made it possible to interfere in decidedly administrative and judicial matters, and in public life as well.

One section of the statute was called "Rules for Areas Not under Emergency Conditions." Logically this category should have included the whole remainder of the empire not affected by the statute. In fact, the statute had a kind of intermediate application: there were regulations somewhere in between normal regulations and emergency ones. "Simultaneously with the declaration of an emergency in a certain area, the following regulations may be introduced at the discretion of the Committee of Ministers in certain precisely-defined, contiguous provinces or areas, or even throughout the remainder of the empire."[73] These regulations gave to police and gendarmes the right to search or arrest for up to seven days any persons suspected of political crimes. Governors and municipal governors received the power to confirm or dismiss officials serving in zemstvos and municipal institutions, and also judges and arbitrators, as in the Statute on Intensified Security. Finally, in these non-emergency areas cases could be tried in military tribunals by agreement of the Ministers of Internal Affairs and Justice. Therefore, besides the "normal, general governmental system," there were three special conditions of government: (a) for localities not under emergency declarations; (b) for areas under the Statute on Intensified Security; (c) for areas under the Statute on Emergency Security.

The final sections of the statute presented the regulations for administrative exile. The question of exile was decided by a special committee of four members—two from the Ministry of Internal Affairs, and two from the Ministry of Justice—under the chairmanship of the Assistant Minister of Internal Affairs. The term of exile was from one to five years.[74]

Such were the contents of the "Statute on Measures to Preserve State Security and Public Order," which constituted a "*de facto* Russian constitution," according to V.I. Lenin.[75] This statute, adopted as a temporary measure by the Committee of Ministers, remained in effect for 36 years—that is, until the February Revolution of 1917. The publication of this statute was not only symptomatic of the crisis of the autocracy, but also of the instability of the political system in general. The statute was a serious infringement on the independence of the judiciary, the one area of the political superstructure that was the most bourgeois in character.

As I noted earlier, the director of the Department of State Police was extremely desirous of swift confirmation of the statute. In the letter quoted earlier Plehve had written to Ignatiev about the law's practical application. "And so the issue arises: in what framework to apply it? Should it remain subject to those prerequisites about which I wrote you earlier and which set the most extreme measures for Petersburg? An emergency declaration of the second order[76] would be prepared for Moscow, Kharkov, Poltava, Kursk, Kiev, Warsaw, Chernigov, Saratov, Samara, Kherson, Odessa, Ekaterinoslav, and Taganrog provinces. Otherwise, it will be necessary, according to the statute, to summon the Governors-General and decide on further steps in consultation with them."[77]

The attempt to declare an emergency situation in Petersburg and invoke intensified security in eleven provinces demonstrated that confusion and anxiety predominated in the government, and that the country as a whole was extremely tense. In my opinion, confusion and anxiety were more in evidence than any pervasive tension in the nation. There were no justifiable reasons to declare an emergency in Petersburg. There were scarcely any good reasons to intensify security in most of the provinces listed by Plehve. Nevertheless, his plan was adopted.

On 4 September 1881 a decree "On the Publication of the Statute on Measures to Preserve State Security and Public Order and the Declaration of Intensified Security in Certain Areas of the Empire"[78] was signed. The decree began with a detailed preamble summarizing the factors that had forced the government to adopt the measure. The first part of the preamble, which incidentally was half the length of the entire decree, spoke about the assassination of Alexander II. It indicated that "the action of regular legislation, which is designed to deal with the normal condition of public life, is insufficient to preserve the order and tranquility that are being disrupted by notorious and extraordinary events." The preamble pledged not to depart from "the basic elements of the great reforms of the preceding reign," and stressed that "the proper and smooth operation of institutions is the best guarantee of the prosperity and progress of our dear fatherland." The decree noted "the sad need to implement temporary emergency measures to restore complete order and eradicate sedition."[79] The decree claimed that the statute defined precisely the limits of administrative emergency powers.

The long preamble was followed by a declaration of intensified security in Petersburg, Moscow, Kharkov, Poltava, Chernigov, Kiev, Volynia, Podolia, Kherson, and Bessarabia provinces. In addition, intensified security was instituted in the Crimean districts and in the city of Berdiansk in Tauride province, in the city of Voronezh, and in the districts of Rostov-on-Don and Mariupol in Ekaterinoslav province, and in the Odessa, Taganrog, and Kerch-Enikalskoe municipal areas. There had been several changes from the original Plehve project. Petersburg was placed under intensified, not emergency, security. Intensified security was introduced only partially in Ekaterinoslav and Tauride provinces, and not at all in Saratov, Samara, and Kursk. On the other hand, Bessarabia, Volynia, and Podolia were affected by the new measure even though they had not been included in Plehve's original list.

Did the government have justification for this measure? As I said earlier, it did not. Despite the tense situation in the countryside, no large mass peasant demonstrations had occurred since the late 1870s. The activity of the Populists after 1 March also was no justification. The government did not face any immediate threats.[80] The declaration of intensified security is to be explained solely by the confusion and disorientation in the government following the assassination of Alexander II, and by the establishment of a reactionary direction in governmental policy.

The decree also announced that articles 28 through 31 of the Statute of 14 August were being extended to the whole empire. These articles dealt with "areas not in an emergency condition," and permitted the use of administrative measures outlined by the section on intensified security. The whole of Russia was at least partially affected by exceptional legislation. Finally, the decree announced that emergency regulations on administrative exile would apply to the entire country.

The Statute of 14 August 1881 applied in one way or another to the entire nation. The final sections of the decree stressed the loyalty of the people to the autocratic principle. "We remain unalterably convinced that, even in these difficult times for the fatherland, the unbreakable unity of all classes of the loyal Russian people with the supreme power will serve, in the affirmation of truth, order and law, as the surest guarantee of popular welfare, which We take as the sole justification for Our plans and actions."[81] It was an old habit; whenever the government adopted a plan directed against the people it always justified the plan by fine sentiments, and explained that it was acting in the popular interest.

The law on police surveillance, published on 12 March 1882, was linked directly to the Statute of 14 August 1881. It set living conditions for administrative exiles. Upon arrival at their places of confinement exiles received a residence permit—that is, a passport, which served as a certificate of the right to live at that place. A person under surveillance could not leave his place of exile.[82] The police had the right to enter and search an exile's apartment at any time. Persons under surveillance could not work in the civil service, nor in any pedogogical or public job. They were required to obtain the governor's approval for their choices of work. Those without means of support were to be subsidized by the treasury at an unspecified monetary level. The Minister of Internal Affairs might deprive an exile of the right to receive direct correspondence. In such cases correspondence went through the police and gendarmes. The entire life of the exile was subject to trivial regulation.

Although the measures outlined here were intended to "preserve the governmental system and public order," they were not drafted because of any direct need to struggle against the revolutionary movement. They were adopted out of fear of revolution. The government tried not only to strengthen the governmental apparatus, but to broaden the limits of its sway.

Among the reactionary measures adopted by the Ignatiev ministry was censorship. During Ignatiev's tenure as minister sixteen administrative sanctions were enforced against various publishers.[83] One can see more clearly perhaps in this area than in any other the hand of Pobedonostsev, who strove to influence Ignatiev from the outset. In a letter on 21 May Pobedonostsev wrote: "It is impossible to move forward constructively unless the newspapers are bridled."[84] He then called the Minister of Internal Affairs' attention to a "seditious" article in *Golos*. On the next day, 22 May, he returned to the same problem. ". . . Look at the current issue. It is difficult to say how the language of the feature article is distinguished from the expressions in proclamations by *Zemlia i Volia*." Pobedonostsev had in mind a feuilleton in the Kharkov newspaper *Yuzhny Krai*. [Southern Area] He continued: "Permit me to note, however, that all this is allowed by the censor and that there is a whole squadron of bureaucrats who supervise the provincial press."[85]

When Ignatiev accompanied Alexander III to Moscow in June 1881, Pobedonostsev urged Ignatiev not to allow journalists to see the tsar. "Do me a favor. Do not allow any journalist, except Katkov, to see him. Katkov alone is worthy of respect and is a loyal and rational man. All the rest are scoundrels or half-wits."[86] The six-month suspension of the liberal *Golos* made Pobedonostsev very happy. On 26 July, the day after the suspension, he wrote to Ignatiev: "Finally, I see that they have stopped *Golos*. I warmly embrace you, Count Nikolai Pavlovich; only for God's sake, don't relent."[87]

Pobedonostsev was upset by the appearnace of new papers, particularly of Suvorin's proposed publication *Russkoe Delo* [Russian Cause]. Again he pressed Ignatiev: "Aren't enough lies and perversions already being spread by journals and newspapers? What can the publication of new papers do, besides cause further problems? . . . Yet we read constantly about new permits for these new papers."[88] In his chauvinistic tone Pobedonostsev gave progress reports to the Minister of Internal Affairs on the daily press. Pobedonostsev's performance suggests that the reactionary party attached great importance to the fight with the press.

In the spring of 1882 Ignatiev drew up a project for the creation of a Supreme Commission on the Press. A copy of this project has been preserved in his personal archive. Ignatiev attempted to prove that the existing legislation on the press unreasonably hindered the fight against the "harmful direction" taken by the press. He noted that at the present time the only method to close a newspaper or journal was a report by the Minister of Internal Affairs to the First Department of the Senate. However, the minister might exercise this right only after three warnings had been administered to the paper—"that is, only after the publication has managed to do significant harm that hardly can be evaluated fully by the First Department, which cannot follow the general trends in journalism." Therefore, Ignatiev wanted to found a Supreme Commission on the Press, consisting of the Ministers of Internal Affairs, Education, the Supreme Procurator of the Synod, "and members appointed by the tsar." This commission would have to give permission to found "religious-ethical and political-literary journals," and also would examine the question of their suspension. According to Ignatiev, "the decisions of the Supreme Commission, as a high collegial institution, undoubtedly would exert a greater moral influence on society and the press than the decision of one man, issued in the name of the Minister of Internal Affairs and the Governors-General."[89] In my opinion, Ignatiev was concerned not only about "greater influence on society," but chiefly to create conditions whereby the government could deal swiftly and decisively with publications that it did not like.

Ignatiev's project was approved by his crony Pobedonostsev. In a letter dated 9 May 1882, the latter wrote: "Tomorrow you will receive from me an official answer to your communication on censorship. Here I hasten to say that I am in complete agreement with your proposals and I would even broaden somewhat the powers of the proposed commission. . . ."[90]

Of particular interest was Ignatiev's answering letter, in which he shared the Supreme Procurator's ideas about the method of creating a new press law. "I am very glad that you agree with the proposals I made to change the censorship. In the current negative climate you will not get such a law through the State Council, no matter how much Russia may need it. Therefore, one must be content with correction of the present system, if only by a temporary measure. There will be much criticism even then, but the matter will at least be discussed."[91] However, Ignatiev's dismissal as Minister of Internal Affairs prevented him from implementing these temporary measures. The Temporary Regulations on the Press were confirmed by Alexander III on 27 August 1882 as a result of a decision by the Committee of Ministers. The Ignatiev project was the basis of these regulations. This new law was one manifestation of the reactionary course heralded by the Manifesto of 29 April. In the period after 1861 the Russian autocracy often resorted to "temporary regulations" which violated existing legislation of a permanent nature.

Another sign of reaction was the "Temporary Regulations on Jews." The pretext for the publication of these rules was the events of Spring 1881, the Jewish pogroms that occurred in a number of southern provinces, basically with the full concurrence of local authorities.

On 19 October 1881 a Committee on the Jewish Question was formed in the Ministry of Internal Affairs under the chairmanship of Assistant Minister Gotovtsev. The staff included Professor of Police Law Andreevsky, bureaucrats Bestuzhev-Riumin, Voeikov, Prince Tseretelev, and several governors (of St. Petersburg, Tauride, Poltava, Minsk, Kovno, and Volynia provinces). At the local level committees were founded to examine the Jewish question and were asked to forward their recommendations to the Committee on the Jewish Question.[92]

The Committee met on 20, 27, and 30 January and 2 February 1881. The anti-Semitic movement in southern Russia in 1881 had been a part of the fight against the Jewish village bourgeoisie (tavern owners, shopkeepers, and creditors). It must be noted that local officials encouraged this anti-Semitic movement in all sorts of ways. Most *pogromshchiki* were drawn from the Lumpenproletariat, as one can clearly see in the example of Kiev. The Committee on the Jewish Question decided to enact four extremely reactionary "temporary measures." The first measure reviewed the prohibition against Jewish residence outside cities and small villages. It "granted to Jewish artisans the right to reside on noble manors or in villages when the village assemblies are in agreement." The second measure prohibited Jews from building or purchasing homes outside cities and small villages. The third forbade land "ownership and use, by purchase, rent, mortgage and management either personally or in cooperation with someone else, in areas outside of the cities and villages of the Pale."[93] The fourth proposal forbade Jews to take part in the liquor trade.

All these measures, with the exception of the fourth, affected only bourgeois elements. The measures were very harsh since they involved relocation of Jews from the areas where their parents, grandparents, and great-grandparents had lived. In addition, it is not difficult to see the clear purpose of this legislation, which was designed to eliminate the competition of the Jewish bourgeoisie, although the members of the Committee did not directly express their concern for Christian tavern owners, shopkeepers, and creditors, but rather began from their reactionary and chauvinistic assumptions. The Minister of Internal Affairs approved these proposals, but altered and added to them. He proposed a complete prohibition against Jewish residence in rural areas regardless of the opinions of the local population. Ignatiev's amendments demonstrated open concern for the interests of Christian tavern owners and shopkeepers. "Trade on Sundays and on Christian holidays will be forbidden to Jews; this will follow the principle that commercial institutions, closed on Jewish holidays, also must be closed on Christian holidays."[94] Thus Ignatiev showed a "touching concern" for Jewish shopkeepers, allowing them to celebrate not only their own, but also Christian holidays.

On 3 March 1882 the Minister of Internal Affairs presented his proposals to the Committee of Ministers, although they should have been discussed in the State Council first. The presentation was designed to acquaint the ministers with Ignatiev's plan and to elicit their responses, which were generally hostile. Minister of Finance Bunge spoke sharply against the proposals. "It must be recognized that these proposals cannot fail to elicit serious objections, even if they are properly implemented; this will be particularly true if they are adopted swiftly not as an organic law, but rather as temporary regulations. These regulations will be applied to hundreds of thousands of people with very extensive commercial operations and agreements, the fate of which is connected in most cases with the interests of the Christian population."[95]

Then the Minister of Finance pointed out that the government had tried many times before to apply strict measures to the Jews, but eventually had rejected these measures because they were financially unwise. Moreover, he indicated that the practical implementation of Ignatiev's plan would lead to all sorts of abuses (bribery, drinking bouts). "In such a situation troublemakers easily could exploit government directives and create more serious disturbances. It must be added that the return to the cities of Jews from rural areas could place in a difficult position, not only the migrants, but also the inhabitants of the cities and the local authorities themselves, for the authorities would have to arrange for the shelter of the migrant Jews. In conclusion, restrictive legislation at the present time will cause more problems for the government and will complicate the political situation in the nation by creating a mass of dissatisfied people, not only among the Jews, but also among the population that has commercial ties with the Jews. . . ."[96]

Bunge insisted that "in any case" such legislation could not be adopted without discussion in the State Council—that is, in the prescribed legal manner. The Minister of Finance decisively rejected Ignatiev's plan. The Minister of State Domains also was basically against the proposals. Without touching on the procedural issue, he agreed that the Ignatiev plan arose out of "the actual demands of the situation." "At the same time, one cannot help but wish that the introduction of these rules would be followed by a reduction of violence, and increase in order, and by the greatest possible limitation on the suffering of tens of thousands of individuals, although they may be Jews." He observed that Ignatiev's proposals did "not satisfy this last requirement."[97]

Minister of Justice Nabokov was also a strong opponent of Ignatiev's plan. He thought that it could not be considered outside of the context of a general solution to the Jewish question. According to the Minister of Justice, this could be done only in the prescribed legislative fashion; it would have to be discussed in the State Council. Nabokov saw a political danger in the adoption of the Ignatiev plan. "In the current intellectual climate, which dictates special care in the publication of government decisions, the migration of the Jews from rural areas, and the removal of their rights to own or use any property in those areas, may increase the number of dissatisfied people, not only among Jews, but also in the native population. Certainly the Jews' loss of property often will affect negatively those persons who have some business connection with the Jews."[98] The Minister of Justice argued that Ignatiev's plan would harm the economic position of a large part of the provincial population living in the Pale. In conclusion, Nabokov again emphasized "the very serious difficulties" that were bound to arise in connection with the migration of tens of thousands of people, particularly if they "resisted" the migration.

All the ministers who reacted to Ignatiev's proposals spoke against them. Discussion of the issue in the Committee of Ministers did not provoke a sympathetic response. Golovnin reported to Miliutin that all members of the Committee had opposed the Minister of Internal Affairs' plan.[99] Ignatiev's chief opponent had been Bunge, who had shown that the plan would have disastrous effects. Solsky also spoke against Ignatiev. Criticizing the inaction of local authorities during the pogroms, the chairman of the Committee of Ministers, Reutern wrote in his summary: "Everyone should be defended against infringements of their rights. Today they bait and rob the Jews. Tomorrow they will turn on the so-called kulaks [rich peasants] . . . . Then merchants and landowners will take their turns under the gun. In other words, given such inaction by the authorities, one may expect the development in the very near future of the most terrible socialism."[100] In the final analysis, Ignatiev himself did not even insist on the adoption of his own plan. He confined himself to proposals to prohibit future Jewish settlement in rural areas and to prohibit the issuance of liquor licenses, and to permit the acquisition of immovable property outside the cities.[101] However, even these proposals were not accepted *in toto* by the committee.

The decision of the Committee of Ministers fell into two parts. The first spoke of the impermissibility of anti-Semitic disorders. It said that the government "must make it absolutely clear to everyone that violation of Jewish persons or property will bring prosecution under the general criminal laws that apply to the rest of the population, . . .that the government will not stop at extreme measures to suppress anti-Semitic disorders. . . ."[102] The second part dealt with measures to guard "the interest of the local populace." As a temporary expedient "until there is a general review of the legislation on Jews," the Committee recommended prohibition of Jewish settlement in rural areas, with the exception of existing agricultural colonies. It was also proposed, again as a temporary plan, to halt the notarization of commercial contracts, mortgages, rent agreements on land, and to prohibit liquor trade on Sundays and holidays. Moreover, there were other restrictions on Jewish trade in wine.

The tsar confirmed this decision on 3 May. As I noted earlier, Ignatiev did not succeed in implementing his plan. Even in the Committee of Ministers, which was at that time a most reactionary group, the project encountered friendly opposition. Alexander III himself, despite his pathological hatred of Jews, did not support his Minister of Internal Affairs. Why? Certainly the opposition to Ignatiev had nothing to do with a positive concern for the fate of Jews. The fact that the government shrank from the Ignatiev plan suggests a fear of its consequences, and not so much the economic consequences as the political ones. Even though the year since the assassination of Alexander II had not witnessed any new serious events, the fear of them was just as great as before. After all, nine years later the government did not hesitate to resettle several thousand Moscow Jews outside the city, notwithstanding all the disadvantages of this move.[103]

Yet it should be noted that the first part of the Committee of Minister's decision condemning pogroms was not at all insincere. The government actually was afraid of such disorders since they might be turned against someone other than Jews. Any kind of mass movement, even one of a reactionary nature, struck fear into the government. Alexander III once told General Gurko: "Deep in my soul I am very glad when they beat up the Jews, but nevertheless, it cannot be allowed."[104]

Ignatiev's activity was not confined to the support of reactionary policies. He also advocated a number of others. Among them were economic reforms which were—whatever their limitations—the realization of Loris-Melikov's policies. These reforms were clearly bourgeois in nature. Secondly, Ignatiev urged several political reforms. During this period the government could not pursue a policy of direct and overt reaction. The fear which had been aroused by previous events was still too great for that. Consequently, the government was forced to "deceive" the public for a time,[105] as V.I. Lenin said. For example, one of Ignatiev's measures—the invitation to so-called "informed persons" to participate in various political discussions—was pure demogoguery. Other steps in zemstvo politics, like the creation of the Kakhanov Commission, were not so obviously demagogic although objectively they also were designed to fool the public.

Let us turn to the government's economic proposals. On 9 May Alexander III examined the minutes of the 27 April Plenary Session of the State Council. He confirmed the decision to transfer temporarily-obligated peasants to redemption payments, and also the general amount of the reduction in annual redemption payments (9 million rubles), as well as the cancellation of arrears on these payments (a sum amounting to 14 million rubles). However, the tsar requested that the distribution of reductions over individual provinces be discussed again in a meeting of the Ministers of Finance, Internal Affairs, and State Domains with experts to be appointed by these ministers. The group would work out its schedule so that its conclusions could be presented to the State Council after the summer holidays.

Thus the opinion of the tsar coincided completely with that of Pobedonostsev and the latter's ideological cohorts.[106] During June the Special Ministerial Committee met with 13 zemstvo experts.[107] In their examination of the distribution of payment reductions over individual provinces, the experts unanimously concluded that reductions in redemption payments could not be limited to non-blacksoil provinces, but would have to be extended over all of Russia, except for the western provinces, where mandatory redemption had been adopted in 1863.[108] The experts also unanimously asked that the annual reduction of payments be increased from 9 million to 12 million rubles.

However, the experts were divided on the issue "of the primary assumptions behind reduction of redemption payments, and the method of reduction itself." According to the majority (Galagan, Dmitriev, Kalachov, Koliupanov, Samarin, and Prince Shcherbatov), redemption payments "should be considered those payments which redeem not a rent on land, but a personal obligation to the seigneur that is sanctioned by the state. . . . Redemption payments, being neither a rent on land, nor a property tax, must be in proportion not only to the earning power of the land, according to which the payments are now fixed, but also to the tax-paying power of the peasants, defined by the totality of indices which measure the extent of their welfare."[109] This opinion expressed the openly seigneurial and feudal outlook of D.F. Samarin, who also defended the notion that redemption payments had no relation to the cost of land, but were the sum of the obligations of a "governmental nature." Based on these arguments, the majority of experts proposed to reduce payments by 20 per cent over the whole nation, excluding the western provinces.[110] Independent of this general reduction in payments, the majority of experts considered it necessary to make additional reductions in individual regions of the country, hard-hit by unfavorable circumstances. The additional reduction of three million rubles would be made in the same manner.

The minority of experts (Gorchakov, Olenin, Naumov, Shatalov) preferred to think of redemption payments in direct relation to the price of land. Therefore, they argued that "redemption payments should be in correspondence with all the benefits received by peasants from the land allotments in each province, where there is an unreasonably heavy amount of payments." (This notion would have required a reduction in payments of 8.5 million rubles.) "Only after payments become more nearly equal to those of other localities, which have a more favorable position, can there be a general reduction of ten per cent in redemption payments throughout Russia."[111]

The experts did not disagree on the issue of cancelling arrears in redemption payments throughout Russia. They all thought this proposal necessary. The special group of three ministers supported the majority opinion, and made its own recommendations accordingly. Thus the annual reduction of redemption payments was to be twelve million rubles. Of this, some seven million would be devoted to the general reduction: this was one ruble per soul in all the provinces affected by "The All-Russian Statute on Peasants Leaving the Status of Serfs." In Poltava, Kharkov, and Chernigov provinces redemption payments would be lower by sixteen per cent. The committee concluded: "The money remaining after this general reduction—about five million rubles in silver—will be used for further reduction in those areas where peasants need a reduction in obligations due to difficult conditions."[112] Data on these conditions would be provided by zemstvo statisticians and examined in zemstvo assemblies.

In October the issue of lowered redemption payments was reviewed in the Joint Bureau of the Main Committee on the Condition of

Agriculture and the Departments of Laws and State Economy. In these deliberations the majority endorsed the proposals of the Special Ministerial Committee,[113] and only four members (Count E.T. Baranov, A.P. Zablotsky-Desiatovsky, K.K. Grot, and N.I. Stoianovsky) insisted that redemption payments be calculated according to the price and earning-power of land. In other words, they argued that payments should be lowered first in non-blacksoil provinces, as the government originally had planned.

In plenary sessions on 30 November, and 7 and 21 December there were again heated arguments over reduction of redemption payments. In the first session eleven members of the Joint Bureau took the minority position,[114] Thirty-four comprised the majority,[115] and two members—A.V. Golovnin and his associate S.A. Greig filed separate opinions. Golovnin and Greig concluded that "the methods of distribution of the allotted sum among separate provinces and localities and the details of the plan in general should be discussed again after the Ministry of Internal Affairs has received data on the degree of economic difficulty of former serfs."[116] Essentially, Golovnin was proposing to begin discussion of how to lower redemption payments all over again.

At the session of 7 December, the constellation of forces had changed. Fifteen members supported the special opinion of Golovnin.[117] Now only twenty-seven members supported the "majority" position, and five supported the "minority" view. Finally, when the minutes were being read at the session of 21 December, the "minority" announced that it too was now in support of the Golovnin plan. In the end, twenty-seven members supported reduction of redemption payments in accordance with the recommendations of the Special Ministerial Committee, and twenty members thought it best to return to the issue of methods to lower payments. On 28 December 1881 Alexander III confirmed the majority position. At the same time he promulgated the law on the transfer of peasants to mandatory redemption, which first had been approved in the spring of 1881.[118]

While transferring the peasants to obligatory redemption the government also displayed its concern for the landed gentry by trying to compensate them for the loss of their assets through a supplemental payment. In this regard there was an interesting memorandum from Ignatiev, dated 24 December, which is preserved in his personal papers. This memorandum stressed the need to guard the rights "of the loyal Russian nobility" and to preserve the nobility's "dominant position in Russia." The memorandum raised the issue of support for the middle and petty nobility which had "retained its unsevered bonds with the country and now serves as the most loyal support and instrument of proper government." Ignatiev proposed to subsidize gentry who owned less than 300 revisional [census] souls, taking into account the total arrears in quitrent run up by former serfs, and the magnitude of reduced redemption payments. "If on such estates the arrears are significant, tax enforcement is of little avail, and the landowner desires to repudiate these arrears and receive hard cash, then it would seem justified to give him a money subsidy of up to twenty per cent of the total redemption loan."[119]

The tsar approved this memorandum, but the proposed plan never was adopted in practice.[120] The issue of subsidies to the gentry was resolved differently in May 1883. A law, published during the coronation period, provided that gentry, whose serfs had gone on mandatory redemption, would receive a subsidy of one-twelfth the total redemption loan.[121] Even though redemption payments were not calculated in accordance with the price of land, the reduction of redemption payments, as well as the introduction of mandatory redemption, was important since it accelerated the growth of capitalism in the countryside.

While the process of economic development demanded the introduction of mandatory redemption, the immediate pretext for the adoption of this measure and for the reduction of redemption payments was the tension in the countryside. Other proposals made by Loris-Melikov and approved by the Joint Bureau and the Plenary Session of the State Council subsequently either were dropped entirely, or else adopted in adulterated form. Among these was the law on the renting of land and migrations, the opening of the Peasant Land Bank and the abolition of the head tax.

On 22 May Alexander III confirmed a decision of the Committee of Ministers "On the Granting to Peasant Communes, as a Temporary Measure, Certain Advantages in the Renting of Land."[122] This law permitted peasants to rent treasury land that had been under auction "regardless of their distance from the land;" it also allowed peasants to substitute community pledges for monetary collateral in land rental. This law was of very little assistance to the peasantry; it did not diminish substantially the land hunger of the peasants.

The law on migrations was similar in nature. On 30 June the Committee of Ministers examined the "Temporary Rules on Peasant Migrations to Free Lands." While formerly only land-poor peasants had been allowed to resettle, now peasants of all categories could resettle. The law did focus on those peasants who had received an unencumbered allotment in the Emancipation. These peasants generally constituted the poorest layer of the rural community. The upper size of the allotment was fixed at not more than eight desiatins per revisional soul. The payment for the land was set in accordance with the price of quitrent on treasury land. On the banks of the Volga, not far from Syzpan, a migrations office was established. This decision of the Committee of Ministers was not published in order to avoid mass peasant resettlement.[123] The Ministry of State Domains was made responsible for granting resettlement permits, regardless of the formal position or status of the peasant family. Later the issue of resettlements was discussed by "informed persons," but this led to no practical results.

Let us turn to the foundation of the Peasant Bank.[124] On 20 May 1881 Alexander III ordered consideration of how to "Facilitate Peasant Use of Credit for Land Purchase."[125] The original draft statute on the Peasant Bank was written toward mid-December. A commission in the Ministry of Finance dealt with the question. Three ministers signed the draft statute: the Ministers of Internal Affairs, Finance, and State Domains. It proposed the creation of a Peasant Bank within the Main Redemption Administration under the aegis of that agency's chairman. Loans could be granted to individual peasant proprietors, as well as to agricultural societies as a whole, and to associations of peasant proprietors. These latter could receive loans only if the majority of members lived in a single district. Individual proprietors were eligible for loans only if there was no communal land tenure in their village, and if the proprietors did not own a full allotment. Loans could be granted up to eighty percent of the total sale price of land. There were two periods for repayment: 24 and a half and 34 and a half years.

The project assumed the preservation of existing forms of land tenure, a matter about which the three ministers spoke directly in their presentation. They noted that the operations of the bank "should not be transformed into an indirect method to change the existing forms of land ownership and use; the loan procedure must apply to the established conditions of land ownership, not shaking the communal system of tenure, where it exists."[126] It was proposed that loans not exceed the sums necessary to obtain land in a quantity not greater than the largest allotment established in a given locality. As V.A. Vdovin justly observed, the project did not satisfy the interests of those whom it was designed to assist: the land-poor and landless peasants. The project set a high interest rate on instalments (twelve percent annually), and required large down payments (twenty percent on the total value).

Having been presented to the State Council, the project was subjected to the usual review; due to the criticisms of some council members, it was amended. The loan ceiling was decreased from eighty to seventy-five per cent of the sale value of land. The amount of loans that could be made to a single revisional soul was now to be based on the form of land ownership. The concept of a peasant "association" was defined more precisely, and so were the preconditions for land acquisition by peasant societies.

In mid-February the amended statute was considered again in the State Council. It was discussed in the Joint Bureau of two departments—the Department of Laws and State Economy and the Main Committee on the Condition of Agriculture. Sessions of the Joint Bureau occurred on 20 and 25 February, and 4 March 1882. Two members of the Joint Bureau, Mansurov and Shuvalov, opposed the project, because they saw it as a threat to gentry landownership. In their opinions, the very principle of making loans for land acquisition would arouse "the fatal expectations of the peasants concerning an additional partition of land."[127] They believed that the opening of the bank would be "tantamount to a fundamental decision by the state on an issue of crucial importance: on the need for the preservation in Russia of any large property."[128] According to Mansurov and Shuvalov, the Peasant Bank would not distract the peasants from the notion that they might receive an additional allotment of land; on the contrary, it would reinforce that notion. The majority of the Joint Bureau endorsed the project, but made a number of amendments. These changes touched every aspect of the original project that the peasants might have associated with a change in the existing sizes of allotments. The members opposed granting loans based on the present land holdings of peasants. In addition, they decided not to make the bank a part of the Main Redemption Administration. At a Plenary Session of the State Council on 26 April, twelve members supported the Shuvalov-Mansurov position. Among them, Pobedonostsev was the most forceful.

Pobedonostsev wrote to Ignatiev: "I myself would like to sink the Peasant Land Bank. I consider it a false institution, one link in the false chain plaited by the policy of Loris-Melikov and Abaza: the salt tax, redemption payments, millions payed to the State Bank and to the Peasant Bank. This is useless expenditure of treasury money and it introduces permissive elements into the popular consciousness."[129] Judging by the beginning of this letter, one can assume that Ignatiev had made "advances" at Pobedonostsev's expense.[130] However, in the Plenary

Session the Minister of Internal Affairs did not support his mentor. There were heated debates in the Plenary Session. Along with Pobedonostsev, a number of other reactionaries spoke: A.E. Timashev, Count D.A. Tolstoy, T.I. Filippov, and others. Describing the arguments in the meeting, Valuev wrote: "Everything centered around how the promise of credit for land purchase might deflect the peasants hope for a 'black partition' and might make them more loyal citizens."[131]

The result of this discussion was the presentation of two opinions to Alexander III: the majority was in favor of the bank, and the minority was opposed. Alexander confirmed the majority opinion. During the Plenary Session the statute had been amended. From it was excluded everything which might have sown among the peasantry the hope of acquiring additional land. There were several changes in the conditions for land purchase: the term for down payment was lengthened, and the annual interest rate on instalments was reduced. While the concept of the Peasant Land Bank was itself a bourgeois notion that would have guaranteed a more rapid development of capitalism, the concrete terms in the organization of the bank suggested a concern about the sale of gentry land. Assistant Minister of State Domains Kulomzin, summarizing in his memoirs a conversation with D.A. Tolstoy about the Peasant Bank, wrote: ". . . I consider this institution to be the salvation of the declining nobles from the usurers; they can sell part of their property to save the rest of it."[132] That is how the law functioned in reality.

To conclude this section, let us examine the issue of the abolition of the head tax. The question of "The Replacement of the Head Tax by Other Taxes" was introduced in the State Council by Minister of Finance Bunge on 29 March 1882.[133] The abolition of this purely feudal tax had been raised much earlier. In 1876 a special commission, chaired by Grand Duke Konstantin Nikolaevich, had been founded on Reitern's initiative to consider this question. However, the war had hindered its deliberations.

Statesmen returned to the problem after the Russo-Turkish war. Minister of Finance Greig had chaired an inter-agency commission on the subject. The commission had concluded that the head tax should be replaced by three other taxes: (1) an income tax of three per cent on net income; (2) a manor tax; (3) a personal tax of one ruble for every male between 18 and 55 years old. Loris-Melikov also had considered the abolition of the head tax and had made it a part of his economic program. Bunge thought it necessary to phase out the head tax, which, according to the budget for 1882 brought in 58,793,358 rubles.[134]

Bunge assumed that the introduction of a state income tax (in all its variations) would yield about 70 million rubles, which would more than compensate for the revenue lost from the head tax. He advocated universal abolition of the head tax over an eight-year period, beginning in 1882. Levies of the tax from the less-prosperous levels of society would cease in 1883, and would be added to arrears. The Minister of Finance's opinion was circulated in the Special Committee, which included Reutern, Count Baranov, Solsky, Ignatiev, Ostrovsky, and Bunge. The Committee approved Bunge's plan, but made several amendments.

The Joint Bureau of the Departments of Laws and State Economy and of the Main Committee on the Condition of Agriculture examined Bunge's plan in sessions on 8 and 21 April. The Joint Bureau endorsed the Special Committee's decisions with the exception of the section on adding to arrears, since that might discourage prompt payment of other duties not yet abolished. On 3 May 1882 the Plenary Session affirmed the decision of the United Departments and observed that the abolition of the head tax "is not charity in the strict sense, but a state action intended to eliminate a taxation system that hinders the development of the popular welfare."[135] However, the discussion of this measure by the Plenary Session was rather lively. Pobedonostsev and M_____ _____ _____ he head tax. Greig insisted on _____ [136] On 18 May the Plenary emperor.[137]

pted during the Ignatiev min-
is in nature. In addition to
accelerated by the crisis of

es defended by Ignatiev that
f the earlier liberal policy.
er demagogic flavor. Dema-
summon "informed individ-
ing. Superficially, this plan
likov's proposals to involve
us state reforms. In reality,
_____ individuals was so much political window-dressing.

In late May Ignatiev issued his first invitation in connection with discussions on the reduction of redemption payments. The thirteen individuals picked by Ignatiev included marshals of the nobility and zemstvo personnel, who were rather reactionary in their political views. It is enough to say that the majority upheld the seigneurial position of D.F. Samarin. Essentially, the "informed individuals" endorsed the opinion of Ignatiev, Pobedonostsev, and Ostrovsky on the method to reduce redemption payments.

The Minister of Internal Affairs was very pleased with this "successful experiment," and he decided to try it again. In late September a second session of "informed individuals" was planned to discuss the liquor and resettlement issues. This time 32 people were invited.[138] Besides marshals of the nobility and zemstvo chairmen, the group included simple landowners and even the Kostroma merchant, Morokin, and a "representative of the peasantry," district elder Kostrov of Rostov district, Yaroslavl province. To open the meeting Ignatiev read a speech full of demagogic statements; he claimed that the group had been called together because "the most vital issues could not be resolved without the contribution of local leaders."[139] This meeting, it must be said, had no concrete results, although the group had put in nearly a month's work. For example, after two weeks of discussion on the liquor question the committee decided that it was necessary to preserve the number of liquor distributors, to replace taverns by eating houses, and it also recognized the legal right of rural societies to open bars.[140]

Another step in the liberal direction was the creation of the so-called Kakhanov Commission. On 4 September 1881 Ignatiev presented to the tsar a memorandum on the need to draft reforms of provincial institutions. "The administrative arrangement established during the existence of serfdom, when the old courts still operated and the government conducted local economic affairs, obviously is unable to function satisfactorily today," wrote Ignatiev.[141] He added that the senatorial inspections then being concluded had gathered data on the needs of local administration, and the Ministry of Internal Affairs had been deluged with various proposals for reform of peasant institutions. "Under the circumstances, I deem it useful to found a new special commission under the chairmanship of a reliable person who works in the high bureaucracy and who is fully experienced in administration."[142] Ignatiev recommended Kakhanov, who only recently had served as an assistant minister. The Commission itself would be comprised of representatives from various departments, and the senators who had conducted the inspections. Ignatiev also thought that "informed persons" should be acquainted with the final recommendations of the Commission. This memorandum was approved by Alexander III.

A month and a half later on 19 October, Ignatiev presented a new memorandum to the tsar concerning the "direction of commission operations." He began by asserting the need "to define as exactly as possible" both the focus of Commission activity and its methods of operation. According to Ignatiev, one might succeed in preparing reform only by simultaneous consideration of the whole structure of local administration and the reconciliation of it with the affairs of the government and the needs of society."[143] Thus Ignatiev proposed to embark on reorganization of the entire system of district and provincial administration. "Without review of the status of all institutions it will be impossible to attain the goals set by the tsar for his commission—the improvement of local administrative institutions in general, with the strengthening of local authority, reduction of the number of separate agencies and of red-tape that hinders local administration, and the involvement of the zemstvo in local administration with a precise definition of its rights, obligations, and responsibility."[144] Alexander III also approved this memo.[145]

It would appear that the organization of the Commission and its purposes were proof that the government continued on its earlier reformist path. This impression is reinforced by the appointment of a liberal bureaucrat, Kakhanov, as chairman, since he was in fact an author of Loris-Melikov's reformist projects. There is no evidence to support the notion that the creation of the Kakhanov Commission was a consciously demagogic ploy, although it certainly was demagogic in objective terms. The fact that such a measure was approved by Alexander III suggests, in my opinion, that there were still uncertainties in the government's political policy, which was an expression of the continuing autocratic crisis.

The Kakhanov Commission began its operations in late November. From then until January the Commission worked out a detailed procedural plan, which was confirmed in April 1882 by the Committee of Ministers.[146] However, even with the Commission's first steps it was clear that the Commission would not be allowed to do anything really substantive. For example, Polovtsov recorded on 23 April the following conversation with Kakhanov: "I dropped in to see Kakhanov, who informed me that in yesterday evening's session[147] Ignatiev's assistant, Gotovtsev,[148] had announced that the Commission must not study the question of the police, which would be considered by another group and discussed in the State Council. At this, the members could only state that the Commission might as well be closed. Gotovtsev also announced that the Commission could not broaden the rights of the zemstvo at the expense of the Ministry's power."[149] The creation of the Kakhanov Commission was essentially the same sort of ploy as the invitation to "informed persons" to participate in government deliberations, since it could not study seriously the vital issues of local administration.

There remains the final matter of political policy *vis-à-vis* the zemstvo. Ignatiev considered it his primary task to frustrate the political ambitions of the zemstvos, ambitions expressed in various petitions that were distributed widely after March 1881. Yet the struggle with the zemstvo took relatively mild forms and did not bring in its wake any serious retributions. For example, after the Tver zemstvo assembly had submitted a petition advocating that delegates be summoned from everywhere in Russia [for a zemstvo congress], Ignatiev sent a circular to all governors indicating that such petitions should not be protested, since by their very essence they already had been protested by the law. Articles thirteen and fourteen on the procedure of business in social and class institutions prohibited enactment and subsequent use of such petitions." According to Ignatiev, "this method of rejecting illegal zemstvo proclamations was most expedient since it prevented a second discussion on the merits of the petitions that inevitably would follow an official protest."[150] Ignatiev solved the problem rather archly by simply ignoring petitions that contained "illegal" demands. Throughout 1881 the Ministry of Internal Affairs abided by this circular, and in only one instance took semi-administrative measures.[151] This liberal approach to "seditious petitions" demonstrated the weakness and indecisiveness of the government, which was still in a crisis situation.

The Ministry of Internal affairs presented an overview of zemstvo institutions in the document quoted above. Ignatiev began by describing the history of the mutual relations between the government and the zemstvo. "Soon after their foundation zemstvo institutions were subjected from various sides to unfair criticism and unfavorable reactions. Consequently, their legally-defined jurisdiction was somewhat narrowed and the prescribed right to petition for assistance did not always achieve its purpose." Moreover, in the late 1870s the "restriction of zemstvo activity reached extreme limits;" in 1880 there was a *volte face* in the government's relations with the zemstvo. According to Ignatiev, "the natural result" of this change in policy was that certain zemstvos exceeded their rights, "an invasion, so to speak, into the field of state administration through various petitions and addresses about the convocation of a Zemsky Sobor, of elected officials from all the zemstvos, and so on." Later Ignatiev stated that the future policy of the government toward zemstvos would not provoke doubts and would conform to the Manifesto of 29 April.

Ignatiev emphasized, however, that to attain this end the government should not proceed by draconian measures, but should seek the kind of relationship "which, without severe repression, will provide the opportunity to hold the zemstvo within its legally-defined jurisdiction."[152] He developed this proposition in detail, citing his circular to the governors and his whole attitude toward the zemstvo. In the zemstvo question Ignatiev took a very moderate position, which testified to the government's fear of making a decisive break with the liberals at that time. In addition, Ignatiev's zemstvo policy was determined by his Slavophile sympathies. Obviously, Alexander III did not share his minister's views on the zemstvo question. Therefore, he did not approve Ignatiev's memorandum, but limited himself to the marginal comment: "Read."

The government's education policy now deserves attention. Almost simultaneously with the Ignatiev circular on 6 May the recently-appointed Minister of Education, Baron Nikolai, sent a communiqué to the trustees of educational districts. This document contained a more or less clear definition of the new minister's attitude toward education. With relation to post-secondary schools, Baron Nikolai began with the Statute of 1863, asserting that "the firm legal establishment of the relationship between the professoriate and the university and its student body will serve as the best assurance of the gradual restoration of order and a return to those conditions of proper scholarly life which alone can guarantee success to the professors."[153]

The minister emphasized the need for communication between high schools and the family, and for public figures to supervise those secondary schools that are maintained at their expense. Baron Nikolai also presented a clear and precisely formulated program for elementary schools, in which a large space was devoted to school councils. "School councils exist for the collective action of the government and local representatives; the significance and rights of the councils must be respected. The director and inspector of public schools must act as symbols of the government's concern for education, and not as instruments to hinder local independence. They must respect and encourage local autonomy."[154]

Nikolai was an advocate of the liberal orientation in public education. Describing the circular quoted above, the newspaper *Strana* noted with satisfaction that the Minister of Education's program was "a direct condemnation of Count Tolstoy's policies at all institutional levels."[155] Naturally Baron Nikolai opposed the Tolstoy program for the rest of his brief tenure as minister.[156] As I noted earlier in this book, Nikolai took a stronger position on the abolition of the 1879 Instruction than his predecessor Saburov, and the State Council abolished the Instruction in early May primarily because of Nikolai's adamant opposition to it. Nikolai succeeded in forcing the complete restoration of the 1863 University Charter. Yet it was not the personal influence of Nikolai so much as the vacillations of government policy after 29 April that made the restoration of the charter possible. The confusion that had gripped the nation's elite after the murder of Alexander II had not passed, and for this reason the tsar confirmed the majority opinion of the State Council on educational policy.

Although the emperor confirmed the 26 May decision of the Plenary Session of the State Council, which reinstituted the 1863 charter, he made a move the day before that directly contradicted the new policy. On 25 May the tsar had empanelled a special commission under the chairmanship of I.D. Delianov, the right-hand man of Tolstoy while Tolstoy had been Minister of Education. The commission was to draft rules for more careful supervision of students.[157] This contradictory step was a result of the continuing crisis of the autocracy, another vacillation in government policy.

The direct pretext for creation of the Delianov Commission was a memorandum submitted to the tsar in May, apparently by Ignatiev.[158] "Nowhere in the world," began the memorandum, "have post-secondary educational institutions become breeding grounds for political criminals to the extent that they have in Russia. Almost all the regicides and a large part of those involved in state offenses are university students. In no other nation where there prevails such disorder in elementary and trade schools is it possible to attain a university education at state or public expense so easily."[159] The author then argued that "in the fight against sedition the condition of post-secondary schools must not be ignored: it is necessary to adopt energetic measures to avoid a repetition of that process which occurred with Podbelsky and Rysakov—that is, to avoid turning the best high school students into dangerous fanatics and criminals in half a year."

The author recommended the following steps: (a) to limit the number of stipends, and to transfer part of them from universities in Moscow and Petersburg to the provinces; (b) to accept "for the time being" in Petersburg post-secondary schools only those persons "able to support themselves, or those who present guarantees of their trustworthiness."[160] The author of the memorandum thought it best that these measures be timed so that they would be fully effective by the beginning of the next school year. Then the author dealt with the condition of elementary and secondary schools. He said that the whole school system was intended to "lead the pupil out of his home and, making him unsuited for his former work, to arouse in him the desire to continue his education in high school and eventually in college." The author noted that there were no schools in Russia of a practical, vocational type which answered the needs of the various levels of society.

Thereupon the memorandum discussed the need to find more effective methods to expel young people from the capital than the existing system of administrative exile. It even noted that politically-unreliable youths had no opportunity to earn money in their places of exile. According to the author, the most satisfactory method would be to "send students to the Turkistan military district as soldiers." If this could not be arranged, he thought that the government should "set up work houses with parcels of land where students would be taught to work, or trained as artisans; then students would be housed outside of the cities in special work settlements in distant provinces."[161] This proposal, as we know, was not original. A similar plan had been debated in the spring of 1878 in the Special Commission. Of course, one must give the author of the plan credit for making another "step forward." While the 1878 proposal had called for the eventual return of student offenders to post-secondary schools, the current plan called for perpetual exile.

The author concluded with a summary and a recommendation to create a special commission for the discussion of measures to hinder the growth of the revolutionary movement in post-secondary educational institutions. Thus it was recommended to discuss the issue of removing "artificial incentives for young people to attain a college education," that is, to establish barriers against matriculation in universities and colleges by members of the democratic elements of society. It was proposed to transfer certain educational institutions from Petersburg to other cities. This plan also was not new. In the 1860s S.G. Stroganov had recommended that individual departments of Petersburg and Moscow universities be moved to other cities.

Finally, two points of the memorandum—the first and the fourth—dealt with the supervision of students. The author wanted to register student apartments and to follow through police channels and through the inspection of apartment owners "the occupancy of the apartments and tenant changes." The last point recommended the establishment of a system "of student work and supervision over students that would reduce the student body to the really serious learners."[162] Less serious students would be sent home. The proposals also advocated abolition of auditors, "except in especially respectable cases." Such were the positions adopted in the memorandum. They were all repressive and were not substantively new, since they repeated proposals made in 1878 and 1879.

Aside from the memorandum, there were other reactionary influences at work on Alexander III. These included reactionary public figures led by Katkov. At about this time Katkov sent to the tsar a voluminous memorandum on the conditions of universities. Unlike other critics, Katkov illuminated and focused critical attention on the internal structure of the universities. "If the situation in our universities continues for some time, if the government remains impassive and ignorant of what is going on there, if the power of the revolutionary party gains strength over the steadily-growing mass of students, the state will soon find itself in real danger."

Lamenting the passage of the time when strict rules had governed the universities, when "university classrooms were like upper classrooms in gymnasia," Katkov nevertheless assumed that it would be impossible to return to this earlier situation. Therefore, he called for changes that would have strengthened government influence in the universities. One idea was to create special commissions to read students' final examinations. These commissions would be set up by the ministries. Katkov's idea was intended to assure that only politically-reliable students received university degrees. In my opinion, even Katkov himself did not hide this intention. "This measure will free professors from political decisions not pertaining to their station." How could one speak about political decisions unless one had a political loyalty test in mind? According to Katkov, this measure would lead the professor to an obligation "to teach what the government demands, in the spirit, amount, and level established in the programs [of the government]."[163] In short, Katkov's idea was an open attempt to police the classroom, and to stimulate university teaching sympathetic to the orthodox official line.

Katkov even spoke against professorial autonomy, granted in the 1863 University Charter. "Professors should be freed from inappropriate administrative and judicial-police obligations which unnecessarily distract them from their research. . . ." He was also an opponent of elected rectors and an elected professoriate. His program had one purpose: to eliminate entirely university independence. Katkov also tried to turn to reactionary purposes such changes as the creation of *Privatdozenten* [lecturers], and the development of competition for lecturer positions —measures that were clearly progressive. Concerning *Privatdozenten,* Katkov noted that "they will make it possible for every loyal and capable scholar . . . in addition to the lectures of state professors, to teach their disciplines on the basis of the examination programs; this will allow students to choose among teachers. . . ."[164] The idea here is clear: "a well-intentioned professor" who reads lectures in accordance with the examination program prepared by ministerial commissions will be successful with the students. Katkov's memorandum was intended to prompt a reexamination of the 1863 Charter, which was a serious pursuit of both Katkov and D.A. Tolstoy.

In late May an inter-departmental commission under Delianov's chairmanship was created. The fact that the Commission was formed without the Minister of Education's consent and without his participation testified to the weak position of Baron Nikolai. The Commission met on 22, 27, and 30 June. While the Commission certainly was influenced by the Ignatiev memorandum and Katkov's reactionary propaganda, liberal society also attempted to influence its decisions. A group of liberals, who were members of the Temporary Council under the Petersburg municipal governor—Beketov, Semevsky, Lamansky, Likhachev, Potekhin, and Istomin—presented a special memorandum.[165] The authors began by observing that "anarchist propaganda" circulated widely among students because of the students' poverty and the emptiness of student life. The authors cited data on the material needs of students and on the inadequacy of the assistance being offered to them. They concluded that the "emptiness" of student life was caused by the absence of communication among students, who were driven to organize all sorts of unauthorized circles and societies. In addition, the authors noted that student dissatisfaction stemmed from the administrations' attitude toward them; administrators saw students as a "mass of disloyal individuals."[166]

The members of the Temporary Council thought it necessary: (1) to assist in the organization of inexpensive dining halls and apartments for students; (2) to ask the Ministry of Internal Affairs to allow students to form associations for self-help and self-education. . . . (3) to establish more rational means to distribute student stipends and grants with the help of patrons for student fellows and of student loan associations. . . ." (4) to create a broad network of professional schools, which "without removing the student from his native milieu would provide necessary utilitarian knowledge that could be directly applied to working life."[167] Naturally all those proposals were rejected by the Delianov Commission.

The Delianov Commission's decisions differed little from the rules laid down by the State Council in 1879. Basically, they were intended to strengthen the power of the trustee, who would be empowered to interfere in university affairs. According to the first point in the

Commission's resolution ". . .the trustee, in all cases when the directives of the university council and the rector proved inadequate to secure order, would have the right: (a) to demand that the university inspectorate make daily reports on the condition of the university; (b) to issue at his own discretion directives and instructions to the university inspectorate; (c) to subject guilty students to sanctions and punishments, including dismissal and expulsion from the university without regard to the charter rules of procedure for such cases." Thus, as in the 1879 rules, the inspectorate was answerable neither to the rector, nor to the university council, but rather to the trustee of the educational district.

Because the Commission wished to strengthen the trustee's authority, it tried to give the trustee power to confirm student stipends. "In order to end the artificial enrollment of students lacking outstanding capabilities and vocations, and of students from the poorer social classes,"[168] the Commission recommended reduction of the number of scholarships, especially in Petersburg and Moscow. In order to decrease the number of students, it was proposed to accept them according to the size of classrooms. The Commission thought it expedient to include in the total number of students the pupils studying in the gymnasia of the educational district. People would be accepted as auditors if they worked in the civil service or had proof of secondary school graduation. Both categories would have to present evidence of their political loyalty. To ease the supervision of students, it was proposed to introduce student uniforms. It was to be prohibited categorically on university grounds to organize reading rooms, dining halls, or any kind of assembly "or other public meeting which did not have an academic character." Student dormitories could be allowed only "under the vigilant supervision of the inspectorate."[169]

The subsequent points of the Commission's decision dealt with the establishment of police supervision of students, and with the mandatory agreement among departments on steps to be taken in this area. The twelfth and final point concerned higher education for women. It spoke about the organization of internal order in women's courses and a "more vigilant supervision over them."[170] None of these proposals were really original. All were drawn from Count Tolstoy's arsenal and had figured in the first period of the crisis of the autocracy.

However, despite the reactionary nature of the Commission's decisions, chairman Delianov did not agree with them. According to Delianov all these measures were mere palliatives and could not bring about any serious changes. He demanded more, considering it necessary to reform the universities in accordance with Count Tolstoy's project, submitted to the State Council on 6 February 1880. In view of the recent restoration of the 1863 Charter, Delianov did not have the right, in his own view, to "propose measures more sweeping than those summarized in the commission's journal, nor to touch on those fundamentals of university life which constituted the root of the evil; meanwhile, only a change of these fundaments can, in my opinion, place the universities in peaceful and orderly conditions."

Therefore, Delianov opposed the 1863 Charter as a whole, and proposed to replace it by a new, reactionary charter. At the same time, he pointed to the most important changes needed in the existing charter. Delianov wanted to make the trustee responsible "for the order and welfare of the university in all areas."[171] In other words, he insisted on the complete and unlimited subjugation of the university to the trustee. Furthermore, Delianov demanded the weakening "of the professors' dependence on each other," that is, an end to the elective element in universities. "Only under this condition will the trustee and the minister be real supervisors, the former over a given university, the latter over all universities in Russia." Delianov posed directly the question of stronger control over the professoriate so that "the government will have full opportunity to learn about those who have such an influential position." Turning to the section on students, Delianov advocated the establishment of a firm "independent authority over them, not an elected authority but one appointed by the government." "The inspector and his assistants are the persons to whom moral and police supervision of students is entrusted. They should be, so to speak, the eyes and the ears of the government. . . ." Delianov cited as a model the inspectorship under the 1835 Charter.

Second, Delianov demanded "concern for the improvement of the quality of students through the elimination of artificial incentives to enroll in institutions of higher education."[172] He proposed to abolish the rank that was conferred upon students at their graduation, and to establish impediments to "state and private philanthropy"—that is, to limit the receipt of scholarships. To reduce the flow into higher education Delianov, like his opponents in the liberal camp, recommended the development of vocational training. Finally, like Katkov, Delianov advocated the creation of special commissions to read final examinations. Delianov emphasized that only such measures could "lead our universities to a normal situation and transform them from hotbeds of radicalism into hotbeds of science."[173]

The Commission journal and the comments of its chairman were presented to Alexander III and approved by him. The measures drafted on supervision of students were remanded to the discretion of the ministers with jurisdiction over higher education. The tsar said that regulations for student supervision should be introduced in the forthcoming academic year. The Department of State Police also sought to implement the rules before the beginning of classes. On 17 July Plehve wrote to Ignatiev: "Concerning the academic question, in view of the slow movement of the Delianov Commission report, the police and the academic administration will not be ready to discipline youths by 1 September—the beginning of the school year. Therefore, a delay of classes until 1 October or 1 November seems desirable."[174] On 14 August Ignatiev assembled representatives from the departments with jurisdiction over higher education to discuss the supervision of students. According to Georgievsky, most recommendations of the Delianov Commission were enforced by the departments, with the exception of the Ministry of Education, which stubbornly opposed them.[175]

In October Baron Nikolai, who had returned to Petersburg after a prolonged tour of educational institutions all over Russia, presented his reactions to the Delianov Commission's decisions. Nikolai was very critical of these decisions. He opposed strengthening the authority of the trustee. On the issue of stipend reductions, the Minister of Education stated that this could be done by raising qualifications for scholarship students, rather than by a flat percentage reduction in support. Nikolai thought it wrong "to set some constant norm of university students in accordance with the size of the classrooms." This he believed unjust and contrary to the interests of science and the students themselves. He also opposed counting gymnasia pupils as a part of the university studentry. He did not agree with the point on prohibition of assemblies and public meetings, calling its formulation unsuccessful. Thus Nikolai disagreed on all issues.[176]

When Alexander III acquainted himself with Nikolai's response he decided to submit the matter to a special commission under Ignatiev, to consist of the Ministers of Education, Finance, State Domains, Communications, and War. This group met in Ignatiev's apartment on 20 January. I was unable to find the minutes of this meeting, which were absent from the Ignatiev papers, Alexander III's papers, and the Ministry of Education collection. Therefore the results of the meeting can be discussed only on the basis of indirect sources. A.V. Golovnin in one of his letters to Miliutin wrote about the situation in the Ministry of Education: "At this meeting [the 20 January meeting] Nikolai was placed several times in the position of a man on trial; he did not agree to many measures which he thought harsh and unjust, and he remained attached to his special opinion."[177]

Baron Nikolai continued to defend the 1863 Charter. He also carried out liberal policies on secondary education. In his letter to Golovnin on 4 March 1882, the Minister of Education wrote: "Under the fortress of our dominating classicism we must place land mines; we cannot take it by storm."[178] In early 1882 preliminary work began in the Ministry of Education on review of the Charter, programs for *Realschulen* [vocationally-oriented schools], and measures to develop technical education in connection with the transfer of most technical schools to the Ministry of Finance's jurisdiction.[179]

Nikolai decided to involve public figures, so-called "informed persons," in the discussion on *Realschulen*. However, this frightened the reactionaries. In a verbose letter to Alexander III on 16 January 1882, Pobedonostsev noted with horror that Nikolai's proposed action fell just short of sedition; it was the realization of Loris-Melikov's program. ". . . It is proposed to begin examination of charters on *Realschulen* and gymnasia[180] in a commission composed of bureaucrats from various departments, *with the participation of zemstvo representatives and public municipal officials*—that is, with the involvement in academic matters of disreputable, philistine elements. One can imagine these elements meeting in the following manner. The municipal groups from Moscow and Petersburg have elected Professor Gerie, a famous Moscow agitator and orator, and Kraevsky, the editor of *Golos*, a newspaper that has not ceased and will never cease to confuse parents and educators by the most unintelligent and unprincipled articles on education."[181] Pobedonostsev implored the tsar "in order to preserve public order" not to permit the commission to open. Pobedonostsev did not stop with this letter; he also appealed to Ignatiev. "If it begins tomorrow, the situation cannot be saved and there will be great trouble."[182] Ignatiev and Ostrovsky associated themselves with Pobedonostsev in opposition to the "seditious measure." On the evening of the same day Pobedonostsev received a soothing letter from Ignatiev, who asserted that "the tsar sent to me through Ostrovsky an order to halt the commission meeting; this answered the letter that I sent this morning in lieu of a personal memorandum."[183]

As Golovnin noted in his letter to Miliutin, Nikolai, having heard about the closing, set off for Gatchina, where he gave the tsar a report, stating that the commission would be cancelled and that he would be forced to resign from the ministry. Alexander III decided to retreat slightly. He selected Pobedonostsev to serve as mediator in conversations with Nikolai. Judging by Pobedonostsev's letters, it was decided that, in case of uncompromising opposition from Nikolai, Delianov would become Minister of Education and Nikolai would take Delianov's former job. [184]

This time Nikolai compromised. Pobedonostsev noted: "I spoke with him from the heart, giving him the impression which Your Majesty retained after yesterday's conversation with him. You said to me that it would be impossible to convince him . . . . But today I did not find Baron Nikolai in a stubborn disposition." [185] As a compromise, he agreed to the elimination of Kraevsky and Gerie from the commission's membership. This satisfied the tsar. As Golovnin wrote to Miliutin, Nikolai received permission from Alexander III to open the commission without the above-named persons. In addition, the tsar forbade the publication in the press of an announcement about the commission's work. However, there were no further developments in this area since the fate of Nikolai was already predetermined.

Katkov also denounced Nikolai. He wrote the tsar on 7 February 1882: "Recently I had the honor of speaking with complete candor before Your Majesty on the situation in the Ministry of Education and about the only solution that I saw to this problem. Your Majesty, save by wise autocratic decision, save your future reign through these children and youths." [186] Katkov was urging the dismissal of Baron Nikolai. In mid-March Pobedonostsev was instructed by the tsar to visit Nikolai and to discuss Nikolai's resignation from the ministry and replacement by Delianov. Pobedonostsev stated: "Understanding the difficulty of his position, he was prepared to resign without protest." Nikolai also refused an appointment as head of the Fourth Section of His Majesty's Chancellery. "So the combination which Your Majesty had envisioned was not possible." [187] Within a few days Delianov became Minister of Education and Nikolai was named chairman of the Department of Laws of the State Council. [188] In the field of education, the triumph of reaction was complete.

Nikolai's education policy was a continuation of Loris-Melikov's policy, and it was clearly bourgeois in character. This was a rather dissonant note given the general direction of the government's policy after 29 April. That this liberal policy was tolerated at all was evidence that Alexander III's government did not yet feel confident enough to adopt an openly reactionary program.

Let us consider Ignatiev's attempt to call a Zemsky Sobor [Assembly of the Land] at the end of his ministerial tenure. According to his memoirs, the first conversations about a Zemsky Sobor were conducted by Alexander III while his father was still alive. Apparently the conversations occurred in 1876 when Alexander II summoned Ignatiev, then ambassador to Turkey, for consultation. Ignatiev notes that conversations on this theme were renewed by the young tsar in March 1882 when it became clear that the coronation would be delayed until the spring of 1883 by the pregnancy of the empress. ". . . I reminded His Majesty of my conversations with him on the Zemsky Sobors and said that the most favorable time to revive this historical tradition was the day of the coronation . . . . This made the tsar smile, and with the permission of His Majesty I drafted a project manifesto to deal with all possible details of this great historical event. In my subsequent weekly audiences we often returned to the theme of the Sobor, and the tsar was favorable, even sympathetic, to it."[189]

We do not know the content of these conversations, but arguments used by Ignatiev to promote a Zemsky Sobor must have been cited later in his report on the subject. This report was partly written by a clerk, partly by Ignatiev himself, and was undated and unsigned. Ignatiev began by indicating that Russia was currently at a "crossroads" and three possible paths of development might be followed. The first path was that of intensified repression. According to the author, this would not yield any positive results. "A firmer application of administrative measures, further restrictions on the press, and the development of police methods would only cause dissatisfaction to deepen." Eventually, this would lead to concessions to "social demands." The second path—concessions—was also unacceptable. "The path of concessions, whatever their nature, always will be fatal. In whatever form the concessions are made there is no doubt that each new step will weaken the government, and will create the need for more concessions."[190] The major danger of this approach was that the intelligentsia would become the dominant influence in public life in Russia. "The Russian intelligentsia comprises all the most dangerous and unreliable elements, and therefore its participation in affairs of state will surely mean a limitation of the autocracy. This would be the source of perennial difficulty and disorder in Russia." In Ignatiev's opinion, both the first and the second path would lead to the same result and would be harmful to Russia.

The only correct "path to salvation" was a return to the ancient "historical form of communication between the autocracy and the land—the Zemsky Sobor." Noting that the autocracy was the only form of government native to Russia, Ignatiev stated that "one should not close one's eyes to the imperfection of this system, which has led us to the present situation." This shortcoming was the separation of the tsar from the people by a barrier of bureaucrats. As a result, the tsar could not learn the truth. "Without diminishing his power, the tsar, having summoned the Sobor, will find a true means to learn about the actual needs of the nation and the actions of his own servants." The Sobor would resolve all contradictions and end the great confusion in national life. "When the tsar and the land enter into direct communication, all misunderstandings and dangers will vanish."[191] Such were the contents of the report on the Zemsky Sobor, the virtues of which the Minister of Internal Affairs probably expounded in his conversations with Alexander III.

According to Ignatiev, he prepared a project manifesto on the convocation of the Sobor on 30 March 1882, and he presented the project to the tsar on 12 April. Alexander III approved the text and "was even touched by reading it. The sovereign thanked me, and said that in the manifesto I had guessed his own thoughts and had said exactly what he had wanted to say to the participants of the Sobor."[192] During this conversation with the tsar on 12 April there was discussion of the number of representatives to be called to the Sobor. Ignatiev wanted the Sobor to meet at the newly-constructed, but not-yet-dedicated Temple of Christ the Savior. Ignatiev testified in his memoirs that he had drafted the plan for convocation of a Zemsky Sobor independently. He asserted that in 1883 the idea to call a Sobor was his own.

In fact, Ignatiev's account of this matter is distorted. In Ignatiev's papers there is a letter to him from I.S. Aksakov, dated 10 January 1882. Aksakov wrote in the beginning of this letter: "My sincere faith in you as the sole man who represents the national historical direction prompts me to ask you—no, not ask—insist that you read my conversation with the bearer of this letter, Pavel Dmitrievich Golokhastov." Aksakov went on to describe the intellectual atmosphere and vastov." Aksakov went on to describe the intellectual atmosphere and its attendant danger, which the government's program could not avert. According to him, the basic danger was that all political groups from aristocrats to nihilists were striving for a constitution. But "the tsar cannot grant a constitution; this would betray the people, it would be treachery." Aksakov believed that a constitution would lead to the destruction of Russia. However, there was "a solution for the problem that would put to shame all constitutions in the world—something broader and more liberal than constitutions and yet something that would hold Russia to its historical, political, and national basis. This solution is a *Zemsky Sobor with direct elections* from all classes: peasants, landowners, merchants, and clergy.

"Now there is an occasion for this—the coronation. The presence of a thousand peasant delegates will suffice, without need for further compulsion, to silence any constitutional agitation and serve as a universal confirmation of autocratic power in the real, national historical sense. Like wax in a flame, all foreign, liberal, aristocratic, nihilistic, and similar notions will melt before the people."[193] Then the author stated that as soon as the tsar announced the convocation of the Sobor, every danger to the emperor would disappear: he could travel calmly to Moscow without fear, since nihilism would be "paralyzed at one blow." Having described the significance of the Sobor, Aksakov turned to the practical question of its organization. "But what is a Zemsky Sobor? How can one organize it? For this I am sending to you P.D. Golokhvastov, who has worked on this idea for fifteen years, and has elaborated all the details, which he has even written out."[194]

Therefore the idea about convocation of the Zemsky Sobor during the coronation was suggested to Ignatiev by Aksakov. Besides, the plan for convocation was written by Aksakov and Golokhvastov. Merely because Ignatiev did not mention the contribution of Aksakov and Golokhvastov in his memoirs, one need not dismiss their roles lightly. In fact, Ignatiev was largely the mouthpiece of Aksakov and Golokhvastov's ideas, which he tried to exploit in his own personal interest. All this is clear from the correspondence of Aksakov and Golokhvastov in the Pushkin House Collection.[195]

As Golokhvastov informed Aksakov, Ignatiev listed him as an official with a special assignment in the Ministry of Internal Affairs.[196] The actual appointment of Golokhvastov as a consultant on the Zemsky Sobor originally was cloaked with secrecy. Even the minister's closest aide, his office manager, Voeikov, did not know about it. To avert attention Golokhvastov wrote articles for the ministry's magazine *Selsky Vestnik* [Village Messenger]. During January and February Ignatiev did not work on the Zemsky Sobor seriously. As Golokhvastov told Aksakov, the minister even contrived to lose the project for convocation of the Sobor given to him in January by Golokhvastov. On 2 March Golokhvastov wrote: "First, he lost my report . . . on elections to the Zemsky Sobor and the change in property qualifications for voters and then he asked me to rewrite it." Golokhvastov noted: "He is not at all serious, or perhaps only slightly serious, about the Zemsky Sobor."[197] It is clear that Ignatiev did not devote much attention to the issue until mid-March.

Let us examine the plans for a Zemsky Sobor. These plans have been preserved in the their most concrete form in a memorandum in Ignatiev's papers. There are rough drafts in ink signed by Ignatiev.[198] One

memorandum, the original variant, developed in a manner akin to Aksakov the notion that the Zemsky Sobor would halt the revolutionary
movement, and completely destroy nihilism. "The tasks of the Sobor
are two-fold: (1) to discover the mood, the thoughts, of representatives of the land; (2) to transmit the tsar's will through these representatives to the people, 'to spread His Majesty's word to the whole land,
to all the people, to the entire society.' "[199] The second of these purposes was considered the more important. The author then dealt with
the question of how to set up peasant representation so that "peasant
delegates will return to their districts and convey to *everyone else
what they themselves have heard from the tsar himself:* concerning
the inviolability of tsarist authority; concerning the inalienability of
the land—of communal land from the peasants, of gentry land from
the gentry, and so on." According to Ignatiev, the peasant delegation
should not be selected from their elected representatives in the third
peasant curia. Not all the electors there were peasants, and "many of
the peasants are kulaks and tavernkeepers."

Therefore, elections from the peasantry should occur "expressly for
the Sobor; delegates should be selected directly by all village elders
and all delegates should themselves be village elders ...." In Ignatiev's
opinion, the election district should not be the administrative unit,
the district, and the district should not be determined by population;
it should be a discrete area. Since the effective radius of peasant contact "within which everyone knows the best people, at least by reputation, is twenty versts, a district should be 1600 square versts."[200]
In the north and in steppe regions where peasants were accustomed to
greater distances, the election district would be 3600 square versts.
Given this rule, there would be not more than two thousand peasant
representatives from the forty-seven provinces of European Russia (not
counting Poland, Finland, and the Baltic states).

The second group of representatives would include one or two landowners from each of the 475 counties of European Russia, or between
475 and 950 members. However, the author doubted that such a large
number of nobles need be elected. He thought that the actual number
could be cut to 141. "This may seem a small group to oppose to two
thousand peasants, but the majority will not rule [at the Sobor], so
the number of delegates will be immaterial. Whatever the nature of
the Sobor's business, 140 landowners should be enough. To add 800
more would produce little but overcrowding." Having spoken so clearly
in favor of the limited landowner delegation, the author nevertheless
opted for elections by county, arguing that this would ensure a more

conservative group. " . . . In the hothouse political atmosphere of the provincial city, the zemstvo will not elect for the Sobor, but for *les états généraux*."[201]

Elections of landowners from counties would follow the model of county zemstvo assembly elections. However, the property requirement for zemstvo elections would be eliminated. "Abolish the difference between small and large property requirements [in different districts] and the minimum holding requirement so that tens and hundreds of desiatins will be equal in voting power; this should be done only where there is a *noble manor and farming activity under way*."[202] Naturally, gentry farmers living in the countryside, particularly the small landowners, were a conservative element that usually had no liberal or constitutionalist tendencies.

Merchants selected from an assembly of all guilds were to represent the urban population. "But why select only merchants, and not other elements of the urban populace? There are two reasons: first, the merchants are the only politically-reliable elements. Second, however broadly one wishes to define the word *zemshchina* (constituency), the municipal *zemshchina* is truly municipal. It consists of traders alone. Now commercial interests are national interests, and in this sense they pertain to agriculture. The other urbanites are raznochintsy [individuals not members of a class or estate]. They may have many personal concerns, but as city dwellers their interests are purely local urban interests . . . ." Therefore the Zemsky Sobor was to consist of peasants, nobles, and merchants picked in direct elections.

The election of representatives from Siberia, Poland, Finland, and other peripheral regions was resolved differently in the report. "Why not select people for the Sobor from Siberia, Poland, and other areas? Siberia is too far away, though it would be nice to have elections if time allows. But since there is no danger of popular uprisings in Siberia, there is no reason to select many delegates from Siberia."[203] Then the author noted that it would not be bad to elect delegates from Poland, Finland, and the Baltic area. "From these areas we will take a few delegates, mostly peasants and specially-elected individuals." In addition, the author emphasized the potential dangers of electing representatives from the zemstvo and municipal assemblies. "If we select persons from the contemporary zemstvo and municipal assemblies, from the partisans of European constitutions, the result will be a parliament on the European model. It will be as great as the Russian God, but not as wise."[204]

Textual analysis reveals that the memorandum was revised and expanded by the author. For example, in the section on gentry elections the author wrote: "Here is my correction."[205] There followed the generalizations on the abolition of the property qualification. In the section on merchant elections the author wrote: "I have no remarks to make concerning this subject."[206] Doubtless, the first variant of the memorandum was written by Golokhvastov; Ignatiev then revised and expanded the original document.

There is another rough draft on the Zemsky Sobor, one that spelled out details of the earlier version. This draft, also in Ignatiev's writing, began by mentioning the reasons for convocation of a Zemsky Sobor. ". . . A Zemsky Sobor is convened immediately at His Majesty's summons, whenever and for whatever purpose His Majesty desires . . . . Self-governing zemstvo units at the county and municipal level may petition for the convocation of a Sobor."[207] There followed a detailed summary of proposed electoral representation to the Sobor.[208]

I. Peasants

a) counties of European Russia [minus the Baltic provinces, Finland, and Poland]

from 277 counties	2 delegates each	554
from 109 counties	3 delegates each	327
from 35 counties	4 delegates each	140
from 29 counties	5 delegates each	145
from 18 counties	6 delegates each	108
from 8 counties	7 delegates each	56

Total delegates from 476 counties of European Russia—1330

b) from 14 counties in Baltic provinces	14
c) from 85 counties in Poland	85
d) from 44 counties in Finland	44
e) from 65 counties in Caucasus	65
f) from 49 counties in Siberia and Turkestan	412
Total of Peasants in the Sobor	1950

II. Other Classes

a) from 476 counties of European Russia	952
b) from 47 provinces of European Russia, Provincial Marshals of the Nobility	47
c) from provincial capitals and 20 county seats with more than 25,000 residents	67
d) special delegates from Moscow and Petersburg (3 delegates each) and from the twelve most important Russia cities	18
e) merchant, burger, artisan heads from Moscow, Petersburg, Odessa, Riga, Warsaw, and Helsinki	18
f) from 3 Baltic provinces, 10 Polish provinces, 8 Finnish provinces (1 gentry, 1 merchant representative each)	42
g) from 12 Caucasian and 13 provinces in Siberia and Turkestan (2 gentry, 2 merchant representatives each)	100
Total Delegates from Other Classes	1244

It was also proposed to invite several hundred "higher representatives of the Church and the government."[209] The total number of representatives from all groups would have been about three thousand five hundred.[210]

In another rough draft there is an additional scheme. The total number of delegates would be increased to 4000. This increase would come primarily from the peasantry in European Russia, whose number would be set at 1831 (counting the three Baltic provinces), and from delegates from provincial cities (marshals of the nobility, mayors, merchants, and artisans)—about 150 to 235 persons. The number of Church and government delegates was to be "no more than 236."[211] These details confirmed and elaborated the positions taken in Ignatiev's earlier report. More than half (in the second variant more than sixty per cent) of the delegates would be peasants. The percentage of representation from national regions was to be significantly lower.

In order to demonstrate the political unity of the Sobor, the unity of all the people of Russia with the tsar—that is, to avoid any demonstration of political opposition—Ignatiev wanted to seat representatives from a given national group in different places in the assembly hall. "Because of the Sobor's size, and in order to preserve order, and also to prevent undesirable displays by the Poles, Finns, or our liberals, . . . I propose to seat members at thirty tables, so that around each there would be about 100 persons. This would enable the elected chairman to deal with the flow of debate and control it . . . . The distribution around tables is thought out carefully and is designed to guard Russian interests and to facilitate the successful conclusion of the assembly meetings. The Finns will be spread over three tables, and the Poles over four; they will sit between pure Russians."[212] That was how the unity of all people in Russia with the tsar would be arranged in practice.

According to Ignatiev, the date for the Sobor's announcement should be fixed by the Kakhanov Commission; this suggested that the Sobor would deal with the reform of local administration (particularly, with the nature of the district).[213] However, Ignatiev did not foresee any business discussions in the Sobor. "In case the Sobor began to drag on and did not reach a solution of the issues at hand, it is proposed that His Majesty allow to be elected a commission of not more than thirty or forty persons at the Plenary Session before the close of the Sobor. This commission would continue to work on the orders of His Majesty in Petersburg under the State Council, to which commission proposals would be submitted before confirmation by His Majesty. Thus, without shaking the pillars of the state, a truly Russian constitution, which

would provoke envy in Europe and force our pseudo-liberals to keep
quiet, will be born."[214] This "Russian constitution" did not infringe
in any way on the autocrat's prerogatives. Ignatiev (or perhaps, more
precisely, Golokhvastov) successfully assimilated the experience of Na-
poleon I, his ill-starred nephew, and Bismarck.

Analysis of this material enables one to argue that the convocation
of a Zemsky Sobor was intended by Ignatiev to serve demagogic purposes, to demonstrate "the unity of the tsar and the people," which
would in turn strengthen the peasantry's faith in the tsar. Ignatiev's
purpose was clear from the proposed representation; the delegates would
be "village elders, landowners, and guild members," that is, the heads
of peasant families, gentry, and merchants. The purpose of the 1883
Sobor was manifest: it was a purely cosmetic political maneuver.

According to Ignatiev, Alexander III confirmed the general outlines of
a project manifesto on the Zemsky Sobor on 12 April 1882. On 15
April Alexander III told Ignatiev that "he had read carefully the manifesto and he finds it excellent," but he asked for a briefer version to be
affixed to the next memorandum along with a special rescript in Ignatiev's name that would give the instructions for the elections.[215] Ignatiev
gave this material to the tsar on 20 April, and it was approved. Ignatiev
wanted to publish the manifesto on 6 May, the bicentennial of the previous Zemsky Sobor.

However, things did not really go so smoothly. On 29 April Golokhvastov wrote to Aksakov that "His Majesty still has not said 'yes' or
'no.' Ignatiev is still *almost certain* (as of yesterday) that the manifesto
will be signed before 6 May."[216] Ignatiev tried to win to his side the
empress, who had great influence over her husband. Golokhvastov noted
in the same letter cited earlier: "He [Ignatiev] was at Gatchina yesterday and all but persuaded the empress (according to Voeikov) that
Varfolomey Kochenov[217] . . . and Katkov are lying, that their attacks
against the Sobor (Liubimov, they say, wrote to His Majesty) are stupid
and even of inferior quality; that she will not become another Marie
Antoinette because of the Sobor." Golokhvastov maintained that several days earlier Ignatiev had prepared for this meeting by talking with
the empress about the French revolution, particularly about the National Assembly, and "he even had written something on paper." Golokhvastov spoke here about the pure intentions "of the champion of
the Zemsky Sobor." "Ignatiev's purpose is to become premier. I learned
about his ambitions thus: he dictated to Voeikov a report on the Zemsky
Sobor which said that it was not a constitution and so on, but concluded

by saying that we need a unified ministry to stand before the Zemsky Sobor, yet not like the disorganized one we have now."[218] This document was to be given to an official for his reaction, more precisely, to Prince Shakhovskoy, who, unable to find time to study it, consulted with Golokhvastov. "I learned what was going on, and kicked myself over the ministry of the future Beaconsfield. And only the other day this same Ignatiev cried in my presence over my speeches on the Zemsky Sobor."[219]

The rough drafts of the manifesto and the rescript had been written originally by Golokhvastov and corrected in the ministry chancellery. Interestingly enough, Ignatiev asked Golokhvastov to write a project charter for the Sobor, but the latter refused. "A written, that is, printed, charter is a constitutional matter that will lead to all sorts of quarrels on top of the substantive debates on issues. I wrote you a design for a Zemsky Sobor on the ancient pattern at His Majesty's command."[220]

As 6 May approached Aksakov grew more and more anxious. In his special-delivery letter to Golokhvastov on 27 April Aksakov asked for an immediate report on the matter of the 6 May manifesto since a special issue of *Rus* was planned for that day. "For God's sake, answer me quickly and in detail. If you have to hurry the response, order the porter to ride on a postal or courier train, not on a passenger train. I . . . am very upset, as one might expect in view of such a great historical event. This is the *last chance*. If it fails, there will be a fiasco."[221]

Let us examine the project manifesto prepared for 6 May. "Praying to God, who will show Us the paths of truth, and having reflected on the ancient days and studied the models of our predecessors, of Our tsars and autocrats, We have decided: to hold the forthcoming celebration of the sacred coronation and anointing before a Sobor of all the hierarchs of the Orthodox Church, the senior officials of the government, the senior delegates of the nobility and of the cities and those especially elected from the land."[222] The Sobor was to meet on Easter 1883, and the plan of representation was to follow the one described earlier. The terms of representation for Siberia, Poland, Finland, and the Baltic provinces, and the areas of the Caucasus and Central Asia were not set out in the manifesto. Elections were to be carried out by special orders to the Minister of Internal Affairs. The manifesto declared that "as in olden days Zemsky Sobors were convened by the sovereign before a holy coronation, but sometimes for the proclamation of the sovereign's will to the whole nation in the presence of its finest citizens, or for the sovereign to hear directly about local needs, and in general for a meeting of the tsar with his subjects, so this Zemsky Sobor will be."[223]

Meanwhile Ignatiev worked hard on the publication of the manifesto. Among his rough drafts on the Zemsky Sobor there was one note dated 3 May, almost on the eve of the scheduled publication. Worrying that the foreign press might interpret the announcement of a Zemsky Sobor as a constitutional act, Ignatiev wrote: "Prepare telegrams to our embassies or direct to foreign newspapers in order that the Zemsky Sobor might receive a proper title in foreign press releases. In French, *conseil nationale, Consil nationale* are colorless, but at least foreigners will not be tempted to use the revolutionary-historical term *assemblée nationale*. In German, *Landtag, Reichstag, Reichsrat* have constitutional connotations. There remains *Volkstag*."[224] This note proves that Ignatiev was convinced of success on the Sobor project. However, a surprise was in store for him.

Despite the secret preparations of the Minister of Internal Affairs the matter received publicity. According to Feoktistov's memoirs, he learned about the Sobor from Ostrovsky, the Minister of State Domains, who was informed in early April by I.N. Durnovo, the Assistant Minister of Internal Affairs. Durnovo was well-briefed on the Zemsky Sobor and told Ostrovsky all the details, including the roles of Aksakov and Golokhvastov.[225] It is difficult to ascertain who told Durnovo; however, there is good evidence that the secret came from within the Ministry of Internal Affairs.

While Ignatiev did not tell anyone besides Golokhvastov of his plans at first, the minister's office was informed in April. Not only the head of the chancellery, Voeikov, but a number of others were involved in writing and editing reports relevant to the Zemsky Sobor. One official involved in this work was Prince Shakhovskoy, whose cousin was married to the daughter of Katkov. This created the atmosphere for a news leak. According to Golokhvastov, Ignatiev tried in early May to attract Count Vorontsov-Dashkov, the Minister of the Imperial Court, to the defense of the Zemsky Sobor, but the Count was not persuaded. The Minister of the Court reacted very cautiously to this strategem.[226] True, he changed his mind within several days. Golokhvastov wrote a detailed account of this to Aksakov in his letter of 6 May. According to Golokhvastov, on 4 May Voeikov was approached in the ministry by a certain Fadeev, who told him "a great secret." Fadeev said that "everyone was pressuring Vorontsov to oppose the Sobor, but yesterday Vorontsov had said that he was in favor of the Sobor, but only of a *real* Sobor that would meet in the fall, that is, after 8 September. Fadeev even indicated the pretext (the formation of the Holy Retinue) used by Vorontsov to meet with Ignatiev and Bobby Shuvalov on the evening of the fourth, perhaps at Ignatiev's office; after Shuvalov had left, Vorontsov would talk with Ignatiev alone. That was exactly what happened."[227] Not everything in this account was exactly true. One suspects Golokhvastov's assertions about the influence he wielded over Vorontsov, which lead Vorontsov to continue to think about a "real" Sobor. Another issue was more important: negotiations of Ignatiev and Vorontsov about the Zemsky Sobor and the Holy Retinue. Apparently, agreement was reached and the Minister of Internal Affairs gave his blessing to the Holy Retinue on condition that Vorontsov and his associates support Ignatiev on the Zemsky Sobor. According to Golokhvastov, Ignatiev insistently but unsuccessfully tried to solicit permission from the tsar for Vorontsov to sit in on a conference about the convocation of the Sobor.

Alexander III also talked with his camarilla about Ignatiev's plan for a Zemsky Sobor; the tsar spoke with his tutor, Pobedonostsev, to whom he sent the project manifesto, probably on 4 May. "On the evening of 3 May His Majesty invited Pobedonostsev to a meeting at Peterhof at noon the next day," according to Golokhvastov's letter to Aksakov on 6 May. "Ignatiev learned about this immediately through the police. Late on 3 May he wrote Pobedonostsev a long letter, requesting an audience the next morning. Pobedonostsev answered that he would get up late and there would not be time before the morning train. Now he has come back from Peterhof, and obviously does not want to see Ignatiev."[228] The tsar probably gave the draft manifesto to Pobedonostsev on 4 May.

The manifesto was like a bombshell to Pobedonostsev. On the evening of the fourth he wrote Alexander III a letter in which he described the horrible consequences of a Zemsky Sobor. "Having read these papers, I was stricken by horror of the consequences should Count Ignatiev's project be executed . . . .   If authority (*volia*) and power (*rasporiazhenie*) pass to any kind of popular assembly there will be a *revolution, the destruction of the government, the destruction of Russia.*" Pobedonostsev wrote about one source through whom he had learned about the preparations for the Zemsky Sobor. "I learned today that Aksakov had sent to Ignatiev Golokhvastov, who is an expert on Zemsky Sobors . . . .   This Golokhvastov came to me yesterday in terror: having heard that Ignatiev is beginning now and the acts may be published within a few days, he became frightened and in his agitation tried to reach Your Majesty to implore You to stop the process."[229]

That is how Pobedonostsev described Golokhvastov's decision. Golokhvastov had a different account, probably more accurate. As we

noted above, Ignatiev had met on the fourth with Vorontsov-Dashkov
and Bobby Shuvalov. Golokhvastov also was invited to the ministry and
he expected orders from Voeikov, the head of the chancellery. At ten
thirty Voeikov was summoned by Ignatiev, who passed on instructions
to visit Pobedonostsev.[230] Golokhvastov summarized his discussion with
Pobedonostsev as follows: "Pobedonostsev met me and said immediately
that he had no time that evening or tomorrow to discuss anything, no
matter what. 'Have you been in Petersburg a long time?' Pobedonostsev
asked. 'I have been here two months. I have been a special consultant
to Ignatiev.' Pobedonostsev then said: 'Oh, so you are the one. Well,
listen. You have been racking your brains over the same nonsense as
Aksakov. Ignore the chatterboxes and windbags like Ignatiev. I know
what is up. I do not want to hear about it (and he closed his ears). The
Sobor is the same as a constitution, the end of Russia. Pray for God's
enlightenment, abandon this liar and swindler Ignatiev, and leave on
Sunday.' "[231]

The advice to leave on Sunday (the meeting occurred on Tuesday)
was rejected, and Golokhvastov's audience ended quickly. On parting,
Pobedonostsev asserted again that the Sobor would not be called, now
or later. In my opinion, Golokhvastov's account of the conversation is
more in accord with the facts than is Pobedonostsev's version. What
would Golokhvastov have profitted by running to Pobedonostsev to
complain about Ignatiev and to ask that the Sobor not be convened?

Having learned about Pobedonostsev's opposition and the hesitations
of the empress, Ignatiev began to recruit allies for himself. According
to Feoktistov, Ignatiev came to Ostrovsky on 5 May and told the latter
about the planned Sobor.[232] Ostrovsky voiced the fear that this measure
might have unpleasant consequences. Ignatiev rejoined: "What is important here? Remember that all that is wanted is to establish a festive
atmosphere; it will be nothing more than a decoration .... Of course,
the Sobor is bound to attract a few loudmouths, but what harm can
that do? After the coronation we government officials will return to
Petersburg, and they will be alone; they will sound off and then disperse .... "[233] Ostrovsky was not convinced by Ignatiev and he divulged
the whole conversation to Pobedonostsev the next day.[234] So, at least,
Ostrovsky reported to his friend Feoktistov. Actually, Ostrovsky's position was more complex. As Ignatiev told Golokhvastov: "He [Ostrov-
sky] is whole-heartedly in favor of a *real* Sobor."[235] Ostrovsky added
that if the manifesto were signed without prior discussion of the ministers he would resign from the government. On 8 May he told Golokhvastov approximately the same thing. Golokhvastov wrote to Aksakov: "I saw Ostrovsky yesterday. He is not an opponent, but a very

conditional supporter." Ostrovsky told Golokhvastov that, first, everything should be discussed fully, and, second, the government should draw together and present a united front."[236] It is difficult to say whether Ostrovsky was actually a supporter of the Zemsky Sobor under certain circumstances, or if this was just a maneuver to gain information for the opponents of the measure.

On 8 May Ignatiev sent the tsar a report in which he asserted that the convocation of a Zemsky Sobor could not be viewed as a concession. "For that section of society which considers it necessary for Russia to adopt the political forms of Western Europe the convocation of the Zemsky Sobor not only will be no concession, it will be clear proof that the government has no intention of following that unpopular and false path."[237] Here Ignatiev admitted that if the Sobor were to consist of delegates from the zemstvo and the cities it would present a real danger. But the composition would be much different. "Its representatives will be the most conservative types, dedicated to the existing order .... The absence of public meetings or public votes makes the Sobor innocuous."[238] Apparently this report had no influence on Alexander III, since the tsar's convictions did not change.[239]

Trying to force a positive resolution of the Sobor issue, Ignatiev recruited allies. One of them was the procurator of the Petersburg judiciary, the future Minister of Justice, N.V. Muraviev. Through Ignatiev, Muraviev sent to Alexander III a memorandum on the need for a Zemsky Sobor as a tool to liquidate the revolutionary movement. Muraviev attempted to demonstrate that a Zemsky Sobor would disorganize completely the revolutionary forces and force them to lay down their weapons. He concluded: "After a Zemsky Sobor sedition will be powerless, its sources will dry up and its foothold will be removed."[240] This memorandum had no effect on the young tsar. On the first page, Alexander III left a blunt marginal comment: "A sad illusion!"[241]

Whereas the actions of Ignatiev and his allies did not bear any fruits, their opponents moved more energetically and effectively. According to Ignatiev's memoirs, on 10 May Ostrovsky sent Feoktistov to Moscow on a courier train to see Katkov.[242] Feoktistov was to brief Katkov concerning Ignatiev's plans for the Zemsky Sobor. As a result of this briefing an editorial appeared in *Moskovskie Vedomosti*. One must give Katkov credit. The editorial was written very quickly. Feoktistov arrived in Moscow on 11 May. The editorial appeared the next day. "Let us imagine that under the present circumstances and in the current intellectual atmosphere a certain influential person got the idea, for whatever reason, to convoke what is euphemistically called a Zemsky Sobor.

This action supposedly would assist the government in its struggle against sedition. But is it not in fact a triumph for sedition that such an idea is even discussed in government circles?" Katkov then argued that this assembly would not have positive results. Ending, Katkov observed that the demand for a Zemsky Sobor always had come from the revolutionary camp. "When the gendarmes led the notorious revolutionary Nechaev from the courtroom after sentence had been pronounced against him, he called out furiously 'Zemsky Sobor,' 'Zemsky Sobor.' Zheliabov did the same thing. Who is more faithful to his chosen cause—Zheliabov and Nechaev, or those fantastic guardians of national interests who have screamed for a Zemsky Sobor?"[243]

Although Katkov had not named any names, it was clear to whom he had referred. Ignatiev also went to the press. On 14 May in Suvorin's *Novoe Vremia* there was a short article, inspired by Ignatiev, called the "Uncelebrated Anniversary." The basic idea of the article, which was dedicated to the bicentennial of 1682, was that a Zemsky Sobor would not mean a diminution of royal authority. "One need not think that the procedure for Zemsky Sobors was defined by any exact juridical norms. Exact definitions were not in the spirit of the Muscovite state. The tsars needed the cooperation of the Russian land. They got cooperation through the Sobors, but no one thought to codify this cooperation in the legal canons."[244]

Despite the prohibition against articles on the Zemsky Sobor, the polemic heated up. On 22 May Aksakov's *Rus* ran an editorial critical of Katkov's editorial. Aksakov wrote: "If Nechaev and Zeliabov 'demanded' a Zemsky Sobor that only proves that they heard a chime, but did not know from where the sound came. They had never read a document from a Sobor, and had no idea what a Sobor is all about."[245] On 25 May Katkov returned to this problem in an editorial. Thus, the issue of a Zemsky Sobor got wide exposure.

On 11 May Valuev wrote in his diary: "Yesterday Mansurov and Makov came over. The former said that Ignatiev was talking about resignation. Makov said that he had heard from Klushin that Ignatiev and Aksakov supposedly had tried to call a Zemsky Sobor, but that Pobedonostsev had intervened and had kept an important memorandum sent to the tsar."[246] Having seen that under the influence of Pobedonostsev and Katkov Alexander III now opposed the Sobor, Ignatiev decided to abandon his plan, and tried to avoid discussion of the issue at government meetings. He admitted this directly in his memoirs. "I wrote a letter to His Majesty asking him not to call any meetings on the issue and to await my personal memorandum. His Majesty immediately returned the letter with the comment: 'Okay.'"[247] However, Pobedonostsev's pressure was very strong; he spoke about a meeting personally with the tsar, and sent a letter on 25 May which evidently solved the matter of the meeting.

In this letter Pobedonostsev wrote: "I dare to tell Your Majesty that to leave this subject unresolved and the Minister of Internal Affair's proposals in doubt is most awkward. Everyone knows about it and discusses it. . . .   This matter should be debated in his [Ignatiev's] presence, so that other people who enjoy Your Majesty's trust may talk about the senselessness of this enterprise to his [Ignatiev's] face."[248] Pobedonostsev wrote that Ignatiev had continued to insist on the convocation of the Sobor. On 26 May Alexander III sent Ignatiev a telegram requesting his presence at Peterhof the next morning. A meeting directed by the tsar took place on 27 May. Its participants included: the chairman of the Committee of Ministers, Reutern, Minister of State Domains Ostrovsky, Supreme Procurator of the Synod Pobedonostsev, Minister of Education Delianov, and finally Ignatiev.

There are two sources on the course of this meeting: (1) Ignatiev's memoirs and (2) Ostrovsky's account as interpreted by Feoktistov. The factual report of the meeting is more or less the same in both accounts. Alexander III opened the meeting by asserting that the issue of a Zemsky Sobor should be decided once and for all. Then Ignatiev took the floor. According to Ostrovsky, Ignatiev assured everyone that he did not see the Zemsky Sobor as a permanent agency, but wanted merely "to heighten the ceremony" of the coronation, but the press had distorted his true intentions. "In a long discourse Count Nikolai Pavlovich tried only to extricate himself from this embarrassing affair, but he did not succeed. His Majesty interrupted twice to say: 'That is not so.' 'That is untrue.'"[249]

At Pobedonostsev's insistence the tsar asked Ignatiev to read the project manifesto and the rescript. Then the participants began to attack the projects. Ostrovsky made a very critical speech. Ignatiev tried in a very long commentary to demonstrate that a Zemsky Sobor was the only way to achieve social peace. According to Ignatiev, "the tsar, in a dissatisfied and angry tone, interrupted me, and said that he had had complete faith in me before the issue of the Sobor arose—an issue that I had pushed with strange insistence. The emperor then announced that he would 'not consent to the Sobor.'"[250] The tsar concluded by saying in impersonal fashion that if any minister was not in agreement with this decision, then he must leave his post.[251] Thus the meeting not only resolved the matter of the Sobor, but precipitated Ignatiev's resignation. On 30 May D.A. Tolstoy was named Minister of Internal Affairs.

Ignatiev's ministry had lasted just over a year. It was the final stage in the crisis of the autocracy. The transition to reaction proclaimed in the Manifesto of 29 April could not have been accomplished immediately. The confusion in the government after the events of 1 March was too great. The government did not yet know the strength of the enemies who threatened it. The situation in the countryside, despite the insignificant numbers of peasant disturbances, remained tense. A veiled transition to reaction was necessary.

The best candidate for the role of transition leader was Count N.P. Ignatiev, a confirmed liar and demagogue, a political shark with a gift for invective. From the circular of 6 May, which defined the tasks of the Ministry of Internal Affairs, to the project for the Zemsky Sobor, all of Ignatiev's enterprises were political ploys, except for the reactionary ones. The most important of the reactionary measures was the Statute on Intensified and Emergency Security; its publication was a decisive step by the government on the path of reaction. It also suggested the instability of the political system as a whole, and exemplified the need to adopt emergency laws.

Ignatiev's ministry could not have existed for long in any case. The failure of the Zemsky Sobor scheme merely hastened the inevitable fall of a ministry which was of a temporary, transitional nature. The Aksakov-Ignatiev notion of a Zemsky Sobor was reactionary anyway. It was designed to strengthen the autocracy by a cosmetic maneuver that would illustrate "the unity of the tsar and the people." Yet, regardless of the intent of its organizers, a Zemsky Sobor, even in such an adulterated form, *might* have had other results. That was why the undeviating and more intelligent defenders of the autocracy, like Pobedonostsev, vehemently opposed the Zemsky Sobor.

CONCLUSION

The crisis of the autocracy which arose late in the 1870s was an integral part of the long-developing revolutionary situation. Its roots may be found in the reform of 1861, which did not abolish serfdom entirely. The miserly land allotments, the burden of redemption payments and various levies and taxes, the existence of the commune which retarded the development of agricultural production—all these factors weighed heavily on the majority of the population, the peasantry. Moreover, the development of capitalism, which accelerated after 1861, introduced new contradictions between capital and labor. In the political superstructure the vestiges of feudalism were also important. The bourgeois reforms of the 1860s and 1870s were merely "one step on the road toward the transformation of Russia into a bourgeois monarchy."[1] The state apparatus as a whole retained its feudal nature.

When the tide of social agitation and revolutionary pressure[2] began to ebb in late 1863 the government had an opportunity to adopt reactionary policies. The Karakozov assassination attempt served as a pretext for this transition to a reactionary policy. Together with economic factors political reaction also contributed to the growth of a revolutionary situation.

While the abolition of serfdom reduced contradictions between peasants and landowners to a certain extent, it did not resolve them *in toto*. The exploitative character of the 1861 reform rendered the amelioration of the needs and elimination of the poverty of millions of peasants impossible. Consequently there were peasant disturbances which did not cease even after the reform. The tension which prevailed in the countryside in the late 1870s was the result of the general deterioration in the peasants' living conditions, and of the circulation of rumors about a "black partition." These rumors, the products of the peasants' naive monarchical illusions, were prompted by the war of 1877-1878. Along with a certain increase of peasant disturbances in 1878-1879, the strike movement became more powerful. In the late 1870s the first workers' organizations were created; they were limited in number and influence, however.

The revolutionary democrats, the Populists, expressed the interests of the peasants. In the late 1870s their movement acquired the character of a struggle for political liberty. This occurred under the tense circumstances prevailing in the countryside and during a certain growth in spontaneous peasant disturbances. The heroic fight of the Populists was the *immediate* cause of disorientation in government circles. One must not forget that the Populists' struggle was merely an expression of the peasants' mood; the Populists reflected the peasantry's dissatisfaction and desire to abolish the vestiges of serfdom. The political crisis of the autocracy would not have become so profound had not the government feared the fusion of the spontaneous peasant struggle with the political struggle of the Populists. This was the government's greatest worry, and it explains the government's scrupulous attention to the peasant question.

The Russo-Turkish war had an enormous influence on the growth of the revolutionary situation, and by extension on the crisis of the autocracy. First, the war led to a deterioration in the rural economy. Second, it tarnished the halo of Alexander II and his circle through incidents in the war theater and diplomatic failures which nearly led to a European war. The liberal opposition became much more powerful in the wake of the war.

The crisis of the autocracy lasted approximately from spring 1878 until mid-1882. The symptoms of the crisis were: (1) the impossibility of government by traditional legislation through the existing state apparatus and (2) the apprehension of the need for certain economic and political concessions. Hence the government changed from the existing laws to emergency laws and established new agencies: the special conferences to devise anti-revolutionary measures, and the institution of temporary Governors-General, who were similar in their powers to Roman proconsuls. During this period there were many vacillations in government policy, and a number of reform projects were elaborated. These symptoms characterized the entire crisis of the autocracy; however, at certain times one symptom was more in evidence than the others.

The crisis of the autocracy may be divided into four stages: (1) from spring 1878 to February 1880; (2) from February 1880 to March 1881; (3) from 1 March 1881 to 29 April 1881; and (4) from May 1881 to mid-1882.

The first stage of the crisis was characterized by a certain increase in peasant disturbances and the circulation of rumors about the division of land. There was also an increase in worker demonstrations, especially in the capital. This stage can be subdivided into three periods. The first period lasted from March until August 1878. A series of terrorist acts in southern Russia, strikes in Petersburg, and finally the trial of Vera

Zasulich and the demonstration in front of the courthouse when she was acquitted—all these events prompted the government to establish in late March the Special Conference to devise anti-revolutionary measures. The repressive steps recommended by the Special Conference had not yet infringed radically on the existing laws. The crisis of the autocracy still had not developed fully.

The second period of this stage lasted from August 1878 until early April 1879. The measures adopted in this period already impinged on the operation of the judicial charters. The transfer of cases involving armed revolutionary opposition to military tribunals, and the elaboration of the regulations of 1 September 1878 which allowed gendarmes to apply administrative exile extensively were in direct violation of the judicial charters. It was no accident that this violation affected that part of the political superstructure that was most bourgeois in nature. In this period the governing classes still lacked an understanding of the need for concessions—for economic and political reforms. The crisis had not reached its zenith.

The third period began in April 1879. It was characterized by the creation of temporary Governors-General, by the division of Russia into what might be called proconsulates. The temporary Governors-General did not strengthen the autocracy; on the contrary, they weakened it. In the third period the use of repressive measures reached its apogee. In this period appeared the first signs of a recognition that reforms might be needed to strengthen public support for the autocracy by attracting liberals to the government's side. The most intelligent of the Governors-General, Loris-Melikov, was the first to achieve this recognition. In late 1879 this conviction permeated government spheres. Consequently in early 1880 there was a discussion of the projects written by Valuev and Grand Duke Konstantin Nikolaevich. Nonetheless, these projects were defeated at the direct insistence of the Crown Prince.

The second and third stages of the crisis of the autocracy comprised its most serious phase. The second stage may be subdivided into two periods: the first from February to August 1880, and the second from August 1880 to March 1881. In February 1880 the Supreme Administrative Commission was founded under the direction of Loris-Melikov, who became a kind of quasi-emperor. In contrast to the first stage of the crisis, characterized by a certain decentralization of power through the Governors-General, this period witnessed a reverse process—the concentration of power in the hands of one person. The rights of the Governors-General were reduced somewhat.

Although the ruthless struggle against the revolutionaries continued, there was a marked reduction of police terror, a change in government policy toward the zemstvo, the press, and the universities. This change in the government's course was a direct result of the heroic struggle of the People's Will, not a consequence of Loris-Melikov's policy. It was the further development of the crisis that transformed Loris-Melikov into a liberal bureaucrat.

The abolition of the Supreme Administrative Commission and the appointment of its head as Minister of Internal Affairs strengthened the authority of Loris-Melikov. The abolition of the Third Section, the creation of the Department of State Police and the consolidation of police and gendarmes in the Ministry of Internal Affairs made these punitive agencies more effective.

The project "constitution" outlined in Loris-Melikov's speech of 28 January 1881 was intended to broaden the social base of the autocracy by involving public figures in the discussion of various reforms. Despite its adulterated nature this project would have facilitated the political activism of the bourgeois element in society, and would have prepared the way for the creation of legal political parties. Loris-Melikov's project did not infringe on the principle of autocracy. However, in an increasingly complex situation and given a certain constellation of forces, it might have served as the beginning of a parliamentary system in Russia.

The reduction of police terror lent the revolutionaries a greater opportunity for work among the people. The Executive Committee of *Narodnaia Volia* did not take advantage of this favorable circumstance, which had been made possible by the heroic struggle of the members of the People's Will. Despite the extensive program designed to involve the masses in revolutionary struggle—a program summarized by Zheliabov in his "Preparatory Work of the Party"—the Executive Committee devoted almost its entire energy to the assassination of Alexander II. Consequently the activity of the People's Will members among the workers of Petersburg as well as the activity of the battle organization of the party were limited.

The third stage of the crisis—its apogee—lasted from 1 March until the end of April 1881. This was the period of greatest confusion and disorientation in government ranks. If the assassination had been accompanied by mass demonstrations, or if the battle organization of the party had maneuvered, the government would have been forced to make concessions. This could have resulted in constitutional forms of government, however limited. This did not occur. The People's Will literally exhausted themselves in the assassination. The party was bled dry in the aftermath of the assassination. The finest leaders of the Executive Committee—Alexander Mikhailov, Zheliabov, Perovskaia—were arrested.

There was no other leader capable of carrying on the fight. The bourgeoisie was weak and unrevolutionary, and hence could not lead the spontaneous peasant movement, which was itself insignificant in size. The working class was still a "class unto itself" and was incapable of fighting the autocracy.

For almost two months Alexander III did not dare to pronounce openly his reactionary political ideals. During this time the liberal and reactionary government factions fought for ascendancy. The absence of mass demonstrations in the city and countryside, and of any new actions by the People's Will, enabled Alexander III and his reactionary advisers, headed by Pobedonostsev, to publish the 29 April Manifesto. However, its publication did not signify the end of the crisis.

The fourth and final stage of the crisis of the autocracy commenced with the publication of the manifesto. This stage was a transition to reaction. The leading figure in this transitional phase was Count N.P. Ignatiev. A number of clearly reactionary measures were adopted: "The Statute on Intensified and Emergency Security," "The Temporary Regulations on Jews," and so on. At the same time there were liberal measures, some of which were avowedly demagogic in nature. They included the invitation to "informed persons," which was a cheap political gambit intended to give the appearance of involvement of public figures in governmental work. The creation of the Kakhanov Commission to prepare reforms of local administration was more serious, but it served the same purposes. The government continued to tolerate zemstvo activism in this period, and made certain vague promises to broaden zemstvo jurisdiction. The government also tolerated the liberal policy of the Ministry of Education.

During this period a number of economic reforms were adopted which instituted in abridged form the program outlined by Loris-Melikov. The transfer of peasants to mandatory redemption, the abolition of the head tax, and other reforms were clearly bourgeois measures and doubtless facilitated the development of capitalism. The crisis of the autocracy had not yet run its course.

The final act in Ignatiev's comedy—the unsuccessful attempt to convoke a Zemsky Sobor—was also the closing scene of the crisis of the autocracy. The dismissal of Ignatiev, somewhat hastened by his demagogic undertaking, and the appointment of Tolstoy signified that the government finally had overcome its crisis. Even so, the residual effects of the crisis prevented Tolstoy from forging a program of unalloyed reaction for some time. This became possible only in 1885 when, with the help of A.D. Pazukhin, the Minister of Internal Affairs managed to formulate his reactionary plan of action.

KEY TO ABBREVIATIONS

ch.—chast (section, part)
d.—delo (volume of archival sources)
l.—listok (leaf of archival material)
ll.—listki (leaves of archival material)
op.—opis (archival register)
st.—statia (article of a law)
t.—tom (tome, volume)
GAKhO—Gosudarstvennyi Arkhiv Kharkovskoi Oblasti (State Archive of Kharkov Region)
GIALO—Gosudarstvennyi Istoricheskii Arkhiv Leningradskoi Oblasti (State Historical Archive of the Leningrad Region)
GIAMO—Gosudarstvennyi Istoricheskii Arkhiv Moskovskoi Oblasti (State Historical Arhive of the Moscow Region)
IRLI—Institut Russkoi Literatury (Institute of Russian Literature, Pushkin House)
PSZ—Polnoe Sobranie Zakonov (Complete Collection of Laws)
ROBL—Rukopisnyi Otdel Biblioteki imeni Lenina (Manuscript Section, Lenin Library)
TsGAOR—Tsentralnyi Gosudarstvennyi Arkhiv Oktiabrskoi Revoliutsii (Central State Archive of the October Revolution)
TsGIA—Tsentralnyi Gosudarstvennyi Istoricheskii Arkhiv (Central State Historical Archive)
TsGIA (Ukraine)—Tsentralnyi Gosudarstvennyi Istoricheskii Arkhiv Ukrainskoi Sovetskoi Sotsialisticheskoi Respubliki (Central State Historical Archive of the Ukrainian Soviet Socialist Republic)
TsGVIA—Tsentralnyi Gosudarstvennyi Voenno-istoricheskii Arkhiv (Central State Military-Historical Archive)

NOTES

INTRODUCTION

1. V.I. Lenin, *Sochineniia*, XXI, pp. 189-190.
2. TsGIA, fond Glavnogo komiteta ob ustroistve selskogo sostoianiia, d. 28, 1881 g., ll. 72-74.
3. TsGIA, fond Glavnogo komiteta ob ustroistve selskogo sostoianiia, d. 104, 1881 g., 11. 174-187.
4. TsGVIA, fond Kantseliarii Voennogo ministerstva, No. 1 (L), op. 2, d. 25, p. 16.
5. I.S. Bliokh, *Finansy Rossii v XIX stoletii*, II, (St. Petersburg, 1882), p. 237.
6. *Ibid.*, p. 245.
7. These data are based on materials from central archives: fondy III otdeleniia s.e.u.v. kantseliarii, Ministerstva vnutrennikh del (kantseliarii ministra i Zemskogo otdela), Ministerstva yustitsii; it is to be expected that not all disturbances were reported. In many cases Petersburg was not informed that disturbances had occurred, although these cases were of minor significance. One can assume with confidence that all peasant demonstrations that were considered dangerous by local authorities were reported to the government and that these reports were deposited in the central archives. The table gives a clear impression of the dynamics of the peasant movement. The figures on the years 1875-1880 are taken from documents that I used in preparation of the collection *Krestianskoe dvizhenie 70-kh godov XIX stoletiia*. The figures on the years 1881-1884 are taken from the collection *Krestianskoe dvizhenie v Rossii 1881-1889 gg.* (Moscow, 1960). It should be noted that I have not counted cases of peasant disturbances where the law was not violated. It should also be noted that disturbances that lasted for several years have been counted separately each year.
8. See the table on peasant disturbances by provinces at the end of this book, Russian edition, pp. 480-481.
9. TsGIA, fond Ministerstva yustitsii, No. 1405, 1878 g., op. 72, d. 1782, ll. 2-21. According to data collected by D.P. Poida, the number of peasants participating in disturbances reached 50,000. D.P. Poida, *Krestianskoe dvizhenie na Pravoberezhnoi Ukraine v poreformennyi period.* (Dnepropetrovsk, 1960)p. 198.
10. TsGIA, fond Zemskogo otdela, 1875 g., op. 53, d. 132, ll. 120-125.
11. TsGIA, fond Zemskogo otdela, 1879 g., op. 53, d. 130.
12. TsGIA, fond Zemskogo otdela, 1878 g., op. 53, d. 119, ll. 9-19.
13. TsGIA, fond Zemskogo otdela, 1878 g., op. 53, d. 98. See also *Agrarnyi vopros i krestianskoe dvizhenie v Tatarii v 50-70-e gody XIX veka* (Moscow, Leningrad, 1936) pp. 343-436.
14. With the exception of one summons to the military in Kazan district in 1878.
15. TsGAOR, fond III otdeleniia, No. 109, 3 ekspeditsiia, d. 51 for 1879. See also the article by V.P. Krikunova, "Krestianskoe dvizhenie na Severnom Kavkaze v period revoliutsionnoi situatsii v Rossii v 1879-1881 godakh," *Uchenye zapiski Kabardinskogo gosudarstvennogo pedagogicheskogo instituta*, 1955, vypusk 7, pp. 57-72.
16. I shall not analyze the causes for the growth of the movement in the 80s, since that would fall outside the limits of this study.

17. TsGIA, fond Kantseliarii ministra vnutrennikh del, No. 1282, op. 2, d. 1081, l. 75.

18. *Ibid.*, l. 338.

19. *Ibid.*, l. 57. In certain cases these rumors took concrete form. According to the report of the Kazan governor, one of the people caught spreading rumors, a retired soldier, stated that "in the siege at Plevna General Skobelev agreed to help only if he were permitted to give awards to all the peasants of Kazan province . . . . " l. 36.

20. Yet simultaneously among the peasants, apparently under the influence of Populist propaganda, there surfaced another attitude to the tsar. According to the Pskov governor, there was a peasant from Gorodishche village, Ostrovsky district, named Vasily Semenovich Krivoy who wrote in his diary: "Although they have shot at the tsar, they unfortunately have failed to kill him. He has not given us land." TsGIA, fond Kantseliarii ministra vnutrennikh del, op. 2, d. 1081, l. 169. It should be noted that I cannot cite other examples of this attitude.

21. TsGIA, fond Zemskogo otdela, No. 1291, 1881 g., op. 53, d. 1, l. 9.

22. See chapter 1, below.

23. *Rabochee dvizhenie v Rossii v XIX veke*, II, 1861-1884, ch. 2 – 1875-1884 (Moscow, 1950), pp. 644-676. Data on large strikes have been taken from the same source.

24. K.D. Kavelin, *Sobranie sochinenii*, II (St. Petersburg, 1908), p. 927.

25. M. Gazenkampf, *Moi dnevnik 1877-1878 gg.* (St. Petersburg, 1908), p. 122.

26. I.S. Aksakov, *Slavianskii vopros 1860-1886 gg.* (Moscow, 1886) p. 308.

27. V.I. Lenin, *Sochineniia*, V, p. 36.

28. See below.

29. *Listok Zemli i voli*, no. 2-3, 22 March 1879.

30. *Literatura partii "Narodnoi voli"* (Moscow, 1930), p. 308.

31. *Ibid.*, p. 305.

32. A.A. Planson, *Byloe i nastoiashchee* (St. Petersburg, 1905) pp. 261-262.

33. TsGIA, fond Departamenta zakonov, 1878 g., d. 18.

34. TsGIA, fond Departamenta zakonov, 1878 g., d. 17.

35. TsGIA, fond Departamenta zakonov, 1881 g., d. 40.

36. TsGIA, fond Glavnogo komiteta ob ustroistve selskogo sostoianiia, 1881 g., op. t. XV, dd. 28 and 104.

37. TsGIA, fond Departamenta gosudarstvennoi ekonomii, 1882 g., d. 173.

38. TsGIA, fond Komiteta ministrov, d. 4180, st. 517.

39. TsGIA, fond Komiteta ministrov, d. 4234, st. 333.

40. TsGIA, fond Komiteta ministrov, dd. 4041, 4042, st. 384.

41. TsGIA, fond Komiteta ministrov, dd. 4046, 4047, st. 505.

42. TsGIA, fond Komiteta ministrov, d. 4036, st. 643.

43. TsGIA, fond Komiteta ministrov, dd. 4163, 4164, st. 73.

44 TsGIA, fond Komiteta ministrov, dd. 4234, 4235, st. 280.

45. TsGIA, fond Komiteta ministrov, d. 4173, st. 448.

46. TsGIA, fond 1275.

47. In addition to these conferences, a Special Conference on the Medical-Surgical Academy's right to hold meetings and its influence on other educational institutions was founded on 4 January 1879. The journal of this conference may be found in ROBL, fond D.A. Miliutina, papka 41, d. 41.

48. TsGAOR, fond III otdeleniia, 3 ekspeditsiia, op. 163, d. 502, t. l.

49. TsGAOR, fond III otdeleniia, 3 ekspeditsiia, op. 163, d. 504. Alexander II's resolution in on the first page. Published by Bogucharsky in the notes to *Dnevnik P.A. Valueva 1877-1884 gg.* (Prague, 1919) pp. 295-301.

50. TsGAOR, fond III otdeleniia, op. 163, d. 504, ROBL, fond D.A. Miliutina, papka 39, d. 38.

51. TsGIA, fond Komiteta ministrov, d. 4042, appendix to st. 384, and also a copy written in Valuev's own hand in Valuev's papers TsGIA, fond 908, d. 395.

52. TsGAOR, fond III otdeleniia, op. 163, d. 502, t. 3 and TsGIA, fond Valueva, d. 395.

53. TsGAOR, fond Verkhovnoi rasporiaditelnoi komissii (fond 94), d. 326; and fond Loris-Melikova, op. 569, d. 96; TsGIA, fond Valueva, op. 3, d. 79; ROBL, fond D.A. Miliutina papka 39, d. 41. Among these journals the journal for the meeting of 1 May is not included. It has survived in one copy in the fond Loris-Melikova in TsGAOR. The first three journals are published in *Russkii arkhiv*, 1915, book 12.

54. PSZ, 2 sobr., LIII, LIV, LV; 3 sobr. I, II.

55. The lithographed reports may be found complete in ROBL, fond D.A. Miliutina.

56. These reports were published regularly.

57. One may assume that these documents perished during the archive evacuation from Petrograd in 1918 to Yaroslavl, where one barge of archival documents sank.

58. Some 377 *dela* have been preserved, but many of them have numbers over 1000. The highest extant number is 1352.

59. Report "O polnom sliianii vyshego zavedovaniia politsii v odno uchrezhdenie Ministerstva vnutrennikh del," in TsGIA, fond 1289, op. 241, d. 81, and the report "Ob uchrezhdenii Kakhanovskoi komissii," in *ibid*, d. 83. Loris-Melikov's report of 3 April 1880 in fond Kantseliarii ministra, op. 1, d. 640.

60. In the fond Aleksandra II there are two memoranda of Loris-Melikov — 11 April 1880 in d. 674, and 28 January 1881 in d. 693. Both were published by Golitsyn in *Byloe*, 1918, kn. 4-5. Minister of Finance Bunge's report of 1880 is in d. 673. Generally there are only a few important documents on internal politics preserved in the emperors' papers. In Alexander II's papers there are 170 *dela*, and in Alexander III's there are 151.

61. A great part of the official memoranda are kept in the personal papers of various officials, most of them in the original with the tsar's marginal comments, and some in rough draft form. In Loris-Melikov's papers there are the following reports: "O likvidatsii Verkhovnoi rasporiaditelnoi komissii ot 26 noiabria 1880 g.," d. 64; "o naznachenii senatorskikh revizii ot 11 avgusta 1880 g.," d. 87; in Ignatiev's papers there is his report on the activity of the Ministry of Internal Affairs, dated 22 December 1881, d. 1455; a report dated 15 March 1882, d. 1452; a rough copy of a memorandum on the inadvisability of subjugating the corps of gendarmes and the Department of Police to the head of the imperial Okhrana, d. 1459; a draft memorandum on the need to create a Supreme Commission on the Press, d. 1462; an original copy of an official report by the Minister of Internal Affairs on zemstvo politics, d. 1642; an official report by the Minister of Internal Affairs on assistance to landowners with the redemption on 24 December 1881, with the resolution of Alexander III, d. 1582; a report on the need to dismiss liberal officials from the government with the emperor's comments, d. 148, and others. In Valuev's papers there is an original copy of Loris-Melikov's report of 2 February 1880 on his activity in Kharkov, d. 409.

62. *Krasnyi arkhiv*, 1930, kn. 3 (40), pp. 176-184.

63. *Krasnyi arkhiv*, 1931, kn. 6 (40), pp. 112-143.

64. *Krasnyi arkhiv*, 1930, kn. 3 (40), pp. 125-175.

65. A series of secret circulars were published by S.N. Valk in the journal *Krasnyi arkhiv*, 1931, kn. 2 (45), pp. 147-164.

66. TsGIA, fond Kantseliarii ministra vnutrennikh del, op. 1, d. 643; TsGAOR, fond III otdeleniia, sekretnyi arkhiv, op. 3, d. 570.

67. TsGAOR, fond III otdeleniia, sekretnyi arkhiv, op. 3, d. 711.

68. TsGAOR, fond Verkhovnoi rasporiaditelnoi komissii, d. 367.

69. TsGAOR, fond Verkhovnoi rasporiaditelnoi komissii, d. 326.

70. TsGAOR, fond Verkhovnoi rasporiaditelnoi komissii, d. 340.

71. TsGIA, fond 1282, op. 1, dd. 640, 641, 643-647.

72. TsGIA, fond Departamenta narodnogo prosveshcheniia, op. 200, 1881 g., d. 25.

73. TsGIA, fond Valueva, d. 395.

74. TsGIA, fond Valueva, d. 396. Report published by V.V. Garmiza in the journal *Istoricheskii arkhiv*, 1958, No. 1. It is dated incorrectly 1862.

75. TsGIA, fond Valueva, d. 168.

76. TsGAOR, fond Loris-Melikova, d. 65.

77. TsGAOR, fond Loris-Melikova, d. 44.

78. TsGAOR, fond Loris-Melikova, d. 71.

79. TsGAOR, fond Loris-Melikova, d. 60.

80. TsGAOR, fond 730.

81. TsGAOR, fond 730, dd. 1457 and 1458.

82. TsGAOR, fond 730, d. 1458.

83. TsGAOR, fond 730, d. 1472.

84. TsGAOR, fond 730, d. 1471.

85. TsGAOR, fond 730, d. 1500.

86. TsGAOR, fond 730, d. 1545.

87. TsGAOR, fond Pleve, No. 586, d. 22.

88. All remaining reform projects not presented officially and not the subject of official consideration have been assigned to the category of journalistic sources. To some extent this distinction may be artificial, but it would seem to be justified on the whole.

89. TsGIA (Ukraine), fond 442.

90. GAKhO, fond 5.

91. GIAMO, fond 16.

92. GIALO, fond 2073.

93. I did not use the papers of the Odessa Governor-General. However, I have compensated for this by using a report on the Odessa Governor-General's activity, a series of orders by General Totleben, and accounts of the Governor-General's activity in the revolutionary press.

94. Wiener Haus-Hof-und Staatsarchiv. Ministerium des Aussen P.A. X−76−1, 76−2.

95. The manuscript of the basic first edition of the diaries is in TsGAOR, fond Kollektsii Zimnego dvortsa, No. 728, d. 2587; the second variant is in TsGIA, fond Valueva. I have used the Valuev diary for 1877-1884 published in 1919 by V.Ya. Yakovlev-Bogucharsky and P.E. Shchegolev. They also made the annotations for the years 1877-1879. The published version has a number of gaps and inaccuracies. For example, in January 1881 there are entries listed for 6, 10, 12, 14, 17, 18, 20, 24, and 28 January. Many entries have been shortened substantially. The publication was done in a slap-dash fashion: there are even a number of semantic errors. For a more detailed review see my article: "Ot redaktora," in P.A. Valuev, *Dnevnik*. I, 1861-1864 gg. (Moscow, 1961), pp. 5-16.

96. The Miliutin diaries are kept in his papers in ROBL. The most interesting section of the diaries, dealing with Miliutin's career as a statesman, have been published in four volumes under my editorship. In this publication there are a number of small gaps not discussed in the preface and indicated by four periods without brackets. The rules for this publication have been described in my article: "Ot redaktora," in *Dnevnik D.A. Miliutina*, I, pp. 73-74.

97. This is clear from comparison with the entries of Valuev, Miliutin, and the accounts by K.P. Pobedonostsev in his letters to E.F. Tiutcheva.

98. TsGAOR, fond Aleksadra III, d. 134.

99. The diaries are kept in TsGAOR, fond Polovtsova, No. 583.

100. TsGAOR, fond Polovtsova, d. 18, p. 65. I believe that the emperor was not so much weak-minded, as weak-willed.

101. The Polovtsov diaries were being prepared by Zaionchkovsky for publication at the time *Crisis of the Autocracy* was written. They were published in 1966 in two volumes under the title *Dnevnik gosudarstvennogo sekretaria A.A. Polovtsova* (Moscow, 1966). [Editor]

102. The diaries may be found in Kireev's papers in ROBL.

103. Grand Duke Konstantin Konstantinovich's diaries are kept in his papers in TsGAOR. They are of great interest for historians of literature and the arts. The diary for 1880 contains an account of meetings with F.M. Dostoevsky, P.I. Chaikovsky, N.G. Rubinstein, N.N. Dubovsky and others.

104. These diaries are preserved in his papers in TsGAOR. The entries made during Alexander's tour in the military theater in 1877-1878 are absent.

105. The diary unfailingly describes evening pastimes, especially the period just before bedtime. Often the daily entry ends with the stereotypical phrase: "Having had a bite to eat, we lay down to sleep."

106. After his accession to the throne, Alexander III did not keep a diary; he made only short entires in his memo books: the weather, the air temperature, his guests, etc.

107. TsGAOR, fond Aleksandra II.

108. As an example of such an error I mention the following fact. In the entry for 28 February 1881, which was the final one, there is this phrase: "Zavt. UK, s det." I originally deciphered this as: "Zavt [ra] Uk [az] o det [iakh]." (Tomorrow ukase on children). If one had in mind Alexander II's desire to change the legal status of his children from a morganatic marriage, then such a phrase would make sense. A more careful analysis of the text, showing that a similar phrase appeared on other days, yielded a completely different reading: "Zavt [rakal] u K [ati] s det [mi]." (Breakfasted with the children at Katia's.) Certain entries could not be read. For example, while I was doing research for my book on the abolition of serfdom, I found it impossible to decipher the entry for 18 February 1861.

109. TsGAOR, fond Ignatieva, d. 161. Ignatiev's memoirs are written partly in his own hand, partly in typed copy with the author's corrections.

110. TsGIA, fond Golovnina, No. 851, d. 16, manuscript.

111. IRL, fond M.I. Semevskogo, d. 274.

112. *Byloe*, 1918, kn. 4-5, p. 193.

113. Laferté, *Alexandre II. Details inédits sur la vie intime et sa mort* (Paris, 1882), p. 23. See also *Dnevnik D.A. Miliutina*, IV, p. 134. Judging by Yurievskaia's letters to Alexander III, preserved in his papers, one can say that she was an unintelligent and petty person.

114. The letters are preserved in the Alexander III papers (TsGAOR, d. 519) and in the Loris-Melikov papers (TsGAOR, fond 143a). They have been published in *Krasnyi arkhiv*, 1925, kn. 1.

115. *Perepiska K.P. Pobedonostseva s Aleksandrom III*, I, (Moscow, 1925).
116. *K.P. Pobedonostsev i ego korrespondenty*, I, part 1, (Moscow, 1925).
117. TsGAOR, fond Ignatieva, d. 3679. Part of the letters have been published in *Byloe*, 1924, kn. 27-28.
118. Pobedonostsev's account of these events is written from a reactionary position, but it is factually accurate. The letters are in Pobedonostsev's papers in ROBL; some of them have been published in *Russkii arkhiv*, 1907, kn. 5.
119. I.S. Aksakov papers. Published in *Russkii arkhiv*, 1913, kn. I-II.
120. M.E. Saltykov-Shchedrin, *Polnoe sobranie sochinenii*, XIX; letters to A.N. Ostrovsky, p. 158, and to Loris-Melikov, pp. 221-222, and P.V. Annenkov, p. 170.
121. ROBL, fond Katkova, d. 48. Letter to N.M. Baranov on 24 March 1881, l. 159; d. 48, l. 26—letter to Alexander III, undated; these letters are copies.
122. ROBL, fond D.A. Miliutina, papka 61, dd. 32, 33, 34.
123. ROBL, fond Belogolovyi, No. 22, papka 6, dd. 3-37.
124. *Katorga i ssylka*, 1925, kn. 2.
125. TsGAOR, fond Polovtsova, d. 18, p. 185.
126. Both reports are published in *Krasnyi arkhiv*, 1928, kn. 6, (31).
127. ROBL, fond D.A. Miliutina, papka 44, d. 12.
128. ROBL, fond D.A. Miliutina, papka 39, d. 33. The manuscript consists of six pages in folio. Author's hand in pencil. There are words crossed out. Published with certain errors in *Zapiski Otdela rukopisei GBL*, No. 2, (Moscow, 1939).
129. Chicherin wrote this report in several copies, two of which he sent to Pobedonostsev: one for Pobedonostsev, and the second for Alexander III. *K.P. Pobedonostsev i ego korrespondenty*, I, part 1, pp. 105-120. Reports by L.D. Gradovsky and the Marquis Wielopolsky have a similar content. They are cited in a brochure *Konstitutsiia gr. Loris-Melikova* (London, 1893). One must also mention the report of Count Bobrinsky on 10 March 1881 in *Krasnyi arkhiv*, 1928, kn. 6 (31).
130. TsGAOR, fond Loris-Melikova, d. 52, l. 12.
131. TsGAOR, fond Loris-Melikova, d. 58. The report is written in the author's hand.
132. TsGIA, fond Kantseliarii ministra vnutrennikh del, op. l, d. 646. The report is in a clerk's handwriting, but it is signed by the author. Dated 9 March 1880.
133. S. Muromtsev. *Stati i rechi*, vypusk V (Moscow, 1910), pp. 11-38. The report was first published abroad in Paris in 1881 as a brochure *V pervye dni ministerstva Loris-Melikova*. In 1881 there was also an unsuccessful attempt to publish this report in *Vestnik Evropy*.
134. *Arkhiv Marksa i Engelsa*, XI, (Moscow, 1948); XII, (Moscow, 1952).
135. *Perepiska K. Marksa i F. Engelsa s russkimi politicheskimi deiateliami* (Moscow, 1951).
136. K. Marks i F. Engels, *Sochineniia*, XIX, p. 158.
137. K. Marks i F. Engels, *Sochineniia*, XXII, p. 451.
138. V.I. Lenin, *Sochineniia*, V, p. 40.
139. Analysis of the text in my opinion shows that the information was received from Loris-Melikov.
140. *Dnevnik D.A. Miliutina*, IV, p. 90.
141. *Revue des deux mondes*, 1 May 1882, pp. 375-404.
142. Leroy-Beaulieu, *L'Empire des tsars et les russes*, II, (Paris) pp. 587-685.
143. V-te. E. Melhiore de Vögüé, *Spectacles contemporains* (Paris, 1891), pp. 225-274.

144. This brochure was published several times abroad. In the Berlin edition of 1904 private letters of Loris-Melikov were published as an appendix. The brochure was published in Russia in 1906.
145. *Konstitutsiia gr. Loris-Melikova*, p. 43.
146. *Byloe*, 1918, kn. 4-5, p. 187.
147. F.V. Volkhovsky, *Chemu uchit konstitutsiia gr. Loris-Melikova?*, p. 16.
148. *Ibid.*, p. 17.
149. In the papers of Grand Duke Vladimir Alexandrovich (TsGAOR) there is no such letter.
150. Chapters 32-34.
151. All of Tatishchev's quotations from the journals of the Special Conferences and Loris-Melikov's memoranda are without references to the source.
152. A.A. Kornilov, *Obshchestvennoe dvizhenie pri Aleksandre II (1855-1881)* (Moscow, 1909), pp. 252, and 257.
153. *Kurs istorii Rossii XIX veka*, ch. III (Moscow, 1914), p. 234.
154. V.Ya. Bogucharsky, *Iz istorii politicheskoi borby v 70-80-kh godakh XIX veka* (Moscow, 1912), p. 244.
155. *Byloe*, 1918, kn. 4-5, pp. 125-154.
156. See S.N. Valk, "Posle 1 marta 1881 g.," *Krasnyi arkhiv*, 1931, kn. 2 (45), pp. 147-160 and "Vokrug 1 marta 1881 g.," *Krasnyi arkhiv*, 1930, kn. 3 (40), pp. 176-180.
157. *Istoricheskie zapiski*, No. 2. See also Yu.V. Gotie, "K.P. Pobedonostsev i naslednik Aleksandr Aleksandrovich. 1861-1881," in *Sbornik No. 2 Gosudarstvennoi biblioteki SSSR im. V.I. Lenina*. Some sections of this article were very useful in my research.
158. I.V. Epaneshnikov used only archival materials from the papers of D.A. Miliutin and A.A. Kireev in ROBL.
159. The author published his dissertation in a shortened and somewhat different format: *Vtoraia revoliutsionnaia situatsiia v Rossii (konets 70-kh—nachalo 80-kh godov XIX veka). Krizis pravitelstvennoi politiki* (Moscow, 1963), 240 pp.
160. M.I. Kheifets, *Revoliutsionnaia situatsiia v Rossii kontsa 1870-kh godov* (Moscow, 1950) p. 2.
161. See the table on the peasant movement below.
162. Incidentally, according to the archival registers in the fond Verkhovnoi rasporiaditelnoi komissii (TsGAOR, fond 94), there are no materials on the peasant movement in that fond. Under the rubric "Peasant Movement" there is only one *delo* (No. 252) concerning a secret society in Chigirinsky district, Kiev province. Information on peasant uprisings could not have gone directly to the Supreme Administrative Commission. They went to the Ministry of Internal Affairs from the provincial administration, to the Third Section from the gendarmes, and to the Ministry of Justice from the courts and procurators. Therefore, if such documents wound up in the Supreme Administrative Commission papers, they came either from central departments or from the Governors-General.
163. See D.P. Poida, *Krestianskoe dvizhenie na Pravoberezhnoi Ukraine v poreformennyi period*. See also the diploma thesis of V. Korostelin, *Krestianskoe dvizhenie 70-kh godov po dannym III otdeleniia*, defended at Moscow University in 1958.
164. Kheifets, *op. cit.*, pp. 277, 279, 362.
165. *Ibid.*, p. 545.
166. *Voprosy istorii*, 1962, No. 2, p. 54.
167. See the end of chapter three in this book.

168. Institut istorii AN SSSR' "Materialy k obsuzhdeniiu." *Istoriia SSSR' Period pobedy i utverzhdeniia kapitalizma (1862-1894),* Ch. 1, (Moscow, 1951) pp. 910-937.

CHAPTER I

1. The acquittal of Vera Zasulich was greeted sympathetically in many strata of Russian society. "The acquittal of Vera Zasulich," wrote Stepniak-Kravchinsky, "was a solemn condemnation of the entire system of arbitrary rule that had compelled this young woman to raise her hand in revenge against the executioner [Trepov]. The press and society unanimously approved the decision of the jurors." S. Stepniak, *Podpolnaia Rossiia* (St. Petersburg, 1906) p. 29.

Despite the composition of the jury, which was far from democratic (ten officials and merchants, one active student, and one artist), the jurors were forced to acquit Zasulich. The chief magistrate at the trial, A.F. Koni, exerted great influence on the jury to acquit. Alexander II was infuriated by the verdict of acquittal and asked the Minister of Justice to dismiss Koni. However, the tsar did not succeed: the existing statutes guaranteed the inviolability of the courts. Koni refused to resign, and there was no basis to try him for misconduct. See A.F. Koni, *Vospominanie o dele Very Zasulich* (Moscow-Leningrad, 1933).

2. TsGAOR, fond III otdeleniia, 3 ekspeditsiia, 1878 g., op. 163, d. 502, t. 1, 11. 1-2.

3. This question was considered by the Council of Ministers at the session on 3 April. See below.

4. TsGAOR, fond III otdeleniia, 1878 g., op. 163, d. 502, 1. 10.

5. TsGAOR, fond III otdeleniia, 1878 g., op. 163, d. 502, t. 1, 11. 12, 14.

6. *Ibid.,* 11. 245-246.

7. *Ibid.,* 11. 250-252.

8. *Ibid.,* 1. 253.

9. *Ibid.,* 11. 268-269.

10. *Ibid.,* 11. 274-275.

11. *Ibid.,* 1. 280.

12. For the Apukhtin project see TsGAOR, fond III otdeleniia, 3 ekspeditsiia, 1878 g., op. 163, d. 502, t. 3, 1. 278.

13. *Ibid.,* 1. 281.

14. *Ibid.,* 1. 283. The projects for a corrective educational institution and military-disciplinary regime were never implemented.

15. TsGAOR, fond III otdeleniia, 3 ekspeditsiia, 1878 g., op. 163, d. 502, t. 1, 11. 284-285. Later it was decided to set up three colonies in Eastern Siberia. *Ibid.,* chast 3, 1. 120.

16. *Ibid.,* 11. 286-287.

17. TsGIA, fond Komiteta ministrov, prilozhenie k zhurnalam Komiteta ministrov, d. 3972, prilozhenie k st. 280, 1. 79.

18. *Ibid.,* 11. 62-63.

19. *Ibid.,* 1. 53.

20. PSZ, 2 sobr., LIII, No. 58610.

21. TsGIA, fond Komiteta ministrov, d. 4024, st. 83. "Otchet ministra vnutrennikh del 13 fevralia 1879 g. o realizatsii zakona o politseiskikh uriadnikakh." Alexander II was impressed by this report. He wrote on the journal of the Committee of Ministers: "My special gratitude goes to St. Secretary Makov. I hope that this useful institution will bring the expected good results in the future." *Ibid.,* 1.

143. In a memorandum on the plans of the Special Conference to draft projects on the reform of local government, given to the Committee of Ministers in April 1882, M.S. Kakhanov wrote: "The new institution of village police, which is not connected organically with the police apparatus in general, has shown very serious disadvantages and has not remedied the shortcomings of the rural police commissaries." TsGIA, fond Komiteta ministrov, d. 4234, st. 280, 1. 141.

22. In September 1879 the number of village police was increased by 550. PSZ, 2 sobr., LIV, No. 59986.

23. *Sbornik tsirkuliarov i instruktsii Ministerstva vnutrennikh del za 1878 g.* (St. Petersburg, 1880), p. 171.

24. Judging by a report on the four-month period in which the village police operated, one can say that the village police concentrated mainly on various forms of criminal activity. Of 2251 cases only 151 involved "violation of regulations on public security and order." TsGIA, fond Departamenta politsii ispolnitelnoi, op. 40, d. 4, 1879 g., 11. 98-99. Of the 2503 persons arrested by village police in this period, only 105 persons were tried "for violation of order—assault, fighting, and other crimes against public order and security." *Ibid.*, 11. 100-101.

25. Aside from the ministers the Council of Ministers included: the tsarevich, Grand Dukes Konstantin, Nikolai, and Mikhail Nikolaevich, Prince Oldenburgsky, the chairman of the Committee of Ministers Count Ignatiev, the head of the Second Section of His Majesty's Chancellery Prince Urusov, and Chief of Gendarmes Mezentsov. To this session the chairman of the Department of State Economy Abaza, the commander of His Majesty's Escort General Cherevin, and a member of the State Council Count Baranov also were invited. TsGIA, fond Soveta ministrov, d. 94.

26. In the original variant of the diary the following words are appended: "But without my advice."

27. *Dnevnik D.A. Miliutina,* III, pp. 41-42.

28. TsGIA, fond Departamenta zakonov Gosudarstvennogo soveta, 1878 g., d. 18.

29. *Ibid.,* 1. 2.

30. *Ibid.*

31. *Ibid.,* 11. 16-17.

32. *Ibid.,* 1. 28.

33. PSZ, sobr. 2, LIII, No. 58488.

34. TsGIA, fond Departamenta zakonov, 1878 g., d. 17, 1. 2.

35. *Ibid.,* 1. 3.

36. PSZ, 2 sobr., LIII, No. 58489.

37. TsGAOR, fond III otdeleniia, 3 ekspeditsiia, 1878 g., op. 163, d. 504, 1. 3. This letter was published by V. Ya. Bogucharsky in the book *Iz istorii politicheskoi borby 70-kh godov XIX veka,* p. 171. It was published a second time by Bogucharsky and Shchegolev in their commentaries on the diary of P.A. Valuev 1877-1884, p. 295.

38. *Dnevnik D.A. Miliutina,* III, p. 83.

39. The official report was composed after 4 August, that is, after the assassination of Mezentsov, since it is signed by Mezentsov's assistant, General Seliverstov. The report was published in the notes to the Valuev diary, *Dnevnik 1877-1884 gg.,* pp. 295-301. The original is kept in the fond III otdeleniia, 3 ekspeditsiia, 1878 g., op. 163, d. 504, 11. 6-17.

40. P.A. Valuev, *Dnevnik 1877-1884 gg.,* p. 296.

41. *Ibid.,* p. 297.

42. However the staffing of the Corps of Gendarmes was very difficult, according to a report from acting Chief of Gendarmes General Seliverstov to the tsar. "Very serious difficulties are being encountered in the effort to fill vacant positions in the Corps of Gendarmes; to my distress almost no one can be found who wants to enter such crucial, responsible, and dangerous service. One way to attract able personnel is to increase significantly salaries, and mindful of Your Majesty's desire to act quickly, I have decided to devote part of the 300,000 rubles allocated to strengthen the gendarmerie to salary supplements for the staff and head officers who serve in the gendarmes." *Krasnyi arkhiv*, 1931, kn. 6, p. 149.

43. P.A. Valuev, *Dnevnik 1877-1884 gg*, pp. 299-310.

44. The assassination was in reprisal for the hanging of the Odessa Populist I.M. Kovalsky. The brochure *Smert za smert* (A Death for a Death) was published in response to this incident.

45. *Golos*, 5 August 1878.

46. *Dnevnik D.A. Miliutina*, III, p. 87. Unfortunately, materials on this session have not been preserved in the Council of Ministers papers. In his diary Valuev discussed this meeting. "With complete incredulity I witnessed the strange conversations of the Ministers of Justice and Finance. . . . The Minister of Justice showed a remarkable inclination to out do Count Pahlen in foolishness. After the assassination of the Chief of Gendarmes in broad daylight on Mikhailovsky Square he was thinking not about the prevention or prosecution of crimes, but about the inviolability of the procurators' rights. Thanks to the acting head of the Ministry of Internal Affairs . . . and the temporary, as it were accidentally-designated Chief of Gendarmes Seliverstov, the Ministry [of Justice] was silenced. . . ." P.A. Valuev, *Dnevnik 1877-1884 gg.*, p. 29.

47. One of the practical measures taken to implement this decision was a circular, published in September. It indicated that on 8 August "His Majesty decided to grant the right of free entry into all factories and workshops at any time to the officials of the Corps of Gendarmes and the police, who would also have the right to conduct searches and make arrests." TsGIA, biblioteka, kollektstiia tsirkuliarov po Otd. korpusy zhandarmov, tsirkuliar No. 18 ot 6 fevralia 1878 g..

48. *Ibid.*, Appendix to circular No. 120, 20 September 1878. These rules did not appear in the Complete Collection of Laws (PSZ).

49. *Ibid.*

50. *Ibid.*, Circular No. 137, 25 September 1878.

51. *Ibid.*

52. PSZ, 2 sobr., XLII, No. 44575.

53. PSZ, 2 sobr., LIII, No. 58778. Article 279 of the Military Penal Code prescribed the death penalty.

54. PSZ, 2 sobr., LIII, No. 58799.

55. According to Miliutin, at the Council of Ministers session on 3 April Count Pahlen said it was necessary to have a court that would rule according "to the directives of government authorities." *Dnevnik D.A. Miliutina*, III, p. 42.

56. PSZ, 2 sobr., LIII, No. 59025. The decision of the Committee of Ministers was affirmed by Alexander II on 19 November.

57. *Ibid.* In allotting the money the Committee of Ministers noted: "From the financial side the Committee of Ministers cannot afford to ignore the fact that, given the present circumstances of the state treasury, any new permanent expediture necessarily will mean a further rise in taxes, which inevitably must increase in order to cover various state requirements for the army, navy, prisons, etc.. A heavy tax burden unfortunately may contribute to the appeal of politically harmful elements."

58. Circular of the Department of State Police, No. 1018, 19 February 1881; a copy is held in the fond kantseliarii kievskogo general-gubernatora, TsGIA (U-kraine), fond 442, op. 831, d. 3. Kollektsiia tsirkuliarov Ministerstva vnutrennikh del za 1881 g., 1. 82. In February 1881 this circular was cancelled: runaways were to be returned to their former places of exile, deprived of their property, and forced to continue their exile.

59. *Pravitelstvennyi vestnik,* 20 August 1878.

60. B.B. Veselovsky, *Istoriia zemstva,* III (St. Petersburg, 1911), p. 231.

61. *Moskovskie vedomosti,* 21 November 1878.

62. This order was mentioned in a circular from the Minister of Internal Affairs, No. 3046, 30 May 1881, which cancelled the order. TsGIA (Ukraine), fond kant-seliarii kievskogo general-gubernatora, op. 831, d. 3, 1. 64.

63. *Dnevnik D.A. Miliutina,* III, pp. 128-129.

64. TsGAOR, fond III otdeleniia, 3 ekspeditsiia, 1878 g., op. 163, d. 504, 11. 47-48.

65. *Ibid.,* 1. 50. In accordance with the temporary regulations of 1 September 1878, this right was granted only to the Chief of Gendarmes by agreement with the Minister of Internal Affairs.

66. *Ibid.*

67. *Ibid.,* 1. 53. Alexander II affirmed the decision of the Special Conference on 18 March.

68. TsGAOR, fond Polovtsova, d. 14, p. 4. In a diary entry on 2 April he related a conversation with Grand Duke Vladimir Alexandrovich, with whom he had gone hunting that day. The Grand Duke stated that "much in the government needed reform, but above all it is necessary to adopt strict measures, so that we can, so to speak, fight terror with terror." Page 5.

69. *Dnevnik D.A. Miliutina,* III, p. 134.

70. P.A. Valuev, *Dnevnik 1877-1884 gg.,* p. 33.

71. TsGIA, fond Valueva, d. 396, 11. 2-3. This entry was published in *Istori-cheskii arkhiv,* 1958, No. 1. It was dated incorrectly as 1862.

72. *Ibid.*

73. *Dnevnik D.A. Miliutina,* III, p. 134.

74. PSZ, 2 sobr., LIV, No. 59476.

75. An ukase to the Senate on 23 April 1879 gave to the Moscow, Warsaw, and Kiev Governors-General and to the temporary Governors-General in Petersburg, Kharkov and Odessa the right to extend their authority to all provinces falling under the local military district "in cases of necessity." PSZ, 2 sobr., LIV, No. 59531. In 1879 there were several decrees placing other provinces under the Gov-ernors-General. On 8 August the Moscow Governor-General got control of Smolen-sk (No. 59920), on 20 October he got control of Riazan, Tula, and Kaluga (No. 60095), and on 12 December of Tambov (No. 60274). The Kharkov Governor-General got control of Chernigov, Poltava, Kursk, Orel, and Voronezh provinces on 13 November (No. 60187). Kherson, Tauride, Ekaterinoslav, and Bessarabia fell under the Odessa Governor-General, while St. Petersburg, Pskov, Olonets, Nov-gorod, and Arkhangelsk fell under the Petersburg Governor-General.

76. Article 46 of the Statute on Field Command of the Army in Wartime, published 17 April 1868, stated: "The commander, who is obliged to watch that public order and tranquility are observed in areas and provinces falling under mili-tary control, has the right: to dismiss local officials, appoint new ones, and in cases of crimes with a political character that may harm the security of the army or public order, to try in military courts these officials and all other inhabitants of these areas and provinces. . . ." PSZ, 2 sobr., XLIII, No. 45729.

77. The Governors-General soon controlled the mails. In a secret circular to postal employees, written in April 1879, it was indicated that all postal institutions in areas controlled by the Governors-General "must be subject completely to them and must fulfill unconditionally all demands and orders of the Governors-General. TsGIA, (Ukraine), fond kantseliarii kievskogo general-gubernatora, op. 828, d. 221, 1. 72.

78. PSZ, 2 sobr., LIV, No. 59476.

79. PSZ, 2 sobr., LIV, No. 59478.

80. *Moskovskie vedomosti,* 7 April 1879. Katkov's idea found its future expression in the proposal to create the Supreme Administrative Commission.

81. *Golos,* 8 April 1879. Other liberal publications (*Novoe vremia* and *Vestnik Evropy*) limited themselves to a dry recitation of the fact that the Governors-General had been appointed.

82. *Golos,* 6 May 1879.

83. At this "reception" the most important representatives of the Russian periodical press were gathered: V.A. Bilbasov, P.A. Gaideburov, M.E. Saltykov-Shchedrin, M.I. Semevsky and others. According to Semevsky, there were 18 to 20 persons at the meeting.

84. IRLI, fond M.I. Semevskogo, No. 274, d. 16, materialy k zapiskam, 1. 417.

85. *Ibid.,* 11. 478-485.

86. *Dnevnik D.A. Miliutina,* III, p. 136.

87. TsGAOR, fond kollektsii biblioteki Zimnego dvortsa, d. 2587, kn. VI, 1. 80. In the published text of the diary two words have been left out: "half-ruined sovereign."

88. TsGAOR, fond Aleksandra III, d. 134, dnevnik E.A. Perettsa (typed copy), 1. 17.

89. TsGAOR, fond Loris-Melikova, d. 60, 1. 27. These figures are cited by S.S. Tatishchev in his book *Imperator Aleksandr II. Ego zhizn' i tsarstvovanie,* II, p. 568. According to a directive from the Minister of Internal Affairs on 19 April, persons exiled to the peripheral provinces under the ukase of 5 April should be sent "into Eastern Siberia according to the imperial decision of 8 August 1878." GIAMO, fond kantseliarii moskovskogo general-gubernatora, op. 69, d. 29, ch. II, 1. 1.

90. *Narodnaia volia. Sotsialno-revoliutsionnoe obozrenie,* No. 3, Editorial.

91. The other twenty persons were exiled for various criminal offenses: burglary, robbery, "an intemperate and undisciplined life," gambling etc. One of them, the peasant Savitsky, was exiled to another district for "falsely accusing another person of a state offense." TsGIA (Ukraine), fond kantseliarii kievskogo general-gubernatora, 1880 g., op. 830, d. 250, 1. 58.

92. *Ibid.,* 11. 1-58.

93. *Narodnaia volia,* No. 2, p. 15. In the second number of the paper in the article "Dva slova o general-gubernatorstve," there is the following: "Citizens of Odessa are convinced that Totleben is no more than a pawn in the hands of that person who controls the fate of millions of people." p. 15. There is a quotation from the document "Predlozhenie vremennogo odesskogo general-gubernatora Totlebena tainomu sovetniku Paniutinu ot 7 maia 1879 goda za No. 152," which shows that Totleben gave most of his authority to his assistant.

94. S.F. Chubarov, D.A. Lizogub, I. Ya. Davidenko, S. Ya. Vittenberg, I.I. Logovenko, V.A. Malinka, L.O. Maidansky, I.V. Drobiazgin.

95. TsGIA, fond Komiteta ministrov, d. 4047, st. 505, 1. 106. Most of the exiles were residents of Odessa (67 out of 104).

96. *Ibid.*, ll. 107-109.
97. *Ibid.* l. 105.
98. *Ibid.*, l. 113.
99. According to the report, Totleben arrived in Odessa and assumed office on 23 April.
100. This quotation from a copy preserved in the fond katseliarii s. peterburg-skogo vremennogo general-gubernatora. GIALO, fond 2073, op. 1, d. 63, l. 2.
101. *Ibid.* Officials of the first four ranks in the civil service, gentry marshals, couriers and "those persons who are working and have permission from their superiors to assemble" were exempt from this search.
102. For a second offense the fine was doubled, for a third offense it tripled. Offenders could also be arrested for 1 to 9 months.
103. IRLI, fond M.I. Semevskogo, d. 16, l. 164.
104. Actually, during Loris-Melikov's tenure in Kharkov there was not a single hanging.
105. *Narodnaia volia*, No. 1, p. 18.
106. Of the 575 persons exiled by the Governors-General Loris-Melikov was responsible for only 37. (TsGIA, fond Valueva, d. 402, l. 12.
107. Unfortunately, this material was not preserved in the Kharkov Governor-General's archive, so we can judge only by the proposals of Loris-Melikov to the Special Conference. (See below).
108. When Loris-Melikov arrived, the provincial gendarmerie consisted of 5 officers, 25 junior officers, and 2 clerks. Loris-Melikov petitioned to increase the staff by one officer and 24 junior officers. Before this matter was decided officially, the requested number of officers and junior officers was sent to Kharkov from Kovno. GAKhO, fond vremennogo kharkovskogo general-gubernatora, op. 2, d. 5, ll. 3-8.
109. TsGIA, fond Valueva, d. 402, ll. 28-29. The original is dated 2 February 1880. Valuev wrote on the first page: "Sent by me to the emperor 6 February 1880."
110. TsGIA, fond Valueva, d. 402, l. 30.
111. *Narodnaia volia*, No. 3, p. 17.
112. One of the first steps of the Petersburg Governor-General was to publish an order that apartment houses be guarded around the clock in order to assist the police in the fight against "sedition." Failure to follow this order made home owners liable to a fine of 500 rubles; a guard who deserted the watch could be fined 25 rubles, or be jailed for a week, and a second desertion was grounds for exile from the capital. "Obiazatelnoe postanovlenie s. peterburgskogo vremennogo general-guvernatora ot 8 aprelia 1879 g." According to information appended to the order, there must have been 5473 house guards falling under the regulations. A similar order was issued by the Moscow General-Governor. *Vedomosti moskov-skoi gorodskoi politsii,* 19 April 1879.
113. Besides Valuev, the Special Conference included: Ministers of War—Miliutin, of Education—Tolstoy, of Internal Affairs—Makov, of Finance—Greig, Chief of Gendarmes Drenteln, and the head of the Second Section of His Majesty's Chancellery Prince Urusov. However, Miliutin was unavailable for the meetings of the Special Conference because from 12 April until 28 May he was with the royal family in Livadia. S.S. Tatishchev, *Imperator Aleksandr II. Ego zhizn i tsarstvovanie*, II, p. 560.
114. TsGAOR, fond kollektsii rukopisei Zimnego dvortsa, d. 2587, kn. VI, l. 75. Valuev diary, In the published version there are several errors.

115. TsGIA, fond Valueva, d. 395, 1. 28.
116. *Ibid.*, 1. 29.
117. *Ibid.*
118. *Ibid.*, ll. 29-30.
119. *Ibid.*, 1. 31.
120. Otnoshenie ot 25 iiulia 1879 g. TsGIA, fond Kantseliarii ministra vnutrennikh del, op. 2, d. 1081, 1. 213. Of the 35 reports by governors to the Minister of Internal Affairs about the spread of false rumors 15 stated that the rumors were spread by soldiers.
121. I could not find this circular. It is mentioned in TsGIA, fond Kantseliarii
ministra vnutrennikh del, op. 2, d. 1081, 1. 25.
122. *Ibid.*, 1. 50.
123. TsGIA, fond Valueva, d. 395, 11. 31-32.
124. *Ibid.*, 1. 32.
125. With the exception of the law of 10 December 1865 which prohibited persons of Polish descent from acquiring estates in these provinces. *Ibid.*, ll. 18-19.
126. The Conference did not make any decision on this matter because of the
absence of two of its members. It limited itself to discussion. In the official memorandum Valuev summarized the question in a brief form. Therefore, I have relied on the journal of the Conference for my summary (The journal is in complete
accord with Valuev's summary, save for several introductory sentences).
127. TsGIA, fond Komiteta ministrov, d. 4042, prilozhenie k st. 384, 1. 353.
128. *Ibid.*, ll. 353-354.
129. *Ibid.*, 1. 355.
130. The Minister of Education presented a "Supplemental Report" on this issue,
criticizing the proposed measure. First, he observed that from 1871 to 1879 only
three persons out of the fifty dismissed from seminary teaching positions had
been indicted for political offenses. Second, it would be hard to improve the material position of the clergy through this measure since the expenses on training
and salary for teachers in the 25,000 elementary schools equalled only one million rubles a year. For each school the expenditure was only 40 rubles per annum,
or just over three rubles a month. At the end of the report the minister wrote:
"One does not even need to comment on the terrible impression that will be
produced among the friends of Russian education by this proposal, which is unprecedented in the annals of Russian and European civilization, to eliminate all
subsidies for rural schools and to destroy an entire category of educational institutions serving the people .... " The citation is from the printed copy, kept
in the fond D.A. Miliutina, ROBL, papka 39, d. 39, p. 4.
131. TsGIA, fond Komiteta ministrov, d. 4042, st. 384, 1. 356.
132. *Ibid.*
133. TsGIA, fond Komiteta ministrov, d. 4041, st. 384, Osobyi zhurnal Komiteta ministrov, ll. 103-104.
134. *Ibid.*, 1. 107.
135. *Ibid.*, ll. 107-108.
136. This issue was finally resolved when Alexander II affirmed the decision of
the Committee of Ministers on 19 August 1979, which accorded with the desires
of the Minister of Internal Affairs and the Chief of Gendarmes. The decision
said: "When offices are being filled in zemstvo and municipal institutions, either
by election or by appointment, the governor should receive all documents relevant
to the background of the prospective officeholders in advance of the assumption
of office. The governor should announce his opposition if he finds, after studying

the documents, that the prospective officeholder is unreliable politically. When the governor is opposed to a person, the person will not assume office. If the governor does not announce his opposition to a candidate within two weeks of the receipt of the background information, this shall be construed as consent to the appointment or election." TsGIA, fond Komiteta ministrov, d. 4044, st. 451, ll. 90-91. This decision, which infringed upon the last traces of independence of zemstvo and municipal institutions, was modified subsequently, although in essence it remained the same. In a circular explaining the application of this rule on 29 October, there was this note: "Persons elected to zemstvo and municipal boards shall not be subject to special confirmation and the system of elections will be the same as that set down in the law. Application of the imperial order of 19 August will be required only if becomes clear that candidates to the elective offices are unreliable or harmful politically." Therefore, the governor had the right not to confirm persons elected by either zemstvo assemblies or municipal dumas.

137. This issue was resolved in September 1879 in connection with the Committee of Ministers' discussion of Totleben's official report. TsGIA, fond Komiteta ministrov, d. 4046, st. 505.

138. TsGIA, fond Komiteta ministrov, d. 4036, st. 643, Osobyi zhurnal za 5 i 13 iiunia 1879 g., l. 141.

139. TsGIA, fond Komiteta ministrov, d. 4038, l. 8.

140. *Ibid.*, d. 4036, st. 331, Osobyi zhurnal ot 5 i 13 iiunia 1879 g., ll. 138-139. Rumors among the peasants concerned not only the land. In a circular to the governors on 26 June Makov wrote: "In the second half of May rumors began to circulate among the peasants of Putivlsky district to the effect that there was a government regulation prohibiting peasants from renting land as sharecroppers, or from hiring themselves out as workers for less than a certain wage: men for less than one ruble and women for less than 50 kopecks. Supposedly there were secret gendarmes writing down the names of everyone who did not follow this regulation." GAKhO, fond vrem. kharkovsk. gen-gubernatora, op. 2, d. 2, l. 145.

141. TsGIA, fond Kantseliarii ministra vnutrennikh del, op. 2, d. 1081, l. 4.

142. Apparently the "Declaration" had some effect on the peasants, and rumors about the partition of land were reduced significantly in number. After the "Declaration" was published, rumors were reported to be circulating in only four provinces: in September 1879 in Novgorod, in October in Smolensk, in February 1880 in Voronezh, and in March in Kazan. TsGIA, *Ibid*. The Kursk governor also reported in late 1879 that "after the publication of the Declaration we observed a greater tendency among the peasants to acquire land as property than before; even in the summer of this year the peasants were afraid to acquire property." *Ibid.*, l. 343. Similar reports came from Smolensk province.

143. The minister had in mind the order of the military commander in the Kiev military district on 4 August 1879, No. 193.

144. GIAMO, fond Kantseliarii moskovskogo general-gubernatora, op. 69, d. 29, ch. 1, l. 310. Letter of 29 July 1879, No. 3637.

145. Published as an appendix to the order to the military in the Moscow military district on 9 August 1879, No. 220. In general, the government used every device to maintain loyalty among the troops. Guided by this intention, the head military procurator sent a secret circular to the Moscow Governor-General asking the latter to avoid the use of troops to carry out death sentences. GIAMO, fond Kantseliarii moskovskogo general-gubernatora, 1879 g., op. 69, d. 29, ch. II, d. 17.

146. TsGIA, fond Zemskogo otdela, 1867 g., op. 53, d. 25, ch. II, l. 22.

147. TsGIA, fond Komiteta ministrov, d. 4041, st. 384, Osobyi zhurnal Komiteta, l. 134.

148. *Ibid.*, ll. 137-138.

149. *Ibid.*, l. 149.

150. In the papers of the First Section of His Majesty's Chancellery (TsGIA, fond 1409) there is a special *delo* containing material gathered by the ministries on this question (op. 3, d. 9333). The material was compiled by the Ministers of Justice, Education, and Communications. On 2 January 1880 the Committee of Ministers heard a report on the course of implementation of the Special Conference's decisions.

151. TsGIA (Ukraine), fond Kantseliarii kievskogo general-gubernatora, op. 828, d. 221, l. 128.

152. *Ibid.* l. 109. This ukase is not cited in the Complete Collection of Laws (PSZ).

153. TsGIA, fond Komiteta ministrov, d. 4046, st. 505, l. 143. The Senate "in examination of reports on the confirmation of justices of the peace has done a careful evaluation and check of the answers sent to it by local provincial officials."

154. One this matter there was complete confusion at the local level.

155. TsGAOR, fond III otdeleniia, 3 ekspeditsiia 1878 g., op. 163, d. 504, ll. 71-73.

156. TsGIA, fond Komiteta ministrov, d. 4057, st. 691, ll. 526-532.

157. ROBL, fond Katkova 12/21, letter of 22 December 1879.

158. TsGIA (Ukraine), fond Kantseliarii kievskogo general-gubernatora, op. 828, d. 221, l. 155.

159. TsGIA, fond Valueva, d. 395, l. 36.

160. *Ibid.*, ll. 36-37.

161. *Ibid.*, l. 37.

162. *Ibid.*, l. 37. Later other measures were adopted to insure that teachers were politically reliable. On 10 November 1879 the Minister of Education wrote: "In order to guard high schools and elementary schools from instructors who are politically and morally unreliable. . .provincial governors must testify to the political and moral soundness of these candidates for teaching positions before the candidates may begin to teach in high schools and elementary schools or in private homes." GIAMO, fond Kantseliarii moskovskogo general-gubernatora, op. 69, d. 29, ch. II, l. 1.

163. *Ibid.*

164. TsGIA, fond Valueva, d. 395, l. 39.

165. *Ibid.*, ll. 40-41.

166. With the exception of St. Petersburg, for which analogous regulations were drafted earlier and approved by the Committee of Ministers on 2 August.

167. TsGIA, fond Departament narodnogo prosveshcheniia, op. 149, d. 423, l. 211.

168. *Ibid.*, l. 212.

169. *Ibid.*, l. 217.

170. Also with the exception of St. Petersburg.

171. *Ibid.*, ll. 224-225.

172. They were first checked with the Governors-General.

173. TsGIA, fond Departamenta narodnogo prosveshcheniia, op. 149, d. 423, l. 209.

174. TsGIA, fond Departamenta zakonov, 1884 g., d. 53, l. 78.

175. See TsGIA, fond Departamenta zakonov, 1877 g., d. 3. One consequence was a deterioration in the position of political prisoners. The circular of 11 June

1879 said that recently there had been cases where "officials conducting prison inspections had not been shown the proper respect by political prisoners." The circular required "strict observation of the prisoners behavior in this respect. Prison regulations must be followed regardless of the reasons for incarceration." GIAMO, fond Kantseliarii moskovskogo general-gubernatora, op. 69, d. 29, ch. 1, l. 267. Former Saratov governor Galkin-Vrassky, a well-known reactionary, was appointed head of the Main Prison Administration.

176. *Plan gosudarstvennogo preobrazovaniia grafa M.M. Speranskogo* (Moscow, 1905), p. 15.

177. Printed in the book N.K. Shilder, *Imperator Aleksandr I. Ego zhizn i tsarstvovanie*, IV, (St. Petersburg, 1908), pp. 499-526.

178. See *Vestnik prava*, 1905, kn. 9.

179. In this chapter I have examined only those projects proposed by government officials.

180. *Vestnik prava*, 1905, kn. 9, p. 228.

181. *Ibid.*, p. 229.

182. He wrote in his diary that on 12 April 1863: "I decided to present my thinking on the question of summoning zemstvo representatives to the State Council" to Alexander II. P.A. Valuev, *Dnevnik 1877-1884*, I, p. 217.

183. *Ibid.*, p. 219.

184. *Vestnik prava*, 1905, kn. 9, pp. 235-269.

185. This report was a subject of discussion in early 1880. I have considered it in greater detail, especially because it is not well known in the literature.

186. TsGAOR, fond Aleksandra III, d. 134, l. 3.

187. *Ibid.*, ll. 3-4.

188. *Ibid.*, l. 4.

189. The project says that assemblies could be called on the national level, as well as in separate regions or localities.

190. TsGAOR, fond Aleksandra III, d. 134, l. 5.

191. *Ibid.*, l. 1.

192. As Valuev noted in his diary in 1876, Minister of Internal Affairs Timashev, frightened by the growth of the revolutionary movement, said to Valuev in fear that "in view of the course of events it would not be unwise to have ready a project of a constitutional sort." P.A. Valuev, *Dnevnik 1877-1884 gg.*, II, p. 392.

193. A.A. Abaza was in this period the chairman of the Department of Laws of the State Council.

194. TsGAOR, fond kollektsii Zimnego dvortsa, d. 2587, kn. 6, l. 75. (In the published text of the diary, which was drafted from the second variant, Abaza's surname was replaced by the letter "A".) Three days later in the entry for 30 April, Valuev spoke about giving to Abaza copies of his 1863 memorandum and that of Grand Duke Konstantin Nikolaevich.

195. Miliutin returned from the Crimea to Petersburg along with the royal family on 28 May.

196. *Dnevnik D.A. Miliutina*, III, p. 148.

197. The article was published in the journal *Rech*, 1879, kn. 1-3.

198. *Dnevnik D.A. Miliutina*, III, pp. 139-140.

199. I have given a short analysis of this memorandum in the biographical essay "D.A. Miliutin" in *Ibid.*, I, pp. 57-60.

200. It seems to me that one must give a negative answer to this question, since no one in the upper bureaucracy discussed it in his diary or memoranda. I have in mind the diaries of Valuev, Peretts, and Polovtsov, and the notes by one of

Miliutin's closest friends, A.V. Golovnin, *Materialy dlia budushchikh istorikov* (TsGIA, fond Golovnina, d. 16).

201. ROBL, fond D.A. Miliutina, papka 44, d. 12, ll. 1-18.

202. Miliutin had in mind the existence of various committees, commissions, and special bureaux.

203. ROBL, fond D.A. Miliutina, papka 44, d. 12, l. 3.

204. *Ibid.*, ll. 7-8.

205. *Ibid.*, ll. 8-9.

206. *Ibid.*, l. 13.

207. *Ibid.*, l. 17.

208. *Dnevnik D.A. Miliutina*, III, p. 184. The second part of the quotation is based on the original.

209. *Ibid.*, p. 187.

210. *Ibid.*, pp. 181, 186.

211. TsGIA, fond Golovnina, d. 16, l. 3.

212. According to Golovnin, Artsimovich in mid-January 1880 told him about the proposal to add several bishops and gentry marshals to the State Council. TsGIA, fond Golovnina, d. 16, l. 3. However, this conversation was obviously the result of rumors circulating in the government, because other sources do not mention such a plan.

213. P.A. Valuev, *Dnevnik 1877-1884 gg.*, p. 47.

214. TsGAOR, fond Aleksandra III, d. 134, l. 1.

215. TsGIA, fond Golovnina, d. 16. Golovnin noted that Grand Duke Konstantin told him about this, but Golovnin dated it not the 13th, but the 11th. (l. 1). Valuev also wrote about this in his diary. In the entry for 15 January Valuev said that Makov came to him on that day (the 15th) and talked with him about Grand Duke Konstantin Nikolaevich. "The tsar has in mind something like the 19th of February. . . ." P.A. Valuev, *Dnevnik 1877-1884 gg.*, p. 48. On 18 January Valuev returned to this issue, discussing a conversation with Grand Duke Konstantin Nikolaevich himself. According to Valuev, he deferred from expressing his opinions on the subject, saying that he would wait for an indication from Alexander II. "I only stated that for me the following three conditions were essential: that the substance of the issues not be trivial; that the advisory role in the preparation of legislation be given to persons specially elected for that purpose from the provinces; and that purpose from the provinces; and that there be no limitations or exceptions based on national origin. I argued not for a body of courtiers, but for one representing the whole Russian empire." (*Ibid.*, p. 49).

216. *Ibid.*, pp. 50-51.

217. TsGAOR, fond Aleksandra III, d. 134, l. 8.

218. *Ibid.*, l. 9.

219. *Ibid.*.

220. *Ibid.*, l. 10.

221. In his diary Valuev wrote about this meeting, dealing only with his speech. Valuev's interpretation coincided completely with Peretts' summary. "I told the Grand Duke," wrote Valuev, "that in view of the absence of the necessary unanimity I consider my proposals to be unfeasible at the present time and therefore I reject any further debate or even discussion." P.A. Valuev, *Dnevnik 1877-1884 gg.*, p. 51.

222. TsGAOR, fond Aleksandra III, d. 134, l. 15.

223. *Ibid.*, ll. 14-15.

224. *Ibid.*, ll. 15-16.

225. *Ibid.,* l. 16. In Valuev's papers (TsGIA, fond 198) there are two memoranda, written in unfamiliar script, unsigned, and dated by Valuev 21 January 1880; these documents deal with the advantages of allowing zemstvo and municipal representatives to participate in one way or another in the State Council. At the end of the first memorandum, there is the following statement: "...One must conclude that the projected step is ahead of its time, that it is not in accord with the current situation in the state and with the state's immediate responsibilities toward the public, and that it is in direct contradiction to the prerogatives and status of the sovereign. Finally, it will impede the fight of the government against the underground rebellion, and it threatens to create grounds for agitation among various classes of society of an even more serious nature—agitation that would be even less desirable to the government and to the better part of society." (l. 77). The second memorandum, which is quite short, notes that even if it became necessary to involve local representatives in the government, then it would be better to do this through special committees that can examine specific concrete questions. (l. 78).

226. Peretts noted that probably the tsarevich had in mind Greig and Prince Liven. TsGAOR, fond Aleksandra III, d. 134, l. 17.

227. *Ibid.,* ll. 17-18.

228. TsGAOR, fond Aleksandra III, d. 307, pp. 312-313.

229. Valuev himself wrote in his diary about this session: "The meeting at the Grand Duke General-Admiral's came to a simple negative conclusion, though not without effort. He tried very hard to push through his idea, and nearly extorted agreement from the tsarevich, who attended this time.... But I stood my ground and did not permit him to pull off his *'tour de prestidigitation.'* In general I can't stand him." P.A. Valuev, *Dnevnik 1877-1884 gg.,* p. 53.

230. TsGAOR, fond Aleksandra III, d. 134, l. 18.

231. P.A. Valuev, *Dnevnik 1877-1884 gg.,* pp. 54-55.

232. Entry for 29 January. TsGAOR, fond Aleksandra II, d. 334, p. 12.

CHAPTER II

1. TsGAOR, fond velikogo kniazia Konstantina Konstantinovicha, d. 16, l. 101.

2. *Ibid.,* l. 108.

3. ROBL, fond Kireevykh, d. 8, l. 112. Kireev's reaction to the bomb explosion in the Winter Palace was curious: "One does not wish to say, but must say nonetheless, that the bestial attempt to kill the tsar on 5 February has hindered the various contemptible constitutional campaigns and this is a good result." *Ibid.,* l. 110.

4. IRLI, fond M.I. Semevskogo, d. 16, ll. 166-167.

5. GIAMO, fond Kantseliarii moskovskogo general-gubernatora, op. 70, d. 3, l. 31.

6. TsGAOR, fond Aleksandra III, d. 307, p. 321.

7. P.A. Valuev, *Dnevnik 1877-1884 gg.,* p. 59. The statement that Trepov was the "originator" of the plan to create the Supreme Administrative Commission can be explained by conversations he had in Petersburg hotels about the need to establish a government agency with emergency powers. Thus in his diary in early February M.I. Semevsky wrote: "In government circles the realization has begun to dawn that reprisals alone [apparently, he means "repression"—PAZ] cannot reestablish public order, that public needs must be understood, and that one must

explain the dissatisfaction that is so rife in society." IRLI, fond M.I. Semevskogo, d. 16, l. 165. Semevsky later noted that during a visit on 3 February with member of the State Council Voitsekhovich, he had run into Trepov, who said that "in order to fight against our adversaries, we must establish two commissions with supreme and extensive powers: one must be permitted to free from prison everyone who wound up there for no good reason, and punish the truly guilty as soon as possible; the other commission would investigate all the reasons for popular dissatisfaction with the regime." These sentiments, which certainly were not the fruit of Trepov's ruminations, characterized the attitude that dominated government circles even before 5 February. They are testimony to the further development of the crisis of the autocracy.

8. *Moskovskie vedomosti,* 7 February 1880. It should be noted that this idea was bandied about by Katkov as early as April 1879 in connection with creation of the Governors-General. See chapter 1.

9. TsGAOR, fond Aleksandra II, d. 334, p. 16. According to A.F. Koni, Loris-Melikov was nominated for the head of the Supreme Administrative Commission by Miliutin. A.F. Koni, *Na zhiznennom puti,* III (Revel-Berlin) p. 5.

10. TsGIA, fond Valueva, d. 305, l. 29.

11. *Ibid.,* ll. 29-30. The discussion was about rumors that nobles had participated in the preparation for the assassination. The head of the provincial gendarmes had sent a special circular about this matter on 28 February 1880. "Concerning the recent criminal events, rumors have begun to circulate, particularly among the peasants, that the criminal assassination attempt was the result of a plot hatched by nobles who were unhappy about the peasant reforms of 19 February 1861." TsGIA, fond Departamenta obshchikh del, Min. vn. del, 1880 g., op. 238, d. 61, l. 24.

12. P.A. Valuev, *Dnevnik 1877-1884 gg.,* p. 60.

13. According to one of Valuev's diary notes: "*I* am responsible not only for the forms in which the so-called 'Supreme Administrative Commission' will be established, not only for its basic outlines, not only for its title, but for the original idea to establish it." He continued: "The idea of the late tsar [Alexander II], if it was not prompted by the present tsar, then it was at least raised by him, was to establish a supreme executive and investigative commission for state security. Proof of this is the fact that both Makov and I supposed after the first discussions that Trepov would be appointed head of this commission. Only after 9 February when the late tsar appointed Loris-Melikov did I realize that authority over royal and state security would be concentrated in the hands of one person. On that day during an additional meeting of the Committee of Ministers I noted the main lines of the proposed institution, and then wrote the late tsar about the results of this meeting. On the 10th I got an affirmative response, and on the morning of the 11th I gave the tsar the main points on the establishment of the commission in a paper written in my own hand." P.A. Valuev, *Dnevnik 1877-1884 gg.,* p. 61. As we have seen, Valuev's account was not entirely correct; the original idea about the need to establish the Supreme Administrative Commission was formulated rather precisely by Katkov.

14. TsGIA, fond Valueva, d. 395, l. 46.

15. *Ibid..*

16. PSZ, 2 sobr., LV, No. 60492.

17. *Ibid..*

18. TsGAOR, fond Verkhovnoi rasporiaditelnoi komissii, d. 229, l. 10.

19. *Dnevnik D.A. Miliutina,* III, p. 217.

20. P.A. Valuev, *Dnevnik 1877-1884 gg.*, p. 67.

21. *Pravitelstvennyi vestnik,* 15 February 1880.

22. This was supported by the diary entries of Alexander Alexandrovich, which treated the private conversations of Alexander with Loris-Melikov and evaluated Loris-Melikov's activity. TsGAOR, fond Aleksandra III, d. 307, and 308, diary for 1880. On 3 March he wrote about Loris-Melikov: "He has set about the task efficiently and energetically. May God grant him success." (d. 308, p. 2). Loris-Melikov wrote Alexander Alexandrovich often, and asked advice on important issues. On 9 April Loris-Melikov gave to the tsarevich a copy of the official memorandum of 11 April. In an explanatory letter he wrote: "From the first day of my appointment as head of the Supreme Administrative Commission I decided to act only in concert with Your Excellency, since your support is necessary for my undertakings and for the restoration of order." *Krasnyi arkhiv,* 1925, kn. 1, p. 113. Loris-Melikov's correspondence with the Crown Prince and later with Emperor Alexander III may be found in TsGAOR, fond Aleksandra III.

23. ROBL, fond Pobedonostseva, karton 449, d. 2, ll. 13-14. In this letter Pobedonostsev, describing Loris-Melikov as an intelligent and clever man, stated: "From the first he showed intelligence by selecting for an assistant the only person who was suitable for the job—Kakhanov, who is also intelligent and well acquainted with all the leading figures in the government and with all the comings and goings from the nest which the present gang of rulers has built for itself." *(Ibid.,* l. 14).

24. Loris-Melikov had the quality of charisma. Even M.E. Saltykov-Shchedrin, who maintained a skeptical attitude toward the actions of the dictator, was charmed when he met Loris-Melikov years later in Wiesbaden. After this visit Saltykov-Shchedrin wrote to Loris-Melikov: "I shall tell you quite frankly that I have always avoided associations with powerful people, and only you have made me want to overcome my restraint." *Polnoe sobranie sochinenii,* XIX, kn. 2 (Moscow, 1939), p. 222.

25. See the first chapter.

26. ROBL, fond Belogolovogo, karton 6, d. 49. This letter was sent by Loris-Melikov to Alexander II.

27. ROBL, fond Kireevykh, d. 8, ll. 111-112.

28. TsGAOR, fond vel. kn. Konstantina Konstantinovicha, d. 16, l. 104.

29. *Moskovskie vedomosti,* 17 February 1880.

30. *Golos,* 15 February 1880, editorial.

31. *Golos,* 16 February 1880, editorial.

32. *Vestnik Evropy,* March 1880. "Vnutrennee obozrenie," p. 396.

33. *Otechestvennye zpiski,* March 1880. "Vnutrennee obozrenie," p. 127.

34. *Obshchee delo,* No. 35 (1880).

35. M.P. Dragomanov, *Solovia basniami ne kormiat.* Brochure.

36. *Literatura partii "Narodnaia volia",* p. 70. *Listok Narodnoi voli,* No. 1.

37. *Ibid.,* P. 77. *Listok Narodnoi voli,* No. 2.

38. *Ibid.,* p. 72.

39. Having learned of the death sentence for Mlodetsky, Vsevolod Garshin wrote a letter to Loris-Melikov asking him to spare Mlodetsky's life. "Your Excellency, pardon this criminal. It is in your power not to take his human life, and. . . at the same time to *destroy* the idea which has caused so much sadness, spilled so much blood and so many tears. . . ." *Katorga i ssylka,* 1925, kn. 2, p. 133. The original letter is in TsGAOR, fond Kantseliarii ministra vnutrennikh del, op. 1, d. 645, l. 166. On this question see Yu. G. Oksman, "Vsevolod Garshin v dni 'diktatury serdtsa,'" *Katorga i ssylka,* 1925, kn. 2. See also the publication by A. Shilov and G. Lappo: "Pismo Garshina k Loris-Melikovu ot 25 fevralia 1881

g.," *Krasnyi arkhiv*, 1934, No. 3 (64), and the article by M.I. Kheifets, "V.M. Garshin i Loris-Melikov," in *Voprosy selskogo khoziaistva, krestianstva i revoliutsionnogo dvizheniia v Rossii*, (Moscow, 1961).

40. TsGAOR, fond Aleksandra III, d. 334.

41. *Literatura Narodnoi voli*, B. Basilevsky, ed. (Paris, 1905) p. 894. In the brochure *Konstitutsiia grafa Loris-Melikova*, published in London, and probably written by M.M. Kovalevsky, it is asserted that Loris-Melikov tried to save Mlodetsky's life but failed. "All the appeals were futile: Alexander II, who had just given supreme power to someone else, decided to set an example of sternness, and insisted on the hanging of Mlodetsky." (See p. 14) However, this assertion is probably not true.

42. TsGAOR, fond Loris-Melikova, d. 33, l. 1.

43. *Ibid.*, l. 2.

44. PSZ, 2 sobr., LV, No. 60609. On 4 March the gendarmes were placed under his control. According to the memoirs of the German ambassador Schweinitz, on 27 February/11 March Loris-Melikov came to visit him and said the following: "I can say that today I have achieved something important for Russia. The emperor has agreed to my proposal that the police be unified under my control; the police formerly had acted not in concert, but in contradiction with one another." *Denkwurdigkeiten des Botschafters General von Schweinitz*, Zweite Band, (Berlin), p. 106. "I must confess to you," Loris-Melikov said to Schweinitz, "that I was not as nervous before the siege of Kars as I was before this audience."

45. *Dnevik D.A. Miliutina*, III, p. 250.

46. Besides these members Loris-Melikov's report showed that N.S. Abaza, the head of the Main Press Administration, was added to the staff of the Supreme Administrative Commission on 2 May. TsGIA, fond Glavnogo upravleniia po delam pechati, op. 20, d. 247, l. 5.

47. TsGAOR, fond Verkhovnoi rasporiaditelnoi komissii, d. 343, ll. 111-112.

48. TsGAOR, fond Verkhovnoi rasporiaditelnoi komissii, d. 367.

49. The involvement of General Fadeev and former Captain Baranov, proteges of the Crown Prince, indicated that Loris-Melikov was trying to stay on good terms with the Anichkov Palace. On Baranov, see below, chapter four.

50. TsGAOR, fond Verkhovnoi rasporiaditelnoi komissii, d. 343.

51. TsGIA, fond Departamenta obshchikh del, op. 242, d. 81, l. 425.

52. The law of 19 May 1871 transferred authority for political surveillance to the gendarmes, who were supposed to work through the procurators.

53. *Russkii arkhiv*, 1915, kn. 12, p. 221.

54. *Ibid.*, pp. 221-222.

55. *Ibid.*, p. 229.

56. *Ibid.*, pp. 235-238.

57. TsGAOR, fond Loris-Melikova, d. 36, ll. 68-69. Journal of the session on 1 May 1880. Original copy.

58. *Ibid.*, l. 69. The original copies of the journals for sessions of the Supreme Administrative Commission are kept in TsGAOR, fond Loris-Melikova, d. 36.

59. TsGIA, fond Kantseliarii ministra vnutrennikh del, op. 1, d. 643, l. 17. Besides this one three positions were vacant. Moreover, this figure did not include the Chief of Gendarmes and the head of the Third Section. In this *delo* (ll. 22-24) there is a list of employees of the Third Section. Among them was N.V. Kletochnikov, who was an agent of the Executive Committee of The People's Will. Kletochnikov was listed as "a senior official with the right to [open] letters" and he got a salary of 900 rubles a year.

60. Data on the internal *agentura* has not survived. Certain information on the *agentura* abroad may be found in the budget of the Third Section for 1878. TsGIA, fond III otdeleniia, sekretnyi arkhiv, op. 3, d. 570, and also in "Vedomosti o polozhenii sekretnykh summ III otd. na 1 iiulia 1880 g.," TsGIA, fond Loris-Melikova, d. 100.

61. Most requests for money came from retired officials, officers, and their wives and children.

62. The jurisdiction of the second *ekspeditsiia* may be defined by analyzing its papers from 1879-1880. Ninety percent of the petitions it answered dealt with questions of money or the right to certain kinds of apartments.

63. TsGAOR, fond III otdeleniia, sekretnyi arkhiv, op. 3, d. 570, l. 4.

64. TsGIA, fond Loris-Melikova, d. 100, ll. 1-2.

65. According to the budget for 1878, 21,000 rubles was paid to P.A. Valuev for newspapers. TsGAOR, fond III otdeleniia, sekretnyi arkhiv, op. 3, d. 570, l. 8. The newspapers receiving money from the Third Section included: *Otgoloski*, published from early 1879. According to data in the secret archive (op. 1, d. 2225), the editor of the journal *Selskaia beseda*, V.V. Kardo-Sysoev was given 5 thousand rubles in 1880. (l. 6). In 1880, probably in connection with the 25-year jubilee of Alexander II's coronation, Kardo-Sysoev published the brochure *Tsar osvobodil, a muzhik ne zabyl* (The tsar liberated, but the peasant did not forget), which was distributed throughout Russia by the Third Section. (l. 3).The manner in which the brochure was distributed is curious. 25,000 copies were sent to Moskow; 20,000 to Petersburg; 20,000 each to Odessa and Kherson; 10,000 each to Vladimir and Nizhny Novgorod; 6,000 to Kiev; 5,000 each to Kharkov and Kursk; 3,000 to Kostroma; and 2,000 to Poltava (l. 7). Thus, most of the brochures went to industrial provinces. The Third Section also distributed the following brochures: *Zhizn za tsaria ili plen u turok; Na chuzhoi karavai rot ne razevai; Golenkii okh, a za golenkim bog; Vsiak Eremei pro sebia razumei.* These brochures were also published in 100,000 copies, and distributed nation-wide. In the above *delo*, there is a note by a famous spy, I. Batalin, who was involved with literary circles, about 1,500 rubles for the journal *Narodnyi list*. (l. 7).

66. PSZ, 2 sobor., XLII, No. 44956.

67. District gendarmeries were set up in the Kingdom of Poland.

68. In Moscow the provincial gendarmerie was somewhat larger: the head, his assistnat, an adjutant, a secretary, and three clerks.

69. PSZ, 2 sobor., XLII, appendix to No. 44956.

70. TsGAOR, fond shtaba otdelnogo korpusa zhandarmov, I otdelenie, op. 1, d. 5559, l. 710.

71. The staffs of provincial gendarmeries differed in numerical size. For example, in Tambov there were 3 officers and 14 junior officers, including clerical help; in Vladimir there were 5 officers, and 35 junior officers; in Penza, 3 officers and 21 junior officers; in Nizhny Novgorod, 4 officers and 29 junior officers; in Perm, 7 and 40 respectively; in Kharkov 6 and 72. Four of these officers were stationed in the city of Kharkov itself: a captain, two assistants, and an adjutant. There was one assistant each in the district towns of Sumy and Izium. The junior officers were also distributed throughout the province: 35 in Kharkov, 6 in Sumy, 4 in Izium, and 4 each in Zmievsky, Starobelsky, and Kupiansky districts, and two each in Akhtyrsky, Bogodukhovsky, Volchansky, Lebedinsky, and Kharkovsky districts. TsGAOR, fond Otdelnogo korpusa zhandarmov, I otdelenie, op. 1, dd. 5522, and 5523.

72. TsGIA, fond Loris-Melikova, d. 100, "Vedomosti o polozhenii sekretnykh summ III otdeleniia s.e.i.v. kantseliarii na 1 iiulia 1880 goda," Prilozheniia Nos. 1 and 4, ll. 3, 6.

73. The staff of the St. Petersburg police consisted of 3 superintendents, 38 police inspectors, 38 senior assistants, 15 junior assistants, 231 district police, and 1500 municipal police. In addition, there was a police reserve consisting of 15 officers and officials and 150 municipal police. TsGAOR, fond Verkhovnoi rasporiaditelnoi komissii, d. 326, l. 96. In 1880 at the insistence of Loris-Melikov, the number of district police was increased "in order to make it possible for the police to keep a really close watch on the populace in the capital." TsGAOR, fond Loris-Melikova, d. 64, l. 4. The number of district police was increased by 200.

74. TsGIA, fond Kantseliarii ministra vnutrennikh del, op. 1, d. 640, ll. 84-85.

75. TsGIA, fond Departamenta obshchikh del, op. 238, d. 61. A circular from the Minister of Internal Affairs on 18 March 1880.

76. TsGIA, fond Kantseliarii ministra vnutrennikh del, op. 1, d. 647, ll. 125-126. Judging by governors' reports, more or less normal relations between gendarmes existed in Kaluga, Saratov, and other provinces. See d. 647.

77. *Ibid.*, l. 134.

78. According to Baranov's statement, the secret *agentura* functioned normally in Rumania; he proposed to set up an *agentura* in Geneva with the help of a person sent from Russia for that purpose. TsGAOR, fond III otdeleniia, sekretnyi arkhiv, op. 3, d. 711, l. 125. As far as Yuzefovich was concerned, there is no information about his role in the mission.

79. *Ibid.*, l. 10. In a report discussing the steps that should be taken to deal with the Russian emigration, Baranov wrote: "I do not know if I will have another chance to suggest steps that should be taken to deal with seditious Russians abroad; here I shall mention several matters which deserve attention. All the most violent radicals, such as Gambetta, Andrier, and even Clemenceau, having attaining wealth and position, become opportunists and ready to exert themselves to crush revolution and preserve and improve their positions." (ll. 13-14). Here Baranov made interesting observations about the publication of the journal *Le Norde*, the official organ of the Ministry of Internal Affairs in France. "Journals like *Le Norde* are completely useless. One does not need a great deal of money or tact to influence a large number of journals, but without making of them official in-house papers." (l. 14).

80. *Ibid.*, l. 12.

81. *Ibid.*, ll. 126-127. Since the foreign press had reported the *complete abolition* of the Third Section (l. 127), Baranov proposed to abolish the *agentura* in the prefecture, and to replace it with a secret *agentura* headed by a certain Savchenko, who had graduated from Petersburg University and who was then living in Geneva. According to a letter from Savchenko, evidently sent to Baranov, Savchenko wanted to become an agent "for ideological reasons .... I shall be not only a spy, but if I must, an executioner." (l. 50).

82. TsGAOR, fond Loris-Melikova, d. 60, l. 3.

83. *Ibid.*, d. 44, l. 2.

84. *Ibid.*, l. 3.

85. *Ibid.*, ll. 5-6.

86. *Krasnyi arkhiv*, 1925, kn. 1 (8), p. 106.

87. On 1 March there were 120 cases in the Third Section; 409 in the gendarmerie and railroad gendarmerie; 668 cases fell under the Ministry of Justice

(excluding the Pribaltic region, the Caucasus, and Siberia). According to the Minister of Justice, these rigures "were only rough estimates," TsGAOR, fond Verkhovnoi rasporiaditelnoi komissii, d. 340, l. 9.

88. Of the 668 cases under the Ministry of Justice, 541 involved this sort of offense. *Ibid.*, l. 9.

89. These cases were classified as "state offenses" according to a tradition that began in the sixteenth century. Senator Markov, a member of the Supreme Administrative Commission, cited interesting comparative data on the people indicted for political crimes as opposed to those indicted under articles 246 and 248 of the Penal Code. Only 5 percent of political offenders were illiterate, while 48 percent of the offenders against article 246 and 248 were illiterate. Of political offenders 88 percent had a secondary and higher education, while only 9 percent in the second category did. TsGAOR, fond Loris-Melikova, d. 71, l. 8. These data suggest that persons prosecuted for verbal criticisms of the royal family were not always revolutionaries.

90. TsGAOR, fond Loris-Melikova, d. 64, l. 4.

91. *Ibid.*, d. 340, l. 1.

92. *Ibid.*, d. 64, l. 4.

93. TsGAOR, fond Verkhovnoi rasporiaditelnoi komissii, d. 340, ll. 8, 11.

94. It should be noted that there was a certain growth in the number of offenses against articles 246 and 248. By 20 July the number of cases was 837. (l. 6).

95. TsGAOR, fond Loris-Melikova, d. 60, l. 2.

96. Circular of the Minister of Internal Affairs on 6 June 1870. Quoted from a memorandum by Senator Kovalevsky to the head of the Supreme Administrative Commission, 22 July 1880. TsGAOR, fond Loris-Melikova, d. 60, l. 2.

97. The pretext for this was the strike of carriage drivers in Odessa. Soon, in a circular dated 15 December 1871, the Minister of Internal Affairs explained that the word "strike" "means not only a disorder caused by cessation of work by factory workers who wish to force their bosses to increase wages in contravention to a written or verbal agreement, but any agreement among workers against employers that halts factory work, or raises prices on products of fundamental importance." TsGAOR, fond Loris-Melikova, d. 60, l. 3. The Minister obliged the governors to "exile strikers as a last resort, only when all preliminary measures to avert the strike have failed."

98. *Ibid.*, l. 3.

99. *Ibid.*

100. *Ibid.*, ll. 6, 8, 27, and 30. The memorandum of Senator Kovalevsky on 22 July 1880. Actually, the number of political exiles was must larger. See below, chapter three.

101. *Russkii arkhiv*, 1915, kn. 12. Journal of the session on 24 March 1880. The number of persons under surveillance, including criminals, was 31,152.

102. *Ibid.* Discussing this data, the Minister of Internal Affairs Makov in a secret circular to the governors on 8 April 1880 even stated that "probably if they were checked, they would be too low." TsGIA, fond Departamenta obshchikh del, op. 238, d. 61, l. 37.

103. See the report from the Chernigov governor to Loris-Melikov. TsGIA, fond Kantseliarii ministra vnutrennikh del, op. 1, d. 647, l. 126. Apparently, neither the Ministry of Internal Affairs nor the Third Section kept exact data on the number of persons under surveillance. In the Kovalevsky memo, there is a statement that in 1875 the number of politically unreliable persons in 27 provinces of European Russia, not counting the people convicted for participation in the Polish uprising,

was only 260. TsGAOR, fond Loris-Melikova, d. 60, l. 4. This figure is an obvious understatement, since in 1874 there were many persons indicted for political propaganda, and many of these were under surveillance. The weakness in record-keeping was further proof of the weakness of the state apparatus and its inability to fight against the revolutionary movement, especially during a growing political crisis.

104. TsGIA, fond Kantseliarii ministra vnutrennikh del, op. 1, d. 640, ll. 222-223.

105. TsGAOR, fond Loris-Melikova, d. 60, ll. 14-15.

106. TsGAOR, fond III otdeleniia, 3 ekspeditsiia, 1880 g., op. 165, d. 327, ch. 1, l. 19.

107. TsGIA, fond Kantseliarii ministra vnutrennikh del, op. 1, d. 640, ll. 134-139. The exiles of Annensky and Pavlenkov were carried out without formal justi-fication. Baranov informed Loris-Melikov about this: "It is quite possible that Annensky and Pavlenkov took part directly or indirectly in the movement against the government, but the police do not have evidence of this participation and both persons deny it." TsGAOR, fond III otdeleniia, 3 ekspeditsiia, 1880 g., op. 165, d. 327, ch. 1, l. 31. Baranov then petitioned to decrease their punishment and to exile them to "a place not so distant" as Siberia. However, this petition was not entirely successful: instead of being sent to Eastern Siberia, they were exiled to Western Siberia.

108. TsGIA, fond Kantseliarii ministra vnutrennikh del, op. 1, d. 640, l. 225.

109. According to the head of the Kiev provincial gendarmerie, Novitsky, the death sentences of Rozovsky and Lozinsky were confirmed by acting Kiev Governor-General Vannovsky, but Loris-Melikov summoned him, Novitsky, to Petersburg to explain the reasons for such a strict punishment. Novitsky admitted that neither man had offered armed resistance. (V.D. Novitsky, *Iz vospominanii zhandarma* (Moscow, 1929), p. 178.

110. TsGAOR, fond Loris-Melikova, d. 286, l. 1. Copy of a telegram.

111. *Ibid.*, l. 3. Later he considered this execution a mistake. He wrote this note on the telegram blank: "The government sometimes is forced to resort to capital punishment, but in the present case, it has made a mistake, in my opinion. The crimes of Kviatkovsky and Presniakov were committed long before the execution and therefore the punishment did not satisfy the masses, but only angered the terrorists and made them more cruel. Zheliabov's statements revealed this clearly."

112. *Russkii arkhiv*, 1915, kn. 12, p. 226.

113. *Ibid.*, l. 226.

114. TsGAOR, fond Verkhovnoi rasporiaditelnoi komissii, d. 343, l. 55. The money for the other 30 students was sent after the abolition of the commission on 13 September. (*Ibid.*, l. 159).

115. If these measures were all intended to "appease" the students, Loris-Melikov might have found it enough to have ordered the Minister of Education to free part of the needy students from tuition payments.

116. TsGAOR, fond Loris-Melikova, d. 84, ll. 1-2.

117. *Ibid.*, l. 3.

118. Later Loris-Melikov, who had become Minister of Internal Affairs, peti-tioned the tsar to give Bogdanovich a salary of 4,000 rubles a year, "for the pur-pose of paying General Bogdanovich for carrying out certain special assignments." TsGIA, fond Departamenta obshchikh del, op. 241, d. 82, l. 105.

119. One of the authors of a plan to save Russia, a certain "school inspector" Rzhanov from Samara, in an excess of loyal sentiments, sent Loris-Melikov a poem that was quite lacking in artistic value.

Let us go to the temple and raise our voices on high
In constant prayer for our tsar and our country:
May Russia prosper, and may the happy dawn unite
All our brothers around the Little Father—Tsar.

TsGIA, fond Kantseliarii ministra vnutrennikh del, op. 1, d. 645, l. 88.

120. See P.A. Zaionchkovsky, *Voennye reformy 1860-1870 gg. v Rossii* (Moscow, 1952), p. 290.

121. TsGAOR, fond Loris-Melikova, d. 58, l. 8.

122. *Ibid.,* l. 9.

123. *Ibid.,* ll. 21 and 26.

124. *Ibid.,* l. 26.

125. *Ibid.*.

126. *Ibid.,* l. 26.

127. *Ibid.,* l. 27.

128. *Ibid.,* l. 28.

129. Bogdanovich took his last journey around Russia in late 1879 "to convince the bishops to set up cathedrals on the model of St. Isaac's in Petersburg" of which Bogdanovich was a church elder.

130. TsGIA, fond Kantseliarii ministra vnutrennikh del, op. 1, d. 646, ll. 5, 7, 17.

131. *Ibid.,* ll. 22-24.

132. *Ibid.,* ll. 32-33.

133. *Ibid.,* ll. 56-57.

134. If we except the various police projects, only one report did not contain some sort of suggestion for reform. This report came from Privy Counsellor Glinka, who wrote from Portugal. According to Glinka, the government would have to change the way "state offenses" were adjudicated, strengthen the police by involving the public, give more severe sentences to political criminals (long solitary confinement, repeated interrogations, deprivation of various comforts). See TsGIA, fond Kantseliarii ministra vnutrennikh del, op. 1, d. 642.

135. *Ibid.,* ll. 67-70.

136. TsGAOR, fond Loris-Melikova, d. 52, l. 37.

137. *Ibid.,* ll. 37-40.

138. Turning to this question, Golovnin wrote: "Among peasants there is the conviction that they have been deprived of land by landowners and officials, who have deceived the tsar, and therefore the peasants will win back this land either by convincing its holders to surrender it or by violence." TsGAOR, fond Loris-Melikova, d. 52, l. 42. Golovnin then argued the strange proposition that the revolutionaries were trying to kill the tsar partly because "during the present reign [of Alexander II] the peasants will not use force because they are grateful to the 'Tsar Liberator.'" It followed that after the accession of a new emperor the peasants would start an uprising.

139. TsGAOR, fond Loris-Melikova, d. 52, l. 43.

140. *Ibid.,* l. 43.

141. See S. Muromtsev, *Stati i rechi,* Vypusk V (Moscow, 1910) pp. 11-38.

142. *Ibid.,* pp. 13-14.

143. *Ibid.,* pp. 18-20.

144. *Ibid.,* p. 23.

145. *Ibid.*.

146. *Ibid.,* pp. 28-29.

147. *Ibid.,* p. 34.

148. *Ibid.,* p. 38.
149. *Byloe,* 1918, kn. 4-5, p. 154. The original is in TsGAOR, fond Aleksandra II, d. 674.
150. *Ibid.,* p. 155.
151. Loris-Melikov himself took part in police investigations. On 19 May 1880 Valuev wrote in his diary: "I have seen Count Loris-Melikov, who says that he has uncovered much through his investigations and he says that earlier inquiries were not very efficient." P.A. Valuev, *Dnevnik 1877-1884 gg.,* p. 96.
152. *Byloe,* 1918, kn. 4-5, p. 156.
153. *Ibid.,* p. 157.
154. *Ibid.,* p. 158
155. *Ibid.,* pp. 158-159.
156. *Ibid.,* p. 159.
157. *Ibid.,* p. 160.
158. *Ibid.,* pp. 160-161.
159. *Ibid.,* p. 161.
160. On the first page of the report Alexander II wrote the following: "Thank you for the candid expression of your thoughts, with which I almost entirely agree. I note with satisfaction that you have understood what a heavy responsibility I have placed on you. May God help you justify my trust." (*Ibid.,* p. 154). Alexander II also made many marginal comments in approval of the sentiments in the report. In particular, beside the paragraph calling for an extension of the powers of the Supreme Administrative Commission, Alexander II wrote: "Da" (Yes).
161. *Krasnyi arkhiv,* 1925, kn. 1 (10), p. 108.
162. *Katorga i ssylka,* 1925, kn. 2, p. 122.
163. ROBL, fond Belogolovogo, karton 6, d. 49. Alexander II wrote on this letter: "We will talk about this."
164. *Ibid.*.
165. On 18 March Valuev wrote in his diary: "Loris-Melikov's attempts to get rid of Count Tolstoy are unsuccessful—they are premature. Apparently, His Majesty is inclined to believe that Count Tolstoy is needed to drive the new university statute through the State Council. Probably Katkov is behind this idea. After the project goes through, [Tolstoy will get] a Vladimir ribbon and retirement." P.A. Valuev, *Dnevnik 1877-1884 gg.,* p. 76.
166. *Krasnyi arkhiv,* 1925, kn. 1 (8), p. 108. This issue was settled on 18 April. On that day Valuev wrote in his diary: "At one o'clock Count Loris-Melikov was here, and His Majesty, still wavering, asked if he did not think it possible to leave Count Tolstoy as minister. Count Loris-Melikov repeated his earlier position, and then the tsar made up his mind." P.A. Valuev, *Dnevnik 1877-1884 gg.,* p. 87. Probably, the tsarevich also spoke with Alexander II on 18 April. One of the direct pretexts for Tolstoy's dismissal was his quarrel with Minister of Internal Affairs Makov, whom he suspected of receiving bribes from the Old Believers. See *Ibid.,* pp. 83-87.
167. Throughout 1880 Loris-Melikov was on good terms with Pobedonostsev. In a letter to the tsarevich on 31 July Loris-Melikov wrote: "K.P. Pobedonostsev returned on the 3rd and told me about his visit to Gapsal. I envy him because I do not have the opportunity to go to Gapsal." *Krasnyi arkhiv,* 1925, kn. 1 (8), p. 114. In early October Loris-Melikov and Pobedonostsev escorted the tsarevich to Crimea. TsGAOR, fond Aleksandra III, d. 307, l. 51. Diary entry for 4 October 1880.

168. ROBL, fond Kireevykh, d. 8, l. 132.
169. *Katorga i ssylka*, 1925, kn. 2, p. 122. Tolstoy's dismissal was decided on Good Friday.
170. *Literatura partii "Narodnaia volia". Listok Narodnoi Voli*, No. 2, p. 3.
171. *Katorga i ssylka*, 1925, kn. 2, p. 120.
172. TsGAOR, fond Loris-Melikova, d. 54, ll. 1-3
173. *Ibid.*, l. 2.
174. *Ibid.*, ll. 5 and 10.
175. TsGIA, fond Komiteta ministrov, d. 4189, st. 474, l. 35.
176. TsGAOR, fond Loris-Melikova, d. 63, l. 2. Letter from Kakhanov to Loris-Melikov on 29 July 1880.
177. TsGAOR, fond Verkhovnoi rasporiaditelnoi komissii, d. 334, l. 1.
178. Describing the attitude of Makov toward the zemstvo, Polovtsov wrote in his diary in summer 1880: "Touring Russia, he played the liberal with the zemstvos, which he hated. . . ." TsGAOR, fond Polovtsova, d. 15, p. 237. Entry of 4 August.
179. P.A. Valuev, *Dnevnik 1877-1884 gg.*, p. 98.
180. *Dnevnik E.A. Perettsa (1880-1883 gg.)* (Moscow-Leningrad, 1927), p. 3.
181. *Ibid.*, p. 4. As Shamshin noted, the only area in which the Third Section functioned perfectly was its surveillance over high government officials. Peretts wrote: "His Majesty gets reports about all this, not excluding episodes from the personal lives of the ministers and other high officials." (p. 4). In addition, Chief of Gendarmes Cherevin studied the problem of the mythical "universal Jewish cabal". A secret circular from the Minister of Internal Affairs on 6 April 1880 said: "The acting head of the Third Section. . .has noted that all Jewish capitalists have entered the universal Jewish cabal, founded with goals that are inimical to the entire Christian population. The capitalists have given sizeable sums. The Jews have in their homes circles to make sacrifices for the sake of the cabal, and they even render material support to the revolutionary party." TsGIA, fond Departamenta obshchikh del Ministerstva vnutrennikh del, op. 238, d. 61, l. 26.
182. He saw the emperor very often. Judging by the memo books of Alexander II, Loris-Melikov saw the tsar almost every day before his trip to Tsarskoe Selo. During the summer Loris-Melikov saw the tsar two or three times a week. TsGAOR, fond Aleksandra II, d. 334.
183. According to Loris-Melikov, the number of state offenses being processed declined from 500 to 65 during the operation of the commission.
184. TsGAOR, fond Loris-Melikova, d. 64, l. 6.
185. Secret circular from the head of the Supreme Administrative Commission to the Governors-General on 26 March 1880. TsGIA, fond Kantseliarii ministra vnutrennikh del, op. 1, d. 640, ll. 78-80.
186. From March through July there was not a single terrorist act.
187. TsGAOR, fond Loris-Melikova, d. 64, l. 8.
188. *Ibid.*, ll. 9-10.
189. *Ibid.*, l. 14.
190. PSZ, 2 sobr., LV, No. 61279.
191. *Ibid.*. As the ukase said, this was to be "until our special order [is issued]." In his memorandum on the need to reform the police, dated 1 August 1880, Loris-Melikov insisted on the complete fusion from top to bottom of the gendarmeries with the Ministry of Internal Affairs. Thus, he proposed to abolish the heads of the provincial gendarmeries, and to replace them with the vice-governors, who control all the police in the province.TsGAOR, fond Loris-Melikova, d. 65, ll. 19-20.

192. According to Peretts, the Ministry of Posts and Telegraphs was created in order "not to alienate entirely Makov, whose patron was [Princess] Dolgorukaia. Without a portfolio he would have lost his lovely house on Bolshaia Morskaia Street and his ministerial salary of 26,000 rubles a year." *Dnevnik E.A. Perettsa,* p. 1. According to Peretts, Loris-Melikov was afraid to appoint Makov to this position "because the head of this agency has a dangerous political weapon at his disposal—the power to read mail. Letters are read, and if something in them is unusual then copies are sent to the tsar. Sometimes only excerpts are sent to the tsar, and worst of all, the letters can be quoted out of context." pp. 1-2. In fact, the perlustration of the mails was widespread. According to data for 1881, some 363,253 letters in the seven largest cities were read, and 3344 copies were made. TsGAOR, fond Ignatieva, d. 1494, l. 1. Even if one discounts Alexander II's love of reading other people's mail, the fears of Loris-Melikov were quite realistic. According to an officer in the gendarmes, V.D. Novitsky, "Emperor Alexander II was most interested in the perlustration of letters, which Minister of Internal Affairs Timashev brought to him every morning at 11 o'clock in a special briefcase with a secret lock." V.D. Novitsky, *Iz vospominanii zhandarma,* p. 71. Obviously, Makov brought the briefcase after Timashev.

193. *Dnevnik E.A. Perettsa,* p. 1.

194. TsGAOR, fond Polovtsova, d. 15, p. 207.

195. *Krasnyi arkhiv,* 1925, kn. 1 (8), p. 112.

196. P.A. Valuev, *Dnevnik 1877-1884 gg.,* p. 106.

197. TsGAOR, fond Polovtsova, d. 15, pp. 234-235. The tsarevich also failed to understand, thinking that this act was one of gratitude by Loris-Melikov. According to the assistant Minister of Internal Affairs Markov, as related by Polovtsov, the tsarevich said the following: "Not everyone in a position like that of Loris-Melikov would have renounced personal power and have become a mere equal of the other ministers." *Ibid.,* d. 17, l. 59. In a letter to Loris-Melikov on 3 August Grand Duke Alexander Alexandrovich wrote: "I read your report to His Majesty with great curiousity and satisfaction. K.P. Pobedonostsev had told me already the essence of your position, and I completely share your view that it is impossible to prolong the existence of the Supreme Administrative Commission in the form which it has had up to now." *Krasnyi arkhiv,* 1925, kn. 1 (8), p. 115.

198. ROBL, fond Kireevykh, d. 8, l. 151.

199. V.I. Lenin, *Sochineniia,* V, p. 36.

CHAPTER III

1. Formally speaking, the Minister of Foreign Affairs continued to be A.M. Gorchakov, who lived abroad almost uninterruptedly. The acting minister was N.K. Giers, whose actual influence was minimal.

2. *Dnevnik D.A. Miliutina,* III, pp. 277-278.

3. A.A. Abaza was relative of D.A. Miliutin. Abaza's sister, Maria Ageevna, was the wife of N.A. Miliutin.

4. On 19 October Loris-Melikov sent a ciphered telegram to Alexander II in Livadia; this telegram revealed Loris-Melikov's role in the appointment of the Minister of Finance. "Allow me to report that Abaza has agreed to accept the post of Minister of Finance and will depart today for Livadia.... As a result of my conference with Greig yesterday, it will not be necessary to summon him." TsGAOR, fond A.V. Adlerberg, d. 605, l. 13. Loris-Melikov tried to hasten the

confirmation of this appointment. In the same telegram, he asked the emperor to order Peretts or Taneev "to prepare the announcement now to save time." *Ibid.*.

5. IRLI, fond Feoktistova, L9122 II[b] 14, l. 33.

6. TsGAOR, fond Aleksandra III, d. 308, p. 79.

7. TsGAOR, fond Loris-Melikova, d. 285, ll. 1-2.

8. From the beginning of October the tsarevich ceased to mention Loris-Melikov in his diary. He wrote to Loris-Melikov much less often. From September 1880 until the beginning of March 1881 there is only one extant letter—a short note from Loris-Melikov to Grand Duke Alexander Alexandrovich dated 22 December. The change in Loris-Melikov's relations with Pobedonostsev also date to this time.

At the very beginning of 1881 Pobedonostsev was unfavorably disposed to Loris-Melikov, if we can judge by the former's letter to Tiutcheva on 2 January. Describing the Minister of Internal Affairs, Pobedonostsev wrote: "With great speed he created for himself two patrons: one in the Winter Palace and one in Anichkov. For His Majesty he became a necessity, a screen against danger. He eased the tsarevich's approachs to His Majesty and offered ready answers to all sorts of difficult situations, an Ariadne's thread out of every labyrinth. At the death of the empress he became even stronger because he untangled an even more confused knot in the stricken family, and as a result of circumstances he found himself a third supporter in a certain woman." ROBL, fond Pobedonostseva, d. 4410/1, l. 1.

9. According to the memoirs of B.N. Chicherin, Alexander II intended to crown his morganatic wife. For this purpose in February 1881 he sent a specialist in church problems named Terty Filippov to Moscow to search the archives for information about the coronation of Catherine I. Having found the archival information in Moscow, Filippov returned triumphantly to Petersburg. In route he found out about the assassination on 1 March. *Vospominaniia Borisa Nikolaevicha Chicherina. Zemstvo i Moskovskaia duma* (Moscow, 1934), p. 118.

Concerning the proposed coronation of Yurievskaia, Grand Duke Alexander Mikhailovich also commented in his memoirs. He had heard about the coronation just before 1 March from his parents. In addition, he related a scene from the palace that he had witnessed, when Alexander II, speaking to his son by his morganatic wife, said half-seriously: "Young man, wouldn't you like to be a Grand Duke?" Vel. Kn. Aleksandr Mikhailovich, *Kniga vospominanii*, ch. 1, Prilozhenie k "Illiustrirovannoi Rossii" za 1933 g. (Paris), p. 53. In my opinion, this set of memoirs as a whole is not trustworthy. However, the conversation cited above seemed plausible.

10. TsGAOR, fond Polovtsova, d. 15, p. 109.

11. V. Laferté, *op. cit.*, p. 52.

12. *Dnevnik D.A. Miliutina*, IV, p. 78. Not without interest in this regard was a statement of Court Minister Adlerberg on the marriage of Alexander II to Yurievskaia. Just over a month after the death of the empress, the tsar mentioned marriage to Yurievskaia. Adlerberg, who was on very close terms with the emperor, tried to dissuade him. Of course, this got back to Yurievskaia. "Within a few days after the period of mourning for the empress, His Majesty again surprised me," Adlerberg told Miliutin, "by announcing his decision to get married soon by secret rite. I again tried to dissuade him by discussing the unpleasant impression that would be produced unless he waited until a year after the empress' death. While I spoke, the tsar was silent, pale, confused. His hands trembled. Suddenly he stood up, and without saying another word, went into the adjoining room. Then the

door opened and in came a woman. Behind her I observed the tsar, who had let the princess into the study and then shut the door behind her . . . . There ensued an emotional scene involving me and the princess. In the middle of our argument, the door to the study opened half-way, and the tsar stuck his head into the room, and asked if it was time for him to enter yet. The princess answered heatedly: "No, let us finish our conversation." The tsar shut the door again, and after a certain time again walked into the study. The princess, who was infuriated with me, rushed out of the room." *Dnevnik D.A. Miliutina*, IV, pp. 78-79. Evidently, Adlerberg did not try very hard to keep this a secret even after the death of Alexander II, since Polovtsov also recounted a similar conversation with Adlerberg.

13. *Byloe*, 1917, kn. 4 (26), p. 36.

14. *Otechestvennye zapiski*, September 1880, pp. 140-141.

15. *Ibid.*, p. 141.

16. S. Muromtsev, *Stati i rechi*, V, pp. 48-49.

17. N. Saltykov (M.E. Shchedrin), *Polnoe sobranie sochinenii*, XIX, kn. 2 (Moscow, 1939), p. 170.

18. TsGAOR, fond Loris-Melikova, d. 87, 1. 2. The original is undated and unsigned. The text has been cited in part in S.S. Tatishchev, *Imperator Aleksandr II. Ego zhizn i tsarstvovanie*, II, pp. 543-548.

19. TsGAOR, fond Loris-Melikova, d. 87, ll. 3-4.

20. *Statistika pozemelnoi sobstvennosti i naselennykh mest Evropeiskoi Rossii*, I, (St. Petersburg, 1880).

21. Loris-Melikov's speech is quoted from Polovtsov's diary. TsGAOR, fond Polovtsova, d. 16, pp. 11-17.

22. TsGAOR, fond Polovtsova, d. 15, pp. 13-15.

23. *Ibid.*, pp. 15-17.

24. TsGAOR, fond Aleksandra III, d. 600, 1. 2. The instruction was a lithographed list without date or signature. It was published with several errors in *Russkii arkhiv*, 1912, kn. 11, pp. 417-429.

25. *Ibid.*, 1. 5.

26. *Ibid.*, ll. 7-8.

27. *Ibid.*, 1. 13, 13[a].

28. TsGIA, fond Departamenta obshchikh del, op. 241, d. 81, l. 414.

29. *Ibid.*, ll. 415, 418.

30. *Ibid.*, l. 417.

31. The staff of the Department of State Police was the following: the director; the vice-director; 3 officials on special assignment; 1 secretary; 1 journalist; 3 managers; 10 senior assistant managers; 9 junior assistant managers; a treasurer; an assistant treasurer; an archive director; 2 assistants for the archive director; 18 officials to read mail. *Sobranie uzakonenii Rossiiskoi imperii 1880 g.*, No. 112, st. 802.

32. In the past Baron Velio had had no direct connection with the gendarmes, if we do not count his tenure as provincial governor in Simbirsk and his year and a half with the Department of the Police in the 1860s.

33. The vice-director of the Department of Police had no relations with the gendarmes or even with the police, since before 1879 he had been a senior manager dealing with construction and appraisal of buildings on state lands in the Kiev branch of the Ministry of State Domains. Obviously, Loris-Melikov did not wish the Department of State Police to be headed by former gendarmes.

34. *Svod zakonov Rossiiskoi imperii*, I (St. Petersburg, 1892), p. 362.

35. TsGIA, fond Departamenta obshchikh del, op. 241, d. 81, ll. 428-429.

36. *Ibid.*, ll. 401, 404, 405.

37. Governors in provinces in the first category received a salary of 5432 rubles to 9900 rubles, not counting housing expenses. Those in the second category got from 4750 to 7504 rubles. TsGIA, fond Departamenta obshchikh del, op. 241, d. 81, ll. 409-413. Later in March 1881, at Loris-Melikov's insistence, the salaries of temporary Governors-General (Kharkov, Kiev, Odessa) were raised to 24,000 rubles a year. This salary was larger than that of members of the State Council.

38. TsGIA (Ukraine), fond Kantseliarii kievskogo general-gubernatora, op. 830, d. 121, 1880 g., l. 14, Circular No. 8363, dated 8 November 1880. This directive was cancelled by the Minister of Internal Affairs, Count Ignatiev, in the circular of 9 June 1881.

39. This directive aroused dissatisfaction among the gendarmes. Proof of this dissatisfaction may be found in a circular letter from Baron Velio to the gendarmeries in Odessa, Kherson, and Ekaterinoslav on 8 November 1880. Speaking about the fusion with the Department of Police, Velio said: ". . . Attempt not only to continue your efforts in such an important matter as the maintenance of order and social tranquility, but with even greater energy and exactitude fulfill your proper obligations, remembering that the new system in no way reduces your importance in the investigation of state crimes." TsGAOR, fond III otdeleniia, 3 ekspeditsiia, 1880 g., d. 737, l. 15[a].

40. TsGIA, fond Komiteta ministrov, d. 4161, st. 33, l. 378.

41. *Ibid.* On this decision by the Main Prisons Administration a special circular was published over two signatures—that of Grot and Galkin-Vrassky. GAKhO, fond vremennogo kharkovskogo general-gubernatora, op. 1, d. 327, l. 1.

42. TsGAOR, fond Aleksandra II, d. 673, ll. 5-6.

43. *Ibid.*, l. 11.

44. *Ibid.*, l. 15. The question of whether to abolish the head tax had been raised already in early 1879, with the establishment of the special commission "to investigate means to abolish the head tax."

45. TsGAOR, fond Aleksandra II, d. 673, l. 16.

46. See R. Yanson, *Opyt statisticheskogo issledovaniia o krestianskikh nadelakh i povinnostiakh* (St. Petersburg, 1878).

47. There is reason to think that this memorandum was not only known to the Minister of Internal Affairs, but was to some extent the fruit of his inspiration, just like the appointment of Bunge had been engineered by him.

48. TsGAOR, fond Loris-Melikova, d. 297. Letter from Loris-Melikov to Alexander II on 14 October 1880, ll. 1-2.

49. This imperial directive was cited by Abaza in his letter to Alexander II. A copy of the letter can be found in Alexander II's papers, dated October 1880. TsGAOR, fond Aleksandra II, d. 676, l. 1.

50. *Ibid.*, ll. 1-2.

51. *Ibid.*, ll. l. 3.

52. PSZ, 2 sobr., LIV, No. 61578.

53. P.A. Valuev, *Dnevnik 1877-1884 gg.*, p. 129.

54. It is interesting to note that the question of whether "to permit the transfer of salt into storage areas without prior payment" was considered by the Committee of Ministers, even though it was a much less important question than abolition of the salt tax. TsGIA, fond Komiteta ministrov, d. 4165, st. 202, session of 31 March 1881.

55. *Dnevnik E.A. Perettsa*, p. 14. Chicherin said approximately the same thing in his memoirs: "The result was that the treasury lost a great deal of income.

The people's lot was not much improved, but the big salt entrepreneurs became richer, and as a result of the disorder on the financial side they made huge windfall profits." *Vospominaniia Borisa Nikolaevicha Chicherina. Zemstvo i Moskovskaia duma*, p. 100. In Chicherin's view, the hastiness that characterized passage of this plan was due to a desire to gain popularity. Such a charge can be levelled not so much at Abaza, as at Loris-Melikov.

56. *Byloe*, 1917, kn. 4 (26), p. 35.

57. TsGAOR, fond Departamenta politsii, op. 249, d. 28, l. 12.

58. TsGAOR, fond Departamenta politsii, op. 166, d. 28, l. 4. Meat prices also went up at the same time. The Petersburg municipal council called a special temporary commission to fight against the "rapid rise in grain prices." Apparently, the commission discharged its assignment. Loris-Melikov, in a memorandum to Alexander III on 4 April 1881, petitioned to give an award to the chairman and the commission members." TsGIA, fond Departamenta obshchikh del, op. 242, d. 81, l. 144.

59. *Dnevnik E.A. Perettsa*, p. 9. The *Vedomosti s.-peterburgskoso gradonachalstva* had an announcement on the matter, which was republished in the *Pravitelstvennyi vestnik* on 28 October in the miscellany section. In this announcement, signed by a group of wholesale merchants, who "desire to help decrease bread prices in the city," there was a statement that prices on 9 poods of bread would drop to between 16 rubles and 16 rubles 50 kopecks after 1 November. Apparently, the bread traders complied with Loris-Melikov's order immediately, rather than on the 1st of November. In a telegram to Alexander II on 27 October Loris-Melikov asserted: "Yesterday the bread traders lowered prices on bread in the capital from 19 to 16 rubles per *chetvert*, and within a few days it is likely that rye bread will sell for 4 kopecks per pound instead of 5." TsGAOR, fond A.V. Adlerberga, d. 605, l. 15. Valuev did not approve of Loris-Melikov's directive. On 11 November he wrote: "Loris-Melikov's authority in provisioning is that of a lieutenant, if not that of a cornet [two low military ranks—Editor]. He spoke to the current heads of the bread trade in the tone of a Pasha, who threated exile. He reminded the merchants, so to speak, of the shores of the Murmansk." P.A. Valuev, *Dnevnik 1877-1884 gg.*, p. 128.

60. TsGIA, fond Komiteta ministrov, zhurnal Komiteta ministrov za iiul 1880 g. Prilozhenie, d. 4108, st. 469, l. 878.

61. As Loris-Melikov informed the committee, the remaining capital for food loans was only 3,100,000 rubles; at that time, the Samara zemstvo had just petitioned for 5,500,000 rubles from the government. TsGIA, fond Komiteta ministrov, d. 4115, st. 619, ll. 196-197.

62. *Ibid.*, ll. 200-201.

63. *Ibid.*, ll. 203-204.

64. Food loans were not always as large as what the borrowers asked. The Samara zemstvo got only 1,000,000 rubles of the 5,500,000 that it asked. Only after a second request from the zemstvo did the Committee of Ministers agree to another 1,500,000 rubles in loans, of which 900,000 rubles were earmarked for seeding of fields. The zemstvo had asked for a supplementary loan to starving peasants of 1,735,210 rubles, of which the government granted 1,200,000 rubles. The government gave between 100,000 and 150,000 rubles of the 450,000 rubles asked for relief of Penza's peasantry. Osobyi zhurnal Komiteta ministrov za 20 yanvaria 1881 g., d. 4161, st. 19, ll. 94-123.

65. Osobyi zhurnal Komiteta ministrov za 12 maia 1881 g., d. 4169, st. 305, ll. 170-171.

66. See the second chapter.

67. These questions concerned the system of selection for permanent district members, the need to elect a candidate for this office, and the responsibility of the permanent member for the actions of the district bureaux, plus the reasonsibility to conduct periodic checks of the volost administrations. It was also recommended that mandatory residence of the permanent member in the district capital city be discussed. GAKhO, fond kharkovskogo vremennogo general-gubernatora, op. 1, d. 319.

68. *Ibid.*, l. 1. According to the memoirs of A.I. Koshelev, "these words provoked in the commissions and zemstvo assemblies sharp and prolonged debate." *Zapiski Aleksandra Ivanovicha Kosheleva* (1812-1883) (Berlin, 1884), p. 256.

69. The special Kharkov provincial zemstvo assembly voted the following resolution on 9 June 1881: (1) to abolish the existing institutions for peasant affairs; to transfer matters now handled by these institutions to existing judicial, economic, and administrative agencies and to such new agencies as will be deemed necessary; peasant societies will be granted an independent administration. (2) To petition the government to draft a plan to resolve this issue in a special assembly of persons appointed by the government and elected by provincial and district zemstvo assemblies." GAKhO, fond vremennogo general-gubernatora, op. 1, d. 319, l. 19. The Tver provincial zemstvo assembly in June 1881 adopted a more radical solution to this problem: "Since neither partial nor general reforms can attain the government's goals without a preliminary examination of the reforms by elected representatives of the whole of Russia, we petition for the calling of a special advisory institution, whose assistance will be necessary for the drafting and introduction of necessary legislation. B. Veselovsky, *Istoriia zemstva*, III, p. 255.

70. *Zemstvo*, 3 December 1880.

71. TsGIA, fond Komiteta ministrov, Osobyi zhurnal ot 10 fevralia 1881 g., st. 73, prilozhenie k zhurnalu, d. 4164, ll. 113-114. In accordance with Loris-Melikov's conclusion a number of zemstvos (Bessarabia, Kherson, Ekaterinoslav, Tauride, Kharkov, Poltava, Kursk) were permitted to send "experts elected by provincial zemstvo boards to discuss ways to control bread beetles." Ibid., d. 4163, st. 73, l. 148. The experts were to meet in Odessa under the chairmanship of the Odessa municipal governor. Simultaneously with this meeting in Odessa there was a conference in Kahrkov on the control of diphtheria.

72. *Zapiski Aleksandra Ivanovicha Kosheleva* (1812-1883), p. 253.

73. According to the "Spisok periodicheskikh izdanii, podvergshikhsia administrativnym vzyskaniiam v 1865-1904 gg.," in Vl. Rozenberg and V. Yakushkin, *Russkaia pechat i tsenzura v proshlom i nastoiashchem* (St. Petersburg, 1905), pp. 193-226. In 1880 there were four warnings and two publications were stopped. In 1881 there were no such actions in the first two months of the year. TsGIA, fond 776, op. 1, d. 171.

74. On 27 October Valuev wired Alexander II in Livadia about this matter. He informed the tsar of Loris-Melikov's request to include Kakhanov on the commission and retain Makov. TsGAOR, fond A.V. Adlerberga, d. 487. Besides Kakhanov and Makov the participants were: the Ministers of Internal Affairs, Finance, and Justice, the head of the Second Section, Urusov, the Supreme-Procurator of the Synod Pobedonostsev, the head of the Main Press Administration, N.S. Abaza, and Senator Frisch.

75. P.A. Valuev, *Dnevnik 1877-1884 gg.*, pp. 122-123. According to A.I. Koshelev, N.S. Abaza did not accept the position offered to him except under the

condition that there be a commission to reexamine the press laws, and new regulations that prosecutions be brought to court for violation of the law. *Zapiski Aleksandra Ivanovicha Kosheleva* (1812-1883), p. 247.

76. P.A. Valuev, *Dnevnik 1877-1884 gg.*, pp. 124-125.

77. *Ibid.*, p. 126.

78. M.M. Stasiulevich's speech was published in *M.M. Stasiulevich i ego sovremenniki*, I (St. Petersburg, 1911), pp. 544-549.

79. *Ibid.*, p. 548. M.E. Saltykov-Shchedrin was skeptical about this project. "I know, I know," he wrote to P.V. Annensky on 18 October, "that there is a new plan to draft a statute on publishing which will eliminate administrative arbitrariness and replace it with trials in court. All the newspapers and journals are in an uproar over this, including *Otechestvennye zapiski*, but I think this: Up to now I have not done time in jail, and I do not know about the future. It seems to me that I will not avoid it. I hear that the trials will be in the court of appeals section of the Senate, where there are people completely indifferent to the discomforts of jail. However, an old man cannot contemplate jail with the same indifference." N. Shchedrin (M.E. Saltykov), *Polnoe sobranie sochinenii*, XIX, kn. 2 (Moscow, 1939), p. 176.

80. P.A. Valuev, *Dnevnik 1877-1884 gg.*, p. 127.

81. TsGIA, fond Valueva, d. 168, l. 11.

82. In August 1866 the Petersburg district court acquitted Yu.R. Zhukovsky as author and A.V. Pypin as editor for publishing articles in the second and third numbers of a journal on the topic "Vopros molodogo pokoleniia." The Petersburg appeals court cancelled this verdict, and on 12 December 1866 there was a law published that removed the press from the jurisdiction of the district courts and transferred it to the appeals court.

83. TsGIA, fond Valueva, d. 168, l. 101.

84. With the participation of the jurors.

85. TsGIA, fond Valueva, d. 168, l. 103.

86. *Ibid.*, l. 106.

87. In the fourth point of the "Checklist" there was mention of a rule dating to the reign of Catherine II that forbade publication of derogatory information, comments, and judgments about the private lives and government actions of the royal family.

88. TsGIA, fond Valueva, d. 168, ll. 107-108.

89. P.A. Valuev, *Dnevnik 1877-1884 gg.*, pp. 146-147. In a note dated 31 May 1881 and entitled "Comments on the Press Question," Valuev wrote: "The commission to draft the basic elements of the new press law could not have come to any practical result. The Ministry of Internal Affairs was the direct and primary instigator of change, but the Ministry began by failing to exert as much pressure on violators as it had formerly, and then attempted the transfer supervision of the law to judicial agencies. The commission was doomed to fail." TsGAOR, fond Ignatieva, d. 1444, ll. 1-2.

90. TsGIA, fond Departamenta narodnogo prosveshcheniia, op. 200, d. 25, 1880 g., l. 2. Report published by G.I. Shchetinina in *Problemyistochnikovedeniia*, Vypusk 9, (Moscow, 1961).

91. TsGIA, fond Departamenta narodnogo prosveshcheniia, op. 200, d. 25, 1880g., ll. 2-3.

92. *Ibid.*, l. 3.

93. *Ibid.*, l. 4.

94. They had in mind Derpt and Warsaw Universities.

95. TsGIA, fond Departamenta narodnogo prosveshcheniia, op. 200, d. 25, 1880 g., ll. 4-5.

96. *Ibid.,* l. 5.

97. One of the copies of this printed report is in the Miliutin papers in ROBL.

98. ROBL, fond D.A. Miliutina, karton 43, d. 27, pp. 1-2.

99. *Ibid.,* pp. 2-3.

100. *Ibid.,* pp. 3-4.

101. *Ibid.,* p. 6.

102. TsGIA, fond Departamenta narodnogo prosveshcheniia, op. 200, d. 25, 1880 g., l. 8.

103. *Ibid.,* l. 8.

104. *Dnevnik D.A. Miliutina,* IV, p. 13.

105. ROBL, fond Pobedonostseva, d. 4410/I, l. 6.

106. *Dnevnik D.A. Miliutina,* IV, pp. 14-15.

107. *Ibid.,* p. 15.

108. ROBL, d. 4410/I, l. 8.

109. *Ibid.,* l. 14. According to many contemporaries, Saburov was actually not an intelligent person.

110. In his memo book on this day there was the following entry: "v ½ 11 dokl[ad] Sabur[ova] ob izmen[enii] v univ[e]r[sitetakh]." (At 10:30 Saburov's memorandum on changes in the universities.' TsGAOR, fond Aleksandra II, d. 335.

111. TsGIA, fond Departamenta zakonov, d. 40, 1881 g., l. 8.

112. *Ibid.,* l. 12.

113. *Ibid.,* ll. 15-16.

114. In this *delo* there are no reactions from the Ministers of Justice, War, State Domains or other persons.

115. TsGIA, fond Departamenta zakonov, d. 40, 1881, g., l. 30.

116. *Ibid.,* ll. 82-83

117. Baron Nikolai was the assistant Minister of Education in the early 1860s under Golovnin. His views were close to those of the liberal bureaucrats.

118. *Byloe,* 1918, kn. 4-5, p. 162. The original is in the Alexander III papers in TsGAOR, d. 693. The author of this document was M.S. Kakhanov. Polovtsov testified directly to this in his diary. On 4 February 1882 he related a conversation with Kakhanov concerning Loris-Melikov's memorandum of 28 January: "According to Kakhanov, the basis of these proposals was a report that he had drawn up after a meeting with the tsar on the day that Mezentsov was buried. At this meeting, in which Kakhanov took part, such wild and stupid things were said that Kakhanov, having returned home, wrote a memorandum including proposals to fight against nihilism. This memorandum was a dead letter until Loris-Melikov revived it." TsGAOR, fond Polovtsova, d. 20, l. 48. M.I. Kheifets also attributed authorship to Kakhanov on the basis of comparisons of various drafts of the document.

119. *Ibid..*

120. After the explosion in the Winter Palace on 5 February 1880, there were two more attacks: one on 20 February by Mlodetsky, who tried to kill Loris-Melikov; the second on 4 March in Kiev by Polikarpov who tried to kill police agent Zabramsky. Neither attack was sanctioned by the Executive Committee of *Narodnaia Volia.*

121. However, rumors about land division were less in evidence in 1880 than in 1879. In the area controlled by the Kharkov Governor-General (six provinces), according to data compiled secretly by the temporary Governor-General, there

were eleven cases of dissemination of rumors about land partition in the first nine months of 1879. During 1880 there were only three cases. In 1879 there were five cases where other sorts of rumors were spread among the peasants. in 1880 there was only one such case. GAKhO, fond kharkovskogo vremennogo general-gubernatora, op. 2.

122. In summer 1880 a mine was placed under the Kamenny Bridge by Merkylov and Teterka. See V. Ya. Bogucharsky, *Iz istorii politicheskoe borby v 70-80-kh godakh XIX veka. Partiia "Narodnaia volia", ee proiskhozhdenie, sudba i gibel* (Moscow, 1912), p. 51.

123. *Byloe,* 1917, kn. 4 (26), p. 34.

124. The so-called Kletochnikov notebooks, containing his communications with the Executive Committee of *Narodnaia Volia,* have been published in *Arkhiv "Zemli i voli",* S.N. Valk, ed., (Moscow, 1932).

125. *Byloe,* 1918, kn. 4-5, p. 163.

126. *Ibid.,* p. 164.

127. *Ibid.,* p. 164.

128. V.I. Lenin, *Sochineniia,* V, p. 39.

129. *Byloe,* 1918, kn. 4-5, p. 165. Alexander II was not certain about this; these words are marked off in pencil, and a question mark is written in the margin.

130. *Ibid.,* p. 165.

131. *Ibid.,* p. 165.

132. *Ibid.,* p. 166.

133. One consequence of this attitude was the memorandum by P.P. Shuvalov in February 1881. Shuvalov wrote about the inevitability of "popular representation" in Russia: "It is difficult to imagine that Russia will long remain the sole exception in the family of European nations, and that it does not deserve from the tsar the trust, which he has shown to his Finnish subjects or to other Slavic peoples." *Krasnyi arkhiv,* 1928, kn. 6 (31), p. 121. Shuvalov wanted to create a bicameral consultative agency, consisting of elected members. The elections for deputies to the lower house would follow the procedures for zemstvo elections. Consequently, the overwhelming majority of members of this house would belong to the propertied classes. The elections to the upper house would be done by a limited number of electors. These electors would actually select only a list of candidates, from which the government would pick delegates to the upper house. Thus, the Shuvalov project was less radical than the proposals by Valuev, Grand Duke Konstantin Nikolaevich, and Loris-Melikov. The Shuvalov plan did not include any timetable for implementation, which was to take place at some undefined point in the future.

134. P.A. Valuev, *Dnevnik 1877-1884 gg.,* p. 142.

135. *Ibid.,* p. 143.

136. TsGAOR, fond biblioteki Zimnego dvortsa, d. 2587, kn. VI, l. 189. In the published version of Valuev's diary part of the sentence has been deleted.

137. *Byloe,* 1918, kn. 4-5, p. 172.

138. *Dnevnik E.A. Perettsa,* p. 35. This letter has not been preserved in the Alexander II papers.

139. According to Pobedonostsev, who did not take part in the conferences that debated Loris-Melikov's plan, the tsarevich asked Loris-Melikov to acquaint the Supreme-Procurator of the Synod with this document. "While Alexander II was still alive," he wrote to Tiutcheva on 3 March 1881, "there were three meetings on some kind of advisory assembly: one in the Winter Palace and two in Anichkov. I

did not take part. The tsarevich did not object, but he told Loris-Melikov to send me the meetings' protocol. Loris-Melikov told me about this two weeks ago, and he received the protocol in my presence. He wanted to send it that day, but he has not sent it yet." *Russkii arkhiv,* 1907, kn. 2, p. 90. Apparently, Loris-Melikov anticipated Pobedonostsev's objections.

140. *Byloe,* 1918, kn. 4-5, p. 174.

141. *Ibid.,* p. 175.

142. TsGIA, fond Valueva, d. 21, l. 1.

143. *Byloe,* 1918, kn. 4-5, p. 177.

144. I did not succeed in finding this circular. It is mentioned in a secret circular of the Main Prisons Administration on 2 April 1881, No. 63. TsGIA (Ukraine), fond Kantseliarii kievskogo general-gubernatora, op. 831, d. 3, 1881 g., l. 46.

145. *Ibid..* The circular also indicated that prisoners who had been exempted from corporal punishment before their sentencing would be subject to the regulations in the general statutes during their transfer to places of confinement.

146. In Nerchinsky district there were five prisons. In the Kariiskaia Prison, according to data of the Main Prisons Administration, there were 60 persons in 1880. TsGAOR, fond glavnogo tiuremnogo upravleniia, op. 1, d. 502. In Eastern Siberia, according to this data, there were 308 political exiles, not counting 4121 persons exiled for participation in the 1863 uprising.

147. TsGAOR, fond III otdeleniia, 3 ekspeditsiia, op. 165, d. 701, 1880 g., ll. 5-6.

148. On the other hand, in a special circular on 10 September addressed to the governors, Loris-Melikov said it was necessary to treat exiles humanely. "Many officials in charge of exiles often fail not only to take the feasible steps to establish a system of supervision and method of treatment of prisons that would be within the confines of law and justice, would maintain a proper relationship between exiles and the government, and would create a spirit of obedience in the exiles, but they [these officials] arouse the exiles to private expression of dissatisfaction and even to disorders, by various trivial, often unnecessary demands and by improper treatment. TsGIA, fond Departamenta obshchikh del, op. 238, d. 61, l. 76. Loris-Melikov went on to say that officials should "avoid even the least hint of abnormal relations" toward political exiles.

149. N. Shchedrin (M.E. Saltykov), *Polnoe sobranie sochinenii,* XIX, kn. 2, p. 158.

150. "Iz avtobiografii Very Figner," *Byloe,* 1917, kn. 4 (26), pp. 63-64.

151. V.I. Lenin, *Sochineniia,* V, p. 59.

152. *Literatura partii "Narodnaia volia",* p. 305.

CHAPTER IV

1. S. Yu. Witte, *Vospominaniia,* I (Moscow, 1960), p. 408.

2. TsGAOR, fond kollektsii biblioteki Zimnego dvortsa, d. 2587, kn. VI, l. 197.

3. In his diary entry for 1 March 1881, Miliutin wrote: "A crowd gathered on the square in front of the palace. I heard stories about several cases where the crowd took revenge on certain careless and rather too obvious nihilists. The crowd wanted to hang one of them from a lightpost: the nihilist was saved by arrest in the gates of the Main Military Headquarters. There were similar incidents in other places, but in general the city is absolutely orderly and even calmer than usual."

ROBL, fond D.A. Miliutina, papka 3, d. 5, ll. 23-24. This passage was not published in the four-volume version of the diary. See also the memoirs of A.A. Bobrinsky, *Katorga i ssylka,* 1931, kn. 3, p. 98.

4. P.A. Valuev, *Dnevnik 1877-1884 gg.,* p. 148.

5. *Byloe,* 1918, kn. 4-5, p. 24. See also the article and publication by S.N. Valk, "Vokrug 1 marta 1881 g.," *Krasnyi arkhiv,* 1930, t. 3, pp. 176-184.

6. Zheliabov's role as party leader was well-known to the government. On 28 February Alexander II wrote happily in his memo book: "Three important arrests, one of them Zheliabov." TsGAOR, fond Aleksandra II, d. 335, p. 22. According to Court Minister Adlerberg, on the morning of 1 March Alexander II spoke to him about the arrest of Zheliabov, and ascribed to this event "great significance." IRLI, fond M.I. Semevskogo, d. 16, l. 592.

7. V. Ya. Bogucharsky, *Iz istorii politicheskoi borby v 70-80-kh godakh XIX veka. Partiia "Narodnaia volia", ee proiskhozhdenie, sudba i gibel,* pp. 67-68.

8. *Ibid.,* pp. 76-78.

9. See the article by R.V. Filippov, "V.I. Lenin i pismo Ispolnitelnogo komiteta 'Narodnoi voli' ot 10 marta 1881 goda," *Voprosy istorii,* Vypusk 1 (Petrozavodsk, 1961) pp. 3-12.

10. *Literatura partii "Narodnaia volia",* section on documents, p. 13.

11. In this memorandum the Minister of Internal Affairs argued in favor of a trial the day after Alexander II's funeral.

12. *Krasnyi arkhiv,* 1930, t. 3, p. 130.

13. *Pisma K.P. Pobedonostseva k Aleksandru III,* I, pp. 318-319.

14. *Dnevnik D.A. Miliutina,* IV, p. 29.

15. P.A. Valuev, *Dnevnik 1877-1884 gg.,* p. 149. The author had in mind the designation of a regent in case Alexander III was killed and the thirteen-year old Nikolai Alexandrovich ascended to the throne.

16. ROBL, fond Kireevykh, d. 8, l. 210.

17. *Denkwürdikeiten des Botschafters General v. Schweinitz,* Zweite Band (Berlin), p. 156.

18. Baranov, who was a captain of the first rank, commanded the ships "Vesta" and "Rossiia" during the Russo-Turkish War. After the peace treaty had been signed it was discovered that Baranov's accounts of military encounters, for which he had been promoted and received the Cross of St. George, were false. He was publically accused of falsifying records. Ultimately, Baranov was forced to resign from the service; yet in 1880 he was named provincial governor in Kovno. According to A.A. Polovtsov, this appointment was made despite the opposition of Loris-Melikov. TsGAOR, fond Polovtsova, d. 18.

19. *Pisma K.P. Pobedonostseva k Aleksandru III,* I, p. 317.

20. *Ibid.,* p. 315. Katkov thought very highly of this adventurist. In a letter to him on 24 March, Katkov wrote: "I believe, I trust in you, Nikolai Mikhailovich, and I trust your intelligence, and your energy, and your political honor (a quality that is very rare these days) and your loyalty to the tsar." ROBL, fond Katkova, d. 48, l. 159.

21. *Russkii arkhiv,* 1907, kn. 2, p. 96.

22. TsGIA, fond Kantseliarii ministra vnutrennikh del, op. 1, d. 1051, ll. 8-9. Published in *Pravitelstvennyi vestnik,* 18 March 1881.

23. TsGIA, fond Kantseliarii ministra vnutrennikh del, op. 1, d. 1052, l. 9.

24. *Golos,* 21 March 1881. Editorial.

25. *Golos,* 22 March 1881. Editorial.

26. *Dnevnik E.A. Perettsa,* pp. 53-54.

27. *Dnevnik D.A. Miliutina,* IV, p. 46. For a description of Baranov's reception see *Golos,* 21 March 1881. The first measure approved—the organization of a military guard around the city and the placement of Cossack mounted patrols —was cancelled in a few days, after it virtually paralyzed the life of the city, especially impeding the flow of produce to market. However, Baranov thought this measure had a salutary effect. In one of the April meetings the municipal governor observed profoundly: "Many reproaches have been made for this step, but in my view it was important because it gave me a chance to see how to close down the city, if that should become necessary in the future." IRLI, fond M.I. Semevskogo, d. 16, l. 383. The second measure was not widely adopted because of its absurdity.

28. *Dnevnik E.A. Perettsa,* p. 52.

29. Elected members were: General-Admiral Trepov; General Admiral Count Vorontsov-Dashkov; State Counsellor Glazunov; the chairman of the Petersburg county court, Privy Counsellor Kvist; Justice of the Peace Likhachev; Collegiate Assessor Count Bobrinsky; Major-General Fredericks; Acting State Counsellor Semevsky; Justice of the Peace Menshutkin; Privy Counsellor Lamansky; Hereditary Citizen Eliseev; Major-General Count Levashev; Commercial Counsellor Krundyshev; Justice of the Peace Major-General Blagovo, Barrister Potekhin; University Rector Bekhetov; member of the Petersburg Appeals Court Acting State Counsellor Khristianovich, member of the State Council Privy Counsellor Zablotsky-Desiatovsky; Major-General Bogdanovich; Justice of the Peace Kotomin; State Counsellor Kraevsky; Major-General Korostovets; Hereditary Citizen Tselbeev; Privy Counsellor Kobeko; and Acting State Counsellor Kamerherr Zhukovsky. TsGIA, fond kantseliarii ministra vnutrennikh del, pop. 1, d. 1051, l. 14. Thus, among the members there were 13 "Excellencies." [All officials with top government ranks were addressed as "Your Excellency."—Editor] The candidates were: Manufacturer-Counsellor San-Gali; Hereditary Citizen Durdin; Hereditary State Counsellor Mikhelson; Privy Counsellor Filosofov; the merchant Glazunov; Colonel Litvinov; State Counsellor Putilin; retired Lieutenant Gorstkin; General-Admiral Glinka-Marvin; Justice of the Peace State Counsellor Trofimov; Justice of the Peace Lermontov; Acting State Counsellor Miasoedov; Court Counsellor Sokolov; Privy Counsellor Vinberg; Hereditary Citizen Lipin; merchant Banukhin; Hereditary Citizens Latkin and Kukanov; merchant Kobyzev; Major-General Dietrichs; merchant Orlovsky; Major-General Fedorov; engineer Kotliarevsky; merchant Lev Koenig. Besides the elected members, the Petersburg mayor [*gorodskoe golova*] and the Petersburg commandant Major-General Adelson were supposed to participate.

30. *Golos,* 22 March 1881.

31. *Strana,* 22 March 1881.

32. IRLI, fond M.I. Semevskogo, d. 16, ll. 353-366.

33. *Byloe,* 1907, kn. 3, pp. 290-302.

34. The Temporary Council drafted a memorandum on the "Causes of Disorders and Disturbances among the Young," and set up a commission "On the Establishment of Internal Surveillance in Domiciles." This commission drafted four projects: (1) "Regulations on Investigation of Violations of the System of Police Notification for Those Arriving and Departing Petersburg;" (2) "Temporary Regulations for General Surveillance of Petersburg Domiciles," (3) "Regulations for Apartment Managers concerning their Police Responsibilities," (4) "Regulations for District Police Appointed to Observe Domiciles." *Byloe,* 1907, kn. 4, p. 300.

35. IRLI, fond M.I. Semevskogo, d. 16, l. 380.

36. *Ibid.,* ll. 394-395.

37. *Ibid.*, l. 359.
38. *Ibid.*, l. 381.
39. TsGAOR, fond kollektsii biblioteki Zimnego dvortsa, d. 2587, kn. VII, ll. 12-13. In the published version the last two sentences have been deleted.
40. ROBL, fond Pobedonostseva, d. 4410/1, l. 43.
41. The reference is to the flight of the French King Louis XVI from revolutionary Paris to Varenne in 1791.
42. TsGAOR, fond Polovtsova, d. 18, p. 218.
43. *Ibid.*, p. 221. Miliutin, who visited Gatchina on 31 March, described it the same way. "In Gatchina the visitor is struck by the sight of the palace and the park surrounded by armed guards, horse patrols, secret agents and the like. The palace now looks like a prison. . . ." *Dnevnik D.A. Miliutina*, IV, p. 51.
44. His youth was relative; Alexander III was 36 years-old.
45. ROBL, fond Pobedonostseva, d. 4410/1, l. 43. On 2 March in a letter to Pobedonostsev, Baranov mentioned the need for the tsar to leave the city for one of the suburbs. *Pobedonostsev i ego korrespondenty*, I, ch. 1, (Moscow-Prague, 1923), p. 99.
46. *Byloe*, 1918, kn. 4-5, p. 185.
47. *Ibid.*, p. 186.
48. TsGIA, fond Glavnogo upravleniia po delam pechati, op. 1, d. 17, 1881 g., l. 4.
49. *Ibid.*, l. 8.
50. TsGAOR, fond Aleksandra III, d. 532, l. 1.
51. On this memorandum Alexander III wrote: "This is long overdue." *Ibid.*, l. 1.
52. TsGIA, fond Glavnogo upravleniia po delam pechati, op. 1, d. 17, 1881 g., l. 12.
53. On this issue there is a brilliant article by Academic Yu. V. Gotie, "Borba pravitelstvennykh gruppirovok i manifest 29 aprelia 1880 g.," *Istoricheskie zapiski*, No. 2, pp. 240-299.
54. *Moskovskie vedomosti*, 3 March 1881.
55. *Strana*, 3 March 1881.
56. *Golos*, 4 March 1881.
57. *Zemstvo*, 18 March 1881.
58. *Rus*, 12 March 1881. Second special supplement.
59. According to B.B. Veselovsky, 31 district and 7 provincial zemstvos sent addresses to Alexander III. *Istoriia zemstva*, III, (St. Petersburg, 1911), pp. 258-261.
60. *Ibid.*, pp. 260-261.
61. *K.P. Pobedonostsev i ego korrespondenty*, I, ch. 1, pp. 105-106.
62. *Ibid.*, p. 108.
63. *Ibid.*, pp. 110, 113.
64. *Ibid.*, pp. 114, 117, 118.
65. *Ibid.*, p. 120.
66. *Konstitutsiia gr. Loris-Melikova* (London, 1893) p. 29.
67. *Krasnyi arkhiv*, 1928, t. 6 (31), p. 142.
68. *Ibid.*.
69. This memorandum was the second version. I analyzed the first version in chapter three.
70. In early March the Marquis Wielopolski also sent a memorandum to the tsar. He tried to demonstrate the need for repression, and to show the advantages

of a certain decentralization of administration that would give individual regions an opportunity for limited self-government. "Centralization only helps to spread the infection to provinces that have been free from it. Societies exist which have not yet been affected, or have been touched less by the illness; yet they are politically weakened, and are not strong enough to offer real resistance to the revolutionary theories of the ruling nationality." *Konstitutsiia gr. Loris-Melikova*, p. 26. Wielopolski's remarks were an attempt to capitalize on the political circumstances to win political autonomy for Poland; he argued that the Populist movement had not made an impression there. The proposal of Paris police prefect Andrier also deserves mention. Andrier recommended that the tsar draft a manifesto that would range the whole society against "sedition" in order to destroy it, and simultaneously to grant limited constitutional rights. *Ibid.*, pp. 32-34.

71. With the exception of proposals to protect cattle raising, which were contained in the list of measures that the Minister of Internal Affairs wanted society to discuss.

72. *Byloe*, 1918, kn. 4-5, p. 180. A copy, signed and dated by Loris-Melikov, is in his papers. TsGAOR, d. 290.

73. Alexander III wrote on the first page: "The project is well put together. I will talk with you about the Council of Ministers. *Ibid.*, p. 177.

74. *Pisma K.P. Pobedonostseva k Aleksandru III*, I, pp. 315-316. On that day Alexander III sent to Pobedonostsev a short letter, in which he wrote: "Thank you from the bottom of my heart for your warm letter, with which I agree completely." *K.P. Pobedonostsev i ego korrespondenty*, I, ch. 1, p. 44. Apparently, this was the answer to the letter quoted above.

75. Grand Dukes Sergei and Pavel Alexandrovich were abroad on 1 March, and they returned home after hearing the news of their father's assassination.

76. *Russkii arkhiv*, 1907, kn. 2, pp. 91-92.

77. *Konstitutsiia gr. Loris-Melikova*, p. 31. This letter has not been preserved in the Alexander III papers in TsGAOR.

78. Miliutin's, Valuev's, and Peretts' testimony may be found in their respective diaries. Loris-Melikov's account is in a note by a historian and journalist, V.A. Bilbasov. *Byloe*, 1918, kn. 4-5, pp. 185-193. The original of Bilbasov's account is in the Manuscript Section of the Saltykov-Shchedrin Library in Leningrad. Pobedonostsev's account is in his letter of 11 March 1881 to E.F. Tiutcheva. *Russkii arkhiv*, 1907, kn. 5. The original is in ROBL, fond Pobedonostseva.

79. P.A. Valuev, *Dnevnik 1877-1884 gg.*, p. 151.

80. *Dnevnik E.A. Perettsa*, p. 32. The course of the meeting has been described primarily from Peretts' diary, since it is the most detailed, and in my opinion, most objective source. In cases where other sources disagree with Peretts or give additional details, I have drawn on them as well.

81. *Ibid.*, pp. 32-33.

82. *Ibid.*, p. 34

83. *Ibid.*, pp. 34-35.

84. *Ibid.*, p. 36.

85. *Ibid.*, p. 37

86. *Ibid.*, pp. 38-40.

87. *Dnevnik D.A. Miliutina*, IV, p. 35.

88. *Dnevnik E.A. Perettsa*, p. 41.

89. *Ibid.*, p. 43. Peretts and Miliutin have given different accounts of Solsky's speech. Miliutin, for example, wrote: "Solsky boldly suggested that an army of bureaucrats is a less solid defense for the regime than representatives of all classes

in the nation." *Dnevnik D.A. Miliutina*, IV, p. 35. Peretts attributed this statement to Saburov. "Now the government relies in all its actions on bureaucrats
alone, that is, on people who may be educated, but who breathe only St. Petersburg air and who assimilate the opinions and biases of the newspapers, which
are not always reliable and not always in accord with the basic interests of the
state. It is necessary to hear the other side. Many people have fundamental
disagreements with the newspaper articles. Zemstvo representatives, especially
around Moscow, think differently than Petersburg representatives. They are much
more conservative and independent, and therefore they constitute a much more
solid support for the government. *Dnevnik E.A. Perettsa*, p. 43.

90. Miliutin was also displeased by this speech. He spoke of Posiet's "vulgar
attacks on progress." *Dnevnik D.A. Miliutina*, IV, p. 35.

91. *Dnevnik E.A. Perettsa*, p. 43.

92. Valuev was contemptuous of Saburov's speech. "Saburov made a half-wit
speech about this proposal, and even looked like a half-wit during the meeting."
P.A. Valuev, *Dnevnik 1877-1884 gg.*, p. 153.

93. *Dnevnik E.A. Perettsa*, p. 45. Neither Miliutin nor Valuev mentioned this
proposal of Grand Duke Konstantin Nikolaevich. Valuev described his speech
very briefly: "The Grand Duke General-Admiral was true to himself, that is, he
spoke in half-truths or outright falsehoods." P.A. Valuev, *Dnevnik 1877-1884 gg.*,
p. 153. Miliutin remarked only that the Grand Duke defended Loris-Melikov's
proposals. *Dnevnik D.A. Miliutina*, IV, p. 36.

94. *Dnevnik E.A. Perettsa*, p. 45.

95. *Dnevnik D.A. Miliutina*, IV, pp. 36-37.

96. *Dnevnik E.A. Perettsa*, p. 47. In Bilbasov's opinion, Loris-Melikov's summary of the meeting was fantastic. Alexander III was purported to have said:
"So, gentlemen, the majority favors the proposal to call a preparatory commission consisting of delegates from all classes, for the good of the state. I agree
with the majority and desire the ukase to dedicate this new reform to the memory
of my father, who is its author. The Minister of Internal Affairs will prepare
the ukase in accordance with the observations that we have made." *Byloe*, 1918,
kn. 4-5, p. 193. I have not been able to determine who was responsible for this
summary: Loris Melikov or Bilbasov, but in any case it is inaccurate.

97. Neither Pobedonostsev nor Count Stroganov were members of the Council
of Ministers, and were invited personally by the tsar. P.A. Valuev, *Dnevnik 1877-
1884 gg.*, p. 151. Moreover, Stroganov was invited on the direct insistence of
Pobedonostsev. On 6 March Pobedonostsev wrote to Alexander III: "Summon
Count S. Stroganov to Your office. He is a man of truth, an old servant of Your
parents. There is no other person with whom You would find it more profitable
to consult in a time of emergency." *Pisma K.P. Pobedonostseva k Aleksandru III*,
I, p. 616.

98. Valuev also shared this view. In notes to his diary entry on 9 March he
wrote: "Although His Majesty allowed everyone to speak, without speaking himself, it was clear that his personal opinion had crystallized. He agreed with Pobedonostsev and his ally Count Stroganov." P.A. Valuev, *Dnevnik 1877-1884 gg.*,
p. 154.

99. V.I. Lenin, *Sochineniia*, V, p. 39.

100. The chairman of the State Council, Grand Duke Konstantin Nikolaevich,
did not participate in the ensuing struggle. His fate already had been decided in
early March. The appointment of Baranov, the officer who had been dismissed
from the Navy, to the position of Petersburg municipal governor showed clearly

enough Alexander III's attitude toward his uncle. In mid-March Polovtsov recorded Abaza's statement that Grand Duke Konstantin Nikolaevich was about to be dismissed from all his offices. TsGAOR, fond Polovtsova, d. 18, pp. 208-209. Alexander III was literally unable to tolerate the Grand Duke, a fact that became clear in a letter from the tsar to Grand Duke Vladimir Alexandrovich. "Today after the requiem Uncle Kostia was very interested to know if you would receive him tomorrow with a memorandum. If you ask my opinion, you should let him see you. He can read the statement with two eye-witnesses present, and consequently, there will be no *tête à tête* and no danger to you. TsGAOR, fond Aleksandra III, d. 738.

Valuev also played no important role in this fight. According to his diary, his role ended with the meeting on 8 March. "From that day I was chairman of the Committee of Ministers in name only." P.A. Valuev, *Dnevnik 1877-1884 gg.*, p. 154.

101. Wiener Haus-Hof-und Staatsarchiv. Ministerium des Aussen. P.A.X. 76-1.

102. In January Pobedonostsev wrote Alexander III four letters, in February—two, in March—nine, in April—twelve. *Pisma K.P. Pobedonostseva k Aleksandru III*, I; *K.P. Pobedonostsev i ego korrespondenty*, I, ch. 1.

103. E.M. Feoktistov, *Za kulisami politiki i literatury* (Moscow, 1929), p. 199. Apparently this passion for lying was a family trait, because it was evidenced in his brother Aleksei Pavlovich. Speaking about the differences between the brothers, the gendarme officer Novitsky wrote in his memoirs: "In a conversation one of the speakers asked: What is the difference between the Ignatiev brothers? The other person answered: "The oldest lies all the time; the other one occasionally speaks the truth." V.D. Novitsky, *Iz vospominanii zhandarma*, p. 66.

104. *Pisma K.P. Pobedonostseva k Aleksandru III*, I, pp. 316-317. Apparently Baranov was included in the category of "loyal person."

105. *Dnevnik D.A. Miliutina*, IV, p. 40. Later Miliutin recorded Loris-Melikov's comment about still another "party" forming around Petr Andreevich Shuvalov, the former Chief of Gendarmes, and then ambassador to England, and around Baranov, who had a very "influential position." However, the "worst of all," according to Loris-Melikov, "may be Pobedonostsev, who by abusing the authority of a former teacher over his pupils, sends the young emperor one memorandum after another with his Pharisaical doctrines and Jesuitical advice." *Ibid*.

106. TsGAOR, fond Polovtsova, d. 18, p. 209.

107. TsGAOR, fond Ignatieva, d. 1437, l. 1.

108. *Ibid.*, l. 2.

109. *Ibid.*, ll. 5-6.

110. *Ibid.*, l. 3.

111. *Ibid.*, l. 4. The idea to summon "zemstvo persons" was expressed in another of Ignatiev's memoranda: "Blizhaishie zadachi nastupaiushchego tsarstvovaniia," written in March 1881 and forwarded by the author to Loris-Melikov. In this memorandum Count Ignatiev wrote: "Now is the best time to summon zemstvo leaders to the aid of the government and to propose that they participate in a preliminary discussion of reforms awaited with impatience by all of Russia. The advice of zemstvo leaders on the question of the day, on the fight against sedition, would be very useful, and I should think that on the day that the tsar finds himself surrounded by these new, but most natural advisers, he will feel as he has never before that there is nothing in common between Russians and revolutionaries." TsGAOR, fond Ignatieva, d. 1492, l. 6. Later Ignatiev stated that provincial zemstvo assemblies should elect zemstvo representatives. According to him, these

elected delegates should be able to take part in the State Council. It is interesting that opposite the phrase about zemstvo representatives Ignatiev has written: "I changed my views on this question somewhat after acquainting myself with the administration and the zemstvos in the Ministry of Internal Affairs." It should be added that Ignatiev's project on zemstvo representatives, even though it was based on a reactionary-chauvinistic point-of-view, was very close in substance to the plan of Loris-Melikov.

112. P.A. Valuev,*Dnevnik 1877-1884 gg.*, p. 161.

113. *Dnevnik E.A. Perettsa*, p. 57.

114. Wiener Haus-Hof-und Staatsarchiv. Ministerium des Aussen. P.A.X. 76-1.

115. According to Peretts and Polovtsov, the dismissal of Makov was connected with the perlustration of mail. According to one version, Makov came to the tsar with a memorandum about the system of perlustration, and the young emperor, having spoken with Loris-Melikov, decided to abolish the Ministry of Posts and Telegraphs (Peretts). Polovtsov's version was different. On 18 March he wrote in his diary: "Today Makov came to the tsar with excerpts from letters. His Majesty informed Makov that if there was something political, then he (Makov) should see the Minister of Internal Affairs. Otherwise, he (Alexander III) did not care to read others' mail." TsGAOR, fond Polovtsova, d. 18, p. 205. Supposedly Makov's dismissal was connected with this matter. Miliutin saw the abolition of the Ministry of Posts and Telegraphs as a result of personal disagreement between the tsar and Makov. *Dnevnik D.A. Miliutina*, IV, p. 41. Finally, Valuev stated that the reason for Makov's dismissal was a disagreement over the Uniate question. P.A. Valuev, *Dnevnik 1877-1884 gg.*, p. 158.

116. *Dnevnik E.A. Perettsa*, p. 54.

117. ROBL, fond D.A. Miliutina, papka 68, d. 6, letter of 4 March 1881.

118. See the article "Papii Podbelskii," *Katorga i ssylka*, 1929, kn. 52.

119. Evidently, after Delianov's candidacy had been dismissed there was a proposal (perhaps from Loris-Melikov) to appoint Nikolai minister. In connection with this suggestion, Alexander III asked Pobedonostsev to speak with Nikolai. In a letter to the emperor Pobedonostsev approved of Nikolai's candidacy. *Pisma K.P. Pobedonostseva k Aleksandru III*, I, pp. 319-321. Upon learning of Nikolai's appointment, Katkov was horrified. "I just received news of Baron Nikolai's appointment as Saburov's replacement," he wrote to Baranov. "Is this true? . . . Can we really be walking so much in the dark that such persons are appointed to important posts at random without motivation?" ROBL, fond Katkova, d. 48, l. 159. Letter of 24 March 1881.

120. TsGIA, fond Departamenta obshchikh del, op. 241, d. 82, l. 225.

121. One indirect indication of Loris-Melikov's role in the appointment of Ignatiev is the proposal to the head of the First Section of His Majesty's Chancellery to prepare the necessary rescript. This proposal was forwarded through Loris-Melikov. TsGIA, fond I otdeleniia s.e.i. v. kantseliarii, op. 3, d. 950.

122. See Loris-Melikov's letter to Alexander III on 10 April 1881. *Krasnyi arkhiv*, 1925, kn. 1 (8), pp. 124-125.

123. *Dnevnik D.A. Miliutina*, IV, p. 40.

124. *Ibid.* Later in the entry for the same date Miliutin spoke about an analogous conversation involving himself, Loris-Melikov, and Grand Duke Konstantin Nikolaevich. *Ibid.*, pp. 40-41.

125. Loris-Melikov circled the words "unified" and "elected."

126. TsGAOR, fond Polovtsova, d. 18, p. 216. According to Polovtsov, Kakhanov stopped Loris-Melikov and said that among these five questions there were

matters that could "not be entrusted to zemstvo delegates, for example the reform of administration or changes in press laws. Loris did not agree with him [Kakhanov], not having a well-defined and firm principle behind his somewhat confused proposals." *Ibid.*, pp. 216-217.

127. *Ibid.*, pp. 223, 225.

128. TsGIA, fond Glavnogo komiteta ob ustroistve selskogo sostoianiia, op. t. XV, d. 28, 1881 g., p. 3.

129. *Ibid.*, l. 2. Abaza added that there "are provinces, namely the blacksoil provinces, where this difference works to the benefit of the persons making payments, since the price of land has risen four or five times." *Ibid.*, ll. 2-3.

130. The commission consisted of the chairman of the Central Statistical Committee, P.P. Semenov-Tian-Shansky, the head of the Zemstvo Section, F.L. Barykov, and the chairman of the St. Petersburg zemstvo board, Prince I.A. Gorchakov.

131. TsGIA, fond Glavnogo komiteta ob ustroistve selskogo sostoianiia, op. t. XV, d. 28, 1881 g., ll. 16, 18.

132. *Ibid.*, ll. 24-25.

133. *Ibid.*, l. 106.

134. *Ibid.*, ll. 117-118.

135. See R. Yanson, *Opyt statisticheskogo issledovaniia o krestianskikh nadelakh i platezhakh* (St. Petersburg, 1877).

136. TsGIA, fond Glavnogo komiteta ob ustroistve selskogo sostoianiia, op. t. XV, d. 28, 1881 g., l. 203. The joint session also decided to forgive arrears on redemption payments, accumulated before 1 July 1881 by villages of peasant proprietors, "for whom future payments will be reduced." *Ibid.*

137. *Dnevnik E.A. Perettsa*, pp. 59-60.

138. According to the Statute on Redemption, a landowner received a loan of 75-80 percent of the capitalized annual money payment [obrok]; the remaining 20-25 percent, if there were a mutual agreement between peasants and landowner to transfer to redemption, would be paid by the peasant to the landowner in the form of supplementary payments. See my book *Provedenie v zhizn krestianskoi reformy 1861 goda*, (Moscow, 1958). In connection with the introduction of mandatory redemption the landowner naturally lost the supplementary payments.

139. TsGIA, fond Glavnogo komiteta ob ustroistve selskogo sostoianiia, op. t. XV, d. 28, 1881 g., prilozhenie, l. 263.

140. *Ibid.*, ll. 257-258.

141. This memorandum, which was probably drafted by Ignatiev or one of his associates, was mentioned twice in letters by Pobedonostsev. TsGAOR, fond Ignatieva, d. 3679, ll. 15-19.

142. *K.P. Pobedonostsev i ego korrespondenty*, I, ch. 1, p. 86.

143. See below.

144. *Dnevnik E.A. Perettsa*, p. 67.

145. After the meeting on 8 March Pobedonostsev sent Loris-Melikov a letter in which he tried to salvage his personal ties with the Minister of Internal Affairs. He wrote: "In the excitement of this morning I did not have a chance to talk with you, most esteemed Mikhail Tarielovich! But I would regret very much if the words that I spoke at the meeting today caused you to be dissatisfied with me." *Byloe*, 1918, kn. 4-5, p. 180. Then he spoke about the difference between his political position and that of Loris-Melikov and the need to express these opinions "according to one's reason and conscience." *Ibid.*

146. *Dnevnik E.A. Perettsa*, p. 51.

147. *Dnevnik D.A. Miliutina*, IV, p. 55.

148. That is, 8 April.
148. That is, 14 April.
150. ROBL, fond Pobedonostseva, d. 4410/1, l. 49.
151. The trial of the conspirators helped relieve some of the tension in the government. The Executive Committee of *Narodnaia Volia* did not react violently to the hanging of Zheliabov and his comrades. This showed the weakness of the revolutionaries.
152. *Byloe*, 1918, kn. 4-5, pp. 180-181.
153. *Ibid.*, p. 181.
154. *Ibid.*, p. 182.
155. *Ibid.*
156. *Ibid.*, p. 181.
157. *Ibid.*, p. 183.
158. *Ibid.*, p. 183.
159. *Ibid.*, p. 184.
160. The memorandum of 28 January addressed only the question of whether to elect members of the general commission.
161. I believe that this memorandum, like its predecessor (that of 28 January), was written by Kakhanov. In confirmation one can cite an entry in Polovtsov's diary about a conversation in late March with Loris-Melikov. Kakhanov pointed out to Loris-Melikov that not all the minister's proposals ought to be examined by zemstvo delegates. He included administrative reforms and press laws in this category. [See above in this chapter.] Literally the same ideas were repeated in the memorandum.
162. *Dnevnik E.A. Perettsa*, p. 61.
163. *Pisma K.P. Pobedonostseva k Aleksandru III*, I, p. 328.
164. Wiener Haus-Hof-und Staatsarchiv. Ministerium des Aussen. P.A.X. 76-1.
165. Chairman of the State Council Konstantin Nikolaevich and Minister of Justice Nabokov were among a number of persons who were invited but did not attend the meeting.
166. *Dnevnik D.A. Miliutina*, IV, p. 55.
167. *Pisma K.P. Pobedonostseva k Aleksandru III*, I, p. 325.
168. *Ibid.*, pp. 326-327. It is apparent that Loris-Melikov informed Pobedonostsev about the course of the meeting.
169. *Dnevnik D.A. Miliutina*, IV, pp. 56-57.
170. TsGAOR, fond Ignatieva, d. 3679, l. 14.
171. Vsesoiuznaia biblioteka im. V.I. Lenina, *Zapiski Otdela rukopisei*, Vypusk 2 (Moscow, 1939), p. 26. The original manuscript is in ROBL, fond Miliutina, karton 43, d. 27.
172. *Ibid.*, pp. 27-28.
173. *Ibid.*, pp. 28-29.
174. Miliutin was not quite accurate: Alexander II did not confirm Loris-Melikov's proposal about participation of zemstvo representatives in the State Council.
175. *Zapiski Otdela rukopisei*, Vypusk 2, p. 29.
176. *Russkii arkhiv*, 1907, kn. 2, p. 98. Evidently Loris-Melikov tried to hide from his associates the fact of his rapprochement with Pobedonostsev.
177. *Dnevnik D.A. Miliutina*, IV, p. 57.
178. Peretts said that Pobedonostsev spoke first.
179. *Dnevnik D.A. Miliutina*, IV, p. 58. Pobedonostsev summarized his speech somewhat differently in the letter quoted above. "I said that it was necessary to agree in general with everything said about unanimity, trust, the need to eliminate

disorganization; but one has to bear in mind the demands of the present: everyone waits and is uncertain. They wait for the government to decide on concrete measures that leave no doubt as to what it wants and what it will not permit." *Russkii arkhiv*, 1907, kn. 2, p. 98.

180. *Dnevnik D.A. Miliutina*, IV, p. 59.

181. *Dnevnik E.A. Perettsa*, p. 65.

182. *Russkii arkhiv*, 1907, kn. 2, p. 99.

183. *Ibid.*, p. 99.

184. *Ibid.*

185. P.A. Valuev, *Dnevnik 1877-1884 gg.*, p. 162.

186. K.P. *Pobedonostsev i ego korrespondenty*, I, ch. 1, p. 49.

187. *Istoricheskie zapiski*, t. 2, p. 287.

188. *Dnevnik D.A. Miliutina*, IV, p. 54.

189. *Pisma K.P. Pobedonostseva k Aleksandru III*, I, p. 328.

190. In it the author said: "Yesterday I wrote Your Majesty about the manifesto." The first letter was dated 23 April; it follows that the second letter was written on 24 April.

191. *Pisma K.P. Pobedonostseva k Aleksandru III*, I, pp. 330-331.

192. There is no information that would suggest that Alexander III asked Pobedonostsev to write the manifesto. In my view, such a request did not occur.

193. *Ibid.*, p. 331.

194. *Ibid.*, p. 332.

195. K.P. *Pobedonostsev i ego korrespondenty*, I, ch. 1, p. 50.

196. My emphasis.

197. TsGAOR, fond Ignatieva, d. 3679, l. 17, letter of 27 April. This letter refutes the widely-believed notion that Ignatiev took part in the preparation of the manifesto. On 27 April Pobedonostsev also sent a note to State Secretary Peretts saying that in connection with his summons to Gatchina, he (Pobedonostsev) could not be present at the meeting in the State Council. *Dnevnik E.A. Perettsa*, p. 67.

198. *Ibid.*, p. 67.

199. Thus Alexander III lied to his own brother when he said that the manifesto was the product of his initiative.

200. *Konstitutsiia gr. Loris-Melikova*, p. 34. A copy of the letter may be found in the diary of E.M. Feoktistov. IRLI, 9122, L 11^b 14, l. 12.

201. *Dnevnik E.A. Perettsa*, p. 68.

202. An announcement of the day of the meeting is published in K.P. *Pobedonostsev i ego korrespondenty*, I, ch. 1, p. 50.

203. *Dnevnik D.A. Miliutina*, IV, p. 61.

204. K.P. *Pobedonostsev i ego korrespondenty*, I, ch. 1, p. 50.

205. *Dnevnik D.A. Miliutina*, IV, p. 62.

206. *Ibid.*

207. Pobedonostsev described this meeting in two sentences, in which he said that all the arguments revolved around "quasiconstitutional institutions." ROBL, fond Pobedonostseva, d. 4389/3, l. 2. Published with certain errors in K.P. *Pobedonostsev i ego korrespondenty*, I. ch. 1, p. 51.

208. "It was senseless," wrote Miliutin, "to continue to argue after the Grand Duke said to us that on the morning of that terrible day 1 March the emperor, having signed the report of the secret commission and waited for Loris-Melikov to leave his office, spoke to the Grand Dukes. He said: 'I have consented to this proposal although I know that we are on the path toward a constitution.' It is

difficult to explain," wrote Miliutin, "just what elements of Loris-Melikov's proposals gave the tsar the impression that we were headed for a constitution; but it is understandable that these words, spoken just before his martyr's death, have had a profound impact on the young tsarevich and have prepared the way for the retrograde theories of Pobedonostsev, Katkov, and company." *Dnevnik D.A. Miliutina*, IV, p. 62. Certain details in Miliutin's account are inaccurate. The assertion that on 1 March Alexander II signed the official memorandum, is incorrect, since the memorandum in question was signed on 17 February. Apparently, Miliutin made this mistake when he was editing the diary because in the original version of the diary this assertion is absent.

209. *Ibid.*, p. 62.
210. *Ibid.*, p. 63.
211. ROBL, fond Pobdeonostseva, d. 4389/3, l. 2.
212. PSZ, 3 sobr., I, No. 118.
213. *Ibid.*
214. *Dnevnik D.A. Miliutina*, IV, p. 40.
215. *Denkwürdikeiten des Botschafters General v. Schweinitz*, Zweite Band, p. 162.
216. *Moskovskie vedomosti*, 30 April 1881.
217. *Poriadok*, 30 April 1881.
218. *Strana*, 30 April 1881.
219. P.A. Valuev, *Dnevnik 1877-1884 gg.*, p. 164.
220. *Ibid.*
221. *Dnevnik D.A. Miliutina*, IV, p. 65.
222. The Austro-Hungarian ambassador devoted a special dispatch to his patron, Hamerlei, about the dismissal of Miliutin and the appointment of Vannovsky. He wrote a detailed description of Miliutin's activity in foreign affairs, emphasizing Miliutin's anti-German orientation. Describing the attitude in military circles to the appointment of Vannovsky, he wrote: "His appointment as War Minister has not been well-received in high military circles, in the War Ministry and General Staff." Wiener Haus-Hof-und Staatsarchiv. Ministerium des Aussen, P. A. X. 76-11.
223. V.I. Lenin, *Sochineniia*, V, p. 40.

CHAPTER V

1. V.I. Lenin, *Sochineniia*, V, pp. 41-42.
2. In addition, in southern Russia (in Kiev, Ekaterinoslav, Chernigov, Poltava, Kherson, and Volynia provinces) there were Jewish pogroms. The attacks were directed against the middle and petty Jewish bourgeoisie, mainly in rural areas. The pogroms were supported and inspired by local government officials. The head of the Kiev provincial gendarmerie, Novitsky, wrote: "The Kiev Governor-General was no doubt behind the three-day pogrom in Kiev and its spread to other districts. . . . Drenteln hated Jews with every fiber of his being, and he gave complete freedom to unruly gangs of 'hooligans' and Dnepr 'vagabonds', who openly smashed Jewish property, stores and shops, bazaars. This went on in his presence, in the presence of soldiers, in the presence of those called out to stop the disorders." V.D. Novitsky, *Iz vospominanii zhandarma*, pp. 180-181. See also: TsGAOR, fond Ignatieva, d. 3605, letter from Pavlov to Ignatiev. However, the pogroms were of serious concern to the central government since at any movement the target of violence might have shifted from the Jews to the landowners.

3. Wiener Haus-Hof-und Staatsarchiv. Ministerium des Aussen. P. A. X. 76-11. Report on 24/12 August 1881.

4. See TsGAOR, fond Polovtsova, d. 18, p. 273, for Kakhanov's account; and d. 20, 1. 48, for the reaction of Dondukov-Korsakov. See also *Dnevnik E.A. Perettsa,* p. 125. L. Kliachko (Lvov), a journalist and contributor to the newspaper *Rech,* stated in his memoirs [*Povest proshlogo* (Leningrad, 1929)] that Ignatiev took more than one bribe from a well-known banker, Baron Ginsburg. [See pp. 137-141 of Kliachko's memoirs.] Although Kliachko's memoirs are generally unreliable, it seems to me that he may have told the truth in this instance.

5. On 4 May Ignatiev had not yet been appointed officially. Pobedonostsev wrote the tsar the following note: "I also fear that Count Ignatiev will break with Baranov if they do not understand one another. This would be a tragedy, and Ignatiev would be without assistance in a very serious undertaking." *Pisma K.P. Pobedonostseva k Aleksandru III,* I, p. 339. This note suggests that Alexander III must have consulted with Pobedonostsev before appointing Ignatiev. It also may mean that Pobedonostsev had not taken the initiative in this matter, since Baronov was his henchman.

6. TsGAOR, fond Ignatieva, d. 3679, 1. 32.

7. Note that behind Cherevin stood Court Minister Count Vorontsov-Dashkov.

8. I know of only one case during this period when Alexander III did not follow Pobedonostsev. This was the matter of the organization of the Peasant Bank (see below). Later the influence of Pobedonostsev over the tsar began to decline. The reason, in my opinion, was that Pobedonostsev had no positive program. He could only criticize what he did not like from the standpoint of orthodox autocratic principles. As the old Count S.G. Stroganov said of Pobedonostsev, "he always knows what not to do, but he never knows what should be done." V.P. Meshchersky, *Moi vospominaniia,* III (St. Petersburg, 1912), p. 66.

9. ROBL, fond Pobedonostseva, d. 4410,/, 1. 139. Even Alexander III, with his limited intelligence, could not fail to see that his foremost minister was a liar. However, according to Grand Duke Aleksei Alexandrovich, the tsar thought that Ignatiev "lies only in small affairs, but the tsar is mistaken because Ignatiev lies as much about important things as he does about trivial ones." TsGAOR, fond Polovtsova, d. 20, p. 62.

10. See the article by A. Pribylovaia-Korba, "Sergei Petrovich Degaev," *Byloe,* 1906, kn. 4, pp. 1=17, and the documents that follow on pp. 18-54.

11. ROBL, fond Miliutina, papka 61, d. 34.

12. TsGAOR, fond Ignatieva, d. 1471, 1. 1.

13. The project said that "amnesty will be given only to persons, who, aside from their crimes against the state, are not guilty of other common criminal offenses. The exceptions to this rule are cases where the commission of common crimes was necessary to carry out a crime against the state or to help such a state offense succeed. *Ibid.,* 1. 1. As we see here, Ignatiev showed a "touching concern" for revolutionaries, giving them amnesty for criminal offense if they were forced to commit these common crimes "to carry out an attack on the government."

14. *Byloe,* 1924, kn. 27-28, p. 63. Letter of Pobedonostsev on 1 November 1881.

15. TsGAOR, fond Ignatieva, d. 1472. Clerical copy without signature and date.

16. *Ibid.,* 1. 2.

17. *Byloe,* 1924, kn. 27-28, p. 53.

18. *Pravitelstvennyi vestnik,* 6 May 1881.
19. A.V. Golovnin was more correct in his analysis of the causes of the revolutionary movement. They were, in his view, the inadequacies of the reforms in 1861, which had not given enough land to the peasants. See the second chapter above.
20. Later in a memorandum given to Alexander III on 15 March 1882, Ignatiev wrote: "Careful investigations of the popular vengeance [sic.—P. A. Z.] that occurred in the provinces show clearly that these disorders had no connection with the socialist movement." TsGAOR, fond Ignatiev, d. 1452, ll. 30-31.
21. *Pravitelstvennyi vestnik,* 6 May 1881.
22. *Ibid..*
23. *Moskovskie vedomosti,* 7 May 1881.
24. *Poriadok,* 7 May 1881.
25. *Zemstvo,* 13 May 1881.
26. *Ibid..*
27. *Golos,* 7 May 1881.
28. TsGAOR, fond Ignatieva, d. 1458, l. 1. Clerical copy. See also the other memorandum in *Ibid.,* d. 1457.
29. TsGAOR, fond Ignatieva, d. 1458, l. 2.
30. *Ibid.,* ll. 2-3.
31. TsGAOR, fond Ignatieva, d. 1443, l. 35.
32. *Ibid.,* l. 30.
33. TsGIA, fond Kantseliarii ministra vnutrennikh del, op. 1, d. 680, l. 3. It should be noted that reports from the Tambov, Poltava, Voronezh, and Kaluga governors gave more optimistic assessments of the situation in the countryside.
34. GIAMO, fond Kantseliarii moskovskogo general-gubernatora, op. 71, d. 3. Circular of 26 May 1881.
35. TsGIA (Ukraine), fond Kantseliarii kievskogo general-gubernatora, op. 831, d. 3, 1881 g., l. 57. I have not been able to discover in which provinces military maneuvers were called off. There was one petition from the Vladimir governor, Sudienko, to the Moscow General-Governor that requested the 11th Pskov regiment to remain in Shuisky district during the summer "as a precaution," since "industrial factories had brought a mass of workers." GIAMO, fond Moskovskogo general-gubernatora, op. 71, d. 3. It should be noted that the district military was also quartered in the town of Shui.
36. TsGAOR, fond Ignatieva, d. 1452, l. 2.
37. TsGAOR, fond Ignatieva, d. 1489. Alexander III wrote the following sentence on the first page: "The memo is drafted intelligently and skilfully, and the main thing is that it tells the complete and unfortunate truth." The memorandum is undated and unsigned.
38. Ignatiev had in mind the privileged elements of society.
39. TsGAOR, fond Ignatieva, d. 1489, l. 2.
40. *Ibid.,* ll. 2-3, 8.
41. *Ibid.,* ll. 10-11.
42. The draft ukase is in the original clerical copy without date or signature. TsGAOR, fond Ignatieva, d. 1488.
43. *Ibid.,* ll. 1-2.
44. As we have learned from Pobedonostsev's letter to Alexander III, the commission debated whether the police as well as the gendarmes should be removed from the governors' power. According to one proposal, the police would have fallen under the gendarmes: jurisdiction. Pobedonostsev attacked this plan sharply in his letter. *Pisma K.P. Pobedonostseva k Aleksandru III,* I, p. 345.

45. See chapter three above.

46. TsGIA (Ukraine), fond Kievskogo general-gubernatora, op. 831, d. 3, 1881 g., l. 216.

47. *Ibid.*, l. 216.

48. This memorandum exists in a clerical copy without signature or date. Comparison of the basic ideas in the memo with the contents of the circular described above indicated that the memorandum was written by Ignatiev.

49. TsGAOR, fond Ignatieva, d. 1458, l. 5.

50. *Ibid.*.

51. Before that time he was assistant Minister of Internal Affairs, and directly controlled both the Department of State Police and the Corps of Gendarmes.

52. TsGAOR, fond Ignatieva, d. 1459, l. 4.

53. I do not think it necessary to analyze the activity of this organization in this monograph since the Holy Retinue did not directly influence internal politics. The role of the Holy Retinue is a subject for specialized research. It seems to me that, aside from its basic goal, the Holy Retinue also served as a sort of right-wing opposition organization. On the Holy Retinue, see the work of the historian M.K. Lemke in Pushkin House.

54. *Pisma K.P. Pobedonostseva k Aleksandru III*, I, p. 357.

55. TsGAOR, fond Aleksandra III, d. 809, l. 2.

56. TsGAOR, fond Ignatieva, d. 3679, ll. 91-92. Letter of 20 December 1881.

57. TsGIA, fond Komiteta ministrov. Prilozhenie k zhurnalu za avgust 1881 g., d. 4181, st. 517, l. 2.

58. *Ibid.*, ll. 2-4.

59. In this project there were two stages of an emergency situation: (a) the stage of disorder; and (b) the stage of potential danger. According to Ignatiev, these terms "may serve to be a source of confusion and misunderstanding, especially among the uneducated masses." *Ibid.*, l. 6. That is why he changed the terms to "intensified security" and "emergency security." Hence, the statute enacted by the government was called the "Statute on Intensified and Emergency Security."

60. TsGAOR, fond Ignatieva, d. 3675. Letter on 17 July 1881.

61. TsGAOR, fond Ignatieva, d. 3679, ll. 43-44. Letter of 9 August 1881. Judging by Ignatiev's letter of response, Pobedonostsev played a direct role in preparing the legislation on intensified and emergency security. See *K.P. Pobedonostsev i ego korrespondenty*, I, ch. 1, pp. 87-88.

62. TsGIA, fond Komiteta ministrov, zhurnal za avgust 1881 g., d. 4180, st. 517, ll. 21-22. The Committee of Ministers directed the Minister of Internal Affairs to give the tsar a draft decree defining the areas that would fall under the emergency laws.

63. PSZ, 3 sobr., I, No. 350, st. 6, point "a".

64. *Ibid.*, point "b".

65. *Ibid.*, st. 15.

66. *Ibid.*, st. 16. Exile without the right to leave the place of exile required "preliminary notification of the Minister of Internal Affairs" in the special manner outlined in the law.

67. *Ibid.*, st. 17.

68. *Ibid.*.

69. PSZ, 3 sobr., I, No. 350, st. 20. Independent of this, the governor was given the right even in normal circumstances to confirm official appointments, aside from members of the judiciary. *Svod zakonov*, 1876 ed., II, ch. 1, st. 511.

70. This measure did not apply to justices of the peace, or to elected zemstvo or municipal officials.

71. PSZ, 3 sobr., I, No. 350, st. 21.

72. With the exception of persons of the three highest ranks.

73. PSZ, 3 sobr., I, No. 350, st. 28.

74. A note to article 33 said that persons who were to be exiled by administrative order could be arrested "prior to a decision about their exile." This provision made it possible to detain persons for a rther long period.

75. V.I. Lenin, *Sochineniia,* XVII, p. 396.

76. He had in mind the state of intensified security.

77. TsGAOR, fond Ignatieva, d. 3675, letter of 17 July 1881.

78. PSZ, 3 sobr., I, No. 382.

79. *Ibid..*

80. It was possible to justify to a certain extent on the basis of official criteria the introduction of intensified security in several southern and southwestern provinces. Here in spring 1881 there were the massive Jewish pogroms. However, the pogroms, as indicated earlier, occurred with the unspoken consent of the local "government authorities."

81. PSZ, 3 sobr., I, No. 382.

82. Prisoners were allowed to leave their places of exile as long as they stayed in the district where they were under surveillance, if they had "especially important reasons." Permission had to be obtained from the head of the local police. Prisoners could visit other districts in the same province only with permission from the governor. Other provinces could be visited only after permission from the Minister of Internal Affairs.

83. TsGIA, fond Glavnogo upravleniia po delam pechati, op. 1, d. 17, ll. 30-75; d. 18, ll. 1-14. These actions against the press involved official warnings, prohibition of retail sales, and cessation of publication of up to six months.

84. *Byloe,* 1924, kn. 27-28, p. 54.

85. *Ibid.,* p. 55.

86. *Ibid.,* p. 57.

87. *Ibid..*

88. *Ibid.,* p. 71, letter of 14 February 1882.

89. TsGAOR, fond Ignatieva, d. 1462, ll. 1-2, 5. Clerical copy without signature or date.

90. *Byloe,* 1924, kn. 27-28, p. 75.

91. *K.P. Pobedonostsev i ego korrespondenty,* I. ch. 1, p. 258. Undated letter in response to Pobedonostsev's letter of 9 May. It must have been written between the 10th and the 15th of May.

92. Local committees were established by imperial order on 22 August 1881 in those provinces with a large Jewish population.

93. TsGIA, fond Komiteta ministrov, Zhurnal za aprel 1882 g., d. 4234, st. 333, ll. 474, 479-480.

94. TsGIA, fond Komiteta ministrov, Prilozhenie k zhurnalu za aprel 1882 g., l. 4235, st. 333, l. 542.

95. *Ibid.,* ll. 586-587.

96. *Ibid.,* ll. 592-593.

97. *Ibid.,* l. 597.

98. *Ibid.,* l. 607.

99. ROBL, fond D.A. Miliutina, papka 61, d. 35. Letter of 30 April 1882.

100. *Dnevnik E.A. Perettsa,* p. 133. This session of the Committee of Ministers is described in detail by Peretts, pp. 130-133.

101. According to L. Kliachko, Ignatiev received a bribe of 100,000 rubles from Baron Ginzburg after rejection of his original proposals. L. Kliachko (Lvov), *Povesti proshlogo,* p. 141.

102. TsGIA, fond Komiteta ministrov. Osobyi zhurnal 20 i 27 aprelia 1882 g., d. 4234, st. 333, ll. 490-491. Published in shortened form in PSZ, 3 sobr., II, No. 834.

103. The emperor was opposed to any improvement in the position of the Jews. He noted solemnly: "Their condition is lamentable, but it was forecast in the gospel." According to E.M. Feoktistov, the emperor made a similar comment after reading Baron Ginzburg's petition for improvement in the position of the Jews in 1890. IRLI, fond E.M. Feoktistova, L 9122 11^b 54. Diary entry on 22 February 1891, l. 26.

104. *Ibid.,* l. 8.

105. V.I. Lenin, *Sochineniia,* V, p. 42.

106. See chapter four above.

107. The zemstvo experts were marshals of the nobility and chairmen of zemstvo boards. These experts were selected by the Minister of Internal Affairs.

108. According to the experts, in the Western provinces the reduction should have affected only those peasants who had transferred to redemption before the law of 1863 was enacted.

109. TsGIA, fond Glavnogo komiteta ob ustroistve selskogo sostoianiia, op. t. XV, ch. 1, 1881 g., ll. 42-43.

110. The majority of experts concluded that reduction of redemption payments on a nation-wide basis was a political necessity. "The reduction of the redemption payments is the first act of the new reign directed toward the improvement of the material welfare of the peasants. If a large part of Russia is left out, the impression made by this measure on the masses will not be satisfactory. . . ." *Ibid.,* l. 43.

111. *Ibid.,* l. 44.

112. *Ibid.,* l. 49.

113. M. Kh. Reitern, N.F. Metlin, F.M. Novosilsky, D.N. Nabokov, D.M. Solsky, G.P. Nebolsin, N.P. Ignatiev, E.I. Brevern, B.P. Mansurov, M.N. Ostrovsky, M.E. Kovalevsky, N. Kh. Bunge.

114. A.A. Saburov, E.T. Baranov, A.V. Adlerberg, A.P. Zablotsky-Desiatovsky, M.N. Liuboshchinsky, K.K. Grot, F.P. Kornilov, L.S. Makov, N.I. Stoianovsky, I.I. Vorontsov-Dashkov, V.M. Markus.

115. Grand Duke's Mikhail Nikolaevich, Vladimir Alexandrovich, E.V. Putiatin, N.F. Metlin, A.I. Gildenstube, F.M. Novosilsky, V.P. Titov, A.I. Verigin, A.A. Barantsov, M. Kh. Reitern, F.L. Geiden, A.E. Timashev, P.A. Shuvalov, V.A. Dolgorukov, A.P. Nikolai, D.N. Nabokov, S.A. Taneev, D.M. Solsky, B.P. Mansurov, M.S. Kakhanov, P.N. Klushin, E.N. Staritsky, V.D. Filosofov, M.N. Ostrovsky, K.P. Pobedonostsev, M.E. Kovalevsky, M.S. Vannovsky, N. Kh. Bunge, N.K. Giers, G.P. Nebolsin, N.V. Isakov, N.P. Ignatiev, K.I. Palen, E.I. Brevern.

116. TsGIA, fond Glavnogo komiteta ob ustroistve selskogo sostoianiia, op. t. XV, d. 104, ch. 2, 1881 g., l. 246.

117. A.V. Adlerberg, M.I. Liuboshinsky, F.P. Kornilov, V.M. Markus, V.P. Titov, A.E. Timashev, K.I. Palen, P.N. Klushin, V.D. Filosofov, N.K. Giers, S.A. Greig, A.V. Golovnin, K.N. Posiet, A.A. Liven, A.M. Dondukov-Korsakov.

118. PSZ, 3 sobr., I, No. 575, 576, 577.

119. Ignatiev thought it unwise to assist these large landowners because "they had decided not to fulfill the intentions of Alexander II and for non-receipt of the 20 percent payments they had awarded themselves as quitrent for twenty years."

120. Alexander III wrote on the first page: "I also share your opinion."
121. PSZ, 3 sobr., III, No. 1584.
122. PSZ, 3 sobr., I, No. 189.
123. TsGIA, fond Komiteta ministrov, zhurnal za iiun 1881 g., d. 4173, st. 448. The "Temporary Regulations" were not published in the complete collection of laws.
124. This question is examined in detail by V.A. Vdovin in this *Krestianskii pozemelnyi bank* (Moscow, 1959). As a result, I have examined this reform only briefly.
125. TsGIA, fond Departamenta gosudarstvennoi ekonomii, 1882, d. 164, 1. 2. Cited by Vdovin, p. 26.
126. V.A. Vdovin, *op. cit.*, p. 28.
127. *Ibid.*, p. 31.
128. *Ibid..*
129. *Byloe*, 1924, kn. 27-28, p. 71.
130. On 13 April Polovtsov recorded in his diary a conversation with Ignatiev about the latter's policy concerning the peasantry, and his attitude toward the Peasant Bank in particular. "His policy is completely conservative, because he wants to increase the number of landowners in Russia. He says that to destroy the communal system is difficult in view of the wide public support for it. However, he was going to move by a different path—that of increasing the number of peasant proprietors by credit." TsGAOR, fond Polovtsova, d. 20, p. 70. As we know, Ignatiev announced himself a defender of the commune on more than one occasion. Therefore it is hard to establish where he lied. But apparently, he lied to Polovtsov.
131. P.A. Valuev, *Dnevnik 1877-1884 gg.*, p. 196.
132. V.A. Vdovin, *op. cit.*, p. 35.
133. TsGIA, fond Departamenta gosudarstvennoi ekonomii, 1882 g., d. 173.
134. *Ibid.*, ll. 14-15.
135. *Otchet po Gosudarstvennomu sovetu za 1882 g.*, (St. Petersburg, 1884), p. 53.
136. *Dnevnik E.A. Perettsa*, p. 133.
137. PSZ, 3 sobr., II, No. 887, 889.
138. For the composition of this group of informed persons see TsGIA, fond Kantseliarii ministra vnutrennikh del, op. 2, d. 971, 1. 166 and *Pravitelstvennyi vestnik*, 25 September 1881.
139. *Pravitelstvennyi vestnik*, 25 September 1881.
140. TsGIA, fond Kantseliarii ministra vnutrennikh del, op. 2, d. 968, ll. 40-43.
141. TsGIA, fond Departamenta obshchikh del, op. 241, 1881 g., d. 83, 1. 211.
142. *Ibid.*, l. 213.
143. *Ibid.*, l. 277.
144. *Ibid.*, l. 277.
145. Alexander wrote on the first page: "I approve." *Ibid.*, l. 275.
146. The commission started its activity on 20 November. An agenda was worked out in sessions on 20 November 1881, and 22 and 26 January 1882. On 6 and 13 April the agenda was examined by the Committee of Ministers. TsGIA, fond komiteta ministrov, d. 4235, st. 280. Osobyi zhurnal 6 i 13 aprelia 1882 g.. Proekt plana zaniatii, d. 4235. st. 280.
147. That is, 22 January.
148. The assistant Minister of Internal Affairs who replaced Kakhanov.
149. TsGAOR, fond Polovtsova, d. 20, p. 42.

150. Quotation from Ignatiev's memorandum to Alexander III of late December 1881. TsGAOR, fond Ignatieva, d. 1542, l. 4. I did not succeed in locating the actual circular. There were illegal petitions in other zemstvos as well: in Kherson, and Pskov provincial zemstvos, and Smolensk and Urzhursky district zemstvo assemblies.

151. This case involved Khvalynsky district assembly in Saratov province. The chairman of this assembly was forced into retirement, and the chairman of the provincial zemstvo board, who had also been a party to this illegal petition, was not allowed to stand for election.

152. TsGAOR, fond Ignatieva, d. 1542, ll. 1-3.

153. *Strana*, 10 May 1881. Circular of 5 May, No. 5562.

154. *Strana*, 10 May 1881.

155. *Strana*, 12 May 1881.

156. He was appointed 24 March 1881, and dismissed on 16 March 1882.

157. The commission included: director of the Department of State Police Plehve, director of the Construction School Berngardt, trustee of the Petersburg educational district Dmitriev, chairman of the Main Administration of Military Academies Lalaev, director of the Department of Agriculture and Rural Industry of the Ministry of State Domains Veshniakov, inspector of the Institute of Communications Kokovtsev and director of the Moscow Technical School Professor Arkhipov.

158. The original of this document, unsigned and undated and written in a clerk's handwriting, is in the Plehve papers, TsGAOR, fond 586, d. 22. Plehve wrote on the first page: "Report to His Majesty, the Emperor, of May 1881 that served as the justification for the foundation of the Delianov Commission." Plehve must have meant another document that may have been affixed to the text on which he commented.

159. TsGAOR, fond Pleve, d. 22, l. 1.

160. *Ibid.*, l. 2.

161. *Ibid.*, ll. 3-4.

162. TsGAOR, fond Pleve, d. 22, l. 4.

163. ROBL, fond Katkova, d. 46, l. 26.

164. *Ibid.*, ll. 26-27.

165. The head of this group was the former rector of Petersburg University, Beketov.

166. In Petersburg University 835 students out of 1825 (or 45.7 percent) had certificates saying they were poor; of the 1168 students in the Technological, Mining, and Communications Institutes, some 533 (or 45.6 percent) were poor. Of the 452 attending the Women's Higher Medical Courses, there were only 100 who had enough private resources to continue their educations. A. Georgievsky, *Kratkii istoricheskii ocherk pravitelstvennykh mer i prednachertanii protiv studentcheskikh besporiadkov* (St. Petersburg, 1890), p. 83.

167. *Ibid.*, pp. 84-85. For materials of the Kakhanov Commission see TsGIA, fond Departamenta narodnogo prosveshcheniia, No. 733, op. 149, d. 552, 1881 g.

168. A. Georgievsky, *op. cit.*, p. 79.

169. *Ibid.*, pp. 81-82.

170. *Ibid.*, pp. 85-86.

171. *Ibid.*, p. 87.

172. *Ibid.*, pp. 88-89.

173. *Ibid.*, p. 91.

174. TsGAOR, fond Ignatieva, d. 3675.

175. A. Georgievsky, p. 93.
176. TsGIA, fond Departamenta narodnogo prosveshcheniia, op. 149, d. 552, 1881, g., l. 34.
177. ROBL, fond D.A. Miliutina, papka 61, d. 35, letter of 2 April 1882, l. 3.
178. ROBL, fond D.A. Miliutina, papka 61, d. 34. Quotation from Golovnin's letter to Miliutin.
179. All these measures were approved by Alexander III on the basis of the Minister of Education's memorandum of 5 December. See the memorandum "O komissii po peresmotru ustava i programmy realnykh uchilishch," in *Sbornik postanovlennii po Ministerstvu narodnogo prosveshcheniia*, VIII (St. Petersburg, 1892), No. 129.
180. Pobedonostsev was not quite accurate: the issue of the gymnasium statute was not raised.
181. *Pisma K.P. Pobedonostseva k Aleksandru III*, I, p. 366.
182. TsGAOR, fond Ignatieva, d. 3679, l. 98. Letter of 18 January 1882.
183. *K.P. Pobedonostsev i ego korrespondenty*, I, ch. 1, p. 84.
184. Delianov was the head of the Fourth Section of His Majesty's Chancellery.
185. *Pisma K.P. Pobedonostseva k Aleksandru III*, I, p. 368. The letter was dated the evening of 22/23 January.
186. TsGAOR, fond Aleksandra III, d. 823, l. 10.
187. *Pisma K.P. Pobedonostseva k Aleksandru III*, I, pp. 375-376.
188. The dismissal of Nikolai was connected to a certain extent with the Liubimov affair. Liubimov was a friend of Katkov and a professor at Moscow University. In 1877, knowing that his contract was coming up for a vote in the University Council, he used the influence of Katkov to get a five-year contract without election. In 1882 Nikolai was asked what to do about Liubimov, since the latter was at the end of the old contract. Nikolai said that Liubimov would have to be endorsed by the University Council. This upset Alexander III, who sent to Nikolai a copy of Liubimov's letter with the words: "Fulfill his request." In other words, the tsar asked Nikolai to reappoint Liubimov without a vote in the University Council.
189. TsGAOR, fond Ignatieva, d. 161, ll. 6-7.
190. *Ibid.*, d. 1527, ll. 1-2.
191. *Ibid.*, ll. 3-7.
192. *Ibid.*, d. 161, l. 7.
193. *Ibid.*, d. 2258, ll. 15, 17.
194. *Ibid.*, d. 225, l. 17.
195. This very candid correspondence was conducted through special express couriers, or through specially trusted persons. The letters were to have been destroyed. In one of the letters Golokhvastov wrote: "Please, dear Ivan Sergeevich, burn this letter just like the others that I sent by courier. It is dangerous to certain individuals and to the Zemsky Sobor to preserve such letters." IRLI, d. 11056, XVII, p. 17, letter of 9 May. This correspondence was published in *Russkii arkhiv*, 1913, kn. I-II.
196. According to the papers of Golokhvastov, his appointment as special official in the Ministry occurred on 12 March. TsGIA, fond Departamenta obshchikh del, op. 51, d. 40, l. 8.
197. IRLI, d. 11056, XVII, p. 17. Letter of P.D. Golokhvastov to I.S. Aksakov, 2 March 1882.
198. It does not follow from the fact that Ignatiev's signature may be found on all the proposals for a Zemsky Sobor that he was their author. In her letter to Aksakov on 27 April 1882 the wife of Golokhvastov wrote: "Everything that my husband wrote and writes Count Ignatiev claimed and claims as his own.

That is why he recopies all those papers and manifestos five times in his own hand after every little correction. And he does this even though he is a terribly busy man," exclaimed Golokhvastova. *Russkii arkhiv*, 1913, kn. 1, pp. 103-104.

199. TsGAOR, fond Ignatieva, d. 1533, l. 3.

200. *Ibid.*, ll. 3-5.

201. *Ibid.*, ll. 11-12.

202. *Ibid.*, l. 8.

203. *Ibid.*, ll. 13-14.

204. *Ibid.*, ll. 14-15.

205. *Ibid.*, l. 8.

206. *Ibid.*, l. 13.

207. *Ibid.*, l. 50.

208. The manuscript says 454, but this is a mistake.

209. *Ibid.*, l. 52.

210. The text mistakenly said 3400 representatives.

211. *Ibid.*, l. 71.

212. *Ibid.*, d. 161, l. 7.

213. *Ibid.*, d. 1533, l. 29.

214. *Ibid.*, d. 161, l. 7. The Zemsky Sobor would last no more than three weeks according to Ignatiev.

215. *Ibid.*, l. 8.

216. IRLI, d. 11056, XVII, p. 17.

217. Liubimov's pseudonym.

218. *Ibid.*

219. *Ibid.* Letter of 29 April 1882.

220. *Ibid.*

221. *Ibid.* Golokhvastov worked out a special code to inform Aksakov about the manifesto. In the 29 April letter he wrote: "If I telegraph you to 'Send a carriage to postcarrier Dmitrievich' that means you should send to Petersburg an express courier so that he can get news to you on the 6th. If I telegraph: 'Don't send a carriage until I telegraph again' that means that the manifesto will not be signed now. If I merely say 'Til the next telegraph" that will mean that the whole affair is cancelled." IRLI, d. 11056, XVII, p. 17.

222. *K.P. Pobedonostsev i ego korrespondenty*, I, ch. 1, p. 261. Published from a copy with Pobedonostsev's signature. ROBL, fond Pobedonostseva, d. 4391.

223. *Ibid.*, p. 262.

224. TsGAOR, fond Ignatieva, d. 1533, l. 29.

225. See E.M. Feoktistov, *Vospominaniia*, pp. 204-211.

226. IRLI, d. 11056, XVII, p. 17.

227. *Ibid.* This "secret" was passed on to Voeikov by Fadeev in answer to a very prosaic favor by Voeikov, who helped Fadeev received an allowance of 500 rubles on that day.

228. IRLI, d. 11056, XVII, p. 17.

229. *Pisma K.P. Pobedonostseva k Aleksandru III*, I, pp. 379-381.

230. The matter of this visit came up earlier as a means to convince Pobedonostsev to support the Zemsky Sobor. Vorontsov apparently also knew about Golokhvastov's visit.

231. IRLI, d. 11056, XVII, p. 17.

232. In his memoirs Ignatiev was also silent on this point. According to Ignatiev, he first found out about Alexander III's hesitations on 8 May.

233. E.M. Feoktistov, *Vospominaniia*, p. 208.

234. *Pisma Pobedonostseva k Aleksandru III*, I, p. 383.
235. IRLI, d. 11056, XVII, p. 17. Letter from Golokhvastov to Aksakov on 6 May 1882. It is unclear what Ostrovsky meant by a "genuine Sobor". Given his reactionary opinions, one may suppose that he had in mind a smaller delegation of conservative elements.
236. *Ibid.*, Letter of 9 May.
237. TsGAOR, fond Ignatieva, d. 1528, l. 5. On the first page of this report was written: "Read to His Majesty the Emperor on 8 May." The fact that the report was read to the tsar on 8 May disproves Ignatiev's assertion that he only found out about the tsar's hesitations on 8 May.
238. *Ibid.*, l. 9.
239. Already Alexander III could not trust Ignatiev completely, since he (the tsar) had a sharply critical attitude toward anything that would have infringed on the autocratic principle. Other members of the royal family were also unfavorably disposed toward Ignatiev. Grand Duke Vladimir Alexandrovich wrote the tsar on 15 March 1882 from Vienna: "Dear Sasha, my conscience forbids me to be silent. Everyone is strongly opposed here, as they have always been, to all the machinations of Ignatiev." TsGAOR, fond Aleksandra III, d. 738, l. 25.
240. TsGAOR, fond Ignatieva, d. 1530, l. 15. Report without signature or date. Ignatiev wrote on the first page: "Report of Nikolai Valerianovich Muraviev (procurator with the St. Petersburg Appeals Court), presented by the Minister of Internal Affairs to His Majesty." At the beginning Ignatiev wrote: "1882, May."
241. *Ibid.*, l. 1.
242. The relationship between Feoktistov and Ostrovsky was rather complicated. Somewhat later, when Feoktistov was appointed head of the Main Press Administration, the poet D.D. Minaev wrote: "Ostrovsky gave Feoktistov horns so that he could madly gore writers with them." Quoted by Yu.G. Oksman in the introduction to Feoktistov's memoirs, *op. cit.*, p. XXIII.
243. *Moskovskie vedomosti*, 12 May 1882.
244. *Novoe vremia*, 14 May 1882.
245. *Rus*, 22 May 1882.
246. P.A. Valuev, *Dnevnik 1877-1884 gg*, p. 197.
247. TsGAOR, fond Ignatieva, d. 161, l. 39.
248. *Pisma K.P. Pobedonostseva k Aleksandru III*, I, p. 385.
249. E.M. Feoktistov, *Vospominaniia*, pp. 209-210.
250. TsGAOR, fond Ignatieva, d. 161, ll. 73-74.
251. *Ibid.*, l. 74.

CONCLUSION

1. V.I. Lenin, *Sochineniia*, XVII, p. 95.
2. V.I. Lenin, *Sochineniia*, V, p. 30.

INDEX

ACADEMIC INTERNATIONAL PRESS

THE RUSSIAN SERIES

1 S.F. Platonov *History of Russia* Out of print
2 *The Nicky-Sunny Letters. Correspondence of Nicholas and Alexandra, 1914-1917*
3 Ken Shen Weigh *Russo-Chinese Diplomacy, 1689-1924* Out of print
4 Gaston Cahen *Relations of Russia with China. . .1689-1730* Out of print
5 M.N. Pokrovsky *Brief History of Russia* 2 Volumes
6 M.N. Pokrovsky *History of Russia from Earliest Times. . .* Out of print
7 Robert J. Kerner *Bohemia in the Eighteenth Century*
8 *Memoirs of Prince Adam Czartoryski and His Correspondence with Alexander I* 2v
9 S.F. Platonov *Moscow and the West*
10 S.F. Platonov *Boris Godunov*
11 Boris Nikolajewsky *Aseff the Spy*
12 Francis Dvornik *Les Legendes de Constantin et de Methode vues de Byzance*
13 Francis Dvornik *Les Slaves, Byzance et Rome au XIᵉ Siecle*
14 A. Leroy-Beaulieu *Un Homme d'Etat Russe (Nicolas Miliutine). . .*
15 Nicholas Berdyaev *Leontiev* (In English)
16 V.O. Kliuchevskii *Istoriie soslovii v Rossii*
17 *Tehran Yalta Potsdam. The Soviet Protocols*
18 *The Chronicle of Novgorod*
19 Paul N. Miliukov *Outlines of Russian Culture* Vol. III (3 vols.)
20 P.A. Zaionchkovskii *The Abolition of Serfdom in Russia*
21 V.V. Vinogradov *Russkii iazyk. Grammaticheskoe uchenie o slove*
22 P.A. Zaionchkovsky *The Russian Autocracy under Alexander III*
23 A.E. Presniakov *Emperor Nicholas I of Russia. The Apogee of Autocracy*
24 V.I. Semevskii *Krestianskii vopros v Rossii v XVIII i pervoi polovine XIX veka*
25 S.S. Oldenburg *Last Tsar! Nicholas II, His Reign and His Russia* 4 volumes
26 Carl von Clausewitz *The Campaign of 1812 in Russia*
27 M.K. Liubavskii *Obrazovanie osnovnoi gosudarstvennoi territorii velikorusskoi narodnosti. Zaselenie i obedinenie tsentra*
28 S.F. Platonov *Ivan the Terrible* Out of print
29 Paul N. Miliukov *Iz istorii russkoi intelligentsii. Sbornik statei i etiudov*
30 A.E. Presniakov *The Tsardom of Muscovy*
31 M. Gorky, J. Stalin et al., *History of the Civil War in Russia* (Revolution) 2 vols.
33 P.A. Zaionchkovsky *The Russian Autocracy in Crisis, 1878-1882*
43 Nicholas Zernov *Three Russian Prophets: Khomiakov, Dostoevsky, Soloviev*
44 Paul N. Miliukov *The Russian Revolution* 3 vols.
45 Anton I. Denikin *The White Army*
55 M.V. Rodzianko *The Reign of Rasputin—An Empire's Collapse, Memoirs*
56 *The Memoirs of Alexander Iswolsky*

THE CENTRAL AND EAST EUROPEAN SERIES

1 Louis Eisenmann *Le Compromis Austro-Hongrois de 1867*
3 Francis Dvornik *The Making of Central and Eastern Europe* 2nd edition
4 Feodor F. Zigel *Lectures on Slavonic Law*
10 Doros Alastos *Venizelos—Patriot, Statesman, Revolutionary*
20 Paul Teleki *The Evolution of Hungary and its Place in European History*

FORUM ASIATICA

1 M.I. Sladkovsky *China and Japan—Past and Present*

THE ACADEMIC INTERNATIONAL REFERENCE SERIES

The Modern Encyclopedia of Russian and Soviet History 50 vols.
The Modern Encyclopedia of Russian and Soviet Literature 50 vols.
Soviet Armed Forces Review Annual
USSR Facts & Figures Annual
Military-Naval Encyclopedia of Russia and the Soviet Union 50 vols.
China Facts & Figures Annual

SPECIAL WORKS

S.M. Soloviev *History of Russia* 50 vols.